Nest of Eagles

Nest of Eagles

Messerschmitt Production and Flight-Testing at Regensburg 1936-1945

CLASSIC

An imprint of
Ian Allan Publishing

The Author
Born in 1952, Peter Schmoll has held an interest in the history of the Second World War since he was a boy. After leaving school, he trained as a mechanic and worked for Audi for two years, before becoming a professional firefighter for a refinery-based fire brigade. He is presently an area fire chief, responsible for the operations of 52 professional firefighters and 180 volunteers in three fire stations attached to the BAYERNOIL company in southern Germany.

His research for *Nest of Eagles* (originally published in Germany as *Messerschmitt-Giganten und der Fliegerhorst Regensburg-Obertraubling 1936-1945* [2002] and *Die Messerschmitt-Werke im Zweiten Weltkrieg* [2004]) took several years, during which he corresponded with and interviewed many former eye-witnesses, workers and pilots at the Messerschmitt Regensburg facility, as well as consulting various archives and collections in Germany and the USA.

Editor's Note
The contents that formed the author's Foreword to his first book and Introduction to his second book have been largely combined into a new Preface in this single volume, to which modified and new explanatory text has been added. The Contents of both the original German-language books have been divided into two separate Parts, each reflecting the aircraft produced at the pertinent Messerschmitt facility and its environs, the Appendices in both books having likewise been reorganised and numbered accordingly. The aim of this revised arrangement is to provide the reader with a greater degree of clarity than would otherwise have been possible with two separate narratives as originally written and to avoid duplication, the aircraft types being related here are as far as possible in chronological order of the year in which production at each Messerschmitt facility commenced.

Nest of Eagles
Originally published as two books by the
MZ Buchverlag GmbH, Regensburg, as:
(1) *Die Messerschmitt-Werke im Zweiten Weltkrieg* (2004)
and (2) *Messerschmitt-Giganten und der Fliegerhorst Regensburg-Obertraubling 1936-1945* (2002)

ISBN 978 1 906537 12 8

Produced by Chevron Publishing Limited
(www.chevronpublishing.co.uk)

Project Editors: Robert Forsyth and Ted Oliver
Translation: Ted Oliver

Chevron Publishing would like to thank Ted Oliver for his kind assistance and advice during the proudction of this book

Cover and book design: Mark Nelson
© 2002 & 2004 Peter Schmoll
© Colour profiles: Fernando Estanislau (pages 106, 116, 124), Tom Tullis (46, 52, 64, 76, 78, 79, 110, 152), Janusz Swiatlon (27, 31, 135)

Published by Ian Allan Publishing
Riverdene Business Park, Molesey Road,
Hersham, Surrey, KT12 4RG

North American trade distribution:
Specialty Press Publishers & Wholesalers Inc.
39966 Grand Avenue, North Branch, MN 55056, USA
Fax: 651 277 1203 Tel: 651 277 1400
Toll free telephone: 800 895 4585
www.specialtypress.com

With effect from 1st February 2010 distribution of all Ian Allan Publishing Ltd titles in the United States of America and Canada will be undertaken by BookMasters Distribution Services Inc, 20 Amberwood Parkway, Ashland, Ohio 44805.

Printed in England by Ian Allan Printing Ltd
Riverdene Business Park, Molesey Road,
Hersham, Surrey, KT12 4RG

All rights reserved. No part of this publication may be reproduced, stored in a retrieval system, transmitted in any form or by any means, electronic, mechanical or photocopied, recorded or otherwise, without the written permission of the publishers.

Visit the Ian Allan Publishing website at:
www.ianallanpublishing.com

CONTENTS

Preface

Acknowledgements

Glossary and Abbreviations

PART I The Messerschmitt-Werke at Regensburg

Chapter 1	Construction and the commencement of production: 1936-1942	9
Chapter 2	The outbreak of war and expansion: 1939-1941	21
Chapter 3	War and Production	47
Chapter 4	'Total War': 1943-1945	53
Chapter 5	The Hardest Years: 1944-1945	67
Chapter 6	'Zero Hour': The end in Regensburg	81

PART II The Fliegerhorst Obertraubling and the Me 262

Chapter 7	Building the Fliegerhorst Obertraubling	83
Chapter 8	'The first beast is now here!': Me 321 mass production 1941-1943	88
Chapter 9	The Me 163 B at Obertraubling: 1942-1944	109
Chapter 10	Me 323 Production at Obertraubling: 1942-1944	113
Chapter 11	Bombing	129
Chapter 12	Messerschmitt Me 262	147
Chapter 13	'Götterdämmerung' – 1945	155

Appendices	169
Sources and Bibliography	191
Index	191

Preface

IN 1936-1937, Messerschmitt AG Augsburg established a new aircraft plant in the western part of Regensburg. In the years 1938-1940, this production facility was known as the Bayerische Flugzeugwerke Regensburg GmbH which, on 13 November 1940, was renamed Messerschmitt GmbH Regensburg. The plant brought about an immense economic stimulus to the town that is comparable today with the establishment of the BMW concern, and whose construction was largely carried out by locally-based construction firms. According to Dr. Helmut Halter, author of the book *Stadt unterm Hakenkreuz* (Town under the Swastika), Messerschmitt GmbH Regensburg became the largest taxpayer in the town's history.

The aviation industry altered the entire social structure in Regensburg, from the labour market right up to the dramatic increase in the number of residents that left their traces to such an extent on the town that these eventually led to Regensburg developing into a major town. As a result of the enormous increase in the workforce and its families, a completely new residential area arose, where the total number of the town's occupants rose from 82,749 in 1936 to 97,969 residents in 1939 and of which only a small proportion was due to the incorporation in it of the surburbs of Prüfening, Dechbetten and Ziegetsdorf.

Where industry in Regensburg had formerly consisted mostly of artisans, the manufacture of aircraft brought about the introduction and application of the newest technological design and production methods. In modern-day language, one could say that Messerschmitt was 'high-tech'. Whereas the old-established firms in Regensburg suffered losses of their workforces in droves, the aircraft firm offered much higher wages. The ability to work in clean, bright, and in large factory premises as well as the unmatched social benefits, were further factors that formed a magnet for the Messerschmitt workforce which could not be overlooked.

Besides the Wiener-Neustädter Flugzeugwerke and the Erla Maschinenfabrik in Leipzig, Messerschmitt GmbH Regensburg was the main production centre for the Bf 109 fighter. Despite the most widespread dispersal production, according to a study conducted by the USSBS after the end of World War II, even though it was heavily bombed in 1944 it remained one of the most capable and most productive German aircraft plants during the war, but it should nevertheless not be forgotten that 35 per cent of production that year came from inmates of the Flossenburg and Mauthausen concentration camps. Between 1939 and 1945, almost 11,000 examples of the Bf 109 E, F, G and K were built at Messerschmitt GmbH Regensburg.

From January 1938, Regensburg-Prüfening manufactured the Bf 108 single-engined 4-seat touring aircraft and from 1939, the Bf 109 fighter. To this was added centralized component manufacture and final assembly of the Me 210 in 1941-42, as well as the experimental series manufacture of the Me 163 B rocket fighter designed by a team led by Alexander Lippisch. Continual increases in production quantities of the Bf 109 that were demanded by the RLM necessitated the transfer of Bf 108 production to France in 1942.

Following the establishment of a new production centre under the aegis of Messerschmitt AG at the Fliegerhorst Obertraubling in 1941, production and factory flight testing of the Me 321 commenced there, and from the end of 1942, was continued with the Me 323 motorized version of the glider. In that same year, final assembly of the Me 163 B also took place in Obertraubling. Subsequent to the first Allied bombing raid on the production centres in Regensburg-Prüfening on 17 August 1943, one of the three final assembly lines of the Bf 109 was transferred to the Fliegerhorst Obertraubling. After the bombing raids of 22 and 25 February 1944, an unparalleled decentralization of aircraft production was put in hand that had already begun on a small scale in 1943. Individual aircraft parts manufacture was divided up among tunnels and bomb-proof galleries that were located all over southern Bavaria and also partially in Austria and the Sudetenland. A vast transport system ensured that the requisite raw materials were delivered to the manufacturing centres so that the parts produced were in turn shipped to the handling centres or to those engaged in final assembly. In the forested areas in the neighbourhood of Regensburg, well-camouflaged 'Waldwerken' ('forest factories') were erected where aircraft manufacture was continued, safe from air attacks, right up until April 1945. Principal production at these locations centred on the Me 262, the first operational jet fighter in the history of aviation.

A particularly shocking chapter during the war was the widescale use of concentration camp inmates in the German armaments industry - not only for Messerschmitt aircraft but also for the V-1 and V-2 weapons, in which human beings died en masse through coercion, brutal ill-treatment, starvation and sheer pressure of work, not to mention the several other deprivations they experienced daily. Not many survived before liberation in the last weeks of April and May 1945.

As mentioned above, those inmates who were set to work on aircraft production for Messerschmitt were drawn from the Flossenburg and Mauthausen concentration camps, their work having been directed by the firm's personnel, the inmates themselves supervised by the dreaded SS who then sold the aircraft items produced by the inmates to the Messerschmitt concern. In addition, a significant number of the firm's workforce consisted of forced labour by foreign nationals from all over Europe, as well as Russian officer PoWs.

It was the aim of the author, after more than 50 years since the end of the war, to attempt to document a significant portion of German aviation history that was founded at the Regensburg and Obertraubling production centres which, despite their involvement in an inhuman epoch, also introduced several advanced technical innovations. A further motivation was the 100th anniversary (on 26 June 1998) of one of the great German aircraft designers, Prof. Dr.-Ing. Willy Messerschmitt.

The documented status of aircraft production in Regensburg was viewed by the author as extremely scarce, but through interviews held with numerous eyewitnesses, several gaps were able to be filled. Over a period of 12 years, he was thus able to assemble a number of hitherto unknown facts and details on production in Regensburg both before and during the war, and to document them based on previously unpublished photographs. For a better understanding of the subject matter, brief references are made by the author in the text to wartime events in the years concerned.

With regard to the Fliegerhorst Obertraubling (the subject of Part II of this volume), it should be mentioned that hardly any trace of its existence remains today. Officially designated during the war as Regensburg-Obertraubling, the Fliegerhorst became involved in aircraft production such as none other in the Third Reich. What still remains are buildings that once formed a part of the former barrack blocks, control tower, and the Werfthalle in what is now Neutraubling. Nothing remains of the 1,200 m-long grass airfield strip that was south of the Fliegerhorst where today there are numerous industrial and commercial enterprises; the former grounds ahead of the production Hallen on the eastern side form a housing estate.

Despite the presence of massive anti-aircraft defences, the Fliegerhorst Obertraubling was heavily damaged in three bombing raids in 1944 and by two in 1945. Even at the present time - as elsewhere in Germany - unexploded Allied bombs are often by chance uncovered during excavations, and extensive precautions have to be undertaken to safeguard the populace in the neighbourhood until the bombs are safely defused, blown-up on site, or carried away.

After the end of the war, the U.S. Army used the Fliegerhorst for only a short period as an interim landing ground and as a base for the repatriation of freed PoWs. At the end of 1946, the first refugees began to settle in, as far as undamaged buildings allowed, on the Fliegerhorst. When the U.S. Army completely cleared out the former Fliegerhorst, an increasing influx of refugees and displaced persons commenced and the work of reconstruction began, where with the most primitive means, the heavily damaged barracks were made habitable. On 1 April 1951, the Fliegerhorst community became self-administrating as the new Neutraubling community, and it is thanks to Edith Frank and Cäcilie Vilsmeier that, in the local Heimatmuseum, there is an interesting small exhibition devoted to the Fliegerhorst and the establishment history of Neutraubling.

Acknowledgements
The author wishes to express his heartfelt thanks to the following individuals for their support and contributions: Gottfried Baron, Leopold Berghammer, Heinrich Binder, Winfried Bock, Carl E. Charles, Prof. Thomas Childers, Gernot Croneiß, Hans-Peter Dabrowski, Josef Dienstl, Rainer Ehm, Arno Fischer, Edith Frank, Martin Gattinger, Karl Geisbe, Josef Haid, Dr. Helmut Halter, Reinhard Hanausch, Josef Herzig, Ulrich Huber, Familie Hübsch-Bodenschatz, Ludwig Kandler†, Rudolf Klemm, Karl Kössler, Rosi Linder, Heinz Lohmann, Rudolf Melzl, Arno Mittmann, Theodor Mohr, Heinrich Obermaier, Heinz Powilleit, Willy Radinger, Josef Sachenshauser†, Adolf Riedmeir, Georg Schlaug, Karl Schmid, Helmut Schulz, Edgar Steinbügel, Flugkapitän Stemmler, Karl Strippel, Flugkapitän Wendelin Trenkle†, Familie Vilsmeier, Prof. Dr. Wedemeyer, Dr. Josef Weißmüller† and Ulrich Willbold, as well as the many others who played an important part in furnishing photographs, documents and reports. Especial thanks are expressed to Rainer Ehm of Regensburg for his energetic specialist support in the realisation and checking of the manuscript for the earlier book.

Glossary and Abbreviations

German enterprise name followed by:

Flugzeug	aircraft, airplane(USA)
-bau	construction, manufacture
-fabrik	factory, plant
-werk	works, company
AG	Aktiengesellschaft = joint stock company
IG	Interessengemeinschaft = community of interests
KG	Kommanditgesellschaft = limited partnership company
GmbH	Gesellschaft mit beschränkter Haftung = limited liability company
eV	eingetragener Verein = registered company

Principal types of aircraft

Aufklärer	reconnaissance
Bomber	bomber
Gleiter, Segler	glider, sailplane
Heimatschützer	home protector
Jäger	fighter
Jagdbomber	fighter-bomber
Lastensegler	load-carrying glider
Großraumsegler	large-capacity glider
Stuka	Sturzkampfflugzeug = dive-bomber
Waffenträger	weapons carrier
Zerstörer	twin-engined heavy fighter

Air Force and Luftwaffe-related

Abteilung	Detachment, department
BAL	Bauaufsicht der Luftwaffe = Construction Inspectorate
BG	Bombardment Group(USA)
Flak	Fliegerabwehrkanone = anti-aircraft cannon
Führer	Leader, unit head, pilot
E-Stelle	Erprobungsstelle der Luftwaffe = Evaluation/Test Centre
Erprobungskommando	Evaluation Detachment
Flughafen	Airport
FuG	Funkgerät = radio or radar set
FAGr	Fernaufklärungsgruppe = Long-range Reconnaissance Wing
Fliegerhorst	Air Base
Geschwader	Group (RAF) or Squadron (USAAF)
GFM	Generalfeldmarschall = Marshal of the RAF, General of the Air Force
GL	Generalluftzeugmeister = Chief of Air Procurement in the RLM
Gruppe	Wing (RAF) or Group (USAAF)
GS	Gigantstaffel = Me 321/Me 323 Squadron *or* Großraumsegler (q.v.)
Heer	German Army
JG	Jagdgeschwader or -gruppe = Fighter Group or Wing
JV	Jagdverband = Fighter formation
Kette	3-aircraft flight
KG	Kampfgruppe = Bomber Wing
Kommando	Detachment
Lieferplan	Delivery Plan
Luftwaffe	German Air Force
Luftflotte	Air Fleet
MG	Maschinengewehr = machine gun (below 20mm)
MK	Maschinenkanone = aircraft cannon (20mm and above)
Ob.d.L.	Oberbefehlshaber der Luftwaffe = Luftwaffe Commander-in-Chief
OKL	Oberkommando der Luftwaffe = Luftwaffe Supreme Command
OKW	Oberkommando der Wehrmacht = Armed Forces Supreme Command
RAF	Royal Air Force
RATO	Rocket-assisted take-off
Revi	Reflexvizier = reflex gunsight
Rotte	2-aircraft flight
RLM	Reichsluftfahrtministerium = German Air Ministry
Rüstsatz	Field conversion set
SKG	Schnellkampfgeschwader = Fast-bomber Geschwader
Schwarm	4-aircraft flight
Sonderkommando	Special Detachment
Stab	HQ, Staff
Staffel	Squadron
TG	Transportgeschwader = Transport Squadron
Troika	3-aircraft towing group
USAAF	United States Army Air Force (redesignated USAF in 1947)
USSBS	United States Strategic Bombing Survey
Wehrmacht	German Armed Forces
WGr	Werfergranate = mortar grenade
zbV	zur besonderen Verwendung = for special use
ZG	Zerstörergeschwader = Heavy fighter (destroyer) Wing

Organisations and other terms

A/A	anti-aircraft(weapons)
Autobahn	motorway
BA/MA	Bundesarchiv/Militärarchiv, Freiburg (photocredits)
Beruftrade	profession
DAF	Deutsche Arbeitsfront = German Workers Front
DAK	Deutsches Afrika-Korps = German Africa Corps
DASA	Deutsche Aerospace AG
DDR	Deutsche Demokratische Republik = German Democratic Republic (former East Germany)
DEST	Deutsche Erd- und Steinwerke = German Earth and Stone Works
DFS	Deutsche Forschungsanstalt für Segelfluge = German Research Institute for Sailplane Flight
DM	Deutsches Museum, Munich (photocredits)
DRK	Deutsches Rotes Kreuz = German Red Cross
EADS	European Aeronautics Defence & Space Agency (photocredits)
Gauleiter	Nazi District Leader *or* Area Commander
Gestapo	Geheime Staatspolizei = Nazi Secret State Police
HASA	Hispano-Aviacion S.A.
Halle	hall, hangar
HJ	Hitler Jugend = Hitler Youth
HWK	Hellmuth Walterwerke, Kiel
KdF	Kraft durch Freude = Strength through Joy (Nazi recreational organisation)
KZ	Konzentrationslager = concentration camp
Lagerhalle	storage hall/hangar
NASM	National Air and Space Museum (USA)
NSDAP	Nationalsozialistische Deutsche Arbeiterpartei = Nazi Party
PoW	Prisoner of War (PW in USA)
Reich	State, nation
RM	Reichsmarks (German currency in the Third Reich)
SA	Sturmabteilung = Nazi Storm Troopers
SD	Sicherheitsdienst = Nazi Security Service
SED	Sozialistische Einheitspartei Deutschlands = DDR Communist Party
SNCAN	Société Nationaledes Constructions Aéronautiques du Nord
Siedlung	community
Strasse	street, road
USA	United States of America
USAF	United States Air Force (photocredits)
USSR	Union of Soviet Socialist Republics
W/T	Wireless/telephone

Equivalent ranks in

Luftwaffe	Royal Air Force	USAAF
Generalfeldmarschall	Marshal of the RAF	General (5-star)
Generaloberst	Air Chief Marshal	General (4-star)
General der Flieger	Air Marshal	Lieutenant General
Generalleutnant	Air Vice Marshal	Major General
Generalmajor	Air Commodore	Brigadier General
Oberst	Group Captain	Colonel
Oberstleutnant	Wing Commander	Lieutenant Colonel
Major	Squadron Leader	Major
Hauptmann	Flight Lieutenant	Captain
Oberleutnant	Flying Officer	First Lieutenant
Leutnant	Pilot Officer	Lieutenant
Stabsfeldwebel	Warrant Officer	Warrant Officer
Oberfeldwebel	Flight Sergeant	Master Sergeant
Feldwebel	Sergeant	Technical Sergeant
Unteroffizier	Corporal	Staff Sergeant
Obergefreiter	Leading Aircraftman	Corporal
Gefreiter	Aircraftman First Class	Private First Class
Flieger	Aircraftman	Second Class Private
Flugkapitän	Flight Captain, title awarded to civilian airline and test pilots	

The Messerschmitt-Werke at Regensburg

PART 1

CHAPTER 1

Construction and the commencement of production: 1936-1942

FOLLOWING the Machtergreifung (Assumption of Power) by the NSDAP (Nazi) Party on 30 January 1933 when Adolf Hitler was appointed Reichs Chancellor, immediate steps were taken secretly to shake off the military restrictions that had been imposed on a defeated Germany by the victorious Allies in June 1919. Although the German aviation industry had gradually re-emerged with the permitted manufacture of civil aircraft as a result of periodic relaxations of Allied restrictions that had been imposed during the first 15 years since the end of the First World War, the new government was firmly set on its path to rebuild a powerful new Luftwaffe (German Air Force), surreptitious work to this end having been conducted in the interim until then by German firms in neighbouring countries in Europe as well as in the USSR. As a first step, the former air ace Hermann Göring, who had been an ardent follower of Adolf Hitler from the earliest days, among his several political functions was appointed Reichs Commissioner for Aviation, tasked with responsibility for establishing a new secret Luftwaffe that in terms of aircraft and equipment, would soon be on a par with the Air Forces of the other major European Powers. For the Messerschmitt concern, whose principal manufacturing centre was at Augsburg, this meant the erection of new plants in order to expand its manufacturing capability for military aircraft.

Still known at the time as the Bayerische Flugzeugwerke GmbH (Bavarian Aircraft Company Ltd.), aircraft production at Augsburg centred in 1936-37 on manufacture of the Bf 108 and Bf 109. During this period, Prof. Dr.-Ing. Wilhelm (Willy) Messerschmitt was head of the Technical and Design Offices of the firm, and under the standardized aircraft designation system which consisted of a firm's identification prefix followed by a sequential number introduced by the newly-created Reichsluftfahrtministerium (German Air Ministry) or RLM in 1934, its aircraft carried the short prefix 'Bf'. In the public domain, however, its aircraft were most often referred to as 'Me' types, which from the historical aspect, is not strictly correct. Leading personalities in the Third Reich had at that time favoured the firm being renamed, and on 11 July 1938, with the approval of the Board and the shareholders the Augsburg company was renamed Messerschmitt AG. Willy Messerschmitt himself simultaneously became its Generaldirektor, and all newer designs from the stable henceforth carried the prefix 'Me' that was applied to the Me 163, Me 210, Me 262, Me 321 and Me 323 described in this volume. There were, of course, several other designs that carried 'Bf' and 'Me' designations as well.

Aircraft production capacity by the Bayerische Flugzeugwerke was expanded by order of the RLM on 27 June 1936, and although the firm had been forced to look for a new location for a manufacturing plant, this was rejected at that time by the town of Augsburg. The new plant was foreseen for mass-production of the Bf 108 as well as the wings and tail surfaces of the Bf 110. The original intention had been to erect this plant at Deggendorf but the Chairman of the Board, Theo Croneiß, was very much in favour of Regensburg, so that a preliminary decision for selection of this location took place in a confidential meeting between Dr. Schotterheim – the Lord Mayor of Regensburg, Willy Messerschmitt, and Theo Croneiß at the latter's country estate in Schrammhof near Laaber.

It should be mentioned here that Theo Croneiß, a pilot during the First World War and owner of the Nordbayerische Verkehrsflug GmbH airline, had already been a good friend of Messerschmitt during the 1920s, when the designer had produced various civil aircraft types such as the M 18, M 20 and M 28. In 1931, however, within the space of six months, two examples of the M 20 in service with Lufthansa crashed, causing a number of passenger fatalities, so that all aircraft of this type were forbidden for civil use. At that time, the Generaldirektor of Lufthansa was Erhard Milch, who held Messerschmitt to blame for the crashes, but no

Construction and the commencement of production: 1936-1942

direct responsibility for this could be established as the entire empennage of one of the aircraft had twisted due to the effects of wind gusts which led to a partial structural collapse. Nevertheless, although as a result of the crashes the strength requirements for aircraft became doubled, Milch still held Messerschmitt fully responsible and cancelled the remaining M 20s that were on order for the airline: a decision which led to the catastrophe that in 1933 Messerschmitt was forced to go into liquidation.

In addition to that, the small airline of Theo Croneiß, equipped with 20 examples of the M 18 (pilot plus 4-passenger), was a serious competitor to Milch's Lufthansa, and at a cost of only RM 0.70 per km, operated considerably more efficiently than the latter's figure of RM 2.00 per km. This then, formed the basis for the enmity between Milch on the one hand and Messerschmitt/Croneiß on the other, which reached its zenith in 1942 when a host of problems was experienced with the Me 210 that eventually led to Messerschmitt being displaced as head of the company.

To recap at this point, in October 1933 Theo Croneiß had received a strictly confidential letter from the then Prussian Ministerpräsident Hermann Göring, who commissioned him to establish an aircraft company in Bavaria (when the Bayerische Flugzeugwerke was in liquidation). At the same time, Göring assigned Croneiß the task of developing a first-class civil airliner and a very fast courier aircraft (see Appendix 1). In practical terms, this led to the birth of the development and manufacture of the Bf 108 and the soon-to-follow Bf 109 fighter designed by Willy Messerschmitt. At that time, Croneiß was also a member of the staff of the SA leader Ernst Röhm, so that he made full use of all his political and business connections to once more draw the Bayerische Flugzeugwerke and Willy Messerschmitt as designer, into the realm of German aircraft production. It was only through good fortune that Croneiß, who had remained in Munich and had been forewarned by Deputy Führer Rudolf Hess not to go to Bad Wiessee, that he escaped the destruction and murder of the SA leadership under Röhm, a 'clean-up' that had been ordered by Adolf Hitler. Croneiß, who thereafter switched his allegiance to Hitler's deputy Hess, also joined the Luftwaffe and the SS. According to the testimony of his son, in so doing Croneiß thereby sought to cover himself on all sides, something which proved necessary for survival in the Third Reich with all its intrigues and power politics.

In further discussions concerning the new aircraft plant, Regensburg was also the choice of the Board of Directors as it possessed the most important criteria for a new aircraft production plant. Although it had an airfield and the necessary potential in terms of a workforce, as it later turned out, it was lacking in skilled workers. In addition, the low economic strength of the town of Regensburg may have played a role in the decision to set up an aircraft industry there. In 1936, the Bayerische Flugzeugwerke acquired an appropriate property in the Prüfeninger Strasse in the western part of Regensburg. Here, south of the Danube between the new hospital of the Barmherziger Brüder (Brothers of Charity) and the racecourse, a completely new aircraft factory was erected on an area of 1 km² (10,751,054 ft²) with its own enlarged industrial airfield that had formerly served as the Regensburg civil airfield. The airfield was made over rent-free for a period of 20 years by the Flughafen GmbH Regensburg to the Bayerische Flugzeugwerke. Already at that time there were warning voices, among others, from the Bishop of Regensburg, who made

Professor Willy Messerschmitt with Works Director Theo Croneiß at the latter's country house at Schrammhof. (Photo Croneiß)

known their views against the building of an aircraft plant in the immediate neighbourhood of a hospital, but they met with no success. On 24 July 1936, a new enterprise for the Regensburg plant was established: the Bayerische Flugzeugwerke Regensburg GmbH, which became renamed Messerschmitt GmbH Regensburg on 13 November 1940.

Tasked with the planning of the Regensburg Werke were the architects Wilhelm Wichtendahl and Bernhard Hermkes, and with their layout proposal, succeeded in embedding an industrial installation within a nature-park landscape. The production Hallen (halls or hangars) were not centrally located in a central zone, but were dispersed over the entire area and connected to one another by concreted roads. This decentralized arrangement resulted in the necessity to establish a transport system within the plant, and although the distances between the buildings were a disadvantage, nevertheless had the advantage in that in an enemy air raid, the entire plant would not be disabled in one blow for a long duration. This fact became very clear when it suffered a devastating bombing raid on 17 August 1943, but despite severe damage, production was able to be resumed after three weeks of repair work.

Construction work at the Regensburg site commenced at the end of 1936 and from the very beginning the site was guarded by the newly-established Works Security Service. The Richtfest (topping-out ceremony) followed on 8 May 1937. Accelerated construction of the large storage warehouse with a railway connection made it possible to complete and equip it from July 1937 onwards. Erection of machine tooling, buildings and various other plant installations in the individual assembly halls and workshops began in mid 1937. This activity was largely carried out by the Regensburg workforce that had received training in the Augsburg plant. In 1936-37, the following preliminary and final assembly halls were erected: a metalwork Halle for presses, milling machines, and lathes; a Halle for the manufacture of wing spars and ribs, as well as Hallen for wings and fuselages. The transformer station and heating works were provided with the most modern technology of the day that was available, and the large central mess hall at the entrance to the Prüfeninger Strasse supplied the several individual canteens that were spread out over the Works grounds.

In an act of financial strength, the town of Regensburg placed the necessary infrastructure facilities

11

Messerschmitt Board Directors Theo Croneiß (left) and Friedrich Wilhelm Seiler view the foundations of the Administration Building in Regensburg in 1937. In the background are the hospital buildings at the Prüfeninger Straße. (Photo Croneiß)

Top right: The Works buildings were erected in 1937 with the most modern technical aids. Their close proximity to the Barmherziger Brüder (Brothers of Charity) hospital buildings in the background is evident. (Photo Croneiß)

such as electric power and water connections at the disposal of the works. There then followed the extension of the Prüfeninger Strasse, and the tram transport depot had to be expanded. For the supply of water, new and efficient pipelines and a new water-well was necessary. For the town, this meant an investment of RM 600,000 which, however, was soon recovered from rates and taxes collected, since the Messerschmitt-Werke was in any case the largest single consumer of municipal supplies in terms of electric power and water consumption. For the hiring of the necessary personnel, an administrative office was rented in the town, which at the beginning of May 1937 was relocated to a barracks on the grounds of the plant. In the first stage of erection, a workforce of 5,000 employees was planned, which in December 1939 was almost attained with a total of 4,850. A deficit in the Regensburg plant was the lack of qualified employees, so that the plant management instituted internal training programmes, partially in Augsburg. The Administration building – currently the Kaufmännische Berufschule (Commercial Trade School), whose construction was begun in March 1937, had advanced so far in November that it was able to be occupied on 15 November.

On 24 April 1937, the Richtfest followed for the employee 'Siedlung' (housing colony) – the 'Hermann Göring Heim', which today is the Ganghofer Siedlung. From the autumn of 1936, 1,500 workers on the Ziegetsberg built, in terrace or step-form, on the slope, a total of 228 houses containing 608 apartments. A second phase followed in summer 1939 with 232 apartments in 20 4-family and 19 8-family houses. These were joined by a Kindergarten and a Volksschule (elementary or primary school) which, however, were only able to be completed in 1941, plus two restaurants and a few shops. Altogether, within a short period of construction, there arose a completely new suburb. These apartments were occupied exclusively by plant employees and had cost RM 4 million. Later on, the Schottenheim Siedlung (currently the Konrad Siedlung) formed an additional extension in the northeastern part of the town. But despite these construction measures, living accommodation remained a bottleneck in Regensburg that became even more acute during the course of the Second World War. As a consequence, numerous barrack blocks arose in almost all parts of the town, which long after the end of the war, served as refugee accommodation.

With great pomp and ceremony, the Richtfest for the new aircraft plant was celebrated on 8 May 1937. From November that year, series production of the Bf 108 Taifun (Typhoon) ran at full speed. Numerous pre-fabricated small parts and component groups for the wings and fuselages were transported from Augsburg to Regensburg. Senior staff from Augsburg instructed the Regensburg workforce on the mating of individual components and final assembly of the aircraft, and in the space of eighteen months, in the true sense of the word, an aircraft plant rose from the ground and commenced with aircraft production that portrayed the apex of technology of the time. The application of the newest technological methods in production was put to use in the most modern assembly halls, in conjunction with a pathfinding method of workplace arrangement.

The Commencement of Bf 108 production in 1938

In January 1938, the very first aircraft built in Regensburg were rolled out of the final assembly halls. Production ran at maximum pace and in that year, 175 Bf 108s were manufactured. On 29 January 1938, the Administration Department of the Bayerische Flugzeugwerke Regensburg GmbH moved out of the Augsburg premises and during the year further Hallen and buildings such as flight-test hangars, upholstery, aero-engine and paintshops were erected, as well as the conically-shaped air-raid bunker completed in 1938. The latter, with room for 450 people, was divided into four layers about 20 m (66 ft) in height, had a diameter of 12 m (39 ft) and a wall thickness of 2 m (6.6 ft). According to American statements, at the end of the war this bunker was the sole undamaged edifice on the Messerschmitt grounds in Regensburg-Prüfening. During the war, it had been used for the storage of documents such as design drawings for the construction of formers or jigs and for aircraft blueprints, as well as by the plant leadership as an air-raid shelter. Further air-raid shelters were located in the cellar of the Administration building, in the cellars of the various canteens, and in some of the assembly halls. These rooms were equipped with steel doors and locks, but because of their conventional steel and concrete roofing, afforded only limited protection.

After Messerschmitt had also won the contest for what became the Bf 110 Zerstörer (twin-engined heavy fighter), preparations followed in Augsburg in 1938 for series production of this aircraft. For the Regensburg plant, this had far-reaching consequences since Bf 109 production, previously at Augsburg, had to be relocated for lack of space there to Regensburg. This thus gave Regensburg a completely new production status which led to the planning of an even further expansion of the plant. Within the framework of this expansion plan, the erection of a second storage Halle, two further production Hallen (as works-internal training workshops became necessary), and purchasing negotiations for

Construction and the commencement of production: 1936-1942

The Messerschmitt Administration Building in Regensburg. The entrance hall was on the east side and above it on the 2nd floor, the large conference room and the Works management's offices. Together with the flight-test building (occupied by Siemens at the time of writing), the former administration centre - currently the Matthäus-Runtinger-Berufsbildungszentrum (Professional Training Centre), are the only two remaining but considerably structurally-modified buildings of the former Messerschmitt-Werke. (Photo Linder)

Left: On both sides of the Augsburger Straße on the Ziegetsberg, a completely new surburb was erected and is still popular today as each house has a garden strip. (Photo Croneiß)

obtaining the required surface area of around 22,000 m² (236,800 ft²) were initiated immediately. The most decisive aspect in this connection was as follows: whereas until that time Regensburg had manufactured the Bf 108 Taifun for commercial use as well as for the Luftwaffe, the decision to produce the Bf 109 fighter here transformed the Regensburg plant into a first-rate armaments production centre.

Further alterations took place at the airfield, since the higher take-off and landing speeds of the Bf 109 necessitated its enlargement. Corresponding approval for this from the RLM was granted immediately and not only was the necessary premises space purchased, but also on grounds of its intended purpose, the hitherto rented airfield. Bf 109 production also required the erection of covered weapon adjustment and centring stands whose completion, however, first became ready in 1939 and for this purpose, an additional 9,000 m² (96,873 ft²) was acquired.

During the period when the last Bf 109 E was rolled out in Augsburg in August and handed over to the Luftwaffe, preparations had begun in autumn 1938 for final assembly of this aircraft in Regensburg. As with the Bf 108, the same procedure was to be followed with the Bf 109. Regensburg personnel were trained by those in Augsburg and materials, construction jigs, component parts and component groups in all phases of manufacture were transported by rail to Regensburg, the Augsburg senior staff assisting in starting-up production. In January 1938, the number of employees rose by 1,477 and

Elly Beinhorn, the internationally renowned pilot, sits on the rim of the cockpit of the Bf 108 D (D-IROS) while in discussion with Works Director Theo Croneiß and other Messerschmitt personnel. (Photo Croneiß)

The Bf 108 B (D-INVJ) in Works livery. The name Taifun (Typhoon) is inscribed beneath the canopy. (Photo Croneiß)

climbed until September to reach a total of 2,603, of which 122 were apprentices and probationers. Due to the commencement of Bf 109 production, the employee total rose to 2,950 at the end of the year, which meant a doubling of the workforce within the space of 12 months.

By virtue of its excellent performance, the Bf 108 had proven to be an outstanding aircraft in its class. On 28 October 1938, the world-famous Atlantic flyer Charles Lindbergh was afforded the opportunity to fly a Bf 108 B in Berlin and after he had landed, said: 'It's the best aircraft in its class that I have ever flown.' Numerous noteworthy flights were accomplished by the Bf 108 during that decade to demonstrate its performance capabilities. On 25 May 1936, a Bf 108 B (D-IONO) was transported by air to Rio de Janeiro by the LZ 129 'Hindenburg' airship. This was followed by a demonstration flight over South America in which it overflew the Andes mountains. In all of the countries where the Bf 108 made its appearance, it generated considerable attention as aircraft types of its size were mainly biplanes. With its elegant lines, its technical novelties of wing leading-edge slats and trailing-edge flaps as well as its retractable undercarriage, it stood out like an aircraft from another planet. Above all, its outstanding performance was due to its overall aerodynamic concept, which for all successive aircraft types of its size right up to the present time, has served as a forbear. In February 1937, the famous German female pilot Elly Beinhorn[1] gained 2nd place in the international Oasis Rundflug (circuit flight) in Egypt in a Bf 108 B-1 W.Nr. 825 (D-IGNY), and in that same year, she made a long-distance flight from Berlin to Capetown and back. In May 1937, Flugkapitän Hans Seidemann won the air race on the Isle of Man with the Bf 108 (D-IOSA). In December 1937, a Bf 108 (D-IBFW) was transported by ship to Rio de Janeiro and from there, took-off on a promotional flight through South and North America, arriving in New York on 5 July 1938. Flown by Otto Brindlinger, it covered a distance of 44,000 km (27,340 mls). In July 1938, the international Queen Astrid Race was won by a Bf 108 and in August, at the international flying contest in Dinard, France, and in the Italian Raduno del Littorio, a Bf 108 gained 2nd place.

These successes, attained through its already-mentioned excellent performance and technical innovations, spurred several countries into ordering examples of the Bf 108 and led to orders from Australia (1), Austria (4), Bulgaria (6), Chile (1), Hungary (1), Japan (1), Rumania (6), Spain (1), Switzerland (12), the UK (1), USA (1), USSR (2), and Yugoslavia (12). It should be taken into account here that several countries only made these purchases in order to examine and test the design and manufacture of this extremely modern aircraft. For Messerschmitt, the foreign purchases meant a significant economic success. The latter enabled later successes to be achieved in as much as Hungary, Rumania, Switzerland, Yugoslavia and others also bought the Bf 109. The largest order, however, was for the Luftwaffe which, in the

[1.] Elly Beinhorn was the first female pilot to accomplish a round-the-world flight in the 1930s. In a historical aviation documentary shown on a German TV station in November 2007, it was mentioned that she celebrated her 100th birthday on 30 May 2007. She died in a Seniorenheim (senior citizens home) on 28 November 2007. (Translator)

Construction and the commencement of production: 1936-1942

A Bf 108 B-1 in Luftwaffe markings on a snow-covered Regensburg airfield in 1938. (Photo Croneiß)

The first Regensburg-built Bf 108 B-1 leaves the final assembly hall in January 1938. The rhyming (in German) placard notice read: 'Wing your way up into heaven's tent / Make known Germany's glory to the whole world / The first, from the bank of the Danube / That emanated from Regensburg' (Photo Radinger)

Flugkapitän Fritz Trenkle posing on Regensburg airfield in 1938 beside Bf 108 B-1 (D-ICRO) which was used by the Messerschmitt Board. (Photo Trenkle)

NEST OF EAGLES

Bf 108 fuselage assembly in Regensburg. Here, a Messerschmitt worker is attaching the cockpit canopy frame to the fuselage. The hollow wing stubs each housed a fuel tank. (Photo Croneiß)

Technicians work on the port wing of a Bf 108. (Photo Croneiß)

A view inside the duel-control, comfortable and very comprehensivley equipped cockpit of a Bf 108. Note the double side-opening canopy. (Photo Radinger)

Construction and the commencement of production: 1936-1942

A Bf 108 B-1 destined for the Rumanian Air Force, pictured in Regensburg in 1939. The blockhouse in the background housed the Flight Operations Control personnel. (Photo Radinger)

unprecedented phase of its build-up (1936-39), employed the Bf 108 as a courier and communications aircraft and as a trainer for Bf 109 fighter pilots.

Bf 108 Taifun production in Regensburg, 1938-1942

Production of the Bf 108 ceased in Augsburg in February 1938, presumably with Werknr 1590 (D-IESH). From autumn 1937 all production jigs, machine tools, partly-built airframe parts and raw materials were transported to Regensburg, and under the leadership of Augsburg specialists, preparations were made for the manufacture, final assembly and works flight-testing for the Bf 108 in Prüfening. Final assembly of the Bf 108 had already begun in January 1938 in Regensburg, where 12 examples were rolled out that month from the final assembly hall onto the airfield, and represented the start of one of the most capable German aircraft plants during the Second World War. Although 175 Bf 108s were completed in 1938, production numbers continually tailed off to make way for the additional manufacture of the Bf 109 from January 1939. Not only was a new aircraft built in Regensburg in 1938, but also repairs on 125 examples were carried out, of which 80 Bf 108s received a strengthened wing main spar in compliance with Alteration Directive 20/21.

At Messerschmitt GmbH Regensburg, a total of 516 Bf 108 B-1s and D-1s were produced from January 1938 until June 1942. Due to the wartime need to concentrate on the Bf 109 in Regensburg, Bf 108 production was thereafter transferred to SNCAN in Les Mureaux, France. The last Bf 108 to be completed in Regensburg was Bf 108 D-1 Werknr 3094 (RE+EM) which was test-flown by Sepp Haid in June 1942. With this, production thus came to an end in Germany of one of the most modern and successful sports aircraft, and even up to the to present time, the German aviation industry has been

Pictured in May 1939 at Regensburg is Bf 108 (HB-EKO) W.Nr. 2064, shortly before delivery to the Swiss Air Force. (Photo Trenkle)

17

NEST OF EAGLES

Bf 108 B-1 final assembly in Regensburg in 1939. This example has a fixed-pitch Schwarz propeller. A Bf 109 E can be made out in the background. (Photo Croneiß).

unsuccessful in evolving a successor in the tradition and weight class of the Bf 108.

The Bf 108 was powered by a 240 hp Argus As 10 C 8-cylinder inverted-V in-line engine that had a cubic capacity of 12.7 litres, weighed 193 kg (425.5 lb), and was one of the most reliable powerplants of its time. The Bf 108 B-1 normally had a series-produced 2-bladed fixed-pitch wooden Schwarz propeller, but could if desired, be equipped with a variable-pitch Me P7 propeller developed by Messerschmitt. The Bf 108 D-1, powered by an As 10 R where the aircraft electrical system was altered from 12 to 24 volts, had the landing light integrated into the starboard wing root, the rudder having a balance weight at its upper end. In those examples that were equipped with the variable-pitch propeller, take-off run was considerably reduced due to its improved acceleration, and climb performance was likewise improved. With its fixed-pitch propeller, the Bf 108 B-1 climbed to 2,000 m (6,560 ft) in 8.1 minutes, whereas the B-2 with its variable-pitch propeller only needed 7 minutes. The cruising speed of around 250 km/h (155 mph) and maximum speed of around 285 km/h (177 mph) are certainly comparable with those of modern-day sports aircraft.

A few examples of the Taifun still exist worldwide that are in flying condition and count among the attractions at every Flying Meet. Among these are the Regensburg-built Bf 108 B W.Nr. 2246 (NF+MP) that was painstakingly restored by Lufthansa and christened 'Elly Beinhorn' and the Bf 108 D-1 W.Nr. 3059 (VE+LI), the latter, at the time of writing, flying with the Commemorative Air Force (CAF) in the USA. A further Bf 108 D-1 (D-EFPT), built in Les Mureaux on jigs furnished by Regensburg, flew as the traditional aircraft of the Flugzeugunion-Süd (DASA) and was stationed in Germany in Manching near Ingolstadt. One airshow commentator once described it as a classical beauty and a technical masterpiece of German aircraft design. In an airshow in Berlin-Johannisthal on 9 September 1995, this aircraft was lost in a crash in which both pilots, Gerd Kahdemann and Reinhard Furrer, were killed. As a substitute, the Messerschmitt Foundation acquired from a Hamburg businessman a flyable Bf 108 that was presumably built in Regensburg in 1939, and as D-ESBH, thrilled the public at airshows. At the time of writing, a further Bf 108 formed an exhibit in the historic aircraft depot in Oberschleißheim near Munich, and yet another at the Deutsches Museum in Munich.

Bf 108 Production in 1938

Accepted in month	Series-built aircraft	Repair-aircraft
January	12	4
February	10	4
March	13	12
April	12 (1)	9
May	22 (1)	10
June	28	15
July	25	10
August	15 (1)	10
September	13 (1)	20
October	9 (2)	14
November	10	9
December	12	8
Total :	**181**	**125**

Construction and the commencement of production: 1936-1942

The total of six (bracketed) examples in the table opposite were completed up to the flight-test stage but were not delivered. 80 of the repair aircraft received the strengthened main spar in accordance with Alteration Directive 20/21.

Total numbers of aircraft types built between 1938 and 1945 at Regensburg are listed in Appendix 2, whilst total personnel employed between 1936 and 1945 are listed in Appendix 3. Details of the Bf 108 and Werknummern of Regensburg-built aircraft are in Appendix 4.

Training of Apprentices

From the very beginning, great emphasis was placed at Regensburg on the training and further education of the workforce. Particular attention was paid to apprentice training and for this purpose a training workshop and later on, an apprenticeship centre with a trade school and apartments were built. The number of trainees rose continuously from year to year and reached its peak of 1,350 in 1944-45. As the Augsburg Town Councillor, Ing. Hans Himmelmeyer, informed the author: 'In 1938, I was among the first apprentices that were engaged by the Messerschmitt firm. At that time, the trainee workshop was still located in a Halle in which the empennages were being built. We initially underwent a one-year basic training in the metalworking shop, which encompassed everything from filing of a workpiece and sheet-metal work right up to working with drilling, milling and turning machines. After this basic training year, one was able to decide what further path one wished to follow, as there were all sorts of possibilities such as metalworking, fitting, jig construction, carpentry, assembly, rotary workshop, electro- and final assembly, works flight-testing, and so on. In the second apprenticeship year, we were then engaged for a time in production. Following the completion of my training period, I joined the Luftwaffe where I completed my training as a pilot and flew the Me 109 on operations. After the war, I started on my engineering course. On looking back, I must say that in the conditions at that time, we were given excellent professional training at the Messerschmitt GmbH.'

Hermann Kronseder, the founder of the Krones firm in Neutraubling, in his book *Mein Leben* (My Life), described his apprenticeship years at Messerschmitt: 'After I left school, which was in 1938-39, there were no apprenticeship opportunities anywhere. I had firmly decided to learn metalworking as a profession. At any rate, I completed the acceptance tests as an apprentice in the Messerschmitt Flugzeugwerke in Regensburg. I knew that out of every ten candidates, at the most two became accepted, whilst the remainder did not find an apprenticeship anywhere for years on end. I was happy that I had passed the examinations and that I was taken on at the age of fourteen. In the first apprenticeship year, we received RM 5 per week, in the

Messerschmitt apprentices in Regensburg. They not only underwent their apprenticeship training there, but also completed military drill. (Photo Croneiß)

The SG 38 glider 'Theo Croneiß' built by apprentices is made ready for take-off. (Photo Croneiß)

19

A view inside the apprenticeship workshop at Messerschmitt Regensburg. (Photo Mirter)

second RM 7.50, in the third RM 10, and finally, RM 12. I can still remember exactly when war broke out in September 1939, and especially since all of us apprentices hoped that our instructors had now to do military service, that we would be left to ourselves as far as work was concerned. Naturally, nothing of this sort happened: on the contrary. Our training was even more rigorously conducted, so that already in our second year, we came into the production sphere. I was allowed to work on the Me 109, one of the most famous fighter aircraft. Soon after that, I was detailed to go to Obertraubling, which at that time consisted only of an enormous airfield and a few barrack buildings – directly alongside the windows of the present-day Krones AG, so to speak. The most important things I learned at Messerschmitt was from our mathematics teacher. He emphasised to us again and again that most of the mistakes were made in the design phase when they were not scrupulously controlled. The training in Regensburg was good, but firm. Whenever we apprentices did something especially stupid, we were slapped over the ears from the head instructor, or else on a Saturday afternoon, had to do a 4-hour long 'punishment exercise'. More than once, I had to pace the length and breadth of the whole Regensburg airfield, through all its puddles and pot-holes. But in my Final Certificate in August 1942, I in fact had a Grade 1 for the practicals and a 2 for theory. My apprenticeship as a metal-aircraft builder thus came to an end.'

Erich Heiss of Amberg also described his apprenticeship: 'I began my apprenticeship on 13 April 1942 in the aircraft plant in Regensburg. Following basic training on the most diverse workpieces, there followed courses in welding, forging, milling and turning. In keeping with a directive, the first aircraft electro-mechanical course was introduced. There were 29 of us apprentices, and on 17 August 1943, when a terrible air raid took place, 14 from my class were killed, and even my valuables and personal documents were destroyed. Following emergency accommodation in a brewery building in Winzer, we had to daily take the ferry over the Danube to get to Obertraubling, where I was engaged in final assembly work until a further air raid on 22 February 1944 changed my activity. Out of damaged Bf 109s which had been parked at the edge of the airfield, we removed the aircraft instruments as well as whatever else was still usable. In the middle of the year we were relocated to Marienthal near Deggendorf. From here, Hans Heim and myself were ordered to go to Weiden with a particular task to perform. Equipped with food coupons, we were assigned accommodation in the railway hotel and on the following day we were made familiar with the control column of the Me 109 by Witt Weiden, i.e., we pushed through its cabling and weapons installations and so forth. When we returned to Marienthal, we taught the other trainees and started on control column production. On 30 January 1944, I took my examination.'

Seen in retrospect, the legacy of Messerschmitt GmbH after the end of the war lay not only the ruins in Prüfening and Obertraubling, but also in a core of well-trained specialist workers who played a very important role in the re-erection of and renewed industrialization in Regensburg.

CHAPTER 2

The outbreak of war and expansion: 1939-1941

1939 – The outbreak of war and Bf 109 E production

ON 1 September 1939, Hitler opened the Second World War with the invasion of Poland, which led, ultimately, to the most total and complete defeat that a nation ever had to face. After the war, German cities were covered by an estimated volume of 400 million m³ (14,125 million ft³) of debris and ashes. Bombing raids caused hundreds of thousands of fatal casualties in the towns and cities of Europe, and millions of fallen soldiers of all nations covered the battlefields. Millions of uprooted people sought a new homeland, and distress, misery and hunger marked the early post-war years.

One aircraft – the Bf 109, made history when in 1939-41 it almost singlehandedly swept from the skies of Europe the Air Forces of the other participants. The German tactic of the four-finger 'Schwarm' that had been tried out in the Spanish Civil War was decisive, as well as the improved technical installment of radio and cannon armament in the Bf 109. The Daimler-Benz DB 601 engine with its fuel injection system gave it a superior performance. With the continuation of the war, the significance of the Regensburg plant continued to rise, for each new campaign that Hitler ordered, swallowed both men and materiel. The Luftwaffe clamoured for ever more fighters, since only these could win air superiority and in this way enabled the remainder of the Luftwaffe's bombers and Stukas (divebombers) to become effective. In the Regensburg plant, this manifested itself in the increase in Bf 109 production and a reduction in Bf 108 production.

The start of large-scale production of the Bf 109 E-3 commenced in Regensburg in January 1939. Only the first 25 aircraft were delivered to the Luftwaffe, as the remainder were released for export. The fact that the export orders of Messerschmitt AG and the Reich were pursued in Regensburg, caused extrordinary problems in the recently commenced production run. The differing variants for export, e.g. for Switzerland and Yugoslavia and those for the Luftwaffe, led to manufacturing problems. What made things more difficult for the overall pursuance of the construction programme was that additionally, in the months of April and May, a taperingoff of skilled workers had to be endured due to their callup for military service. The skilled workers thus had to be replaced by men and women who had to be trained in the internal works training centres. In order to counteract the ever-increasing deficit in skilled workers, the projection and construction of new manufacturing plant ensued. Thus, in the Regensburg plant, in the space of eight months, a new full- and semi-automatic riveting machine was developed that was classed by the RLM as 'secret' and it introduced a novelty into aircraft production. Manufacture in the form of Takten (component completion stages) was further reduced and converted to a conveyor-belt method of production and the entire manufacturing process was undertaken via a new, so-called production-control system which, by virtue of corresponding workshop workforce tier plans, ensured a largely problem-free manufacture. In 1939, the manufacturing capacity could not be fully utilized because of the lack of production manpower. For assembly, a new type of pre-assembly system was introduced in which the manufacturing times were able to be considerably reduced. All components put together in the pre-assembly stages, as far as it was possible anywhere, were fully equipped for final assembly. For the year 1939, the RLM had drawn up a total of six different Delivery Programmes which ensured considerable chaos and constantly led to changes in plant operation and manufacturing.

In order for simultaneous production of the Bf 108 and Bf 109 to become possible at Regensburg in 1939-40, the erection of further Hallen and buildings proved necessary, and included one for the design of construction and production equipment, one for the production of stamping-machine parts, one for preassembly, a weapons-checking and calibrating stand, a fire

21

NEST OF EAGLES

The Bf 109 V25, W.Nr. 1930, coded D-IVCK (factory code VK+AC) during final assembly at Regensburg in 1939. Powered by a DB 601A engine it was an attempt at a more streamlined engine/cowling design. Instead of the normal oil cooler beneath the engine, the V25 featured an annular cooler directly behind the propeller. First flight was on 4 March 1939. It was later converted to a Bf 109 F-2 on 23 November 1939 and sent to Tarnewitz for weapons trials. In the background at left is Bf 109 E-3a (J-305) destined for the Swiss Air Force. (Photo Trenkle)

station, and concreted aircraft parking pens covered by camouflage netting on the southern bank of the Danube. Numerous groups of visitors from abroad came to Regensburg, and despite the already clearly recognizable danger of war in Europe, a delegation from the French Air Force visited the plants in Augsburg and Regensburg. Visiting groups from Brazil, Bulgaria, Yugoslavia, Japan, Switzerland, Hungary and the Soviet Union followed. All of them showed interest in the Bf 109 and its production methods, and even 3 examples of the Bf 109 E were sold to Japan and 5 to Russia.

The state of production as of 31 December 1939 was as follows: 100 Bf 108s were in the course of manufacture, of which 50 were 82% complete and 50 were less than 20% complete. Of 312 examples of the Bf 109 E, 45 were over 50% complete, the remainder less than 50%. Also, 20 of the Bf 109 F-0 model were undergoing manufacture. Due to several alterations being demanded, it no longer became possible at the end of 1938 to deliver the already-started Bf 109 F-0 series, and only 3 examples were completed.

Factory test flights flights were led by Chief Pilot Wendelin Trenkle, who was joined by Works pilots Eichelmann and Mühlenhausen. Acceptance pilot for the Bf 109 was Hauptmann Obermeier from the Luftwaffe Bauaufsicht (Construction Inspectorate) or BAL. The aircraft were accepted directly by the BAL at the industrial airfield and subsequently flown by ferry pilots as well as some fighter pilots to Luftwaffe units. On 1 November 1939, Mühlenhausen crashed near Sinzing on the Danube in a Bf 109 E-3a that was earmarked for export. He had taken off in the aircraft at Prüfening and had flown above a thick cloud layer. During the descent through the clouds, his altitude was too low to level out and the Bf 109 crashed into a forest at 1000 hrs, his body being found in the wreckage. As successor to Mühlenhausen, the Works specialist, Werkmeister Josef 'Sepp' Haid was appointed as Works test pilot. As early as 1935, Haid had begun his pilot training and until then had carried out several factory flights in the Bf 108 and during the war, checked out Bf 109s in a total approaching 5,000 take-offs and landings without serious mishap.

Bf 108 and Bf 109 production in 1939

In contrast to 1938, plant production rose by 100%, where the following aircraft were produced:

For the RLM:	154 Bf 108 B
	25 Bf 109 E-3
For Switzerland:	10 Bf 108 + 5 airframes
	79 Bf 109 E-3a
For Yugoslavia:	17 Bf 108 airframes
	40 Bf 109 E-3a
For other countries:	6 Bf 108
For Germany:	6 Bf 108 + 5 airframes

Total: 193 Bf 108s + 10 Bf 108 airframes (fuselages) 144 Bf 108s

The aircraft and storage depot at Regensburg was expanded by an omnibus, 7 passenger-carrying vehicles, 2 trucks, an ambulance and the Bf 109 B-2 Werknr 1999 (D-ICRO). The financial turnover in 1939 was RM 18.7 million, the private business return comprising 60% of the total turnover, of which 90% in turn was delivered abroad by the Messerschmitt AG in Augsburg. The Works Director was Theo Croneiß in his function as Wehrwirtschaftsführer (Total-War Organisational Leader); the Technical Department was led by Karl Linder; the Commerce side by by Otto Thieme and the Administration Head was Dr. Wedemeyer. In contrast to December 1938 with 2,950 employees, the total rose to 4,850 in December 1939, women accounting for 24% of the total.

In 1939, the Bayerische Flugzeugwerke Regensburg GmbH was declared a 'Nationalsozialistische Deutsche Arbeiterpartei Musterbetrieb' (Model or Exemplary Enterprise). Without doubt, wages and social amenities of the aircraft firm set a good example, since it had a swimming-bath and sports grounds within the plant premises and a recreation centre near Salzburg, etc., which served as exemplary amenities, in addition to above-average wages. The employees considered themselves as an elite, and were proud to be members of this plant. In this regard, Josef Kellnberger of Sandsbach stated: 'At the age of 16 and a half in 1939, as a result of

Standing beside a Bf 109 E-3 at Regensburg are (left to right): Flugkapitän Trenkle, the Italian world record pilot, Francesco Agello and Sales Director, Brindlinger. (Photo Trenkle)

The outbreak of war and expansion: 1939-1941

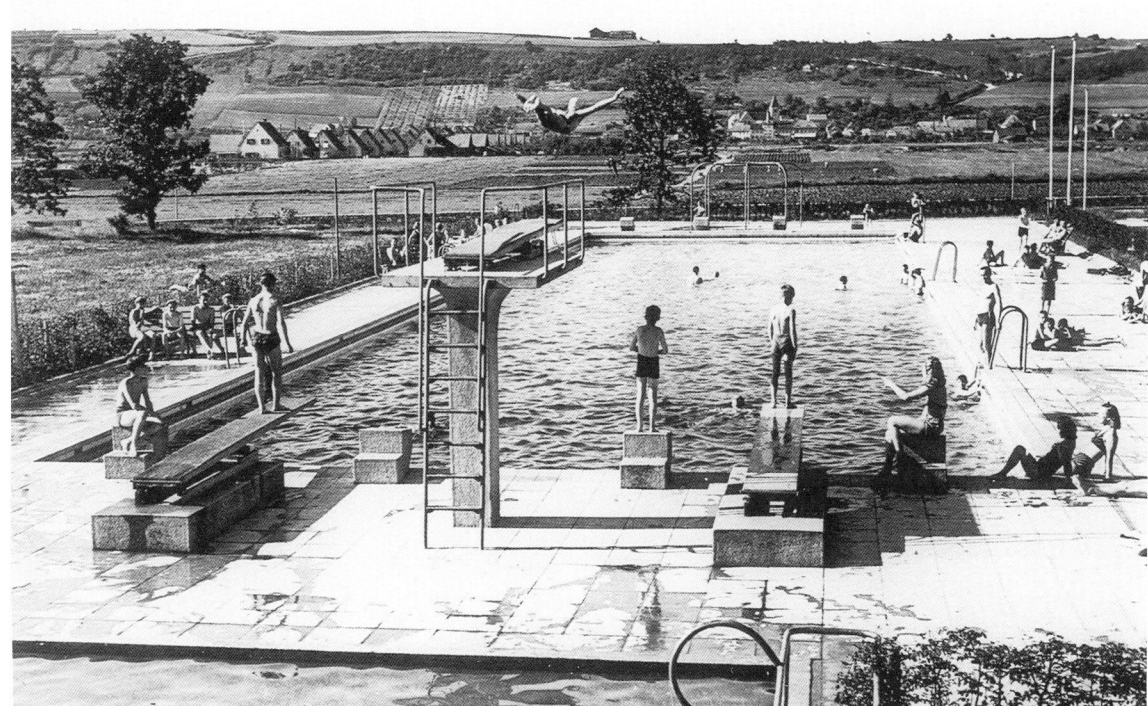

The swimming pool in the Messerschmitt grounds in Regensburg. In the background is the Westheim Siedlung (housing community). (Photo Linder)

The Messerschmitt sports arena. The wall in the background belonged to the metalworking hall in which aircraft wings and fuselage final assembly took place. (Photo Linder)

The Mitteregg-Gaisberg guest house near Salzburg, which served as a recuperation centre for Messerschmitt Regensburg personnel. (Photo Linder)

As the war progressed, more and more women worked in the German armaments industry. They partially replaced the men who had been called-up for Wehrmacht service. (Photo Mirter)

good marks, I was allowed to complete my Gesellen-prüfung (Associate Examination) as a Machine Builder at the Landmaschinenfabrik Käser & Moser in Langquaid. My wages at that time were RM 3 per week. As my father was a disabled war veteran of the First World War, our family finances were not exactly the best. I therefore applied for a job at Messerschmitt in Regensburg and was hired immediately. The hourly wage at the beginning was RM 0.48, which meant for me, in a 48-hour week, a good RM 23 per week. This was more than sevenfold what I was previously paid. Not only that, I was able to work in a bright Halle engaged in final checks on the Me 109, and even in my search for a dwelling – I lived in a single room in the Ludwigstrasse – the plant rendered assistance. The social amenities were exemplary. In any case, I was very proud to be working for Messerschmitt. When I look back on it today, my activities at Messerschmitt in Regensburg and my later period in the Luftwaffe, seen from the specialist aspect, were the high points in my working career.'

But in all areas of the plant, the NSDAP was also represented in its various organisations such as the SA, SS, HJ, DAF, KdF and so on, and hardly any employee could avoid this thick-meshed net. All official activities of the workforce both inside and outside the plant were organised and controlled by the Party organisations. Even the work-breaks in the plant and vacation in the recreation centre in Salzburg consisted of organised freetime by the DAF or KdF. Even if not constantly recognised as such by all concerned, they were subject to control, supervision and ideological indoctrination according to the motto: 'Whoever is not for it, is against the current system.' In countless events, it was continually striven to harness and identify the workforce with the Party, something that was not so easy, given the Bavarian mentality. All work and thought took place under the symbol of the Swastika. Utterance of free political opinion was not tolerated and for the individual concerned, highly dangerous. The Regensburg NSDAP leadership was supported in this strategy by the visit of several prominent NSDAP leaders and Party such as Rudolf Hess, Hermann Göring and the DAF leader Robert Ley, who were received with much pomp and ceremony in the Regensburg Messerschmitt-Werke. This was meant to create the impression that all honours surrounding the plant were due only to Adolf Hitler and his Party. In hindsight, today we can assume that not only aircraft, but also a healthy zeal for National Socialism was 'manufactured' and fostered at the Regensburg plant. This was comparable with the later conditions in the DDR (East Germany) for there also, the SED (Communist Party) exerted massive ideological influence on the nationalized enterprises.

There were also instances of typical NSDAP influence on people and of their effects. A Frau Meier describes the bombing raid on 17 August 1943, in which she lost her 16-year-old son: 'My son Josef worked as an apprentice at Messerschmitt in Regensburg. In the air raid on 17 August, there were hundreds of dead and wounded among the workforce, among whom was my son who was fatally hit, just like several other apprentices. Because of his funeral, I had to visit the Amt (Official Department or Office) concerned in order to take care of the necessary formalities and requested the supply of a coffin for Josef. In response, I was informed that I was not a member of the Party and hence would not receive a coffin. That made me fly into a rage and I asked the men there: "For what purpose has my son been killed?" That worked, and after some humming and hawing, I was supplied with a coffin.'

Frau Mirter reported the ill-treatment of Ostarbeiter-Frauen (female workers from the East): 'In the Messerschmitt-Werke, I was employed as an instructor for the apprentices. Among my duties in 1943 was teaching the Ostarbeiter-Frauen who came to me at the end of their workshift and in the realm of sheet-metal work, received training in filing, riveting, drilling, honing, and so on. The women and young girls always made a very shy and intimidated impression, but gradually, a certain amount of trust was built up. One day, they came to me with tears in their eyes and asked me to obtain for them some bandages or wraps. When I asked what these were needed for, they showed me their blood-covered heels. The women wore wooden shoes that were open at the back, and each time that they did something wrong, their Meister or supervisor kicked them in the heels with his shoe until they turned bloody. I naturally reported that to my superior, but whether the guilty ones were ever punished, is something I do not know. For many, these were only women from the East, and goodness only knows, they did not have an easy time of it. In this connection, I also made yet a further observation. Because of an illness, I was quartered in a recuperation centre for one or two nights, when I was awakened in shock from my sleep by loud screams. I straightaway put on my bathrobe in order to investigate what was happening. When I entered the corridor, I could clearly hear a woman groaning in one of the treatment rooms. The night-nurse later showed up and I asked her what had been going on there. She at first did not want to spit it out, but under the strictest of confidentiality, she told me that among foreign women who became pregnant, the Works doctor performed abortions. This later led to arguments between the head doctor of the hospital and the Works doctor.' (Author's note: The reason for the abortions by the Works doctor is not known. One can, however, assume that this was to prevent the long-term fall-out of female workers.)

On the subject of working conditions in the aircraft plant, Otto Liebl from Regensburg remembered: 'With the commencement of production in 1938, I was involved with final assembly of the Me 108 Taifun. As long as only the Me 108 was being built, it was really nice work. I can well remember that in the summer, due to the large windows, an unbearable heat sometimes developed. With the commencement of large-scale series-production of the Me 109, the demands were set ever higher, which increased still more during the war. The Takt method of production which allowed for a certain pause for rest, was eventually replaced by a conveyor-belt method of production. As an electrician, it was no simple matter to lay the masses of cabling in the constricted fuselages, and work safety hardly existed at the time. During the pre-assembly and metal construction phases, an indescribable noise pervaded where here, workers from the East were primarily engaged later on. The large sheet-metal parts reacted like resonance plates when the riveting hammers went into action. From the outside, a worker pushed the countersunk rivet heads into the bored holes and pressed the heavy metal stampings against them, whilst from the inside, another worker using a compressed-air riveting hammer shaped the rivet heads such that the noise droned around one's ears. Later on, even though this was accomplished by introducing automatic riveting machines, the noise remained. Following final assembly, in the paintshop the camouflage coat and factory call-signs were sprayed on by the paint crews to the fuselages and wings. Due to the use of Nitrolacquer, there was the constant presence of solvent gases in the air and especially in winter there was an indescribable smell in the paintshop. Here too, several forced-labourers were set to work. When at one time a position in the works flight-test area was advertised, I had myself transferred there.'

1940 – Bf 109 E production expands

The war of 1940 extended like a widespread conflagration over the whole of Western Europe. In a contest against the British that began on 9 April 1940, the Wehrmacht was successful in occupying Denmark and Norway, whereby the battles around Narvik stretched until the middle of May. The Western Campaign began on 10 May 1940 and within a few weeks German troops overran Holland, Belgium, Luxemburg and France. Even the use of the British Expeditionary Force could not hold back the German armies. A significant contribution to the success of the German troops was made by the Luftwaffe and in particular by the Geschwader equipped with the Bf 109, which were successful in gaining absolute air superiority within the shortest period of time. Even when losses were suffered, the Bf 109 became the guarantor of victory over the Armée de l'Air (French Air Force) and the Royal Air Force. The Battle of Britain commenced on 12 August 1940 and with it, a further blood-letting in personnel and aircraft for the Luftwaffe. The effect on the Regensburg production plant was that twice as many Bf 109s left the Regensburg final assembly halls as in 1939 and in turn, manufacture of the Bf 108 was reduced by around 50%.

In 1940, considerable construction activity took place at Regensburg-Prüfening where the Lagerhalle II, a sheet-metal cutting and mechanical shop, an instruction building, appren-tice lodgings, office barracks and air-raid shelters were erected. Taken as a whole, until summer 1943, a host of new halls and buildings were erected in order to to keep pace with the constantly increasing volume of aircraft production. The firing-practice stand north of the final assembly hall, which was used for training of the Works guard crew and the SA Works contingent, from the end of 1940 on grounds of air raid protection, was converted into a further storage building. Because of the earthen walls that were already in place, the shooting-stand offered a significant measure of protection from bomb shrapnel and the installation was partially covered over with camouflage netting to hide it from the air. In 1940, a total of RM 4,430,000 was invested in the property. The housing construction programme was expanded by the addition of 232 apartments in the Hermann Göring Siedlung II and 50 apartments in the Dr. Schottenheim Siedlung, in which most of the workforce's needs were catered for.

Particular attention was further paid to systematic training and re-training of unskilled workers to compensate for the call-up of skilled workers into the armed forces and to a certain degree, maintain the high standard of production. On the other hand, the workforce had to do overtime to overcome the need for the extra work required to replace those that had left. For the additional effort to produce more aircraft, the RLM paid special premiums to the tune of RM 235,000 which was distributed in the form of special payments to the workforce and an increase in the Christmas bonus. On 16 August 1940, Rudolf Hess visited the plant in Regensburg, and besides Director Croneiß, Prof. Messerschmitt and chief test pilot Willi Stöhr, the entire Nazi senior hierarchy from Regensburg were in attendance, among them Kreisleiter Weigert,

On 1 June 1939, the Messerschmitt Regensburg air-raid bunker at the Prüfeninger Straße was given a camouflage scheme. In 1942, a 2-cm flak position was installed on its roof. (Photo Croneiß)

Rudolf Hess, Willy Stöhr and Willy Messerschmitt seen in August 1940 beside the Bf 109 E-4 (CI+EG) W.Nr. 3741. (Photo Croneiß)

NEST OF EAGLES

An engine test involving four Bf 109 E-3s out of the first production run in Regensburg in January 1939. The aircraft coded BY+ bears the words 'Glysantin eingefüllt' (glycol filled) on the engine cowling. (Photo Trenkle)

Lord Mayor Schottenheim and the Director of Police Popp.

The total workforce in December 1939 of 4,850 reduced in December 1940 to 4,275, of which 380 were apprentices and 842 were women. Upon the order of the RLM, the Works Protection and Fire Brigade were quartered in barracks. In 1940, 19 employees were awarded the Kriegsverdienstkreuz II.Klasse (War Service Cross, 2nd Class). The Regensburg plant was awarded the performance decoration for exemplary professional training and for its accommodation facilities. Within the scope of the KdF (Strength through Joy) organisation, 130 men and women visited the Bayreuth Festspiele (concerts). In June 1940, a Sports Evening was held in the Works and for the DRK (German Red Cross) and the Winterhilfswerk (Winter Support organisation), appreciable sums were donated by the workforce. But wartime events also threw their shadow on the workforce, for in 1940 the first of their colleagues who fell were Josef Matysiak in operations in the North and Hans Peller in the Western Campaign. By taking over the patrimony of the Reservelazarett (reserve field hospital) in the new hospital, every 14 days there took place entertainment afternoons encompassing the Apprentice's Fanfare parade, the Works Band, the String Orchestra, the Men's Choir and the Sports Group. Numerous letters were exchanged with relatives of the Works employees who were serving at the Front and parcels were sent by Messerschmitt GmbH to the soldiers as a sign that they were thought of in the homeland.

Back in mid-1938, preparations had been made to relocate Bf 109 production from Augsburg to Regensburg, as more space than before was needed in Augsburg to make room for the start of Bf 110 production there. As had already happened with the relocation of Bf 108 production from Augsburg to Regensburg, the same proven method was likewise applied, where all the necessary machines and tooling and completed groups of parts were transported from the former location together with the transfer of employees, whose task was to train the workforce in Regensburg to ensure a smooth commencement of Bf 109 production. At the beginning of 1939 the first Bf 109 E-3s were rolled out of the Regensburg final assembly hall in Prüfening, which meant that Regensburg turned out one of the world's most modern and capable fighter aircraft.

In the Bf 109, Prof. Messerschmitt had incorporated all the experiences gained in the manufacture of the Bf 108, so that its design and manufacture was essentially similar to its forebear in being of semi-monoque construction with riveted longerons, single-spar wing with Handley-Page leading-edge slats and of all-metal construction. The Bf 109's powerplant of the Bf 109 was a 12-cylinder 1,100 hp DB 601 A of 34 litres cubic capacity. It was with this engine that the Bf 109 attained a performance which made it not only famous but also feared. Its sole weakness lay in its narrow-track main undercarriage which very often led to take-off and landing accidents. For a time, losses through accidents were higher than those due to enemy action, which became noticeable as the duration of the war continued, when more and more pilots with few flying hours in the Bf 109 arrived at operational units.

Even today, the question is asked why Prof. Messerschmitt designed such a narrow-track

The outbreak of war and expansion: 1939-1941

A short series of Bf 109 E-3s was built for the Luftwaffe at Regensburg in 1939. All other examples were exported to Yugoslavia and Switzerland. This factory fresh Bf 109 E-3 (BY+HI) is camouflaged in RLM 70/71 over 65. (Photo Croneiß)

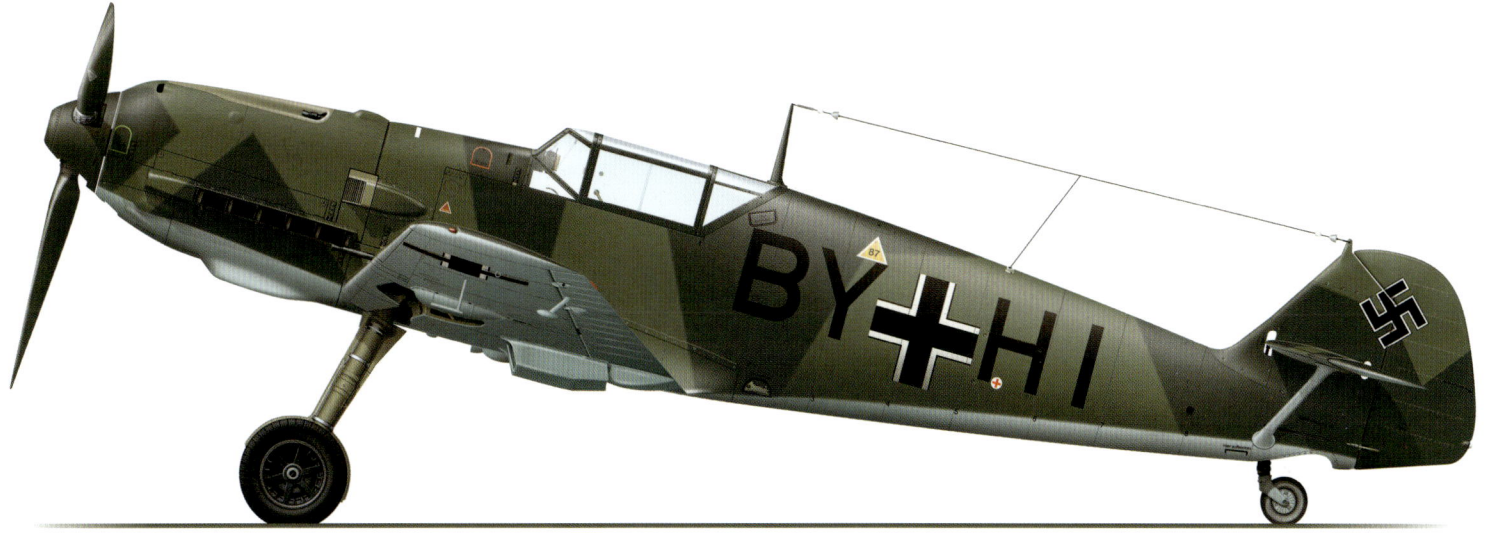

Messerschmitt Bf 109 E-3, BY+HI, Regensburg, 1939

undercarriage. He too, naturally recognized the disadvantage of such an undercarriage, but in the project description for the new fighter, the RLM had laid down the following requirement: after acceptance of the wings, the fuselage had to be capable of being transported on its main undercarriage - also a feature of the Arado Ar 80, the Focke-Wulf Fw 159 and the Heinkel He 112, and a decisive factor for this requirement must have been experiences during the First World War.

Like the Bf 108, the Bf 109 was also demonstrated in air races and flying meets abroad. In a flying meet in Switzerland, the Bf 109 won all the contests for aircraft of its class, and in the Spanish Civil War, it revolutionized air fighting where its speed, rate of climb and armament were not attained by any other fighter. Although its W/T equipment functioned somewhat unreliably at the beginning, it opened completely new tactical possibilities on operations. The tactical flight formation consisting of the 4-finger 'Schwarm' that had been developed by German pilots in Spain, proved its superiority to all other types of formations. This was even recognized during the war by the RAF and the USAAF and led to its introduction by them. By virtue of its performance capabilities that had often been demonstrated, in the period 1938-39 when it ruled the skies over Spain, the Bf 109 E generated considerable interest abroad. Several countries placed orders for it and in 1939, despite approaching war clouds, the Third Reich delivered the Bf 109 to the air forces of Switzerland (79), Spain (40), Yugoslavia (73), Bulgaria (19), Rumania (69), USSR (5), Hungary (40) and Japan (3). In 1939, a total of 144 Bf 109 Es were built in Regensburg, of which only 25 went to the Luftwaffe, 79 to Switzerland and 40 to Yugoslavia. There is thus no question that these deliveries abroad counted as a huge economic success for Messerschmitt and the Reich, since the earnings per Bf 109 from exports was higher than that made on deliveries to the Luftwaffe.

NEST OF EAGLES

This photograph, taken on 28 June 1939, shows Swiss Air Force Bf 109 E-3a (J-325) W.Nr. 2173 at Regensburg. (Photo Croneiß)

A Bf 109 E-3a in Regensburg in 1939 ready to be ferried to the Yugoslav Air Force. (Photo Croneiß)

A Japanese Colonel in civilian clothes visiting the Messerschmitt-Werke at Regensburg in December 1939. The apprentices are dresssed in Hitler Youth uniform and form an Honour Guard. (Photo Croneiß)

The commencement of the Second World War also resulted in a new era for the Messerschmitt GmbH Regensburg, which in 1943-44 led to the total destruction of the plant. It suddenly dawned on several of the workforce that the so aesthically-appearing metal war machines brought about death and destruction. But the mood of ecstasy still reigned over the successes of the German armed forces, and in particular of the Luftwaffe. The RLM issued new delivery plans to the aviation industry and for the Regensburg plant, this meant a significant increase in production of the Bf 109. Whereas Bf 108 production was reduced by 50%, the Bf 109 E-4 variant was now turned out, mainly equipped with an improved 20 mm MG/FF cannon in the wings and was recognizable from the angular cockpit canopy. Whereas in January 1940 only 7 Bf 109 Es were completed, production rose in July to 55 aircraft, all of which were blocked for export and had to be brought back to Luftwaffe standards. Bad weather in the spring of 1940 influenced factory test-flying, but despite this, it had to be established that the RLM had planned aircraft production without any far-seeing strategy. During the peak of the Battle of Britain in August and September 1940, more Bf 109s were lost than industry was capable of producing. This resulted in the fighter squadrons having 20% less aircraft than they should have had, and this at a decisive phase of the war. At the end of 1940, Regensburg began to turn out ever increasing numbers of the Bf 109 F, the successor model to the Bf 109 E.

As the table opposite shows, 144 examples of the Bf 109 E were produced in Regensburg in 1939, 317 in 1940, and 4 in 1941 of the Bf 109 E-7 variant. In the spring of 1941, the latter were ferried from Regensburg to 7./JG 26 in Sicily, led by Hauptmann Joachim Müncheberg. As recorded by Hauptmann Dr. Josef Weißmüller, one of the ferry pilots: 'With three other pilots, I was tasked in March 1941 to fly four Bf 109 Es to Italy. We flew from Regensburg to Munich-Neubiberg, settled the necessary paperwork there and had the aircraft fitted-out with 300-litre drop-tanks.

Production at Regensburg in 1940

	Bf 108	Bf 109 E	Bf 109 F-0	Bf 109 F-1
January	3	7	-	-
February	1	16	-	-
March	15	8	-	-
April	18	43	-	-
May	9	49	2	-
June	9	30	-	-
July	9	55	-	-
August	6	41	-	-
September	5	32	-	1
October	1	15	7	8
November	-	7	-	1
December	3	14	2	11
Totals:	**79**	**317**	**11**	**21**

A Bf 109 E-3 during final assembly at Regensburg in 1939. Its large three-bladed propeller had a diameter of 3,100 mm (10 ft 2 in). (Photo Croneiß)

From Munich we took the direct route to an airfield near Venice. From there we then took off for the flight to Rome, and although it was expressly forbidden, we flew at very low level over the Vatican (Author's note: A fact also confirmed by photographs). We then proceeded via Naples to Sicily and on the airfield at Gela, handed over the Bf 109s to Hauptmann Müncheberg's Staffel. After a stay of a few days, we returned to Germany in a Ju 52.'

One Bf 109 E-3 from the Regensburg production machines survived the war and is today in a museum in Lucerne, Switzerland. Built in 1939, this Bf 109 Werknr 2422 was in Swiss Air Force service from 1939 to 1948, and today serves as the world's most original surviving Bf 109 E. At the time of writing, a further very well maintained Bf 109 E was in the Deutsches Museum in Munich. Although built in Augsburg, all its parts were manufactured in Regensburg. It was used by the Spanish Air Force and was returned to Germany in 1958.

As seen in the table above, 11 Bf 109 F-0s were delivered in 1940, in which year according to RLM plans, 98 were to have been completed. Because of technical problems with the airframe, the cooler installation and armament as well as alterations made to the wings and empennage, to fuselage frame 9 and to the engine (reduction of oil pressure at high altitude), only 21 Bf 109 Fs were able to be delivered in 1941. As a result, alteration costs for the F-series amounted to RM 2,321,968.80 and due to bad weather, in January and February, only a few machines slated for export were able to undergo works flight tests. In March 1940 the RLM decided to reduce the number of export aircraft ordered, so that 75 export Bf 109 Es had to revert to RLM standard. In order to raise the number of aircraft produced, the newly-established assembly method, which consisted primarily of pre-assembly of all group components for final assembly, played an important role. In the business year 1940, earnings amounted to RM 1,059,186.68 and total manufacturing time amounted to 4,353,229 hours.

Of interest to note at this point is that already in 1940, production at Regensburg was dependent upon

NEST OF EAGLES

Bf 109 E-4s (GA+HP) W.Nr. 2782, and KF+SO W.Nr 2755, photographed on the industry airfield at Regensburg in June 1940. (Photo Trenkle)

Bf 109 E wing manufacture. Visible is the bulged covering for the MG/FF cannon on the wing underside. (Photo Croneiß)

This Bf 109 E-3a (D-IWKU, ex L-55) had to make an emergency landing in 1940 near Lappersdorf, north of Regensburg. Originally intended for export, it subsequently reverted to Luftwaffe standard. (Photo Croneiß)

numerous subcontractors. The following is a list of the delivery firms that year which, spread out over the entire Reich, supplied items to Messerschmitt GmbH Regensburg:

Wiener-Neustädter Flugzeugwerke – aircraft parts
Vereinigte Deutsche Metallwerke, Hamburg – variable-pitch propellers
Schäffer & Budenberg, Magdeburg – thermostatic control equipment
Karl Fischer, Nuremberg – aircraft parts
Treiber & Co., Graz (Austria) – exhaust-gas nozzles
Hartmann & Braun, Frankfurt/Main – fuel contents indicators
Eberspächer, Esslingen – stampings and castings
C.O. Raspe & Co., Berlin – fuel tanks and rubber plates
Schelter und Giesecke, Leipzig – undercarriage oleo legs
Vereinigte Deutsche Metallwerke, Frankfurt/Main – aircraft parts
Union Gesellschaft, Fröndenberg – aircraft parts
Erla Maschinenfabrik, Leipzig – aircraft parts
Elektron-Co., Stuttgart – wheel rims
Neue Kühler und Flugzeugteile, Berlin – coolers/radiators
Arado Flugzeugwerke, Babelsberg – aircraft parts
Robert Bosch, Stuttgart – electrical equipment
Siemens-Apparate, Berlin – electrical equipment parts
R.O. Meyer, Stuttgart – electrical equipment insulation materials
Süddeutsche Kühlerfabrik, Stuttgart – coolers/radiators
Dr. X. Herberts, Wuppertal – lacquer and paint
Vereinigte Leichtmetallwerke, Hannover – metal sheeting and profiles
Argus Motoren GmbH, Berlin – aero-engines and spare parts
Deutsche Benzinuhren, Berlin – instruments (indicators) and spare parts
Chr. Mansfeld, Leipzig – accessory parts
Wilhelm Hermes, Wuppertal – Plexiglas
I.G. Farben, Bitterfeld – raw materials
Gustav Rafflenbeul, Schwelm – raw materials
Daimler-Benz AG, Stuttgart - aero-engines and spare parts
Brown, Boverie & Cie, Mannheim – spare parts
AGO, Oschersleben – aircraft parts
Helmut Nestler, Eilenburg – aircraft parts
Pilz & Hayard, Glashütte – rivets and screws
Fieseler Flugzeugbau, Kassel – aircraft parts
Rhenania Ossag, Munich – fuel and oil
Feinmaschinenbau, Weinheim – aircraft components
Vereinigte Kugellagerfabriken, Schweinfurt – ball-bearings
Uher & Co., Munich – hydraulic cylinders
Rathgeber AG Waggonfabrik, Munich – airframe spar fittings

As the war progressed, especially from 1943, the supplier firms were bombed, dispersed and decentralized, which led constantly to bottlenecks in production since particular components, e.g. propellers, tyres or engines, were lacking. The number of production centres rose continually and for each component, it was attempted as far as possible to create a second manufacturing location resulting in dispersal into small and miniscule manufacture. A huge transport system therefore became absolutely essential to ensure a

The outbreak of war and expansion: 1939-1941

Bf 109 V 24, W.Nr. 5604, VK+AB was the fourth series prototype of the Bf 109 F. Whilst incorporating the new low drag wing design, it lacked the new detachable semi-elliptical wing tips found on the production F-series. The V 24 did however introduce the definitive supercharger air intake design and the deeper oil cooler bath beneath the engine cowling.

Messerschmitt Bf 109 V 24, W.Nr. 5604, VK+AB, Regensburg, 1940

The new look for the Bf 109 F. With its large, characteristic airscrew spinner, the F-series had considerably improved aerodynamics compared to the E-series. Here, Einflieger (acceptance test pilot) Josef 'Sepp' Haid is about to enter the cockpit of an F-0, W.Nr. 2180 (BY+KA) prior to a test flight in Regensburg on 14 August 1940. (Photo Croneiß)

NEST OF EAGLES

Another photograph showing Josef 'Sepp' Haid, now taxing the Bf 109 F-0 on 14 August 1940 prior to a test flight. The entire engine cowling is unpainted, whilst the fuselage is probably finished in RLM 02. Interestingly the Werknummer of this aircraft indicates that it was an E-series fuselage, that was taken over and modified for the F-series. In the background can be seen a Bf 109 E-series aircraft. (Photo Croneiß)

The Bf 109 F-1 (SG+EI) W.Nr. 5640 after its crash landing on 14 November 1940 near Mannheim. The undercarriage wheels sank into the soft ground and led to the aircraft somersaulted, pilot Unteroffizier Lohmann surviving slightly injured. The damaged aircraft was taken apart and transported by rail to Regensburg. (Photo Lohmann)

The final assembly hall at Regensburg in May 1940. Parked at right is Bf 109 E-4 (KF+SA) W.Nr. 2741. (Photo Linder)

more or less smooth-running production. Constantly increasing bombing raids on the German transportation system led to drastic production cuts at the end of 1944 and 1945, because the requisite materials could no longer be transported due to a dearth of railway freight wagons or because the transported goods were either destroyed or damaged, or because they reached their destinations after considerable delay.

1941 – Worldwide war

At the beginning of 1941, German forces were stationed from the North Cape down to the Spanish border along the Atlantic coast. The Battle of Britain was in its terminal phase, and following large losses on both sides, was broken off by Germany without success in March 1941, so that bombers flew only at night on missions against British industrial targets. In the OKW, preparatory plans for 'Unternehmen Seelöwe' (Operation Sea-Lion) – the invasion of the British Isles, were abandoned and instead, maximum effort was expended on 'Unternehmen Barbarossa' – the invasion of the Soviet Union. At the beginning of 1941, however, Italy came under such military pressure in North Africa, Albania and Greece, with retreats on all Fronts, that Hitler felt compelled to rush to the aid of his ally Benito Mussolini. German troops commanded by General Erwin Rommel were dispatched to Tripoli in North Africa, and in the Balkans, German forces commenced the campaign against Yugoslavia and Greece on 7 April 1941. Here also, the Bf 109 secured mastery of the skies ahead of the advancing troops or alternatively, intervened in the battle zones. A particular novelty in the history of warfare was the conquest of Crete from the air where, beginning on 20 May 1941, paratroops and mountain troops that were dropped from Ju 52 transports suffered bloody losses. On 2 June 1941, the OKW announced the victorious end of the fighting on Crete. Not announced, however, was the fact that close to 5,000 German soldiers had been killed.

The Russian campaign began on 22 June 1941, when German divisions stormed into the wide plains of the Soviet Union. In great encircling battles, numerous Russian armies were destroyed and hundreds of thousands of Soviet troops were captured. Again, it was the Bf 109 that had secured mastery of the skies and had enabled the bombers and Stukas to reach their targets unhindered. On Russian airfields, aircraft were lined up in rows as if on parade and in countless low-level attacks, hundreds of them were destroyed by the Luftwaffe, so that during the first weeks the Red Air Force was unable to play a significant part in the fighting. But then came the period of mud and slush which severely hindered the advance of the German troops. One of the most bitter winters caught the Wehrmacht almost unprepared and shortly before the gates of Moscow, the advance came to a standstill in temperatures of minus 35°C and below. Elite Russian divisions from Siberia, best equipped for the low temperatures, attacked the frozen German armies and threw them back. The Germans were thus faced with a repeat of the fate that had befallen the armies of Napoleon; even the Luftwaffe suffered enormous losses through technical problems and became very limited operationally due to the low temperatures. From 22 June to 31 December 1941, the Luftwaffe lost

Manufacture of Bf 109 F spinner back plates in December 1940. Of interest is the apprentice's armband bearing the Messerschmitt emblem 'LW' for Lehrwerkstatt (training workshop) and the '3' for the third training year. (Photo Croneiß)

The Bf 109 could be a tricky aircraft to land or take-off in and even the experienced could be caught out. Though the circumstances of this crash are unknown, it occurred on 26 February 1941 at Regensburg airfield to Bf 109 F-2 (NA+YM) W.Nr. 5698. To the right of the tail lies its DB 601 engine, wrenched free in the crash. The fate of the pilot, however, remains unknown. (Photo Croneiß)

NEST OF EAGLES

*An Italian government delegation inspected the Messerschmitt-Werke in Regensburg on 12 January 1941, and is seen here showing a special interest in the Bf 109 F's retractable tailwheel which initially caused enormous problems as it often jammed during retraction and extension. Even the later Bf 109 G-1 was equipped with this tailwheel.
Photo Croneiß)*

*On 10 May 1941, Japanese officers inspected Bf 109 F production at Regensburg.
At this time, negotiations were underway to produce the Bf 109 under licence in Japan.
(Photo Croneiß)*

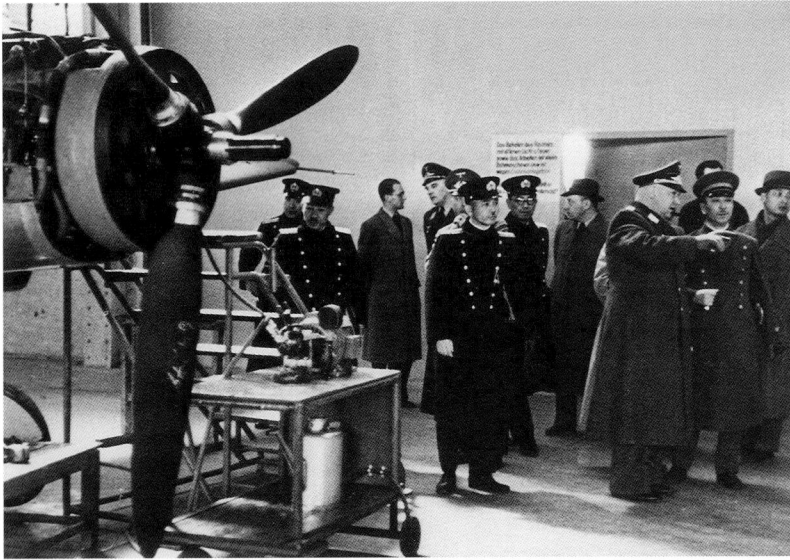

568 Bf 109 Es and Fs in the East and a further 413 Bf 109s were reported as damaged. Losses in bombers, Stukas and various other types amounted to 1,242 aircraft. On 11 December 1941, Germany declared war on the USA.

Despite immense losses on the Eastern Front, conveyor-belt production of the Bf 109 continued unabated at Regensburg, but only 353 aircraft rolled out of the assembly halls, only four more than in 1940. The reason for this was the commencement of Me 210 production at Regensburg. This twin-engined two-seater multi-purpose aircraft had been ordered for quantity production by the RLM without waiting for the results of front line flight trials and had been hurriedly put into production by Messerschmitt. Its flying characteristics were unsatisfactory; it tended to spin and there were several crash-landings by inexperienced young pilots, which for the Luftwaffe and for Messerschmitt, were to have catastrophic consequences.

Also in 1941, extensive construction was carried out in the plant grounds at Regensburg-Prüfening. The airfield was enlarged, its extent comprising 623,000 m² (6,705,754 ft²) and the works premises 451,230 m² (4,856,880 ft²). When building the concrete apron ahead of the flight-test hangar, the compass adjustment platform was covered over and replaced by a swinging compass base. In the spring of 1941, 13 barrack buildings were erected to serve as accommodation for German and foreign workers in the Prüfeninger Strasse, plus three barracks for French prisoners of war and a further seven for Works use. Engaged on construction work were the firms of Hans Schricker, Josef Riepl, and Sechser & Klug, all from Regensburg as well as Lenz & Co. of Munich, and Wolfferts of Mannheim. For the business year, RM 229,000 was expended on lathes, milling and boring machines as well as a new press. The Messerschmitt GmbH vehicle depot was expanded by five trucks, nine electric vehicles with trailers, two trailers, one tipper, a hand tanker, two cars, a motorcycle and a Bf 109 (W.Nr. 2277, TI+EC). The Works leadership consisted of SS Brigadeführer Theo Croneiß, Commercial Director Otto Thieme and Technical Director Karl Linder. Compared to 1940, the workforce as of 31 December 1941 climbed from 2,154 to 6,429, of which 1,527 were women, 225 PoWs and 80 Italians. Fifty-two skilled workers were called-up to serve in the armed forces.

Bf 108 production transferred to Les Mureaux

With the ending of the campaign in the West, the RLM in Berlin considered to what extent the French aviation industry could be utilized to assist in German armaments production. In collaboration with German aircraft firms, the RLM made contact with French aircraft manufacturers. At the beginning of 1941, this led to initial discussions between Messerschmitt AG and SNCAN in Les Mureaux for licence production of the Bf 108 D-1. In order to accelerate the transfer of production from Regensburg to Les Mureaux, an office was set up in Paris under the leadership of Ranft of Messerschmitt. The capacity thus freed up at Regensburg was to be immediately utilized for the much needed Bf 109 and Me 210 so as to increase their production. Because Bf 108 production continued meanwhile in Regensburg, the Regensburg templates were first sent to SNCAN, so that everything required for production of the Bf 108 could be completed. As quickly as 20 March 1941, Regensburg received the loaned templates back from SNCAN, but on 3 April, the original templates had to be sent once more to Les Mureaux because SNCAN had forgotten to measure the newly-completed templates against the originals! Likewise in April, the ready-for-assembly part groups for 30 aircraft were sent by Regensburg to Les Mureaux, including the equipment components that were needed for final assembly. Prior to that, on 28 March, the Messerschmitt office in Paris was handed detailed instructions for the external surface protection of light metal and steel, needed for the chemical composition of acid baths, galvanized zinc, and cadmium etc. In a Messerschmitt document dated 17 May 1941, it records that the RLM Department LC 2 IA had drawn up a delivery programme for 234 Bf 108 D-1s from SNCAN, in addition to an test order for five Bf 108 D-1s that had to be built in advance.

Production in Les Mureaux faced considerable difficulties in matching and fabricating the cockpit framework and its transparent panels. In a letter dated 19 May, Regensburg Technical Director Linder described in detail the method they used there. According to this, the cockpit frame was adjusted to fit each individual fuselage. The Plexiglas panels were heated to a temperature of 150°C in an oven of its own design by Messerschmitt GmbH Regensburg, whereby hot air was directed by a blower onto the panels. After warming, these were given their curvature by being bent over a buckskin-covered forming block and after cutting, were

Seen here in May 1942 is Bf 108 D-1 (RE+EM) W.Nr. 3094, the last of 516 examples of this type that were built at Regensburg. Because of the need for space for increased production of the Bf 109, its further manufacture was transferred to SNCAN in occupied France. (Photo Wedemeyer)

shaped to fit into the cockpit framework. In a letter dated 27 June from SNCAN to Regensburg it transpires that between the drawings, templates and manufacturing instructions, large deviations had been established. With the engine covering panels, for example, the difference was as much as 30 cm (12 in). In view of these catastrophically large deviations in the construction of these aircraft, Les Mureaux requested that a complete fuselage be delivered in its finished state.

On 25 July 1941, Bf 108 W.Nr. 2101 was transferred by the Reichsbahn (German Railways) from Freising to Les Mureaux and with it, the SNCAN technicians were once more given the opportunity to check all the instructions and construction processes. The result of this control was so depressing that all SNCAN-built templates and construction jigs were transported to Regensburg and had to be thoroughly modified there. This led to serious consequences for a part of the leadership at Les Mureaux who were dismissed, as sabotage was suspected. What other stern measures were taken and whether confirmable sabotage actually played a role, has not been established by this author.

On 17 June 1941, SNCAN ordered light metal for the production of 184 Bf 108s via Messerschmitt AG Augsburg. Since the construction of formers in Regensburg was totally overloaded due to Bf 109 F production and start-up preparations for Bf 109 G and Me 210 production, the revised templates and construction gear were able to be delivered only from Augsburg after considerable delays and repeated demands to SNCAN. In written exchanges between SNCAN and the Messerschmitt office in Paris on the one hand and Messerschmitt AG and GmbH on the other, it can be seen what enormous problems were faced for series-production of the Bf 108 in France, where passive resistance and sabotage were certainly the principal reasons. Production figures for the Bf 108 at SNCAN in the W.Nr. 5000 and 6000 blocks amounted to 50 in 1942, 108 in 1943 and 12 in 1944, hence a total of 170 Bf 108 Ds. Up to the end of the war, two examples of the further development of the Bf 108, the Me 208, with tricycle nosewheel undercarriage, were completed. After the war, the French continued to manufacture this model as the Nord 1101 Noralpha.

Bf 109 F Production in 1940-1941

At the end of May 1940, two Bf 109 F-0s were completed in Regensburg. On 14 August 1940, Josef Haid made the first take-off in an F-0 on a thorough test flight. Work was in full swing for the manufacture of Bf 109 F jigs and machine tooling. As opposed to the Bf 109 E-series, the F-series incorporated a considerable number of aerodynamic refinements that optically, were noticeable in the large propeller spinner which blended into the engine casing, the cantilever elevators, rounded wingtips, revised ailerons and flaps, as well as an aerodynamically improved radiator beneath the wings. Cooler regulation took place via split flaps which served as auxiliary landing flaps. The upper and lower engine nacelle coverings which were also reshaped, were now hinged and made servicing easier. The control cables for the rudder were no longer visible at the rear fuselage and were integrated into the fuselage. The undercarriage track was widened from 1975 mm (77.76 in) to 2062 mm (81.2 in), whilst propeller diameter was reduced to 3,000 mm (118 in) with rather wider blades than on the Bf 109 E-series. Its DB 601 N, which delivered 1,200 hp but which required 100 octane fuel, was later replaced by the more powerful 1,300 hp DB 601 E that used 87 octane fuel. When considered in detail, except for the fuselage, the Bf 109 F was of completely new design and as it turned out, was not fully matured. Whereas the Bf 109 E took about 9,000 working hours to produce, through production simplifications, this was able to be reduced to 6,000, and paved the way for large-scale manufacture of the F, G and K versions. In 1940, Regensburg turned out 11 Bf 109 F-0s and 21 F-1s that were immediately ferried to front line units in the course of which a not inconsiderable number of problems surfaced.

On 28 October 1940 for example, Unteroffizier Lohmann of 3./JG 51 fetched Bf 109 F-1 W.Nr. 5640 from Regensburg and flew the aircraft to Pihen in northern France. After a sortie over England a few days

Italian 'guest workers' stood in for those specialists that had been called up for Wehrmacht service in 1941 in the metalworking section on the wings and fuselages of the Bf 109 F.
(Photo Croneiß)

later in which it had to be dived to around 750 km/h (466 mph) in order to shake off a Spitfire, it was established after the landing that the wing skinning had become wrinkled. This led initially to considerable astonishment and surmise as to the cause. Following consultation with the responsible Luftflotte (Air Fleet) and with Regensburg, it was decided to return the aircraft to the latter production plant. Lohmann, who flew it back, submitted the following report: 'On 14 November 1940, I took-off at 1400 hrs in W.Nr. 5640 on a flight from Pihen to Regensburg. Since I did not trust putting too much load on the wings any more, I flew at only 300 km/h (186 mph) in a south-easterly direction. Shortly after take-off I encountered bad weather and lost my orientation. At 1530 hrs, the fuel slowly but surely ran out; the red light on the instrument panel had already been on for some minutes when in the direction of flight a large field appeared. I did not hesitate for long, and with undercarriage and flaps extended, I prepared to land. Shortly after touchdown, the wheels sank into the soft earth and the tailplane rose inexorably high. What followed was a classic nose-over. It was only due to the fortunate circumstance that my crash-landing, which had been observed by the occupants of a bus that was passing by on a nearby road, led to my rescue. The people lifted one wing to a height where I was able to open the canopy roof and in this manner, had firm soil beneath my feet. As I recall, my emergency landing took place in the neighbourhood of the Rhine near Rochenhausen. The Me 109 was later dismantled by a recovery team and I continued by rail to Regensburg. On my arrival there, I was given a new F-1, W.Nr. 5629 (SG+GX), which I ferried to Pihen on 22 November and delivered it to the Geschwader where, because of the unhappy emergency landing, I was given a real dressing-down by Oberst (Werner) Mölders because I had not followed regulations in making the emergency landing in the wheels-up condition. Smiling, he then stated he was pleased that I had not broken my neck and that I returned to the Geschwader.'

The problems with W.Nr. 5640 however, were not isolated. With other aircraft, the empennage had ripped at fuselage frame No.9. Problems also existed with the tailplane and the elevators. Still others experienced a fall in engine power. Fastening bolts for the wingtips became damaged and vibrated, and aileron covering fabric twisted. Because of the widened undercarriage track, on take-offs and landings on concrete runways, there was increased tyre wear. A further problem occurred with the retractable tailwheel which continually jammed and on landing did not extend, and led to damage to the rear fuselage and tailplane. As if that was not enough, the armament also caused problems. In the F-series, it consisted of two 7.9 mm MG 17s above the engine and a 15 mm MG 151/15. Many pilots rejected this reduction to a single MG 151 and regarded it as a step backward in the development of a modern fighter aircraft. The MG 151, however, had a considerably higher rate of fire and muzzle velocity than the wing-mounted MG/FFs in the E-series. Whereas the E-series carried 120 rounds of 20 mm ammunition, the F-series had 180 rounds. In addition, the effectiveness of the MG 151 rounds was considerably better. In the Bf 109, they were

Unteroffizier Lohmann in the cockpit of his Bf 109 'Yellow 4' surrounded by comrades of 3./JG 51 at Abbeville, France in February 1941. In 1940, Lohmann took part in the Battle of Britain and flew several sorties over London.
(Photo Lohmann)

held in a belt container in the port wing, and this constituted the problem. Under particular flight load conditions, as happens during dogfighting, the belt jammed and blocked the ammunition feed. On forward airfields, maintenance crews inserted small wooden chocks as an aid, but the problem was not completely resolved until the 20 mm MG 151/20 became available. From mid-1941, flying units equipped the F-series on all fronts with the MG 151/20, with which the extremely effective Minengranaten, containing a Hexogen filling, could now be fired. The MG 151, now positioned directly along the fuselage longitudinal axis and firing through the propeller boss, was to prove itself a deadly weapon in fighter-versus-fighter combat. German fighter aces such as Werner Mölders, Adolf Galland, Hans-Joachim Marseille, Hermann Graf, Joachim Müncheberg and others, attained the majority of their victories with the Bf 109 F.

Following a thorough examination of the reported deficiencies with the Bf 109 F, work was immediately started at Regensburg to resolve them. Some involved subcontractors, whilst others were eliminated by design modifications for which on-going material checks and load tests were necessary. All experiences gained flowed into current production but caused an enormous increase in financial outlay. The almost completely new design of the Bf 109 F-series had, of course, been calculated in detail, but showed that the airframe material requirements in air combat and in take-offs and landings at forward airfields far exceeded the normal loads. Following the elimination of all deficiencies, according to several pilots, the F-series was the best of the Bf 109 series that they had ever flown.

In a report of experiences dated 28 January 1942 by JG 2 'Richthofen' concerning the Bf 109 F-4, the Technical Officer reported that at high speeds up to 650 km/h (404 mph), no wing deformations occurred anymore. Oberleutnant Riedmeir of JG 52 reported of the Bf 109 F: 'With its thermostat-controlled radiator flaps and automatic variable-pitch propeller, the Bf 109 F pilot was significantly less burdened. In addition, it had balanced flight characteristics and a high maximum speed coupled with a greatly increased climb rate. In terms of acceleration, no other aircraft could keep pace with it, and its service ceiling of over 10,000 m (32,800 ft) was impressive. As opposed to Russian fighters, in 1941-42 we undoubtedly had the advantage, and as a rule could determine the outcome of a dogfight.'

At Regensburg, 32 Bf 109s were built in 1940 and 347 in 1941, hence a total of 379, of which 16 were F-0s and 363 F-1/F-2s. This shows a difference of 3 from the RLM Lieferplan (Delivery Plan) which reports figures of 157 F-1s and 209 F-2s, and with the 16 F-0s gives a total of 382 aircraft. Presumably, 3 F-0s were modified to F-1

Bf 109 F-2 W.Nr. 8906 (PK+IK) takes off from Regensburg on its acceptance flight in April 1941. (Photo Trenkle)

Bf 109 F-2 (PK+IK) now seen in low-level flight over Regensburg airfield. The camouflage scheme on the wings and tailplane are clearly visible in this photograph. (Photo Trenkle)

NEST OF EAGLES

On 9 October 1941, a Rumanian delegation was flown to Regensburg in a Fw 200 Condor belonging to the German Regierungsstaffel (Government Staffel). At centre in this photograph is Messerschmitt Director Fritz H. Hentzen. (Photo Croneiß)

or F-2 standard, as the F-0 does not appear in this Lieferplan. At least one Bf 109 F crashed in a landing accident during Works flight-testing. One Bf 109 F survived the war and, at the time of writing, was in the South African War Museum in Johannesburg. In November 1941, the successor to the Bf 109 F, the first Bf 109 G, already stood outside the Regensburg production halls and was to become the most-built version of the Bf 109. For a technical description of the Bf 109 G and Werknummern for the Bf 109 E to K versions see Appendix 5.

The Me 210 fiasco: 1941-1942

Without doubt, from its shape and overall technical concept, the Me 210 was an extremely modern and progressive design but from the very beginning, its flight characteristics were unsatisfactory. With the Me 210, the Messerschmitt concern suffered its worst economic setback. The result was the removal from power of Willy Messerschmitt because, following this setback, the RLM exerted massive influence on the entire enterprise and all activities were supervised by Generalfeldmarschall Erhard Milch or by his delegate. Me 210 final assembly was to have taken place in Augsburg and Regensburg, but after only a few aircraft, production was terminated at both plants in May 1942. Augsburg manufactured the main fuselage and empennage, whilst Regensburg the wing and rear fuselage, a comparable division of component manufacture having later occurred with the Me 262.

The Me 210 was intended as the successor to the Bf 110 and was designed as a Zerstörer (twin-engined heavy fighter) capable of dive-bombing. Against the original plan of Chief Designer Woldemar Voigt, Prof. Messerschmitt had shortened the fuselage by about 900 mm (35.4 in), and the originally intended leading-edge slats were cancelled by the RLM on grounds of cost. Already in early flights with Me 210 prototypes, test pilots criticized the aircraft's flying characteristics which were caused by its shortened fuselage. Flight stability around the vertical or yaw axis was not in accordance with calculations. At that time, in 1939-40, test pilots had already demanded a longer fuselage for the Me 210. It took almost two years until Prof. Messerschmitt gave his approval for the fuselage to be lengthened, but by then it was too late to save it. Additional built-in equipment such as more powerful armament and armour-plating for the pilot caused its flight characteristics to deteriorate even further. It was typical for the Luftwaffe leadership to have an aircraft designed and to then demand special installations that were not part of the overall design, to be retrospectively incorporated. In German aircraft developments of the Second World War, this concept-less method ran like a red thread through almost all projects. Despite the known problems, preparations for largescale production ran at full speed in Augsburg and Regensburg. Without waiting for the results of flight trials, the RLM ordered 1,000 Me 210s straight from the drawing board. In September 1941, Me 210 final assembly was on-going in Regensburg, and in November, the first 16 aircraft were delivered to the experimental Erprobungskommando 210 which was formed from II./ZG 1.

In his book '*Meine Flugberichte* (My Flight Reports) 1935-1945', Johannes Kaufmann of ZG 1 related his

The Me 210 in flight. After production was stopped in April 1942, those examples that had not yet been accepted by the Luftwaffe were parked on the airfield at Obertraubling. (Photo Schmoll)

In September 1941, the first Me 210s were rolled out of final assembly in Regensburg-Prüfening. With their teardrop-shaped canopies, the engine nacelles mounted far forward and their mighty three-bladed airscrews, the Me 210 displayed an extremely dynamic appearance. (Photo Croneiß)

experiences with the Me 210: 'The Me 210 certainly impressed us. However, instruction could unfortunately only be carried out very superficially, as suitable personnel were not available. One had to proceed cautiously in order to capture its novelties as opposed to the Bf 110, and to learn how to deal with them. In comparison with the Bf 110, the Me 210 was faster, the bombs could be housed internally in the fuselage, climb performance was much better, the diving characteristics conformed to the demands placed on it; the weapons were more effective, and the radio and navigational equipment had been improved. Overall, the Me 210 was a more racy aircraft in which we had placed all our hopes and consequently I eagerly looked forward to the first take-off. This took place on 14 November 1941 when the initial take-off, conducted with extreme caution due to the predicted danger of veering off the runway, took place without any mishap. This warning of danger on take-off was justified, as it needed some corrections to be made with the rudder and the engines in order to stay on a straightline course. The second take-off went off better, and I remained airborne for 26 minutes to test out the new aircraft in flight. The flying characteristics were good, and better than the Bf 110. In particular, the Me 210 possessed higher manoeuvrability and rapid acceleration. The approach and landing caused no problems, and in this respect it naturally differed from the Bf 110, which in no way constituted a disadvantage. We practised bomb drops, weapons-firing in the air, dives, and formation flying, and soon became familiar with its peculiarities, which led to optimistic expectations.

'The first problems were encountered by our younger-generation pilots. As a consequence, we relocated from Landsberg to Lechfeld, in order to have a longer take-off and landing distance at our disposal. Unfortunately, the abundant winter snow crossed through our plans, so that we were only able to fly from Lechfeld between 13 January and 2 March 1942, and on the afternoon of 2 March, we relocated to Tours. The flying programme encompassed 91 flights with around 27 flying hours on the Me 210, to which came an additional 4 hours for the ferry flights from Lechfeld to Tours and from Regensburg-Obertraubling to Tours. In the overall programme of conversion, 82 airfield flights took place, plus 3 for firing practice, 3 bomb drops, 1 dive, and the 2 ferry flights. Coming from Regensburg, on the landing approach to Tours, I saw a most unusual picture. There were some crashed aircraft lying on the airfield which were evidently new and consisted of Me 210s. In the first moments, I could not precisely identify them but upon landing, I came to hear what had happened. These crashes were due exclusively to the young, still inexperienced pilots, so that a revised decision was forced about the aeroplane. This came relatively quickly. The Me 210 was withdrawn, and we had to revert back to the Bf 110 and go along with it to Russia in the summer offensive of 1942. The whole airfeld was gripped with deep disappointment.'

(Author's Note: Johannes Kaufmann's report again shows the Luftwaffe's dilemma. Not enough qualified personnel from industry or from the Luftwaffe were available for instructing new pilots, who had to familiarize themselves with the characteristics of this aircraft. For experienced pilots this caused few problems, but the young and inexperienced faced their share of

An Me 210 that made an emergency landing near Obertraubling following engine damage on 25 August 1941 is towed by a Luftwaffe tracked vehicle to the Fliegerhorst. The outer wings have been detached and for reasons of security, the aircraft has been covered over. (Photo Croneiß)

39

NEST OF EAGLES

Seen on the production line at Regensburg are cockpit canopies being fitted to Me 210s W.Nr. 2316 to 2318. (Photo Croneiß)

Equipping and wiring the Me 210 instrument panel and cockpit side consoles was accomplished almost exclusively by women. The fully-equipped components thereafter merely had to be fitted during final assembly to the aircraft's systems. (Photo Croneiß)

problems. The OKL transferred the re-equipment and training to Upper Bavaria in the winter, which led to weather-related problems, and it was too late when training was relocated to France. The necessary coordination was lacking between the RLM, Messerschmitt and the operational units, one of whom was relocated during wartime to the homeland, where the corresponding preparations were only partially completed. Today, it would be described as 'woefully unprofessional', yet at that time this 'mismanagement' was paid for with the blood of German airmen!)

As a result of such incidents, one crisis conference after another was held at the RLM and at Messerschmitt, and on 9 March 1942, Göring, Milch and Vorwald decided to terminate production of the Me 210. This resulted almost in a panic at Messerschmitt, as it threatened losses in terms of millions. At a conference held on 12 March at the RLM in Berlin, Prof. Messerschmitt had to admit that in its current state the Me 210 was not ready for operational use. At this conference, it was decided to rebuild the Me 210 with a longer fuselage and to fit the wings with leading-edge slats. Of these, the first ten experimental aircraft were to become available by 1 April, a date that from the very outset could not be adhered to. But Prof. Messerschmitt attempted to save what could still be saved. All subcontractors and the entire plants in Augsburg and Regensburg had converted to Me 210 production as well as their manufacture by three licence firms: the Lutherwerke at Braunschweig, Erla at Leipzig-Mockau, and the Gothaer Waggonfabrik at Gotha. After the deadline of 1 April 1942 had passed and the ten experimental aircraft had not been completed, Milch ordered that Prof. Messerschmitt be removed. This was the high point in the long-existing enmity between the two men and it was soon determined that the ten aircraft could not even be made ready for delivery before 1 May. On 19 April, Generalingenieur Roluf Lucht of the RLM was sent by Milch on an inspection visit to Messerschmitt Augsburg, where he reported on the desolate state of the Works and the totally depressed condition of Prof. Messerschmitt. Upon an RLM directive of 25 April, all further work on the Me 210 was, for the time being, to be stopped. Theo Croneiß, Chairman of the Board at Messerschmitt, attempted feverishly to negotiate between Prof. Messerschmitt and Milch.

Up until the cancellation of production, 94 examples of the Me 210 had been completed in Augsburg and 258 in Regensburg. At both plants, a total of 540 Me 210s were in a more or less advanced stage of manufacture. Futher materials for the largescale series had been delivered to the plants, where close to 4,000 employees stood around with nothing to do. At full speed, work was put in hand on the jigs and machine tools in both plants on lengthening the Me 210 fuselages. Following detailed negotiations with the RLM, work on lengthening the fuselages of 95 Me 210s was taken up (per the Messerschmitt AG letter of 13 June). Of these, four were to have been delivered by Regensburg in July and one in August, whilst Augsburg was to deliver ten, plus 20 aircraft per month from September to December 1942. For this purpose, the aircraft had to be dismantled; the outboard and centre wings, empennages and forward fuselages had to be modified and the new lengthened fuselage added. These were then mated together and the aircraft flight-tested, the work involved amounting to around 3,400 hours per aircraft.

In a letter dated 4 August 1942, Messerschmitt AG advised the RLM that ten Me 210s with lengthened fuselages had been delivered to the Luftwaffe. The total number on the Lieferprogram was thus raised to 534 aircraft, included 12 with the lengthened fuselage that had been completed up to this time in Regensburg, seven of which were delivered to Augsburg. The remaining five were ferried to Lechfeld and together with some modifications, were partly taken over by the BAL. Based on these facts, it can be assumed that the lengthened fuselage Me 210s were delivered ready for operational use. Delivery of the Me 210 C version (with the DB 605 A) was delayed until at least November 1942 since procurement of materials and production installations could not be delivered earlier. (Author's note: The Me 210 C was manufactured under licence in Hungary from the end of 1942 and established itself admirably). The completely modified Me 210 was equipped with more powerful engines and as the Me 410, was introduced from 1943 by the Luftwaffe, proving itself as an excellent Zerstörer, bomber, and reconnaissance aircraft.

For the Messerschmitt firm, there remained economic damage to the tune of RM 38 million and resulted in the removal of Prof. Messerschmitt, who was now made responsible only for design and development work. Theo Croneiß took over the chairmanship of the Board. According to accounts from former Messerschmitt employees at Regensburg, after the decision to stop production of the Me 210, a veritable chaos reigned in the production halls, where completed aircraft and aircraft parts in all stages of manufacture stood around. The two final assembly lines for the Me 210 that had been in operation since September 1941 had to be dismantled, for according to the latest RLM production plans, only the Bf 109 would be turned out in Regensburg. The first steps on further extension of the airfield at Prüfening had already been started, as industrial space for the Me 210 was insufficient. Regensburg thus began production of an aircraft despite the fact that the requisite larger airfield for it did not exist, a similar situation applying at the end of 1944 with the Me 262 in Obertraubling.

In the aftermath of the RLM decision, a huge clearing-out took place in the manufacturing halls in Regensburg. Entire goods trains with semi-completed

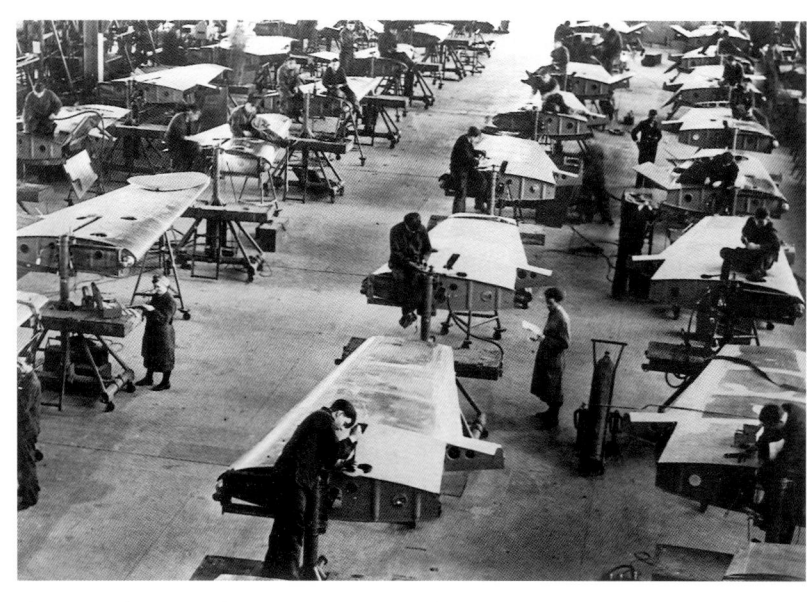

Me 210 wing final assembly took place on movable and rotatable jigs. (Photo Croneiß)

The raised working platforms that surround Me 210 W.Nr. 2294 made final assembly at Regensburg much easier. Photo Croneiß)

aircraft and parts, construction jigs and also a quantity of raw materials left the Prüfening plant heading in the direction of Augsburg. A portion of the materials were stored in some of the production halls at the Fliegerhorst Obertraubling. Feverish work was undertaken for largescale production in Regensburg of the Bf 109 G in order to achieve the required turn-out of 250 aircraft per month. It was only after the passage of several months that this target was attained, because the subcontractors had likewise to raise their manufacture of components to match the increased production numbers.

Aircraft mechanic Martin Gattinger recorded of Me 210 production at Regensburg: 'From September 1941, there remained only a single assembly line for Bf 109 production in the finally assembly hall. Here, since mid-1941, erection of two production lines for the Me 210 had begun, and in September the first Me 210s rolled off the conveyor belt. My work at that time consisted of installing the undercarriage, followed by a functional test of the undercarriage installations. Continual modifications to the aircraft led to on-going delays in its manufacture, as the aircraft had significantly more complex technology than the Bf 109. The hydraulics alone for the Me 210 undercarriage was far greater in extent than in the Bf 109. A novelty was the electrically remote-controlled machine guns for the rearward-aimed defensive armament. Hardly had production got started, when a few months later it again had to be stopped. It was said to us at the time that because of continual additional installations such as the heavier armament (originally the 15 mm MG 151/15, replaced by the 20 mm MG 151/20), additional amour-plating and so forth, the aircraft that flew on operations had become too nose-heavy. A consequence of this was the stoppage of production and ensuing chaos at Regensburg. Everywhere, there lay aircraft components, group-construction parts, production jigs and materials that had been delivered. The two Me 210 assembly lines were dismantled again and in their place the conveyor-belt assembly lines for the Bf 109 were erected. As a result, there was a certain amount of loss in Bf 109 production, and aircraft parts and other components were thereafter stored in a large hall in the Fliegerhorst Obertraubling'.

Elektromeister (Master Electrician) Otto Liebl who worked on the Me 210 at Regensburg recalled: 'From its very beginning, the Me 210 was a much more modern aircraft than the Bf 109. The electric and hydraulic systems alone were far more comprehensive and the aircraft as such was an extremely modern design. As far as I can remember, the Me 210 was a fast aircraft with initially uncomplicated flying characteristics. Because of constant additions such as armament and larger bomb suspensions, the Me 210 became heavier than was probably originally intended. I can still remember quite well that production had to be stopped once again because additional armour-plating had to be added to

The size comparison between man and machine emphasizes how much larger the Me 210 was as opposed to the Bf 108 and Bf 109. At the extreme centre right can be seen the upper and lower wing-mounted dive brakes. (Photo Croneiß)

A 3-bladed airscrew is here being attached to the port engine of Me 210 Werknummer 2276 with the aid of a crane. To the right of it, a main undercarriage is being prepared for installation. (Photo Croneiß)

the cockpit and to the engines. In discussions with our technicians, there were covert whispers about the critical situation with the Me 210. After some serious accidents had occurred with this aircraft in the flying units, the 'big bang' then happened, when production of this modern aircraft was halted at Regensburg. There was chaos throughout the entire plant. Production of the Bf 109 was to continue immediately whilst at the same time the halls were cleared-out of the Me 210; it was indescribable. Production of the 108 also continued simultaneously. We were occupied for weeks with conversion work until the 210 could again be built at Regensburg. A large portion of the workforce thus became unemployed, which meant that no aircraft came off the final assembly lines, and the resulting damage for the Messerschmitt plant must have been immense.'

Hermann Kronseder also recalled: '... soon afterwards, I was ordered to go to Obertraubling. The first thing we were ordered to do was to chop up 100 Me 210s. The Luftwaffe had refused to accept this aircraft as it was too nose-heavy and in every third landing, had nosed-over. Nothing much happened to the young, inexperienced pilots, and we apprentices were always the first to show up at the wrecks. We sometimes removed the aircraft clock with its illuminated numerals and took it home, and whatever appeared to be still usable from the 100 aircraft. Engines and tyres were removed, and we then set to work with the axe. Just as we had hacked 12 aircraft to pieces, came the order: "Stop, stop!" The designers had found another solution: the fuselage was lengthened by one metre, the nose-heaviness had disappeared and the aircraft flew faultlessly. In the shortest possible time, we modified the remaining aircraft.'

According to eyewitnesses, at the Fliegerhorst some 12 to 15 Me 210s that were parked were destroyed in June-July 1942. From these, all reusable parts were first removed and then the wings and fuselages were destroyed. A blind-flying clock that was removed from a Me 210 by Leopold Berghammer is today in the author's possession.

The Me 210 A-1s built at Regensburg were in the Wrknummer range 2251 to 2354 and the following call-signs are known: 2251 (VC+GA) to 2276 (VC+GZ); 2321 (GF+CA) to 2346 (GF+CZ), and 2347 (GE+KS) to 2354 (GE+KZ). W.Nr. 2350 (GE+KV) was delivered to Japan in 1943, and the majority of Me 210 production at Regensburg was delivered to I./ZG 1 and III./ZG 1 as well as to I./SKG 210.

(Author's note: Information given in previously-published literature on Me 210 production needs an emphatic correction. The fact is that Prof. Messerschmitt

Seen here is the manufacture of Me 210 fuselages and semi-fuselages, which followed the same construction methods as used on the fuselages of the Bf 108 and Bf 109. Note the circular cut-outs into which the aircraft's defensive rearward-firing remote-controlled barbettes were inserted. The confined working space under with which the Regensburg workforce had to contend is evident. (Photo Croneiß)

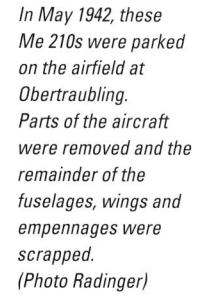

In May 1942, these Me 210s were parked on the airfield at Obertraubling. Parts of the aircraft were removed and the remainder of the fuselages, wings and empennages were scrapped. (Photo Radinger)

A Me 210 with its outer wings removed, being towed with the aid of a Lanz vehicle to a parking spot at Obertraubling. (Photo Croneiß)

NEST OF EAGLES

This photograph from August 1942 shows the worried faces (from left) of Director Karl Linder, Theo Croneiß, Prof. Messerschmitt and Works Director Rakan Kokothaki with regard to the problems experienced in introducing the Me 210 to the Luftwaffe. The bomb-bay doors are open and clearly visible are the openings for the forward-firing MG 17 and MG 151/20 weapons. (Photo Croneiß)

Me 210 losses from September 1941 to April 1942

	Damaged	Destroyed
I./SKG 210:		
Crashes	-	3
Engine damage	1	-
In landings	5	1
For I./ZG 1:		
In take-offs	1	1
Crashes	-	2
Engine damage	-	3
In landings	9	-
E-Stelle Rechlin:		
In landings	-	1
Luftzeugamt:		
Crashes		1
Total:	16	11

ordered the fuselage to be shortened in conjunction with the use of wing leading-edge slats. In air combat with enemy fighters these measures were expected to provide a higher degree of manoeuvrability to the Me 210, the lack oh which on the Bf 110 had been cause for criticism. On grounds of expense, the leading-edge slats had been rejected by the RLM for the Me 210. Despite reports by test pilots concerning its unbalanced flying characteristics, the Me 210 went into production in this configuration, and the accounts that continually appear in literature on Me 210 crashes at the front line which led to the termination of production are likewise not correct. The loss reports in the author's possession from I./SKG 210, I./ZG 1, the E-Stelle Rechlin and from the Luftzeugamt from September 1941 until April 1942, occurred during test-flying and conversion training, as in the table (top right).

From this list, it can be seen that six aircraft were lost during this period through crashes, but about which no further details are known. A further six Me 210s were destroyed due to other causes, and 14 aircraft were damaged in landings alone, which were for the most part due to poor instruction and training of the pilots. The losses occured during a period of around eight months and viewed under wartime conditions, were certainly not that high. A further point was the continually rising tension between the management of the Messerschmitt firm and the RLM which had existed for some time due to the insufficient productivity of the Augsburg plant.

Gernot Croneiß recalled: 'At that time, my father was on the Messerschmitt Board of Directors and he told us in 1941 after a visit to the Augsburg plant, that the management there first appeared in the Works on a Tuesday and left on a Thursday for the weekend. The work performance in the whole of the Augsburg plant at that time lay below that of Regensburg. Moreover, the relationship between Prof. Messerschmitt on the one hand and Milch of the RLM on the other, who continually won more influence with Göring, worsened dramatically. Messerschmitt's position at this point of time (1942) was that it was the sole aircraft producer in the German Reich that did not stand under the direct influence of the RLM. Heinkel, for example, because of the problems with the He 177, had to go the same way. The problems with the Me 210 for the RLM were hence a welcome opportunity to put Messerschmitt down. All this naturally took place with the full approval of Göring, who allowed Milch and Generaling. Lucht a free hand to eliminate the chaos at Messerschmitt after production of the Me 210 had been stopped by order of the RLM.'

A further previously little-considered aspect concerning the Me 210 was its eight-month operational use by III./ZG 1. Those Me 210s built, because of their supposedly inferior flight

From left to right: RLM Generalingenieur Roluf Lucht, Reichsmarschall Hermann Göring (seen without decorations following an argument over fighter strategy with the General der Jagdflieger, General Adolf Galland) and Generalfeldmarschall Erhard Milch. Göring and Milch were the chief advocates for halting production of the Me 210. (Photo Wedemeyer)

characteristics, were not scrapped but instead were operated by III./ZG 1 in Tunisia from November 1942, and in Italy until June 1943, and therefore for about half a year after Me 210 production had been stopped. As to exactly what extent the Me 210 – with lengthened fuselage – saw service, has not up to now been ascertained.

Losses by III./ZG 1 from November 1942 to June 1943

	Damaged	Destroyed
Losses without enemy action:		
On take-off	2	1
In landings	15	3
In crashes	-	7
Engine damage	2	8
Taxiing damage	3	1
Blown up	-	
Total:	**22**	**21**
Losses through enemy action:		
Air combat	2	28
Bombing raids	10	7
Through flak	1	5
Total:	**13**	**40**

As can be seen above, seven aircraft were lost in crashes, while eight losses were due to engine damage – and this with a twin-engined model. It can thus be concluded that the Me 210 was just as good or as bad as the engines delivered by Daimler-Benz.

In March 1941, a Hungarian delegation visited the Messerschmitt-Werke in Augsburg and Regensburg and obtained manufacturing licences for the Bf 109 G and the Me 210. In accordance with the licence agreement, half of the aircraft built were to be delivered to the Luftwaffe, which were then designated the Me 210 Ca. The Hungarians commenced Me 210 production at the end of 1942 which they modified, the DB 601 F engines being replaced with the DB 605 A. The forward-facing armament was reduced to two MG 151/20s and the entire additional built-in armour-plating by the Germans in the cockpit was dispensed with, so that only the standard 8-mm thick armour-plating remained. In 1942-44, a total of 302 Me 210s were built by the Dunai Repülögépgyar RT (Danube Aircraft Plant) near Budapest. The Hungarian-built Me 210s were given a higher combat rating by the German pilots than the German version. Until far into 1944, the Me 210 equipped with GM-1 injection was flown as an early-warning aircraft by the Luftbeobachtungsstaffeln (Air Observation Staffeln). Fitted with a 300-litre auxiliary fuel tank beneath each wing, these aircraft, flying at high altitudes, chased American bomber formations and reported continuously on the numbers and course of the bombers to the ground stations. With the help of GM-1, the Me 210 was able to overcome almost all attacks by USAAF fighters, and only one loss, by the Luftbeobachtungsstaffel 3 on 11 Februray 1944, has been identified.

The production run of the Me 210 at Regensburg caused enormous problems in the manufacturing run of the Bf 109 E, which ended in March and that of the Bf 109 F in September 1941. From October to December, no Bf 109s left the final assembly lines and only two experimental examples of the Bf 109 G-1 (W.Nr. 14001 and W.Nr. 14002) were flight-tested, whilst a further six aircraft were under construction.

Ground crew carry out engine tests on an Me 210 of III./ZG 1 based in Tunisia in March 1943. (AMC)

Ground crew load the standard dinghy (in its container) into the fuselage of an Me 210 just forward of the MG 131 remote-controlled gun barbette. It could be released from the cockpit by either crew member by pulling a lever which activated a powerful spring which ejected it out of the fuselage.

NEST OF EAGLES

Aircraft Production in 1941

	Bf 108 B	Bf 108 D	Bf 109 E	Bf 109 F-0	Bf 109 F-1/F-2	Bf 109 G-1	Me 210
January			3	1	9		
February	9				26		
March	10		1	1	45		
April	2				91		
May				2	80		
June	1			1	30		
July	4				29		
August	7				20		
Sept	2				12		5
Oct	3	1					10
Nov	9						6
Dec	11					2	11
Totals	**58**	**1**	**4**	**5**	**342**	**2**	**32**

In addition, within the scope of centralized deliveries, 172 sets of wings and 278 fuselage rear sections for the Me 210 were sent to Augsburg. For series manufacture, a total of 3,090,895 and for centralized manufacture, 2,650,300 production hours were expended. Technical data for the Me 210 are in Appendix 6.

Regensburg-built Messerschmitt Me 210 A-1 W.Nr. 2102251, 2N+DD, ZG 26 at Diepholz, Germany in 1943. The aircraft has been fitted with a pair of WGr 21 mortar tubes under each wing. Note the white tail fin and rudder.

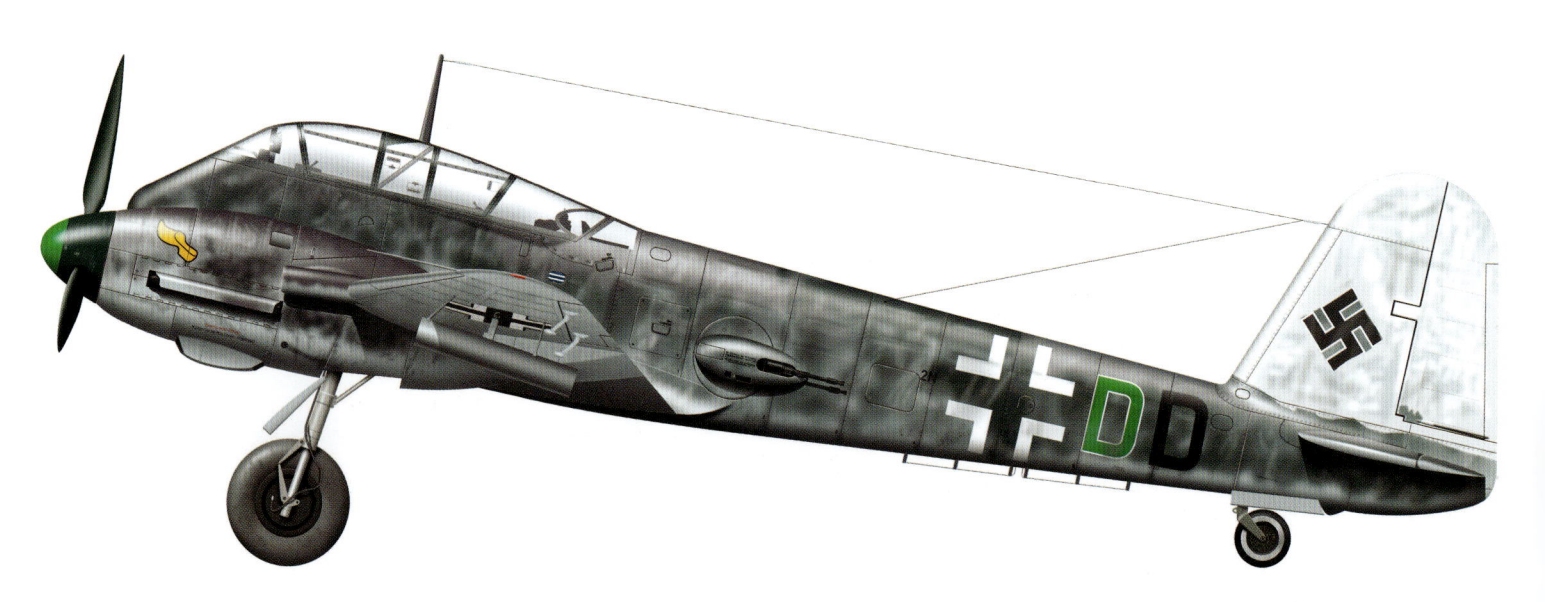

Messerschmitt Me 210 A-1, W.Nr. 2102251, 2N+DD, ZG 26, Diepholz, Germany 1943

CHAPTER 3

War and Production

Stoppage of the Me 210 and Series-Production of the Bf 109 G

IN the winter of 1941-42, under great personnel and materiel losses, some stability was introduced to the Eastern Front. Yet the Soviet Army had brought the Wehrmacht to the verge of defeat. The year 1942 saw German troops close to Murmansk, at Stalingrad, and on the Elbrus in the Caucasus. The Deutsche Afrika Korps (DAK) was poised before El Alamein ready for a leap to the Suez Canal. However, on the completely overstretched German battlefronts, the first setbacks became apparent when at the end of October, the DAK faced ever-increasing enemy sterngth. On 8 November, the British and Americans landed in Algeria to the rear of the DAK which resulted in a retreat of 2,000 km (1,242 mls) to Tunisia. At Stalingrad, the 6.Armee under GFM Friedrich Paulus became encircled and was to have been supplied from the air. By 31 May, the first RAF 'thousand bomber raid' took place over German soil and resulted in the destruction of Cologne. On 17 August 1942, the US Eighth Air Force based in England flew its first air assault with 12 Boeing B-17s against the Sotteville-les-Rouen railway marshalling yards and exactly one year later, this was followed by a raid with 126 B-17s on Regensburg. The pendulum of the war had swung back. On 17 April 1942, 12 Avro Lancaster bombers of the RAF's 44 Squadron flying in daylight at low level attacked the MAN (Maschinenfabrik Augsburg-Nürnberg) Motorenwerke in Augsburg. Of these, seven were shot down. Although their aim to destroy the production of U-boat engines was unsuccessful, this raid nevertheless caused a considerable stir in Germany. As a consequence, additional 2-cm anti-aircraft guns were positioned on the Works premises at Regensburg, and all fronts demanded Luftwaffe support. Without air superiority, no firm operative war leadership of the Army was possible. Due to catastrophic planning in the RLM, at a decisive turning point in the war, hundreds of fighters and bombers were lacking at the various fronts, and it has to be said that the Messerschmitt-Werke in Regensburg also played a considerable part in this state of affairs.

In the first three months of 1942, only nine Bf 109 G-1s and two Bf 109G-1/R-2s were delivered from Regensburg. These did not go to the front line but instead, to the Luftwaffe Erprobungsstelle at Rechlin. Why? The fiasco had already surfaced at the end of 1941, when increasing problems with the Me 210 appeared. In May, the RLM had ordered the stoppage of Me 210 production in Augsburg and Regensburg. At the latter location, in 1941-42, only 94 Me 210s were produced, of which 62 were in 1942. Production of the Bf 110, which was to have been replaced with the Me 210, was nil. Luftwaffe units that were making preparations to convert to the Me 210 relinquished their aircraft in order to revert to the Bf 110 once more. Completely new production programmes had to be drawn up by the RLM for industry so that Bf 110 production could be resumed. This, however, did not take place within a matter of a few weeks as all of the subcontractors had to change over from their production of the Me 210. Now, very late in the day, the alarm bells rang in Berlin. Not only was the Me 210 not available, but because of the twice-over switch of production in Regensburg, production of some 200 Bf 109s was also lacking. Over a space of six months, from October 1941 to March 1942, not a single Bf 109 left Regensburg for the front line. As a result of detailed research, it can be assumed that the problems with the Me 210 came as a not unwelcome excuse for the RLM to displace Prof. Messerschmitt and to take over control of the firm.

It was now GFM Milch at the RLM who took up the reins and set the targets. In three aircraft plants, a monthly output of 1,000 Bf 109 Gs was to be attained. The firms intended to accomplish this were the Wiener-Neustädter Flugzeugwerke at Vienna, the Erla Maschinenwerke GmbH at Leipzig, and Messerschmitt at Regensburg. According to this directive of 15 April

47

NEST OF EAGLES

Parked on the concrete apron at Regensburg in March 1942 were these Bf 109 G-1s (BD+GP) W.Nr. 14021, (NI+BW) W.Nr. 14053, and (NI+BK) W.Nr. 14041. (Photo Seitz)

On 13 June 1942, DAF (Deutsche Arbeitsfront - German Workers' Movement) Leader, Robert Ley, (with cap in hand) visited Regensburg. Ley was known as the 'Zahnradgeneral' (gear- or toothed-wheel General). (Städtische Bildstelle 183-34)

1942, Regensburg was to produce 50 Bf 109 Gs per month, rising to 100/month from May 1943 and 200/month from June 1944. In Regensburg, the Technical Department evaluated the possibility of producing up to 250 Bf 109 Gs per month, but this bordered on the uppermost limit of its productivity capabilities. The greatest problem in surmounting the construction programme was the bottleneck in having sufficiently large manufacturing buildings. Regensburg helped itself by constructing a connecting building between the metalworking and the final assembly halls, which provided an additional manufacturing area of about 410 x 40 m (1,345 x 130 ft). As a result of the largescale manufacture of the Bf 109 in Regensburg, Bf 108 production was transferred to France, with the relocation of the Me 163 pre-production series to Obertraubling becoming necessary. Ever since April 1942, three Hallen in the north-eastern area of the plant had housed 'Abteilung L' ('L' for Lippisch) which was engaged in work on the Me 163. This area within the plant was cordoned-off and could only be entered with special identification. The eight Me 309 prototypes that were in the original construction programme of 1942-43 were not manufactured in Regensburg.

Production of the Bf 109 G took place in two full shifts. Even so, production could only be gradually raised to a maximum, since such an increase could only be coordinated with the subcontractor firms. Due to the higher production rate, acceptance testing had to be strengthened so that technically trained and experienced Luftwaffe pilots could support the Messerschmitt test pilots. Up to the middle of the year, manufactured parts and groups of parts, machinery and various other materials for the Me 210, still lay around in the Prüfening manufacturing halls. Removing these items proved to be extremely tiresome and caused a not inconsiderable hindrance to Bf 109 production. At the Fliegerhorst Obertraubling, a portion of the final assemblies and works flight-testing of the Me 321 had been in progress since 1941, as well as preparations for series-production of the Me 323 under the leadership of Messerschmitt AG Augsburg. From January 1942, this plant was taken over by Messerschmitt GmbH Regensburg. The Fliegerhorst Obertraubling, erected in 1936-37, had been assigned cost-free for use by the Messerschmitt firm and it was here in 1942 that seven Me 163 B-0s plus seven prototypes and 16 Me 323 series aircraft were completed.

In the take-over of Obertraubling, the workforce had increased by 3,811 and through the expansion of production at Prüfening, had risen to 7,604, so that the total Messerschmitt GmbH workforce rose to 11,415 employees. Bolstering the workforce was accomplished mainly by PoWs, 'Ostarbeiter' (workers from the East) and other foreign labour. The presence and engagement of 2,997 PoWs and 1,713 foreign workers in such a sensitive area of military aircraft production caused a considerable security problem. Sabotage could not be excluded, and the Gestapo was always present in both plants. The technical management was faced with almost insurmountable problems, and whilst 4,018 men worked in Prüfening at the end of 1941, this figure reduced to 3,510 at the end of 1942, caused by the increased call-up for military service. Replacing 500 skilled workers by Ostarbeiter and other foreign workers within a short period of time and maintaining high-quality production with its high standards, was certainly a notable achievement. An additional disturbance was the long-prevailing bad weather period in November and December 1942, which virtually brought acceptance flights to a halt. Production aircraft that were turned out congested the snowed-in airfield parking area. Since new machines were continually and urgently required at the front, however, at least some of the wings of the Bf 109 G-4/trop were dismantled and the aircraft were loaded onto heavy goods rail wagons. These Bf 109s were then transported to Bari in southern Italy, where the aircraft were again put together by Messerschmitt mechanics for the Luftwaffe front line contingents and test-flown by Regensburg pilots such as Josef Haid and later, Oberfeldwebel Semmler.

For the completely unexpected death of Director Croneiß on 7 November 1942, funeral ceremonies took place five days later in the large hangar. Ever since the removal of Prof. Messerschmitt as head of the firm by the RLM, Croneiß had been Chairman of the Board of the entire enterprise and simultaneously Betriebsführer (Works Head) of the AG and GmbH, Reichsamtsleiter (Department Head) of the NSDAP, SS Brigadeführer, Gaujägermeister (District Hunting Head) and Major in the Luftwaffe. The chairmanship in the governing body of Messerschmitt GmbH Regensburg that thus became vacant was filled by the Munich banker, F.S. Seiler, with lawyer Michael Konrad of Munich appointed as deputy chairman. Newly elected to the governing body was Frau Baroness von Michel-Raulono of Bamberg. Responsibility for business leadership was for a time passed to Karl Linder, who handed this over to RLM Generalstabsingenieur Lucht in May 1943, but which reverted to Linder in April 1944 when Lucht took over new tasks on the Jägerstab (Fighter Staff). Lucht was also one of the initiators of the 'forest construction trains' which comprised railway carriages that were equipped with appropriate personnel and materiel ranging from electric power generators up to dismantled barracks and construction equipment suitable for installation in small hangars. These trains were sent to the bombed-out aircraft plants and later also to other industrial firms to overcome the most urgent damage suffered or else to imediately reinstate production in dispersed centres in forests (as stated in a report by Dr. Wedemeyer to the author).

Production of the Bf 109 G-1 to G-4

From the DB 601, Daimler-Benz had developed the higher-performance DB 605 A of 1,475 hp at take-off. Following initial problems with the exhaust valve which often overheated and then caught fire, the introduction of an exhaust valve containing a sodium-filled valve shaft and one with an increased chrome-nickel content led to one of the most reliable powerplants. Flight trials of the new Bf 109 G-1 began at Regensburg at the end of November 1941. It had a pressurized cockpit, and was built there in a small series of 148 aircraft from November 1941 until June 1942, which included 81 Bf 109 G-1/R-2 interim high-altitude fighters. The first G-1s were partly still fitted with the retractable tailwheel of the F-series. The task of the G-1 variant was to match the superior high-altitude performance of the Spitfire on the Channel coast.

In March 1942, the following G-1s were ferried from Regensburg to the Erprobungsstelle Rechlin to enable training of an Erprobungsstaffel: W.Nr. 14002, 14005, 14007, 14009 and 14018 to 14021, as well as the G-1/R-2s W.Nr. 14010 and 14011. These were put

Overview of Messerschmitt GmbH Regensburg Personnel in December 1942

	Werk I and II	Werk I Regensburg	Werk II Obertraubling
Plant Employees			
German - men	4,278	3,510	768
German - women	1,268	1,075	193
Eastern workers - men	595	595	
Eastern workers - women	189	189	
Other foreigners	929	929	
Prisoners of war	2,997	241	2,756
Total	10,256	6,539	3,717
Office Employees			
German – men	679	600	79
German – women	480	465	15
Overall total	11,415	7,604	3,811

In 1942, production by the Messerschmitt GmbH comprised the folowing numbers of aircraft: 58 Bf 108s, 486 Bf 109s, 7 Me 163s, 62 Me 210s and 23 Me 323s. The last Bf 108 completed in Regensburg was flown in June, after which production was transferred to France. Together with this, when production of the Me 210 was stopped, the decision to go for largescale Bf 109 production and incorporate Me 323 production in the Fliegerhorst Obertraubling, resulted in a total reorganisation of production by the Messerschmitt GmbH. Despite the introduction of the Bf 109 largescale construction programme, only 142 more aircraft were built in 1942 than in 1941. The required 50 aircraft/month, however, was able to be met from May 1942.

Bf 109 Variants Produced in Regensburg in 1942

Bf 109 model	G-1	G-1/R-2	G-2	G-2/trop	G-4	G-4/trop	Total
January							0
February	9	1					10
March		1					1
April	23	2	2				27
May	28	40					68
June	1	33	18				52
July		2	48				50
August	3		27	20			50
September	1	1	3	3	38		46
October					54		54
November					48		48
December					42	38	80
Total:	65	80	98	23	128	92	486

Because of space considerations and technical interruptions, in acceptance flight trials the following incidents occurred, where all the aircraft involved were the Bf 109 G-4
    Werknr 16118 – crashed 03.11.42
    Werknr 16126 – crashed 06.11.42
    Werknr 16123 – emergency landing 07.11.42
    Werknr 16129 – destroyed 09.11.42
    Werknr 16095 – destroyed 30.11.42
    Werknr 16172 – emergency landing 11.12.42.

through their paces at Rechlin, in the course of which several weaknesses became apparent. At low outside temperatures and at high altitude, the rev-counter shaft broke; the cockpit pressure gauge had too small a measurement range and for checking the pressure of the cockpit on the ground, a closure lock on the pressure-maintainence valve was lacking. The compressor for cockpit pressure delivered too little power, so that with the slightest leak the cabin pressure sank and the vision panels iced up on the insides. Because of its pressure-tight construction, the cockpit hood had become very heavy and its ejection became questionable. The cabin sealing held for about 15 hours in operation, after which the sealing lips deformed despite treatment with a special fat; the putty, with which the vision panels were sealed,

NEST OF EAGLES

Photographed in August 1942 at Regensburg, from left to right, of Technical Director, Karl Linder, Hauptmann Anton 'Toni' Hackl, Staffelkapitän of 5./JG 77, and Works Director Theo Croneiß. Hackl, who flew Bf 109s with JG 77 and had recently been awarded the Ritterkreuz mit Eichenlaub (Knight's Cross with Oakleaves), was a Regensburger and successful fighter pilot who would end the war with a total of 192 aerial victories, among them 34 four-engined bombers.
(Photo Linder)

Hinged engine cowlings introduced from the Bf 109 F onwards considerably eased service and inspection of the DB series of engines. This DB 605 A seen here in a Bf 109 G was able to be rearmed and serviced within 30 minutes.
(Photo Schmoll)

became brittle and crumbled away. At high altitudes, the oxygen supply was insufficient, and the wormscrew for the dry cartridge for condensation protection on the panels was judged to be too sensitive. For the MG 151 weapons covers, guide-rails were found to be necessary, otherwise the sealing of the covers became damaged. At low altitudes, cockpit ventilation was insufficient, and on the cockpit front armoured panels the seals were badly installed (assembly errors). The built-in GM-1 – the so-called 'Göring Mischung' (mixture), an auxiliary fuel consisting of nitrous oxide liquid under pressure as an oxydiser – had no check manometer. In the Bf 109 G-1, it was housed in two double-walled high-pressure bottles in the fuselage. A conduit led from the bottles via an electromagnetic valve to the air scoops of the main engine. By means of a special duct, the GM-1 was vaporized and injected at the rate of 100 gm/sec, so that at high altitude the engine power was increased by around 280 hp. For the Bf 109 G-1/R-2, this meant at 12,000 m (39,370 ft) a speed increase of some 100 km/h (62 mph) – from 560 to 660 km/h (348 to 410 mph). With such a performance, albeit available for only a short duration, no Spitfire was able to compete.

The problems that surfaced at that time would appear to us today to be incomprehensible, but it has to be borne in mind that steps were being made here into totally new technological fields and into high altitudes and speeds which only a few years before, had been regarded as utopian. Further problems existed with the new DB 605 A-1 engine which also displayed a number of faults. For this engine, the concluding verdict in April 1942 was that when delivering full power, it was not operationally ready. In addition, it ran so rough that vibration cracks appeared on the airframe and engine sheet-metal panelling. In the ventral engine panelling, cracks 100 mm (4 in) long were measured. Despite the presence of chafing protection, coolant and lubrication conduits became thoroughly chafed after only a few hours in operation, and only by an enormous amount of maintenance and repair was the operational readiness of the aircraft maintained.

For the fighter units that had been deployed on air defence in the West, the introduction of the Bf 109 G-1/R-2 to counter enemy high-altitude bombers and reconnaissance aircraft had been assigned far above the numbers planned. As a result of the multitude of faults in the Bf 109 G-1 and G-1/R-2, operational limitations were placed on these by the RLM. On training missions, altitudes higher than 11,000 m (36,090 ft) for health safety reasons had not to be exceeded. Despite the pressurized cockpit, the high-altitude breathing system had to be utilized to enable the oxygen supply to be maintained. 'Alarmstart' (emergency take-off) for missions at low altitude was forbidden. The Bf 109 G-1/R-2 variant was siphoned-off the main G-1 series in limited numbers and was hence equipped with a pressure-cabin whose function was not yet fully ready for operational use. The service ceiling of 13,000 m (42,650 ft) actually flown was attained through reducing the cockpit and fuel tank armour-plating and the amount of ammunition carried. A temporary increase in ceiling altitude, climb and level speed through the use of GM-1 was intended at the conclusion of flight trials.

Missions by the Bf 109 G-1 were conducted in special high-altitude fighter Staffeln with JG 2 'Richthofen' and JG 26 'Schlageter'. These G-1s, operated on the Channel coast, also provided high-altitude protection for the Focke-Wulf Fw 190 whose BMW 801 twin-row radial engine could not keep up with the Spitfire's Rolls-Royce Merlin engine at heights above 8,000 m (26,250 ft). In JG 1 on the Dutch and German coasts and in JG 5 on the Norwegian coast, the high-altitude fighters were poised ready for action in 'Schwarms' – as a rule consisting of four aircraft. In May 1942, the G-1 entered operational service with 11./JG 2. One of the first losses at the Front was probably W.Nr. 14052 (NI+BV) of I./JG 1 which, following an engine fire on 21 June 1942, was 90% destroyed. Of the G-1s built at Regensburg from December 1941 to April 1942, a total of 67 were G-1/R-2s and from January to June 1942, 60 aircraft were built and flown. All the experiences gained with the G-1 were later incorporated in the manufacture of the G-3 and G-5 high-altitude fighters. As a follow-on to the Bf 109 F models, the first two G-2s, W.Nr. 14029 and 14036 built at Regensburg in February 1942 were used for test purposes. As with the G-1, faults were experienced with the G-2, but these were primarily due to the strong engine vibrations. From June to August 1942, a total of 141 G-2s was built in Regensburg. Of these, from August to the beginning of September 1942, 23 were the G-2/trop scheduled for operations in North Africa with sand filters ahead of the supercharger intake as well as others modified with auxiliary equipment necessary for desert operations. In addition to equipment for desert operations, the series-produced aircraft for tropical use also incorporated a rifle holder on the starboard inner fuselage wall for a 98K carbine, tropical equipment in the baggage space, protective sheets for covering the engine bay, airscrew hood, shock-absorber undercarriage legs, a surface coat of tropical camouflage (the undersides remaining in their original colour), as well as coverings for the thermostats for the coolant and lubrication systems. To prevent the

War and Production

Bf 109 G-2 (CC+PG) W.Nr. 14236 undergoes a full-load test-run of its DB 605 A engine on Regensburg airfield in July 1942. Note the ballast weight near the tailwheel. (Photo DM Munich)

Bf 109 G-2 (CC+PK) W.Nr. 14240 on the compass base at Regensburg in August 1942. (Photo Seitz)

Bf 109 G-2 (CC+PU) W.Nr. 14250 rolled out of the final assembly hall at Regensburg in August 1942. The G-2s with Werknummern 14246 to 14268 were converted into the G-2/trop and in September 1942 were sent to North Africa or to the Mediterranean. (Photo Seitz)

entry of sand, the operating cylinders for the coolant and lubricant cooling flaps were covered by a leather sheath, likewise the operating cylinders of the undercarriage legs. For those aircraft parked out in the open, the sand filter had to be covered with a sailcloth and the engine exhaust stacks with caps. To prevent the cockpit from overheating in the hot sun, parked aircraft were also covered with an umbrella attached in two places to the port fuselage wall and clamped with the aid of butterfly nuts at the upper ends, the side walls on both sides of the cockpit each having a movable flap for auxiliary ventilation.

51

NEST OF EAGLES

Below: A Bf 109 G-2/Trop of JG 53. Clearly visible in front of the supercharger intake is the sand filter fitted to the tropicalised versions of the aircraft. The sand filter consisted of two Delbag air filter units and two switchover flaps which were operated by cable from a hand operated lever on the left hand side of the cockpit. The Delbag filter units removed impurities from the air by means of a thin coating of oil, and because they soon became choked, they had to be changed or cleaned after every two flights. The cleaning was achieved by dipping the filters in a solvent, such as petrol or paraffin etc. and allowing them to dry. They were then re-dipped in used engine oil and allowed to drain. Note also one of the two dear drop shaped lugs below the port-side windscreen for attaching an umbrella for shading the cockpit when parked between operations.

Above: These Bf 109 G-2s, stand ready for acceptance check flights at Regensburg in July 1942. They are: (DN+YO) W.Nr. 14176, (DN+YW) Werknr 14184, (DN+YK) W.Nr. 14172, (DN+YE) W.Nr. 14166, (DN+YU) W.Nr. 14182; G-1/R-2 (DF+CJ) W.Nr. 14130, G-2 (DN+YT) W.Nr.14181, and G-2 (DN+YQ) W.Nr. 14178. (Photo Seitz)

Although the Werknummer of this Bf 109 G-2, 'Black 3' of 2./JG 53 photographed in Russia in July of 1942, is unknown, it displays typical Regensburg-applied camouflage on the upper fuselage and rear cockpit area. This style of camouflage can often be seen on particular batches of Bf 109s from the factory, up to and including the early K-series. See for example the Bf 109s above and the Bf 109 G-6/Trop on page 134.

Messerschmitt Bf 109 G-2 'Black 3' of 2./JG 53, Russia, July 1942

52

CHAPTER 4

'Total War': 1943-1945

The 'Heimatfront' (Homeland Front)

AT the Casablanca Conference of 14-25 January 1943, the Allied leaders decided upon the future strategy of the air war against the Third Reich. The resulting plan for the 'Combined Bomber Offensive' set out the following target priorities: (1) U-boat bases and production centres, (2) the aircraft industry, (3) principal traffic nodal points, (4) oil refineries and synthetic fuel plants, and (5) the ball-bearing industry. It was also at Casablanca that the Unconditional Surrender decision was born. In 1943, Germany experienced not only setbacks on individual fronts similar to 1941-42, but also suffered military catastrophes of major dimensions. At Stalingrad, GFM Friedrich Paulus' 6.Armee surrendered on 2 February 1943, and on 12 May, Heeresgruppe Afrika (the Afrika Korps) capitulated in Tunis. In the 'Battle of the Atlantic' a total of 36 U-boats were sunk in May 1943. On 2 August, US bomber formations, setting out from Benghazi, flew their first mission against Hitler's largest source of oil – the refineries at Ploesti in Rumania. The greatest tank battle of all time, in the Kursk 'bulge', was broken off from the German side when Sicily was invaded. But Germany itself came to be a War Front leading to the term 'Heimatfront' (Homeland Front). On 17 May, the Möhne dam had been destroyed by RAF Bomber Command and thus was lost as a provider of electric power for the industrial region of the Ruhr. Night after night, strong formations of RAF bombers flew into Reich territory and turned one German town after another into rubble. The amount of bombs dropped by the RAF on German towns in 1943 amounted to 110,000 tons and resulted in tens of thousands of civilian fatalities. In increasing measure, the US Eighth Air Force flew its precision daylight raids on important industrial targets in Germany, including Regensburg which came in for a massive 'dose'. Because of the extremely over-extended German battlefronts and the air attacks on German territory, the need for fighter aircraft climbed rapidly. The General der Jagdflieger, Adolf Galland, anticipating what was coming, feverishly sought to establish a 'Reichsverteidigung' (Reich defence infrastructure) with new fighter formations, including the formation of JG 11 and the experimental JGr 25 and JGr 50. These were later supplemented by the dedicated Reich defence units JG 300, JG 301 and JG 302. Furthermore, by dividing the component Staffeln and Gruppen in almost every Jagdgeschwader, there was a IV.Gruppe set up from 1944 onwards. But for this, however, yet more fighters were needed.

As mentioned previously, the possibility had already been examined in April 1942 to produce 250 Bf 109 Gs per month in Regensburg. In fact even this target was exceeded in the months of July and December 1943. After termination of the Bf 109 G-3 and G-4 series, production rose continually with the series-built G-6 in accordance with the RLM Lieferprogramm 222. A noticeable setback in Bf 109 production took place after the air raid of 17 August 1943. Despite this, the total turn-out of 486 Bf 109s in 1942 was raised to 2,166 in 1943, which represents a production increase by a factor of 4.46. The planned RLM turn-out figure of 2,570, however, could not be fully achieved. The RLM's Lieferprogramm 223 of 15 August 1943 envisaged a further considerable increase in production for the year 1944. Since by the end of 1942, the Works civilian acceptance test pilots had reached the limits of their capabilities, this activity was enhanced by Luftwaffe pilots who had been granted leave from duties. These pilots had amassed a wealth of flying experience, and some of them were even able to show that they had received professional training in the aviation industry. Several pilots of Flieger-Sonderkommando Ob.d.L. were assigned to transfer from Jüterbog 2 Altes Lager (Old Camp) to Regensburg. The pilots concerned no longer received their military pay from the Luftwaffe, but were paid as acceptance pilots by Messerschmitt GmbH. As such, they were paid between RM 800 and RM 900 per month – far in excess of their Luftwaffe pay.

The Messerschmitt Regensburg Industriestaffel

Upon an order from the Luftwaffe's 'Jagdführer Süddeutschland' (Fighter Leader Southern Germany), the 'Industrie Jagdeinheiten Messerschmitt Regensburg' (Industry Fighter Unit Regensburg) was formed with effect from 14 January 1943. Its operational radius was limited to 30 km (18 mls) and any mission outside this radius was only possible upon a directive from the Sub-sector Leader of 5. Jagddivision. Initially known under the abovementioned title, on 14 February 1943 the unit was renamed the 'Industriestaffel Messerschmitt Regensburg'. Personnel for the Industriestaffel comprised civilian acceptance pilots as well as authorized soldiers from the Flieger-Sonderkommando from Jüterbog. Its military head was Oberleutnant Ladegast and his deputy, Flugkapitän Trenkle. Tactically, the Industriestaffel was subordinated to the Kommodore of JG 104 at Fürth. Its Command Centre was the Flugleitung (Flight Operations or Air Traffic Control) in Regensburg-Prüfening which, from 15 minutes before sunrise to 15 minutes after sunset, had to be continually occupied and for which the following alert stages applied:

Stage 1: Aircraft to be airborne in 3 minutes
Stage 2: Aircraft to be airborne in 15 minutes
Stage 3: Aircraft to be airborne in 30 minutes.

During the day, two Bf 109 Gs always had to be on call at Stage 3. Furthermore, four reserve Bf 109 Gs, fully fuelled and armed, also had to be ready for action at Stage 3. Despite on-going acceptance flights, these four reserve aircraft and the corresponding number of pilots had to be on stand-by, ready to take-off within 30 minutes. Upon the approach of a small-scale enemy formation at range 300 km (186 mls) heading for Regensburg, the Industriestaffel was warned by the codeword 'Mückenstich' (midge or gnat-bite), whereupon the two Bf 109 Gs were alerted to warning Stage 1.

In an anticipated large-scale raid when the 300 km mark was approached, a warning was given under the codeword 'Vogelzug' (bird migration). In this case, the four reserve aircraft were raised to alert Stage 1. The warning, take-off order and command in the air was overseen by 5. Jagddivision. After take-off, the four aircraft assembled over Prüfening airfield at combat altitude and when it became apparent that a raid was directed at Regensburg, the combat formation remained on course at altitude and flew towards the enemy. The basic principle was that before they reached Regensburg, the enemy was to be engaged in battle and destroyed, being pursued up to the limit of the fighters' range. Tactical radio communication was to take place over air- and ground-based FuG 16 and run under the code 'Signaltafel für die Tagjagd' (signal table for day fighting). In the aircraft, maps to 1:500,000 scale and an on-board emergency map to scale 1:1,000,000 were always to be carried. Ammunition belts consisted of a sequence as follows: for MG 131s – 2 armour-piercing rounds and 2 incendiary rounds; for MG 151/20s – 2 armour-piercing incendiary rounds, 2 incendiary rounds, 2 armour-piercing rounds and 4 high-explosive rounds. The military commander was responsible to see that two sets of ammunition were constantly on hand in each aircraft. Ammunition supply for the operational flights, air-firing and signal-recognition ammunition were provided by Luftgaukommando (District Air Command) XII/XIII, the ammunition requirements being directed to the airfield detachment in Obertraubling.

For cooperation with the artillery, the following directives were in force: the fighters had to avoid the effective range of the area Flak and to engage the enemy before it reached the Flak zone. In combat that promised to be successful, this could be continued into the Flak zone. As soon as the Flak crews recognized that a fighter was located in the Flak zone, firing was to be suspended. In the cordoned-off military aerial zone, light Flak artillery was accorded priority. If enemy aircraft entered the Flak zone, the Flak were to fire at those aircraft of the enemy formation that had penetrated the furthest. The heavy Flak was instructed to aim its fire frequently at high altitudes during daylight raids, even when the enemy was outside effective range so as to make enemy identification easier for the fighter units, to which these directional shots were signified by using visible red smoke-trail training rounds.

The operational readiness reports by the Industriestaffel were passed daily until 1500 hrs to the Sub-sector Nuremberg and included the number, aircraft type and series model of the parked aircraft ready for day fighter operations, as well as the number of pilots available for them. The availability and maintenance of these aircraft were provided by Messerschmitt GmbH Regensburg. The very first Industriestaffel training flight over the bomb-dropping practice ground in Siegenburg has been documented as having taken place on 14 March 1943, followed by at least nine further flights until the end of the year. With regard to operational missions, the following have been documented:

On 14 April 1943: an Alarmstart at 1323 hrs of two Bf 109 G-6s directed to a Mosquito reconnaissance aircraft at 6,000 m (19,685 ft) above Regensburg, but without contact with the enemy. The Bf 109s landed at 1315 hrs in Regensburg-Prüfening.

On 17 August 1943: an Alarmstart at 1231 hrs with the entire Staffel of six Bf 109 G-6s at an approaching B-17 bomber formation. At least four B-17s were shot down. One bomber crashed near Hemau; another made an emergency landing in Switzerland and two crashed on their way to North Africa. The Industriestaffel landed from 1327 hrs onwards at the Fliegerhorst Obertraubling, since, due to bombardment of the aircraft plant, the Industrie airfield at Prüfening was no longer clear for landing (see the report on the 17 August air raid elsewhere in this book).

On 14 October 1943: an Alarmstart for the whole Staffel. The six Bf 109 G-6s, equipped with underwing WGr 21 air-to-air mortars, were directed to an approaching enemy flight from the west which had Schweinfurt as its target. With the exception of Josef Haid, the Staffel flew over the blocked-off Regensburg zone. In Haid's case, his engine did not start immediately, so that the others took off without him. When the engine finally started, in the belief that his comrades had headed in the direction of Schweinfurt, he followed. Because of the radio silence that had been ordered before take-off, he had no contact with his fellow pilots. Whilst over Schweinfurt, Haid made contact with the enemy and fired both of his air-to-air mortars at a bomber formation and, according to his testimony, hit one of them. But after his Bf 109 received hits from the bombers' defensive fire, he had to make an emergency landing on a sports field near Schweinfurt, in whose immediate neighbourhood some Americans had also landed by parachute. At Regensburg he was regarded as missing, but shortly after being downed, he was able to report by telephone to Karl Linder. Following Haid's return, there were accusations levelled against Oberleutnant Ladegast, who with his Staffel, had only flown in defence over Regensburg and not flown to Schweinfurt to attack the bombers, although the mission order had specified this (Haid's testimony). Ladegast, in turn, referred to the Operations Order for the Industriestaffel (the 30 km radius around Regensburg), and only with effort was a War Tribunal case avoided.

On 24 January 1944: an Alarmstart was made at 1200 hrs at Obertraubling against approaching bombers. No contact was made with the enemy and the aircraft landed in Obertraubling at 1255 hrs. The bombers that had been reported had Frankfurt and nearby Rüsselsheim as their targets.

Since hardly any documentation exists on the Industriestaffel, unfortunately this narrative is therefore patchy. To date, no proof has been found of sorties made on 22 and 25 February 1944, when the Messerschmitt-Werke at Prüfening and Obertraubling were attacked. The last entry dated 6 March 1944 states that the Regensburg Industriestaffel stood ready with two Bf 109 G-6s, and on this day, US bombers made their first daylight raid on Berlin.

The personnel list for the Regensburg Industriestaffel as of 1 January 1944 comprised: Oberleutnant Ladegast (Staffel Leader), Feldwebel Lohmann, Leutnant Riedmeier, Feldwebel Mrotzek, Oberfeldwebel Breunig, Feldwebel Richter, Oberfeldwebel Sorgatz, Feldwebel Stuhrmann, Oberfeldwebel Stemmler, Feldwebel Wolf, Feldwebel Bergmann, Unteroffizier Häussler, Feldwebel Bessler, Unteroffizier Posemann, Feldwebel Hessler and Obergefreiter Schreiber. These airmen came from various Luftwaffe flying units and had been freed from their duties in order to fly the Bf 109 G and later, the Me 262 at Regensburg on test and acceptance flights for the RLM. In this way, Leutnant Riedmeier arrived from JG 52 with 15 confirmed combat victories. In a low-level attack in the Crimea, he lost his left eye through enemy defensive fire and was no longer 'usable at the Front'. After his wound had healed, he was transferred to Regensburg as a works test pilot, and although unable to exercise the necessary visual depth with only one eye, he flew the Bf 109 and even later on the Me 262. Feldwebel Lohmann went to Regensburg with two confirmed victories scored while with JG 51. Before the war he had worked in the design office at the Fieseler Flugzeugbau in Kassel. Feldwebel Mrotzek was likewise an experienced fighter pilot and on 17 August 1943 had shot down a B-17 over Hemau. The number of works test and acceptance pilots was increased in 1944 and among the civilian pilots who belonged to the Industriestaffel were Flugkapitän Trenkle (Deputy Staffelkapitän), Bauer, Eichelmann and Haid. Notable in this connection is that civilians were assigned to fly military missions together with Luftwaffe pilots and that a civilian (Trenkle) functioned as the Deputy Staffelkapitän of a military unit.

Bf 109 G-6 production at Regensburg-Prüfening

Production of the Bf 109 G-6, the successor model to the G-4, commenced in February 1943 with W.Nr. 16313, and which left the final assembly lines in Prüfening that month with a total of 42 aircraft. Externally, the G-6 was recognizable from the structural bulges which accommodated its MG 131 armament. Whereas the G-4 still had two 7.62 mm MG 17s above the engine, the G-6 had two 13 mm MG 131s each with 300 rounds. The MG 131 had a larger breech and a different type of ammunition feed that necessitated bulges on both sides of the forward fuselage engine casing. In addition to the two MG 131 bulges which had to be added to the G-6, teardrop-shaped bulges were required on the wings because of the altered main undercarriage. Luftwaffe pilots hence somewhat disrespectfully referred to the G-6 as the 'Beule' ('bulge'), and this variant was the most-built in Regensburg. From February 1943 to November 1944, Regensburg built a total of 5,564 G-6s, although in the bombing raids on 17 August 1943, 22 and 25 February and 21 July 1944, the entire plant installations at Prüfening and Obertraubling were destroyed, and production, with few exceptions, was dispersed among numerous small manufacturing centres spread over the entire region of eastern Bavaria.

In the National Archives in Washington, an exact description of Bf 109 G production from the beginning of 1943 has been preserved. From Messerschmitt GmbH Regensburg documents covering conveyor-belt production, the following production run is visible: in the sheet-metal cutting department, piecework was in operation, where out of large metal sheets the parts for the large presses were cut out, from which the construction components for the fuselages and wings were formed. As far as possible, it was attempted by means of cast and pressed parts, to relieve work on the lathes and milling machines. In the realm of wing spar manufacture, boring and automatic riveting machines were employed. In electrical pre-assembly, cable clusters and instrument panels were mostly pre-assembled. Hence, in the final assembly stage, a considerable amount of man-hours were saved through previous made-to-measure pre-assembly. In the metalworking area, the construction parts delivered were formed into wings and fuselages, and it was here that 80% of the workforce consisted of forced labourers (men and women) from the East. For space reasons, the conveyor belts in the pre-assembly area were U-shaped. The separate manufacturing groups for the wings were pre-assembled

Acceptance test pilots of the Regensburg Werkschutz (Works Protection) Staffel, known as the 'Industriestaffel Messerschmitt Regensburg' in front of the flight-test building in the spring of 1943. From left to right (seated): Fw. Richter, Lt. Riedmeir, Fw. Heller, Obgfr. Schreiber, (standing): unknown, Ofw. Sorgatz, Uffz. Posemann, and Ofw. Breunig. (Photo Riedmeir)

NEST OF EAGLES

Right: This June 1943 photograph shows 'Ostarbeiterfrauen' (female workers from the East) working on fuselage skinning of the Bf 109 G. The flush rivets were set with the aid of hand tools. In the background can be seen the assembly of a fuselage half made up from fuselage components; for final shaping, hardwood moulds were used. (Photo BA-Koblenz 638/4222/33)

Below: Preparing a DB 605 A motor for installation in a Bf 109 G-6 at Regensburg. The annular oil tank is located ahead of the reduction gearing. The engines were suspended on rotatable assembly jigs that were moved along by a ventral conveyor belt, and after leaving it, were installed in the aircraft. Fuselage assembly can be seen at left. (Photo Wedemeyer)

Fuselage final assembly on the raised and moving conveyor belt, which enabled work to be done simultaneously above and below the engine and on the fuselage itself. The drive unit for the conveyor belt itself is at lower right of the picture. (Photo Wedemeyer)

Right: Bf 109 G-6 fuselage final assembly in June 1943. Between the fuselages are work platforms which moved with the conveyor belt. The fuselages are mounted on jigs which could be rotated into any desired position by a handwheel. (Photo BA-Koblenz 638/4222/24)

and thereafter, in moving and swivelling structures, were screwed and riveted together. All the parts needed for this process were held in readiness directly beside the conveyor belt, and fuselage assembly was likewise conducted on the conveyor belt method. In special working operations, individual half-fuselage sections were joined together by longerons and subsequently clamped and riveted. These two conveyor belts ended in a construction unit for fuselage final assembly, where up to 28 fuselages were located. Engines and propellers were likewise equipped on conveyor belts for the final assembly of the aircraft. The fuselages arriving from the metal-working shop were lifted onto rolling conveyances in the final assembly area and turned through an angle of 90° to the conveyor belt which moved at 1.2 km/h (1.09 ft/sec). Between the fuselages were the working platforms from which the engine, electrics, control rods, etc., could be mounted. Each worker had his fixed workplace and set tasks to perform.

By having ready all the aircraft parts that were needed ensured a continuous work process. Since the rolling conveyances raised the level of the fuselages, engine installation without any problems was thus made possible. After final assembly, the fuselage was turned through 90 degrees and placed on special transport stands which likewise enabled the aircraft to be raised horizontally and suspended on one of the three conveyor belts in the final assembly hall. The

'Total War': 1943-1945

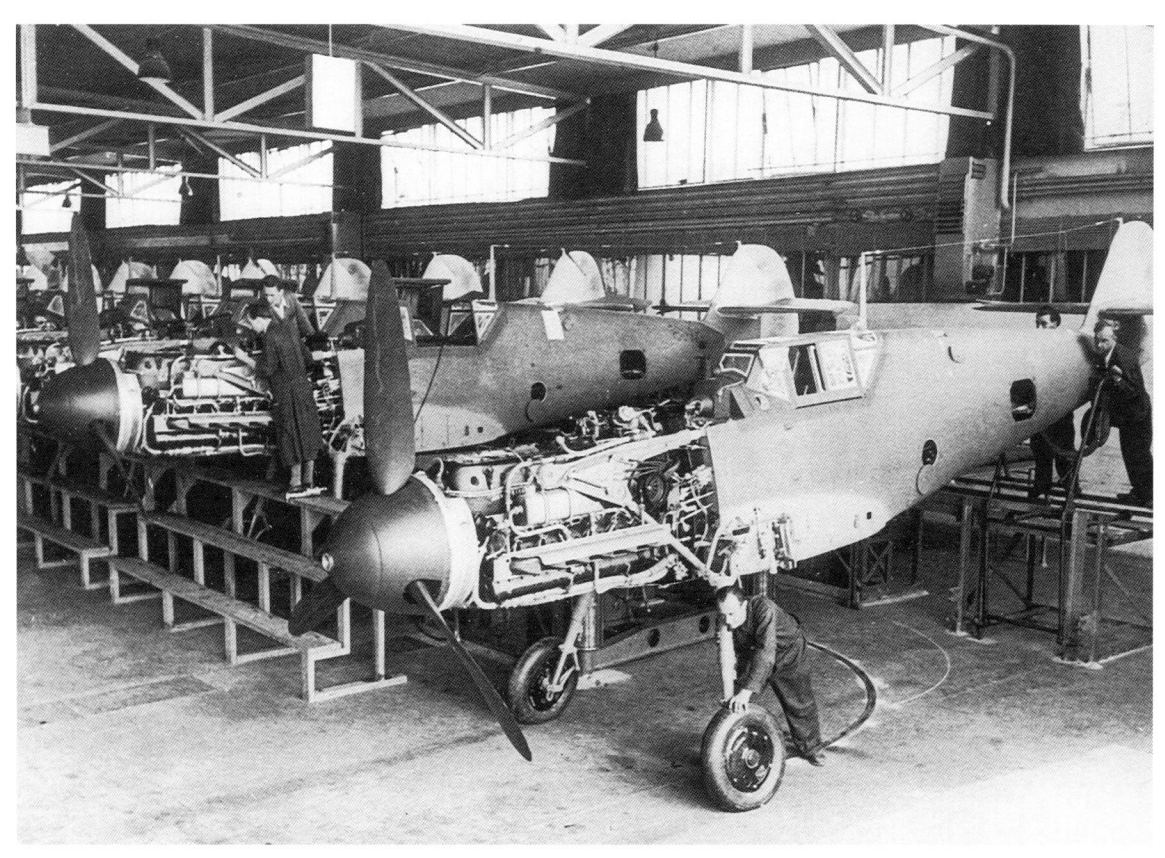

At the end of the conveyor belt, a Bf 109 G-6 is lowered to ground level and rests on its main undercarriage. Clearly visible is that the rear fuselage is supported on a special trestle equipped with small wheels that move forward with the belt. The ability to attach the undercarriage directly to the fuselage, instead of having to wait for the fitting of the wings (as in most contemporary fighter designs) greatly facilitated the ease of moving semi-completed airframes around. (Photo Wedemeyer)

wings, also coming from the left and right from assembly lines, were attached to the fuselages and all leads and conduits attached. In the final phase, all necessary equipment in the shape of fuel tanks, instruments, armament and radio were installed. The fuselage as well as the wings were already lacquered with the later RLM 76 Hellblau (light blue). The engine received its upper and lower covering panels and the oil cooler in the ventral part of the engine casing was attached to the engine circuit. Undercarriage tests followed before the aircraft was lowered onto its wheels and rolled out of the final assembly hall. It was then led to the firing stand to test its weapons as also for centring the compass on the rotatable compass adjustment stand. After fuelling and a last check of all functions, the engine was subjected to a test run, whereafter the Bf 109 stood ready for a works flight. In the initial test flight where it was climbed to 8,000 m (26,250 ft), the aircraft and the engine was thoroughly checked out and performance data compared with that required. In the event that faults were found, these would be recorded and eliminated after the landing. This was then followed by a works test flight in which it could be established how many of the faults had been rectified. Where no further faults were determined on this flight, the aircraft was then released for acceptance by the BAL. In Regensburg, several pilots (Obermeier, Riedmeier, Lohmann and others) were authorized by the RLM to carry out Bf 109 acceptance flights for the BAL. After their acceptance by the BAL, the aircraft were then taken over by the Luftwaffe. Those Bf 109s that had been accepted in Prüfening were parked on the south bank of the Danube in camouflaged parking pens until they were collected by pilots from a fighter unit or an aircraft ferry Geschwader and flown to the front line.

That works test-flying did not pass without incidents, is recalled by Josef Haid: 'In a test-flight with a Bf 109 G, I experienced that the aircraft hung with one wing to starboard. After landing, I mentioned to the Leading Mechanic that he should check the trimtabs on the ailerons and eventually adjust them as the aircraft hung to starboard. On the same day, I flew this Bf 109 which again hung to starboard. Anyway, I thought to myself, the mechanic had not correctly ironed it out. Upon landing, I went through the whole problem with him once more and he assured me that he had ironed the trim-tabs with the ironing pliers. I must mention here that these trim-tabs on the ailerons were merely sheet-metal strips which, with a special pliers according to the need, could be altered in shape such that the aircraft would fly straight and level. I therefore took the pliers and adjusted the trim-tabs myself this time. A short time later I took the aircraft up into the air, but the same phenomenon again manifested itself. After landing, I went straight to Flugkapitän Trenkle and reported this. He said to me: "What? You as well?" Other pilots had also complained that their Bf 109s hung to one side. Following conversations with the Technical Directorate, the problem was soon identified; because of the high

A view of the raised conveyor belt from another perspective. In the foreground is Bf 109 G-6 (TL+DQ) W.Nr. 18377. (Photo Wedemeyer)

57

NEST OF EAGLES

Bf 109 G fuselages neared completion in close proximity to each other, as shown here in June 1943. (Photo Wedemeyer)

This photograph of a Bf 109 G-6/Trop has been previously published, but unfortunately always with an incorrect caption. It is in fact a Bf 109 from the June/July 1943 production batch at Regensburg and was test-flown by acceptance pilot Lohmann. For a brief period, such aircraft bore the initial letter(s) of the pilot's name on the rudder, and confirmed in photographs are Lo/Lohmann, M/Mrotzek and R/Riedmeir. In flight above this parked aircraft at Regensburg is another Bf 109 under full power, recognizable from the black exhaust trail. (Photo BA Koblenz 638/4219/18a)

production rate, not enough formers during wing manufacture were available, so that the sheet-metal coverings on the undersides had to be riveted outside of the jig. As a result, a deformation or twist in the wing and hence of the wing profile occured. This had the effect of generating a higher drag in the airstream so that the aircraft turned around its longitudinal axis.'

A further incident occurred during works flight trials of a Bf 109 by Flugkapitän Trenkle, which he described as follows: 'After making a works test flight, when I was making my landing approach and wanted to extend the undercarriage, a control lamp lit up showing that only one main leg had extended normally and had locked. So, I retracted the undercarriage again and extended it once more, but the same thing happened. Flying as low as possible, I thundered over the airfield and explained my problem by radio to the control tower. From below, the answer came back that one leg had extended and that the other was hanging half out beneath the wing. Since I still had enough fuel, I took the Bf 109 up to 4,000 m (13,120 ft) and went into a steep dive at full power. I thought to myself, when pulling up sharply the second leg must now extend because of the acceleration force. But no, even after several attempts, it was all in vain. Even retracting both undercarriage legs to prepare for a belly landing was not possible, as one of the legs stuck fast halfway out and could neither be further extended nor retracted. Slowly, my fuel was getting low and from the tower I received the instruction to jump out with my parachute over the airfield. But it not easy for any test pilot to give up the aircraft entrusted to him. In this case, however, a landing could have resulted in a somersault at high speed. I therefore climbed to a safe height for making a parachute exit, jettisoned the canopy, switched off the engine and jumped out of the Bf 109. Whilst hanging in my parachute, I could see how the aircraft went into a spin and crashed on the racecourse bordering on the airfield, whilst I landed safely on the airfield. Because the Bf 109 was totally destroyed on impact, it was not possible to ascertain the cause for the undercarriage blockage.'

A little later, at the beginning of 1943, Josef Haid experienced a similar incident: 'At the end of a works test flight with the Bf 109, I was making my landing approach to Prüfening when I discovered that only one undercarriage leg had extended. I immediately recalled the incident that happened to Flugkapitän Trenkle who had likewise experienced the same problem. On arrival over the airfield, I asked the control tower people to take a look at my undercarriage. They in turn promptly shot up a red flare to signal to me that something was wrong with it. I was advised by radio that one one leg had extended and that the other was still inside the wing. I now attempted several to dive times to get both legs out, but was unsuccessful. After I had advised the tower that I was coming in for a landing, I was told not to risk anything and to exit with my parachute. However, I felt that a landing with only one oleo leg extended was acceptable, and that perhaps the technical people could discover the reason for the fault. The fire brigade and first-aid vehicles were already standing-by when I made my landing approach. Against expectations, I was able to hold the aircraft for a relatively long time on one undercarriage leg until the speed had reduced so far that the Bf 109 sank down on to its port wingtip. Then, ignition off, canopy away, and I was out of the cockpit. Somewhat trembling, I accepted the congratulations on the extremely difficult landing. On the aircraft itself, only the wingtip and the propeller were somewhat damaged and could be easily repaired without too much effort. The cause for the undercarriage sticking was attributable to the fact that as a consequence of the bad weather during the winter of 1942-43, several Bf 109s had been parked out in the open for a long time and because they could not be test-flown due to the weather, the locking bolts of the undercarriage legs had oxidised and on retraction, had locked fast. All parked aircraft were then checked immediately and the locking bolts superficially covered with a layer of cadmium were installed. From the plant senior management I received a certificate of recognitiön and a monetary bonus.'

Due to the bad weather conditions mentioned above, flight-testing was moved at the beginning of 1943 to Bari in southern Italy, but even here, flight trials were not without mishap, as Sepp Haid described: 'Together with Oberfeldwebel Semmler, I was transferred to Bari to test-fly the Bf 109s that had been transported there by rail. One series of Bf 109s had a Bosch horn that blew when the pilot set out to land with the undercarriage retracted. I wanted to test this out with a Bf 109. I reduced speed and waited for the horn to blow but nothing happened, and when I next looked round, I found the aircraft on its belly – a very embarassing thing to happen to any pilot. After I had recovered from the initial shock, I proceeded with the mechanic to check why the damned horn had not sounded. To our amazement, we established that no horn at all had been installed. Upon asking Regensburg about this, we were casually told that from Werknummer so-and-so, no horns were installed anymore.'

Oberleutnant Adolf Riedmeier described an accident that had taken place during a works test flight at Prüfening: 'It was a fine summer day in 1943, and I was underway on a check flight in a Bf 109. On this particular day a west wind was blowing, and I floated over the western housing area on coming in to land. During the approach flight, I noticed beneath me numerous rabbits that were hopping about. This small diversion was enough to distract me, so that I flew too far on my landing approach. The airfield in Prüfening was as small as a handkerchief anyway, and just sufficiently long for the Bf 109. In any case I touched down too late; using full brakes was not enough, and I collided with two parked aircraft. Three damaged Bf 109s stood on the edge of the airfield, and when Director Linder approached, I must have had a rather unhappy face. He looked at the damage and uttered in the finest Swabian accent: "We can repair that" and turning to me he said: "Well, Riedmeier, the sun must have blinded you." If only he knew; but for me at least, the incident had no repercussions.'

Until August 1943, Bf 109 production went ahead relatively undisturbed, with a monthly increasing output. After the Bf 109 G-4 series ended in accordance with RLM Lieferprogramm 222, the G-6 and G-6/Trop started-up in February 1943. At least six aircraft were damaged or destroyed during works flight-testing. As a result of the bombing raid on 17 August 1943, the planned figure of 2,570 Bf 109s for that year could not be met. Whilst production was running in Prüfening at top gear, Obertraubling was engaged in final assembly and works testing of the Me 163 and Me 323. In 1943, 62 Me 163s and 80 Me 323s were built. The following table shows the production figures for the Bf 109 G-3, G-4 and G-6 variants for that year.

Flugkapitän Trenkle and Leutnant Riedmeier discuss the selection of pilots for acceptance testing of flight-ready Bf 109 G-6s in May 1943.

Bf 109 G Production in 1943

Variant:	G-3	G-4/Trop	G-6	Monthly
January	19	30	–	49
February	31	12	42	85
March			170	170
April			196	196
May			205	205
June			237	237
July			268	268
August			241	241
September			77	77
October			166	166
November			202	202
December			270	270
Totals:	50	42	2,074	2,166

Up until 31 July 1943, 1,118 G-6s were produced. In the heavy bombing raid on Regensburg-Prüfening on 17 August 1943, 401 of the workforce were killed.

A view inside a late Bf 109 F or early G cockpit. At the level of the pilot's eyes can be seen the Revi gunsight with its cushioned rear surface. To the left beside it are the three ammunition counters. The main instrument panel housed the essential instruments for flying - compass, turn-and-bank indicator, altimeter, tachometer, boost gauge and revolution counter. The smaller instruments to the right are the thermometer, fuel gauge and fuel/oil pressure gauge. Between the rudder pedals is the covering for the breech of the MG 151/20 cannon. (Photo Fischer)

An assembly worker installs an MG 151/20 in a Bf 109 G-6/Trop on the production line at Regensburg. When fitted, the cannon breech, which was enclosed in a metal fairing extended into the cockpit either side of the rudder pedals. (Photo BA-Koblenz 638/4221/17)

Below right: A June 1943 photograph showing the conveyor belts for Bf 109 wing manufacture in the metalworking hall at Regensburg. Here too, one has the impression of a confined workspace. (Photo Wedemeyer)

Bf 109 G-6/Trops in July 1943 shortly before rollout. On the raised port engine cowling of the aircraft in the foreground, the sand filter has not yet been completely affixed ahead of the supercharger air intake. The cover for the breech of the MG 151/20 is lying on the port wing. (Photo BA-Koblenz 638/4222/4)

The 17 August 1943 Bombing Raid

Exactly one year after the US Eighth Air Force had carried out its bombing raid over the northern region of occupied France, it undertook a spectacular double blow against the German armaments industry that had not hitherto been considered possible. On 17 August 1943, flying in two successive waves, B-17 Flying Fortresses attacked the Regensburg production plant which suffered heavy damage, as well as the ball-bearing industry in Schweinfurt. [The Regensburg plant layout is shown in Appendix 7 and the bomb damage inflicted on it in Appendix 8] The bombing strategy was that both bomber formations would fly into Reich territory shortly after each other so that the German defence with its fighter and Zerstörer units would be unable to attack both bomber formations. This tactic did not work however, as thick ground fog delayed the take-off plan, so that the second bomber formation scheduled for Schweinfurt only took off after considerable delay. The German Geschwader thus attacked the first bomber formation with all the aircraft that were available, and when the second bomber formation flew in in the direction of Schweinfurt, the defending fighters and Zerstörers had already been re-armed and refuelled, ready to go into the attack. On that day, 60 bombers were shot down and several more were heavily damaged. Whilst the USAAF could easily replace its materiel losses, the loss of 600 flying personnel was a cause for concern and thus for the Americans too, was not so easy to cope with. The tactical checkmate move brought

'Total War': 1943-1945

An overhead perspective of the Regensburg final assembly area shows three such lines in June 1943. In the foreground is Bf 109 G-6 (CH+IX) W.Nr. 18462. About 27 G-6s could be assembled simultaneously in this Halle. As soon as the fuselage was raised onto the traversable final assembly jig and suspended in the ventral belt, the wings as well as other equipment were attached. (Photo Wedemeyer)

Bf 109 G-6s from the 18300 Werknummer block with their typical Regensburg-production camouflage pattern. The aircraft here in front of the final assembly hall in June 1943 are Bf 109 G-6 (TL+DR) W.Nr. 18378, (TL+DU) W.Nr. 18381, (TL+DT) W.Nr. 18380, and (BJ+HL) W.Nr. 18346. (Photo Seitz)

about the expectations placed on it, because the assault force on Regensburg did not fly back to England but instead, after the bombing raid set course for North Africa and after crossing the Alps, as anticipated, was no longer attacked. The assault on Regensburg was made by the 4th Bombardment Wing – later designated the 3rd Air Division. The bomber formation was divided into three Combat Wings (CW) at whose apex was the 403rd Combat Wing, which consisted of 96th, 388th and 390th Bombardment Groups. They were followed by the 401st Combat Wing, consisting of the 94th and 385th Bombardment Groups, which were to follow the 403rd CW to bombard the target three minutes later. The 402nd CW formed the tail with 95th and 100th BGs, which followed the 401st CW at an interval of three minutes. Out of 21 aircraft lost on the mission, nine were from the 100th BG. It was here that the name 'Bloody Hundredth' was born, as it was the Bombardment Group that suffered by far the highest losses in the war.

Delayed and hindered by bad weather, take-off of the 146 B-17s of the Regensburg assault formation commenced only at 0645 hrs, as the whole of East Anglia lay under a blanket of ground fog. Because of technical problems, seven B-17s had to drop out and in addition, 12 B-17 Fs were shot down before reaching the target. The flightpath led from Lowestoft via Eupen, with several changes of course intended to mislead the German defences. The last IP (Initial Point) or marker point towards the target lay above Beilngries, about 40 km (25 mls) west of Regensburg, from where the target could already be recognized due to good visibility. Before reaching Beilngries, however, the bombers were already expected and were attacked by nightfighters of NJG 101 from Manching. Shortly before Regensburg the 390th BG, which flew as the upper echelon in the 401st, were attacked by 5 or 6 Bf 109s. These must have come from the Messerschmitt-Werke's Industriestaffel, for at this point of time, no other Jagdverband was over the town. The 390th BG lost six B-17s on this mission. Shortly before the target, one B-17 F was shot down at 1257 hrs near Hemau by the Alarmrotte (stand-by pair) of the Industriestaffel led by Feldwebel Mrotzek. An analysis made by the USAAF indicated that Flak fire at the target was not particularly accurate and fired only sporadically, and that the bomber losses were primarily

Parked on Obertraubling airfield in July 1943 are these Bf 109 G-6/Trop's in the Werknummer range 18802 to 18853. (Photo BA Koblenz 650/3408/17)

61

An aerial photograph of the Messerschmitt plant on the Prüfeninger Straße prior to the bombing raid of 17 August 1943. At left is the racecouse, at lower right the Reichsbahn (German railways) area. On the right edge are the Barmherziger Brüder (Brothers of Charity) hospital buildings and nearby, three small Hallen in which Me 163 B fuselages were manufactured. The two larger Hallen to the left were those of the Leichtmetallbau GmbH Regensburg. The almost white Halle, still under construction at the centre of the photograph, was to have taken up Bf 109 wing production, but was totally destroyed in the raid. As a result, a connecting building between the Metallbauhalle (recognizable beneath the sports field) and the final assembly hall was erected. (Photo USAF)

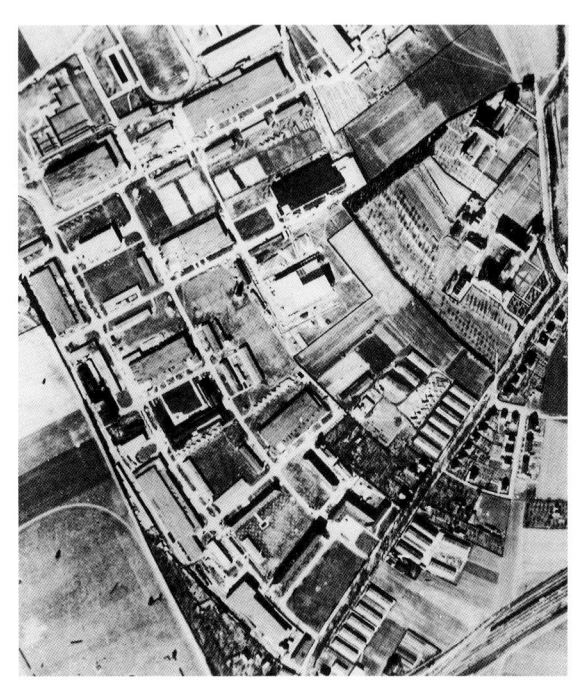

attributable to the defending fighters. Also, despite the massive attacks by the fighters and insufficient barrage fire by the Flak, it could not be avoided that the bombers were able to continue their approach to perform an extremely precise bomb drop. The 96th BG, which flew at the head of the 401st, was the first to release its bombs at 1143 hrs (1243 hrs local time), and 43 tons of bombs from 19 B-17s were released simultaneously. This was in accordance with the USAAF tactic in that when the lead aircraft dropped its bombs, all the other bomb-aimers likewise released their loads. This led to the dreaded carpet-bombing with its immense destructive power.

In all, the attack lasted 20 minutes and hence longer than planned. The reason for this lay with the 401st CW which, because of the smoke and dust clouds raised by the bombs dropped by the 403rd CW, was robbed of

A B-17 from the 4th Bombardment Wing pulls away from its bomb run over the Messerschmitt plant at Regensburg on 17 August 1943. Below, smoke drifts into the sky from the burning target.

target visibility. The 40lst CW flew in a large left circle north of Regensburg and undertook a second flight to the target, whereupon the 385th BG had to again fend off tenacious attacks by fighters. South of Regensburg, the Combat Wings assembled for their further flight to North Africa, the aim of which was to further confuse the German defences. The German fighter controllers, however, recovered very quickly from the surprise and set some Bf 109s of JG 27 and JG 51 onto the formations that were flying away. These attacking fighters came from the Ostmark (Austria) and Munich areas, even if with little success against the disappearing bombers.

Altogether, from heights of 17,000-20,000 ft, 126 B-17 Fs dropped 971 500-lb demolition bombs and 448 250-lb incendiaries. During the attack on Regensburg, the US Eighth Air Force lost a total of 24 B-17s with about 220 crew members. Two B-17s had to make emergency landings in Switzerland. One crashed on landing in North Africa as a result of battle damage and 50 others were heavily damaged. On board the aircraft that landed in North Africa were four fatalities. The bombing raid was one of the most notable precision raids carried out. Around 70 per cent of all bombs dropped fell on the plant premises and on the airfield, the rest falling in the immediate neighbourhood. The hospital that was directly adjacent to the plant did not receive any direct hits and suffered only slight damage. A large number of the bombs fell to the western area of the plant and on the racecourse adjoining it, among them several duds. Only a few of the domestic houses in Regensburg were destroyed or damaged. The aircraft production plant was the heaviest hit, and a gigantic smoke and dust column rose over the plant installations.

In the Regensburg plant, a three-stage air raid warning system had been installed. A green light lit up in the offices of each of the department heads in the various halls and represented the first alarm stage. This signified the entry of enemy bomber formations into Reich airspace. When a red light came on it signified immediate danger from the air (bombers approaching) and when the sirens sounded, the workforce had to make its way immediately to the air raid shelters. These consisted of strengthened cellar rooms equipped with air ventilation ducts, but which afforded insufficient protection against the explosive effects of heavy bombs. A small number of air raid dug-outs in the shape of steel bells and air raid trenches that were partly covered over were also available. When the air raid siren sounded, the plant gates were shut and no-one was allowed to leave. For immediate protection against air attacks, the Heimatflakbatterie 2./XIII provided anti-aircraft defence with five 2-cm anti-aircraft guns spread over the entire plant, plus a gun on the roof of the administration centre, one on the elevated bunker, and three on the wooden towers at the northern end of the premises. A part of the workforce was assigned to man the anti-aircraft guns when the alarm was given. In terms of heavy Flak, batteries were located in Regensburg at the Rennplatz (racecourse), Königswiesen, Napoleonstein, Reinhausen and Oppersdorf.

On 17 August 1943, the air raid sirens sounded in Regensburg at 1224 hrs. At 1213 hrs, the plant's Schutzstaffel (protection flight) had already been alerted and at this moment, the first Alarmrotte took off heading for Kelheim to provide anti-aircraft defence. The heavy Flakbatterie 3/484 (Rennplatz) located at the western edge went into position and at 1250 hrs opened fire on the bombers after the first bombs had already fallen. The Regensburg Flakbatterie command centre was in the

Flak barracks, where absolute chaos reigned. All batteries waited upon the order to open fire, but the Commander refused to do so, as he took the approaching aircraft to be He 111s of the Luftwaffe. When the first bombs fell, the Flak batteries opened fire of their own accord. A further remarkable incident was that on this day, all the Regensburg Flak batteries' distance-measuring instruments were undergoing checking in the Reinhausen Batterie, so that only barrage fire was able to be opened. In all, the Flak fired off about 600 rounds, of which Napoleonstein fired 264. The Flak's firing position and the housing area at the Rennplatz was hit by incendiaries, and the light 2-cm anti-aircraft guns were not able to participate in defence because the bombers flew too high. Four guns of the 2./XIII were destroyed in the raid and No.1 gun on the roof of the admininstration building received a direct hit just as the position was about to be vacated. When the bomb impacted, a 16-year-old apprentice was already on the steps leading downstairs and was the only member of the gun crew who survived. A few days later, the Regensburg Flak Commander, a Major, appeared at the Regensburg plant and upon being asked why the heavy Flak had opened fire so late, replied that it could have turned out that the bombers would merely be flying past. On inspecting the Batteries, he ordered the crews to step forward and in the most despicable manner, cursed the sole 16-year-old survivor of No.1 Battery for his supposed cowardice.

During the second wave of bombing, panic broke out among the Russian PoWs. Some 600-700 of them fled to the surrounding fields or to the nearby forests, but were soon rounded up or else returned by themselves. One surviving record reveals that outside of the air raid shelters, only 16 people were killed and two were wounded. In the inadequately-protected shelters, 245 were killed, 243 were injured and 42 went missing. A record of 7 September 1943 cited 392 killed, and in all, around 400 people lost their lives. In the area of the heavily-hit apprentice workshop alone, 91 apprentices were killed. After the last bombers had departed, the all-clear was given at 1413 hrs. Immediately thereafter, the fire brigade crews at Cham, Naab, Vils and Altmühl were alerted, and all available First-Aid units of the Wehrmacht and the DRK (German Red Cross) were sent to the Messerschmitt-Werke. The fire brigade's fire-fighting vehicles were either covered with debris or had been destroyed by bomb shrapnel. Rescue and fire-fighting work was made difficult as a result of six direct hits in the main water supply circuits in Regensburg-Prüfening, so that water from cisterns had to be pumped via flexible tubes over long distances. Indescribable scenes took place. People who were trapped could not be freed and died in the hands of their rescuers, as no heavy clearing equipment was available. In the canteens, the hot water pipes had burst, and those who had sought shelter there were scalded. Whilst the injured were being cared for, Kreisleiter Weigert showed up and forbade the use of bandages for those PoWs who had been injured. His cynical order at that time was 'Paper bandages are good enough for them!' The Wehrmacht cordoned-off the entire area and 400 soldiers of the Regensburg garrison helped with clearing-up work. At the Upper Catholic Cemetery, 100 soldiers began to dig graves, and when the numbers of dead increased, an excavating machine began to dig out larger mass-graves.

Half of the raw materials stored (dural sheets) and completed aircraft parts had been destroyed by fire, and one third of all machine tooling and construction jigs had been destroyed by fire or by bomb shrapnel. Representative of the 17 August 1943 events are two reports. One, by August Obermeier who was 18 years of age at the time stated: 'Ever since I started working at Messerschmitt in Prüfening, I was engaged as an aircraft mechanic in the works flight-test section. When the air-raid alarm sounded, I had to be at the parked Bf 109s of the Industriestaffel at the new flight-test hangar that was still under construction in the western area of the plant. I always found that a first-rate job because after the pilot had got into the cockpit, until the order to take-off was given I had a chance to rest, which I undertook on the starboard wing with the starting handle in my hand. All the aircraft of the Schutzstaffel were marked with a white number from 1 to 10 as well as a yellow fuselage band. The Bf 109s at the edge of the airfield were always fully fuelled and armed. In accordance with the appropriate alarm phase, the control tower immediately ordered two pilots to be ready in their cockpits. Other pilots stood by on call as there was a readiness plan which Oberleutnant Ladegast had worked out. On 17 August, when the first alarm sounded, no-one really wanted to believe the seriousness of the threat. On that very morning Feldwebel Mrotzek had said to me: "If they don't come today, when then?" – as we had long feared an attack on our plant. On this day, Mrotzek was on the readiness crew and was the first to take-off and head towards the approaching bombers.

'As soon as the alarm was given, we mechanics immediately made our way to the Industriestaffel's Bf 109s and effected all the preparations for take-off.

Inside the 'Leichtmetallbau Regensburg', a subsidiary of the Messerschmitt firm. Taken in 1942, the photograph shows the sea-mine and torpedo casings produced there. Light metal components for U-boat towers were also built there in 1943. In the bombing raid on 17 August 1943, both production halls were destroyed. (Photo Croneiß)

Another photograph taken during the afternoon of 17 August 1943, showing the destroyed Messerschmitt plant in Regensburg. Bomb craters over the entire plant and the adjoining racecourse are clearly visible. The smoke column at centre is from the burning main storage area. (Photo USAF)

NEST OF EAGLES

The remains of early production Me 262 airframes lie amidst the wreckage of the Messerschmitt Regensburg factory following the USAAF raid on 17 August 1943. In the middle distance is the old Zeppelin hangar, whilst behind that is the fuselage and wing assembly hall.

The pilots of the Alarmrotte (two Bf 109s) were there right away. When the rest of the pilots showed up, the Alarmrotte was already taxying to take off. Shortly afterwards, the control tower fired another green flare – the take-off order for the remaining aircraft. One after the other the engines were started, and there was one hell of a noise. As I remember, at that time almost all the aircraft of the Staffel were ready for take-off. Hardly had they disappeared on the horizon, when the control tower ordered us to leave the airfield immediately. "They mean us; let's beat it!" There only remained the question as to where we should go to, but in any case, it had to be away from the airfield and the plant. Not even five minutes later, I ran with a colleague over the race course in the direction of the Prüfeninger Strasse. One could hear the approaching bombers, and just as we stood still for a moment, we were able to recognize them over Mariaort. We had reached roughly the centre of the race course when the first bombs came howling down. I had taken full cover just as a high-explosive bomb impacted closeby. Clumps of earth and stones were thrown on my back so that my breath was momentarily taken away, but this could also have been caused by the pressure wave. Suddenly, I heard my work colleague calling for help. He had been hit badly in the leg and was not able to walk anymore. Despite my pains, I lifted him up and carried

Messerschmitt Bf 109 G-6, W.Nr. 18807, 'Yellow 6' of 9./JG 3, Bad Wörishofen, September 1943

Bf 109 G-6, W.Nr. 18807, 'Yellow 6' was produced at Regensburg and is see here in the markings of 9./JG 3 at Bad Wörishofen in September 1943. It was flown by Ofw. Alfred Surau, one of the most successful non-commissioned officers to fly with III./JG 3. Alfred Surau gained most of his victories in Russia and when the Staffel was withdrawn from Russia to take part in the defence of the Reich in August 1943 he had achieved 41 victories. He was awarded the German Cross in Gold on 31 August. He succeeded in destroying two B-17s on 6 September bringing his victories up to 43. On 1 October he was credited with two more B-17s and possibly a third on 14 October. On this day he was hit by defensive fire from a B-17 and was seriously wounded. He died of his injuries the same day.

64

him across the race course to the tram stop terminus in Prüfening, which I reached completely exhausted. Anyhow, it was not a moment too soon, as the second wave unleashed its loads. There was an indescribable crescendo. The deep, sonorous humming of the bombers' engines mixed with the howling of the falling bombs which exploded with massive thumps; in the middle of that the barking rounds of the Flak whose fire, however, was without any visible effect. Over the plant premises I saw a huge column of dust and smoke that had formed. The administration building was also hit, and I became extremely worried about my brother who worked in the purchasing department.

'After the last bombers had flown off, it all seemed to me as still as a graveyard. We could still not grasp that we had survived it all; the shock was so great. Since more and more Messerschmitt people appeared, we hurried in the direction of the plant premises in order to help. The administration building really looked a mess. The receptionists' building and the canteen were destroyed. A heavy high-explosive bomb had exploded in the middle of the administration building where the 2-cm Flak gun had been mounted. On the east side also, severe damage was evident. To my good fortune I found my brother uninjured, for this week he was not on Flak stand-by duty. In his blue overalls he attempted to set up a First Aid station as there was just chaos and nobody had any clear picture of everything. Walking along the race course, I eventually got to the flight-test centre, and on the way to the new flight-test hangar that was still under construction, in the middle of the entrance path I found a dead construction worker who had been hit. The flight-test area looked pretty grim and the hangar had been hit. Several Bf 109s were damaged, but only a few had been destroyed. My most prized possession at that time – my new bicycle – had not so much as a scratch.'

Rudolf Metzel, at that time only 14 years old, also recalled: 'When the air raid siren sounded in Regensburg, I happened to be at home in Neuprill. My father had a pair of binoculars which I fetched so as to be better able to observe the aircraft. It did not take long before the first formation appeared. The Flak began to shoot, and through the glasses I could clearly make out how the bombs were released, and beneath them also, smoke bombs (as target markers – Author) which during their descent left a grey-blue pillar of smoke. The typical noise of falling bombs could be heard which then exploded with muffled thuds, such that the floor beneath me trembled. After they had dropped their bombs the aircraft flew over the town and turned southwards. The sky over Prüfening had turned dark with the clouds of dust and smoke. Two or three days later, as I made my way home from school which led me past the upper Catholic cemetery, I observed that the dead lay in the hall of blessings on top of each other in rows of five and covered with paper sacks. Two excavators were digging out the mass graves. Due to the summer heat, there was a strong smell of decaying flesh in the air, and soldiers with gas masks buried the dead.'

Because of the large number of personnel losses, new directives were issued to the workforce on how to conduct itself in the event of an air raid warning. When the sirens sounded, the workforce was to leave the plant premises and assemble outside the area in specific rooms made available, until the all-clear could be given. In the works, only an emergency contingent consisting of the fire brigade and security service remained. In two test alarms in August and October 1943, the new instructions were checked out.

After the attack, no new aircraft were produced for three weeks, since the entire workforce was engaged in clearing away the debris and making repairs to buildings and installations. Repair work was carried out with a high degree of efficiency and a minimum amount of effort. In order to prevent further damage to the machines that had been affected by the air raid, hastily built and assembled wooden roofs coated with tar sheets were put in place over the damaged buildings. Lighting was again in operation after three days and the usual electric power supply was repaired within a week. In the second week of September, Bf 109 G-6 production commenced once again. Of the three final assembly lines in Prüfening, one was relocated to the Fliegerhorst in Obertraubling. Since the paintshop in Prüfening had been destroyed, those aircraft that had been sprayed only in RLM 76 (Hellblau), were transferred to Obertraubling. In December 1943, with an output of 270 Bf 109s, the turn-out rate from July had again been achieved.[1]

The 21 July 1944 bombing raid

At the beginning of July, following the Allied Invasion of Normandy on 6 June 1944, the US Eighth Air Force again undertook bombing raids on Reich territory. Since almost all Jagdgeschwader were engaged on operations along the Invasion Front, only a few units were available for Reich defence. In the southern region of Germany, JG 300 and IV./JG 3 'Udet' were operational and were occasionally supported by II./JG 27 or ZG 26.

On 21 July 1944, one day after the abortive attempt on Hitler's life, bombers of the US Eighth and Fifteenth Air Forces penetrated deep into the Reich and this time, Regensburg was once more on the list of targets. The attacks were directed against the aircraft and ball-bearing industry, Regensburg and Schweinfurt being bombed on the same day (as previously on 17 August 1943). Again, it was the 3rd Bomber Division with 134 B-17s, escorted by 73 P-47s and 97 P-51s that made its way to Regensburg. The bomber formation first headed for Rottenburg near Landshut and then turned to the north. Shortly before Regensburg, it split up into two groups which approached the targets at 6,000-7,000 m (19,700-23,000 ft) altitude. The smaller bomber group with 44 B-17s in two waves attacked the Messerschmitt Werk I in Prüfening with 106 tons of bombs. The other maintained course to Obertraubling where 90 B-17s dropped 233.5 tons of bombs on Messerschmitt Werk II. The already heavily damaged Fliegerhorst became once more thoroughly ploughed up. The concentrated attack lasted from 1110 to 1115 hrs, and hence was of only five minutes duration.

From 1015 hrs onwards, the air raid alarm was in force at Regensburg, and it was only at 1247 hrs that the

Victims of the 17 August 1943 bombing raid were interred in mass graves in the Upper Catholic Cemetery. (Photo Wedemeyer)

---

[1]. Further details and reports on this air raid can be found in the author's book: *Luftangriff – Regensburg and the Messerschmitt-Werke im Fadenkreuz (Air Raid – Regensburg and the Messerschmitt-Werke in the Bombsights)*, MZ Buchverlag, Regensburg.

From second from left, Lucht, Göring and Messerschmitt pictured in Regensburg on 2 November 1943. At the conference held that day, the earliest possible start of Me 262 production was discussed. Visible are the provisional repairs made to bomb damage caused by the 17 August 1943 raid. (Photo Wedemeyer)

all-clear could be given. The air situation on this day was thoroughly confused, because another 15th Air Force formation of 483 bombers had set course for Regensburg, but then turned at Burghausen to head for its target – the refineries at Brüx in the Sudetenland. Due to the simultaneous penetration of the Reich from the south and from the west, for the German fighter controllers of the 7. Jagddivision in their bunker in Oberschleißheim in the south, it was no easy task to follow the bomber formations with their variations in course and recognise their presumed targets. On the German side were the so-called Air Observation Staffeln which, equipped with GM-1-boosted Me 210s, set course for the bombers. In running commentaries, the Me 210 crews radioed the course, speed, altitude and numbers of bombers to the command centre, but because of increasing USAAF air superiority and lack of fuel, this extremely effective reporting system could not be maintained until the end of the war.

Some 100 large demolition bombs and around 15,000 incendiaries had been dropped on Messerschmitt Werk I in Prüfening. As a result of the early air raid warning, the entire plant's workforce was able to be brought to safety, and besides two wounded, 350 became homeless, among whom were 300 Italian PoWs whose barracks burned down. The carpet of bombs had once more hit the plant installations heavily. Half of the roof framework of the admin building was set ablaze; the works security building was heavily damaged; the plant's First Aid station and the main manufacturing hall were severely hit. The storage hall and five barrack buildings were burnt down, and a further storage area was destroyed through a direct hit. In the Werk I plant, five large and four medium fires raged. Putting out the fires was extremely difficult since, due to the long-duration air raid alarm, the firefighters were not able to get to work immediately. In addition to that, as a result of the bombing raid of 19 July 1944 on Munich, a portion of the Regensburg fire brigade had been sent there. A fire-fighting readiness unit and two HJ fire brigade groups from Regensburg, a fire-fighting group from Amberg, a Wehrmacht water-sprayer unit, the 3. Kompanie of the motorized air-raid defence Abteilung 22 and all works air raid protection personnel of Messerschmitt Regensburg fought the fires. Bomb damage done on this day at Messerschmitt Werk II in Obertraubling and its surroundings is related separately in Section II of this volume.

The first dispersed production centres in operation

The continually increasing air raids on Reich territory, the ever-increasing turn-out of aircraft at Regensburg and the lack of space associated with this in Prüfening caused the plant management to set up the first dispersal centres (see Appendix 9). Already in March 1943, work was begun on the manufacture of lathes, milling machines and moulded parts in Untersteinbach near Pfreimd in an area that occupied 750 m² (8,073 ft²). Also, in the Flossenburg concentration camp, aircraft parts (radiator hoods) had been produced since April 1943. After the air raid of 17 August 1943, one of the three final assembly lines for the Bf 109 and that for Me 262 fuselage construction was likewise heavily damaged and were relocated to Obertraubling. At the Fliegerhorst, there now stood 12 large Messerschmitt aircraft assembly halls available for production. In Neustadt on the Waldnaab, work was begun in November 1943 on the partial completion of 3,000 m² (32,290 ft²) of space, and a portion of the acceptance flight trials were carried out at the airfields at Obertraubling and Vilseck. This marked the beginning of large decentralization of production in the history of the industry. At the end of 1943, the entire workforce comprised 11,463 employees and the two-shift system, each of 10-12 hours per day from Mondays to Saturdays, was in force.

Otto Liebl of Regensburg recalled: 'As war became ever longer, the burden on us armaments workers became ever greater. In the plant the 12-hour day was announced... That meant for me a 72-hour week, and it often turned out to be much more. We very often worked to the limit of our human load capabilities. A particular factor that affected us was the bad provisions supplies the longer the war lasted. Workers who openly complained about conditions ended up being sent to the front line, or found themselves in prison or in a concentration camp. Since a large number of foreigners were employed in the plant, the SD and the Gestapo and their informers were continually present there. After the air raid of 17 August 1943, the works flight-testing activity was moved to Obertraubling. Here, Russian PoWs, all of them officers, were assigned to us, and they made an excellent impression on me. We often shared what little we had with them in the way of food which we brought from home, because what these prisoners were given was merely juice and food without any nourishment. The food for the Russians was prepared in large troughs and containers and consisted mostly of an undefinable soup, which was accompanied by Ersatzbrot (bread substitute) – a damp, dark brown mass which was stretched with finely-ground straw. The prisoners at the Fliegerhorst were housed in a barrack-like camp opposite the main guardpost, and in which indescribable hygenic conditions prevailed. Even today I can still remember the permanent stink that pervaded in the neighbourhood of the camp, especially in summer, because the sanitary installations for the more than 1,500 prisoners were totally inadequate.'

The procurement of workers, not only in the aviation industry, had in the meantime become Problem No.1. The Messerschmitt GmbH workforce had meanwhile become international and symbolized also that of German-controlled Europe in which the following nationalities were represented: Germans, Hungarians, Russians and Ukranians (each with men and women), and French, Belgians and Italians (men only). PoWs consisted of Frenchmen and Russians (in aircraft construction, the latter were officers only). With the arrival of ever more workers in Regensburg, the housing situation became so acute that the town administration only approved the entry of more workers when the Messerschmitt GmbH plant management made the corresponding need for accommodation available.

CHAPTER 5

The Hardest Years: 1944-1945

German Reverses on all Fronts

THE year 1944 brought further military catastrophies on all fronts. The whole of southern Italy was lost. After the hardest of battles, Monte Cassino was given up when, in the back of the German Front, US forces landed at Anzio and Nettuno. Later, Rome, the 'eternal city' was acceded to Allied troops without a fight. The US Fifteenth Air Force, established on airfields at Foggia, Bari and Taranto since November 1943, began strategic assaults against southern Germany, Ostmark (Austria), the Protectorate of Bohemia and Moravia, Hungary, and the Rumanian oilfields at the beginning of 1944. The Luftwaffe's Reichsverteidigung thus found itself between two millstones. In increasing measure it had to defend itself against assaults by two US Air Forces – the Eighth from England and the Fifteenth from Italy. In June 1944, most of the Luftwaffe's Jagdgeschwader were relocated to the Invasion Front in France. The airfields that they had been intended to operate from had, however, been largely destroyed or else were under continual attack by bombers and low-flying fighters and fighter-bombers. These inflicted heavy losses among the German fighters before they even became operational. The result of the Allies' total air superiority meant the relocation of German units to emergency combat airfields, which in turn required the setting up of communications links to the operational airfields. A further problem was caused by the relocation of ground personnel and supplies – especially of fuel, because the transport columns could only really travel at night as by day they became victims of immediate attacks by constantly active enemy aircraft.

Concentrated assaults by German air units was thus not possible, and despite fierce counter-measures and a very high loss in pilots and aircraft, air superiority was not regained. Totally exhausted, the once proud Jagdgeschwader for the most part returned without aircraft to the Reich in August/September 1944 to be re-equipped. The Reich was thus almost defenceless against the heavy, continually increasing Allied air raids consisting of up to 1,500 four-engined bombers as the Luftwaffe no longer had powerful formations at its disposal and the few operational Staffeln were constantly short of fuel supplies. It was only in November 1944 that German fighter units again became available in numbers, which were then sacrificed uselessly in the 'Unternehmen Bodenplatte' operation of 1 January 1945. In the meantime, large areas of German cities and towns were destroyed and at the end of the war, what had formerly been the focal points of civilian life were covered by some 400 million cubic metres of rubble. On 22 June 1944, the Red Army started its greatest offensive codenamed 'Bagration'. Within a space of 17 days, Heeresgruppe Mitte (Army Group Centre) was destroyed, and between 350,000 and 400,000 German soldiers, among them 31 Generals, were lost, either fallen, wounded, missing, or captured – a catastrophe which by far exceeded the disaster at Stalingrad. The Russians were able to make an operative breakthrough with devastating consequences for the German Divisions. Tens of thousands of German PoWs were paraded through the streets of Moscow on their way to Siberia. The residue of German troops were only able to close the roughly 450 km (280 mls)-wide gap in the front line with difficulty. This only became possible because the Russian troops were totally exhausted after a their 500 km (310 mls) march and had to first regroup their forces.

Bad news from the battlefronts had not ceased when, German propaganda announced the bombardment of London with V-1 (Fi 103) flying-bombs which began on the night of 12/13 June 1944. This was followed by the deployment of the V-2 (A4) rocket against London on 8 September. The first Me 262 jet fighters flew their initial sorties on the Western Front in the autumn of 1944. The superiority in the quantity of war production by the three Allied Powers against that produced by German industry stood in a ratio of about 15:1, so that

67

even the most modern weapons had no effect. Raw material stocks in nickel, manganese, chrome, copper, tungsten and raw rubber dwindled drastically, although in June 1944 they were still sufficient to cover around 18 months' war production needs. Reinforcements only arrived in small quantities into the Reich which was now surounded on all sides.

The USAAF's 'Big Week' air offensive at the beginning of 1944 had as its target the destruction of the German aviation industry and other key industrial centres such as the ball-bearing and tank producing plants. This however, was only partially successful as the striking power of the Luftwaffe had hardly diminished, so that the USAAF encountered increasing problems with its bomber crews. Following the raid on 24 April 1944 on various targets in southern Germany, 14 American bombers made emergency landings in Switzerland. On the Swiss airfield at Dübendorf, it was not known what should be done with the increasing number of bombers gathering there and by the end of the war, no fewer than 186 four-engined American bombers had landed in Switzerland. Their crews preferred to be interned rather than fly further sorties over Germany. Several landings of American bombers took place in neutral Sweden. In April, there was a decisive change in target priority: it was now the turn of the oil refineries and hydrogenation plants – something that had long been feared by the OKW, for without fuel, no tanks could operate and no aircraft could take off to attack the enemy. On 5 April, the US Fifteenth Air Force began its 'Oil Strike' and attacked refineries and tank factories in the Balkans. These were followed on 12 May with attacks by the Eighth Air Force on German refineries and hydrogenation plants and these continued until the end of the war. The results of the attacks on fuel production were to have been decisive for the downfall of the Reich. The year 1944 also witnessed the highest production in the German armaments industry during the war. Now, when it was already too late, Hitler decided that fighter production would be accorded absolute priority and handed over this task to the Jägerstab. Hitler demanded fighters, and still more fighters, for the defence of the Reich in an effort to prevent the systematic destruction of the entire fuel and armaments production infrastructure. It was pure cynicism on the part of the Führer to imagine that the destruction of German towns and cities was acceptable on the basis that they could be rebuilt after the war was won. At the end of 1944, much to the surprise of the Americans, the Wehrmacht launched its counter-offensive in the Ardennes. As long as the period of bad weather lasted and prevented concentrated missions by the USAAF, the elite Panzer forces of the Waffen-SS and those of the regular Army were able to make deep inroads in the American front line. When the weather improved and enabled operations by the US tactical air forces to be conducted, and ground forces to be reinforced, they fought back and destroyed a large part of the last operative German Panzer forces. At the beginning of 1945, this armour was thus not available to be used to defend the German eastern territories against the advancing Russian armies.

In June/July 1944, when the first Me 262s appeared in the skies over southern Germany and were able to shoot down a few de Havilland Mosquito reconnaissance aircraft, it was believed in Regensburg that the leaf could once more turn over. But these jet fighters still suffered from numerous technical problems. Without doubt, with the Me 262, the Luftwaffe gained an enormous technical advantage over the Allies, but they came too late and in too few numbers to turn the tide in the air war. The measures planned by the Jägerstab now began to take effect, and from Messerschmitt GmbH Regensburg alone, far in excess of 6,000 Bf 109s were manufactured in 1944. Whereas aircraft were now sufficiently on hand for operational use, it was fuel that was not. Because of the shortage of fuel, oxen and horses were employed on the airfield at Obertraubling to tow aircraft to their camouflaged parking areas – though Obertraubling was one of several airfields to resort to such measures. A grotesque picture emerged, where oxen prevailed as tugs over the most modern aircraft in the world, and it must have felt as if one was being turned back to the Middle Ages.

The status of dispersal production in 1944-1945

Where not otherwise stated, all information below stems from the Survey of Messerschmitt Factories and Functions (as held at the US Air Force Museum, Dayton, Ohio); only the most important dispersals are listed here.

Prüfening, Messerschmitt Werk I. Except for the manufacture and storage of small parts, production was stopped. In an area of 1,500 m² (16,145 ftt²) occupying the only partially damaged final assembly hall, damaged Bf 109s coming from the front line were repaired and test-flown. In the administration building, everything functioned as normal. Responsible for the smooth running of production were Direktor Linder and his deputy Widmann. Because of his qualities of leadership and organisational talent, Linder was chiefly responsible for the Me 262 production towards the end of 1944. A few departments, for example Purchasing, were housed in barracks or houses in Regensburg. The continual inflow of materials of all kinds to the production centres and the onward transportation of completed parts to the next production line or pre-assembly right up to final assembly, required an extensive transport system. Today this would seem a relatively simple matter but at that time, some almsot insurmountable problems existed. Kurt Obermeier of the Purchasing Department recalled: 'The Purchasing Department had up to 100 convalescent soldiers available, who were operating across the entire Reich as couriers with special authority to procure the most urgent bottlenecked parts needed for production. The extent of transportation of these couriers ranged from the document briefcase for small parts, up to accompanying the railway freight cars with a special identification pass from the manufacturer, as far as Regensburg, and in the most important cases, the Luftwaffe provided help with Ju 52 transport aircraft. Everything was procured – from aircraft instruments and undercarriages to fuel tanks. The material and part deliveries transported by rail from one assembly location to the next were also accompanied by Messserschmitt couriers to ensure that production could continue free of problems wherever possible. In every production centre, forced labourers, PoWs, and even some concentration camp inmates were employed.'

Obertraubling, Messerschmitt Werk II. At the Fliegerhorst, there remained a part of Bf 109 production spread over a 2,500 m² (26,910 ft²) area in partially destroyed and makeshift/repaired Hallen as well as a technical flight-test section. Those Bf 109 G and K aircraft that had been delivered from the Waldwerk 'Gauting' and parked on the road had their wings

The Hardest Years: 1944-1945

Above: Two US servicemen stand on overgrown railway tracks leading into a camouflaged assembly line built in the forest south of Regensburg in the early summer of 1945. Assembly trolleys lie abandoned in the foreground and an Me 262 can be seen in the trees to the left.

Left and above: Partially completed Me 262 airframes lie in the open air in a forest clearing at the Waldwerk 'Stauffen', hastily and ineffectively camouflaged with tree branches. A single-track railway passes close by, which would have provided a connection to other Messerschmitt plants.

Looking out from the assembly line at an Me 262 'Waldwerk' – probably Gauting, south of Regensburg.

69

attached, the radio equipment installed and the armament centred and test-fired. Following successful acceptance, the aircraft were flight-tested or ferried by acceptance pilots to Puchhof near Straubing. These pilots, around six to eight of them, were brought from Puchhof to Obertraubling in a Fw 58 Weihe (Kite) to fetch the Bf 109s. The works airfield was cleared every day and the Bf 109s that had been parked there, had to be parked on the edge of the airfield with a considerable safety distance between them. The aircraft were partly taken over by 3./Süd FlüG 1 based in Landau/Isar and flown to the operational units. Final assembly and works flight-testing of the Me 262 took place in Obertraubling from September 1944 onwards.

Eschenlohe. The Eschenlohe 'Olympia Tunnel' (see Appendix 10), built during the construction of the Reichsstrasse 2 motorway, was divided into two sections: a northern section of 60 m (132 ft) and a southern section of 230 m (755 ft) length, where the entire manufacture of turning and milling work, the sheetmetal cutting shop, punching und moulding machines as well as the welding shop were concentrated. For this purpose, the Reichsstrasse 2 was cordoned-off and traffic through Eschenlohe diverted. The North Tunnel at both ends had an extension by means of a 17 m (56 ft)-long gate edifice and by this means, was expected to be secure against air attacks. At both ends in the region of the North Tunnel, two plateaus were built. The South Tunnel had a corresponding gate edifice only at its southern end. Between the two tunnels were barracks for the construction management, kitchens and canteens as well as a heating plant. On the mountain side of the tunnels there were two underground galleries for heating and storage, each of 20 m (55 ft) or 25 m (82 ft) in length. The construction costs for the additional installations amounted to RM 4.9 million and in November 1944 were 80 per cent complete. The construction of air raid protection galleries for the population of Eschenlohe were planned. The production floor area in both tunnels amounted to a total of 6,000 m² (64,580 ft²) and all parts for the Bf 109 G and K were were produced here as well as those for the Me 262 fuselage. From here, all further Messerschmitt GmbH assembly lines with the pre-assembled parts needed for further assembly were furnished. The bringing of materiel and the taking-away of manufactured parts was done via the Murnau-Garmisch-Partenkirchen railway line that lay directly adjacent to the site. Power supply was obtained from the Walchensee power station. Production began in May 1944 and continued undisturbed until the end of the war.

Obernzell near Passau. As a result of the air raids of 22 and 25 February 1944 on Obertraubling, there were further delays to production of Me 262 fuselages. A consequence was the dispersal of fuselage production from Obertraubling to Obernzell. Production here started from April 1944 over an area of 3,500 m² (37,670 ft²) and remained completely undisturbed until the end of the war. According to documents in the Regensburg Manufacturing Control (Eisenbeiß Collection, Regensburg State Archive) at least 2,036 Me 262 fuselages were completed in Obernzell.

Waldwerk 'Gauting' near Hagelstadt, south of Regensburg. According to the USSBS data, this was one of the most important forest factories, the decision to build it having been taken on 28 February 1944. In an area of forest between Hagelstadt and Alteglofsheim, lying directly beside Reichsstrasse 15, an extensive branch factory was erected within three months having a narrow-gauge railway and a Wegenetz (network of roads) which still exist today. The whole estate was a strictly forbidden area, strongly guarded, and was only allowed to be entered with a special identification pass. An integral part of the Waldwerk was a lodgings camp for foreign workers and PoWs. Some 1,275 workers were occupied in production there and the entire assembly took place in halls or barracks. Like a concealed town, it was not recognizable from the air, and from June 1944 it manufactured the Bf 109 G-6, G-6/AS, G-14, G-14/AS, G-10 and K-4 - all undisturbed from air attacks. Delivered Bf 109 components were put together here. For wings and fuselages, there were respective pre-assembly and final assembly halls. Aircraft engines were also prepared here for installation in the Bf 109 and transported by the narrow-gauge railway to the fuselage final assembly hall. After engine attachment, the aircraft, standing on their undercarriages but without wings, were parked on the forest paths and covered with camouflage netting. The production area covered a total of 5,000 m² (53,820 ft²) and at peak times, daily production was around 16 aircraft, which in 26 workdays corresponded to a monthly production of 416 Bf 109s. At dusk, the Bf 109s were transported on their mainwheels (the tailskid was mounted on the back of a lorry) over the Reichsstrasse 15 to the Fliegerhorst Obertraubling. From January 1945, the Waldwerk 'Gauting' also undertook production of the Me 262. The completed components were then transported from 'Gauting' to the second Waldwerk 'Stauffen' that lay east of Obertraubling, where final assembly of Me 262As took place. In September/October 1944, at least some Bf 109 production was dispersed to Bodenwöhr and Cham.

Waldwerk 'Stauffen' near Obertraubling. East of Obertraubling, this forest factory lay in a commandeered portion of forest belonging to the Thurn & Taxis family and was situated directly next to the stretch of Reichsautobahn to Passau that was under construction. Encompassing a production area of 4,400 m² (47,360 ft²), it was used from October 1944 for Me 262 final assembly until far into April 1945. The completed Me 262s were loaded onto special wagons and transported by rail to the Fliegerhorst, where final acceptance and works flights were conducted. No air raids took place at 'Stauffen', so that production was halted only a few days before US troops on 25 April 1945 reached the Danube near Regensburg. According to USSBS documents, some 345 Me 262 As were built in this Waldwerk, and it is presumed that the last Me 262 from Regensburg was flown out of Obertraubling by works test pilot Lohmann to München-Riem for JV 44 (statement Lohmann, confirmed in his flight log-book).

Waldwerk near Neuburg/Donau-Brück. Within the scope of production of Messerschmitt GmbH Regensburg, Me 262 final assembly was undertaken here since February 1945. The floor area was roughly the same as in the Waldwerk 'Stauffen', and since it lay in the immediate neighbourhood to the Fliegerhorst at Neuburg, it was heavily damaged in an air raid a few weeks later and led to the stoppage of manufacture.

Flugplatz Vilseck. Production commenced here in March 1944 with pre- and final assembly of the Bf 109

The Hardest Years: 1944-1945

An American military convoy drives along a deserted motorway deep into Germany at the close of the Second World War. On either side of the road can be seen completed Me 262 airframes manufactured in a Waldwerk, possibly 'Stauffen', still awaiting their engines.

The scene in a typical forest-based Me 262 manufacturing facility shortly after its discovery by US troops.

G and K and without any disruption from air raids, production continuing over an area of 8,000 m² (86,110 ft²) until March 1945. A change to Me 262 production was planned. At Vilseck airfield, fuselages and wings that came from the Flossenburg concentration camp were kitted-out and underwent final assembly. The aircraft produced here were works flight-tested and transported for hand-over to the Luftwaffe at the forward combat airfield at Schafhof near Amberg.

Cham airfield. After Me 262 fuselage final assembly was undertaken at the Waldwerk 'Gauting' from September 1944, final assembly of the Bf 109 – or at least a part of it, was relocated in the same month to Micheldorf airfield near Cham. It can be assumed today that the wings were delivered here from Regensburg and that the fuselages came from Bodenwöhr. Final assembly of the Bf 109 G-14/AS and K-4 commenced here in October 1944 over an area of 5,000 m² (53,820 ft²) and ran largely undisturbed by air raids. It was only on 4 November 1944 that bombs fell in the Micheldorf area, but did not have any effect on production. Cham airfield suffered an air raid in April 1945, but by then, production had already been stopped.

Waldwerk near Bodenwöhr. Because of Me 262 fuselage manufacture in the 'Gauting' forest factory in September 1944, production of the Bf 109 fuselage was transferred that same month from 'Gauting' to the Bodenwöhr forest factory. The fuselages built here were delivered to Cham or Regensburg. Until April 1945, production over this area of 4,500 m² (14,764 ft²) took place without any interruption from air raids.

Besides the abovementioned main production lines, the following semi-manufacture locations existed:
   Neustadt on the Waldnaab, where in November 1944 production of aircraft parts and equipment began over an area of 3,000 m² (32,290 ft²).
   Untersteinbach near Pfreimd, where in March 1943 production over 750 m² (8,070 ft²) commenced.

71

Taken by US Fifteenth Air Force personnnel, these photographs illustrate the ruidmentary and primitive component storage conditions at the Waldwerk 'Stauffen' near Mooshof, north-east of Obertraubling. Seem here are nose sections (complete with 30 mm MK 108 cannon installed), fuel tanks, engine panels and engine units, wings and tail sections, many of which would have been off-loaded from railway wagons. (USAF)

Sinzing near Regensburg. In August 1944, the manufacture of construction jigs and formers occupied an area of 1,500 m² (16,145 ft²).
Frontenhausen near Landshut. On an area of 1,000 m² (10,765 ft²), manufacture of construction jigs and formers also took place since September 1944.
Franzensthal. From April 1944 onwards, manufacture of aircraft equipment parts for electrical and hydraulic systems took place over an area of 1,000 m² (10,765 ft²).
Schafhof airfield near Amberg, where Bf 109 G and K acceptance flight tests and hand-over to the Luftwaffe were conducted.
Puchhof airfield near Straubing. The same activity was performed here as at Schafhof.

There were also manufacturing centres in Linz and Suben (Austria), Dingolfing, Straubing, Bayreuth, Mistelgau and Marienthal near Deggendorf in Germany, as well as in Budweis in Czechoslovakia for Me 262 conversion to the reconnaissance role. Besides these production locations, in eastern Bavarian there were innumerable material storage depots – four in Regensburg alone and two in Prüfening, as well as further ones at Oberalling, Sinzing, Winzer, Obertraubling, Großberg, Köfering, Burgweinting, Regenstauf, Geiselhöring and Schloß Eggmühl.

The most noticeable point on decentralized manufacture was that the individual assembly centres were almost never the subject of air raids. Even so, on a long-term basis, work was in train on the dispersal of production to underground bunkers or caves. An enormous bunker for Messerschmitt GmbH was under construction at Mühldorf on the Inn, but was just as incomplete as the caves in Ringberg near Saal on the Danube. It was only when air attacks began to disrupt the German transport system that this had a paralysing effect on the course of production.

Operations by 3. Staffel/Gruppe-Süd, Flugzeugüberführungsgeschwader 1

Flugzeugüberführungsgeschwader (Aircraft Ferry Geschwader) 1 belonged organisationally to

Messerschmitt Regensburg, but was responsible for the ferrying or transfer of aircraft to Luftwaffe airfields from the Industry airfields at Obertraubling, Prüfening, Cham, Schafhof, and Puchhof. In September 1944 Flugzeugüberführungsgeschwader 1, under the command of Hauptmann Dr. Josef Weißmüller, was moved from Landau on the Isar to Prüfening. The Staffel had 60 to 80 pilots whose task was to ferry the Bf 109 G and K aircraft accepted by the RLM to the operational units.

Dr. Weißmüller recalled to the author: 'From Messerschmitt, we received lists of Bf 109s that were parked at the various airfields ready to be fetched. My small planning staff then assigned the works test pilots who were to accomplish this task so that in accordance with RLM requirements, the aircraft were flown over to operational airfields or to airfields where they were deposited. For a time, we had three Bf 108s and a Siebel Si 204 to take the ferry pilots to the Industry airfields, or alternatively, the Bf 109s stood ready for collection at Prüfening or Obertraubling. Those pilots who ferried the aircraft to operational units travelled back by rail or truck, or with a bit of luck, with a courier aircraft to Regensburg. This worked quite smoothly with some of my people, whilst others took advantage of the war-imposed conditions and were two or more weeks underway. More than I was inclined to, I was occupied holding the Staffel together and it often transpired that I was unable to say where half of my pilots currently happened to be. Bad weather, air attacks or technical problems with the aircraft were gladly used as excuses, and these could hardly be refuted. I often tracked down the nighthawks and those industrious pilots already believed to be missing, mostly in Regensburg at the Café Heuport – a very popular meeting-place for the charming girls of the town. There was hardly anyone of my people who, on their ferry flights across Germany and the occupied territories, was unable to organize something or other which his girlfriend or wife could not use. From the human nature point of view, I could fully understand that, but discipline suffered thereby, and it became unavoidable at times that disciplinary measures had to be taken, especially as our Gruppenkommandeur Oberstleutnant Fachner in Neubiberg always mistrustfully exercised control of my Staffel. One of the highlights of the short history of my Staffel was the ferrying of twelve Bf 109 G-6s to Switzerland in May 1944. Even I was allowed to fly, and naturally each of my pilots wanted to go along. But the anticipated 'shopping trip' did not take place as the pilots, shortly after landing, were packed into a bus and driven back to the border. Already in Landau/Isar, some Russian pilots who belonged to the Vlasov Army, alias Russian Liberation Army or ROA, had been assigned to my Staffel. When we relocated to Prüfening in September 1944, there were some 20 to 25 Russian ROA pilots in my Staffel. These men made an excellent impression on me, not only in terms of discipline but also because of their flying abilities. Almost all of them spoke fluent German. Among these pilots were two Russian officers who had been decorated with the 'Hero of the Soviet Union' medal and who always carried the award in their trouser pockets. Unfortunately, we also suffered high losses that were not caused by enemy action and which were partly due to technical problems. I can still remember very well a crash that took place on the Arber, when one of the Russian pilots flew into a mountain in bad weather and I had to travel to the crash site to identify the pilot.'

Hauptmann Dr. Josef Weißmüller, commander of Flugzeugüberführungsgeschwader 1, poses for a photogrpah in front of a Bf 108 B-1.

In emergency landings and crashes not due to enemy action, from April 1944 until March 1945, 3./Süd FlüG 1 lost 42 Bf 109 Gs and Ks and a total of 31 pilots killed and 11 wounded, with another 5 killed or injured by bombing or low-level attacks. The pilot mentioned by Dr. Weißmüller was Leutnant Alexei Tschassovnikov of Novosibirsk, who was killed in a crash with a Bf 109 G-14 W.Nr. 782159 on the Arber on 03.09.1944 and who was buried two days later in the cemetery in Bodenmais. The first loss of Russian pilots dated from 18 August 1944, when the Staffel was still based at Landau on the Isar. Leutnant Ilya Sevkin in Bf 109 G-14 W.Nr. 780698, and Leutnant Alexandr Yakovlev in Bf 109 G-14 W.Nr. 780807 collided in the air over the Fliegerhorst Darmstadt and were killed. The next loss of a Russian pilot took place on 11 September 1944, when Leutnant Cyrill Karelin of Moscow was killed near Panyofö in Hungary in Bf 109 G-14 W.Nr. 782211. On 20 November 1944, Hauptmann Peter Voronzow crashed fatally 4 km north of Olmütz in Bf 109 G-14/AS W.Nr. 785730, and Oleg Gorbachov of Moscow was killed on 6 January 1945 in Bf 109 K-4 W.Nr. 332519. (Source: WaSt Berlin.)

Largely unknown is that within the framework of the Vlassov Army, preparations were being made at the end of 1944 to set up a Jagdbomberstaffel. In December 1944, the Ritterkreuz-holder Major Hartmann Grasser began with the establishment of Jagdgeschwader 210 in which all Russian pilots fighting on the side of Germany were brought together. In 1945, this unit was assigned the following: 3 Bf 109 G-6, 17 Bf 109 G-10/U4, 4 Bf 109 G-12, and 4 Fw 190 F-8s which had been previously used but repaired (data via Quartermaster Reports in the Bundesarchiv-Militärarchiv, Freiburg).

Bf 109 G-6/AS to K-4 production

Of the total of 5,564 Bf 109 G-6s built at Regensburg, 326 were of the G-6/AS variant which had a more powerful DB 605/AS equipped with the larger DB 603 supercharger which delivered 1,800 hp at combat power. Because of the larger supercharger, a modified engine mounting on the left side was necessary. The decision was also taken to install a completely new engine upper cowling, so that the well-known bulges of the G-6 disappeared. The engine cowlings of the G-6/AS and the subsequent G-14/AS, G-10 and K-4 were thus considered to have been aerodynamically improved. Due to the higher engine performance, the larger fin and rudder of the series was adopted as well as a larger oil

NEST OF EAGLES

Messerschmitt Bf 109 G-6s undergoing final assembly and painting during the mid-afternoon at Regensburg, some time in 1944. Note the hand-written 'note' on the fuselage of the Bf 109 second from right - which states 'fertig zur Bahn' - 'Ready for rail'.

Ground crew pull a Bf 109 G-6/AS, fitted with a DB 605/AS engine, from its wooded dispersal in France in the summer of 1944. (Photo: BA-Koblenz 486/3477/05/502)

cooler, of the Fo 987 type. In the first half of 1944, the a total of 39 Bf 109 G-6/AS powered by the DB 605/AS were built at Regensburg in April, with 60 following in May and 50 in June. This version was able to attain a maximum speed of 660 km/h at 9,000 m (410 mph at 29,530 ft). In that year, a new full-view cockpit hood was introduced that offered better vision. Since the tendency to swing on take-off and landing still remained a big problem, it was fitted with a larger fin and rudder and a lengthened tailwheel leg.

In some of the series-produced Bf 109 Gs, instead of the 20 mm MG 151/20s, these were fitted with the 30 mm MK 108 cannon. Arno Fischer, a pilot with JG 53, recalled of the Bf 109 with the 30 mm cannon: 'At the end of 1944, we received the first Bf 109s with the MK 108. This weapon had only one weak point, namely, that when operated in curving flight during a dogfight, centrifugal force blocked the ammunition feed. This happened to me many times, when a maximum of only one or two rounds left the barrel and then nothing more. One had to fly completely acceleration-free for it to function, but at the front line nobody told us that; we had to find that out for ourselves. On one occasion, I came behind a Russian LaGG fighter straight ahead of me and thought to myself: now it's time to test out the new cannon. It fired without any problems, and I scored three or four hits on the Russian fighter. An explosion then followed such as I had not experienced with any shoot-down. The whole thing took place so quickly that I had no time to take evasive action and ploughed through the a mass of debris. My Bf 109 shook violently, and it was only with much effort that I was able to make the return flight. From this air battle, my aircraft received several dents and holes and parts of the Russian fighter were even embedded in it, and had to be subsequently taken to the depot for repairs. The effect of the 30 mm projectiles was phenomenal and was certainly more suitable for combat against bombers. After this experience, I only used the two heavy MGs in combat with a fighter.'

A further modification to increase the performance of the Bf 109 was the installation of MW-50 (a 50/50 volume ratio of methanol/water injection) in the aircraft, with which a short-duration engine emergency power could be achieved and which was built in gradual stages into the Bf 109 G. Peter Duttmann, a pilot with II./JG 52, still possesses at the time of writing a datasheet for the DB 605 D, which with MW-50 injection, could produce 2,200 hp. He related to the author: 'With the auxiliary MW-50 installation in my Bf 109 G-10 in which I flew till the end of the war, I was able to save

The Hardest Years: 1944-1945

myself in all of the prickliest air combat situations, of which there were several in April 1945. When no methanol was to hand, we used distilled water which functioned just as well, except that we were not able to fly so high, otherwise the whole installation froze. In the sorties we flew shortly before the end of the war in low-level flight in the Cham area and east of Regensburg, we often met US fighters, and although they were superior to us in numerical terms, we were able to get away from them. The fastest Bf 109 that I ever flew in, I handed over to the Americans on 8 May 1945 in Neubiberg.'

Arno Fischer of I./JG 53 recalled of the MW-50: 'At the beginning of 1945 we received the Bf 109 G-10 with MW-50. In my first sortie with the Bf 109 G-10 on 27 January 1945, I was in an air battle with 20 Yak 9s – four German fighters versus 20 Russians. For almost 20 minutes, we fought a turbulent air battle over Stuhlweißenburg in which much shooting took place, but nothing was hit by either opponent. During the course of this engagement, I used my MW-50 for brief periods many times. The engine turned at higher revs and made such a noise that it made me believe it would explode at any moment. In fact, it transpired that by longer use of the emergency power, the base of the pistons burned through. I used MW-50 injection most unwillingly since, as I said, the engine was being taxed to its limit and made a peculiar noise whch did not sound very reassuring. In dangerous air combat situations, however, you had a short-duration power increase available to you and could raise your speed near the ground to a good 600 km/h (373 mph).'

In order to save on war-important raw materials – in this case aluminium – a wooden empennage was designed and fitted to the Bf 109 in 1944. When the wooden surfaces, manufactured by various firms, were introduced, several major problems arose which led to the total loss of the aircraft In a report dated 11 July 1944, during a flight at 4,000 m (13,125 ft) and at a speed of 600 km/h (373 mph), the entire empennage of Bf 109 G-6 W.Nr. 163247, which was built in Regensburg and in service with I./JG 302, was torn off. Already on 5 June 1944, with W.Nr. 163738 and W.Nr. 163740, the balance weight on the rudder was reported to have torn off in flight. The cause of the breakaway was found to have been due to the bad glueing of frames and skin sheeting. In the winter of 1944/45, the Erprobungsstelle Rechlin carried out several control checks with Bf 109s that were fitted with wooden empennages. The result was devastating. In 70 cases, cracks in the elevator horn balances varying in length from 10 mm up to a complete breakaway of the horn nose was established. In 44 cases, the skin at Rib 1 worked loose due to gluing. In 26 cases, the skin between Ribs 1 and 2 had worked loose, and in one case, over a length of 200 mm (8 in). On 15 aircraft there were cracks in the region of the skinning on the outer end of the elevator joint, and in 200 aircraft, the tailplane trailing-edge strip in the region of the elevator horn balance had partly worked loose. A further 42 aircraft showed damage to the fins and rudders. In 36 aircraft, operational use was made extremely dangerous due to the exceedingly large swelling of the elevator horns which had ripped away the nose skin sheeting. These faults, that were due to bad gluing and conservation, and only a small proportion due to poor aircraft maintenance, were determined during the period 8 to 13 December 1944 with aircraft of JG 26 and JG 27. When the first incidents became known, a conference was held in Regensburg on 19 July 1944 at which representatives of Messerschmitt, the BAL and manufacturers of the wooden empennages (Schempp-Hirth, Deutsche Edelmöbel AG in Bučovice and Oberlechner in Spittal) participated. On the 11th, and from 18-20 July 1944, test-flights and experiments were carried out in Regensburg to determine the cause of the damages to the wooden empennages. Following flight trials and after being subjected to nine hours of artifical rain-sprinkling, the elevators delivered by the Wolf Hirth firm, which had 1.5 mm-thick skinning, there was no damage established. All of the elevators in Regensburg that had developed problems had a skin of only 1 mm thickness and hade been manufactured at Bučovice. When subjected to an artificial nine-hour rain-sprinkling, these developed heavy damage, and also in the area of conservation. In a test-flight carried out by Hauptmann Obermeier of the BAL with a Bf 109 whose empennage was subjected to adverse weather conditions, such extreme vibrations set in at 720 km/h (447 mph) that the pilot's control column was difficult to hold. Insufficient glueing was the cause of the damage. In the empennages from Bučovice, it was further determined that the wood screws were not turned during fixing, but hammered in, so that the anchoring of the screw in to the wood was considerably weakened. In general, insufficient glueing and conservation were responsible for the damages. The first measure taken was that all Bf 109s which had the 1 mm-thick skin between tailplane Ribs 4 and 6 and where the racks did not possess the minimum dimensions, were blocked off. The Luftwaffe units were given instructions on maintenance, conservation and storage of wooden empennages, but even at the beginning of 1945, the problems with wooden empennages had not been fully solved.

Bf 109 G-6, W.Nr. 163824, is a most interesting machine. It is a Regensburg-built airframe produced in May 1944, originally carrying the Stammkennzeichen NF+FY. It was later converted to a G-6/AS, and subsequently suffered damage in a ferry flight. It was extensively repaired and converted back to a standard G-6, though retaining some aspects of its 'AS' configuration. This airframe has two unique features. Firstly it is the only surviving Bf 109 still in an original (unrestored) factory-applied camouflage scheme. Secondly this scheme was applied when it was repaired following the ferrying accident and documents (apart from the Bf 109 F, fin and rudder) the camouflage style applied to early production Bf 109 K-4s at Regensburg. This aircraft is currently on display at the Australian War Memorial in Canberra, Australia.

75

NEST OF EAGLES

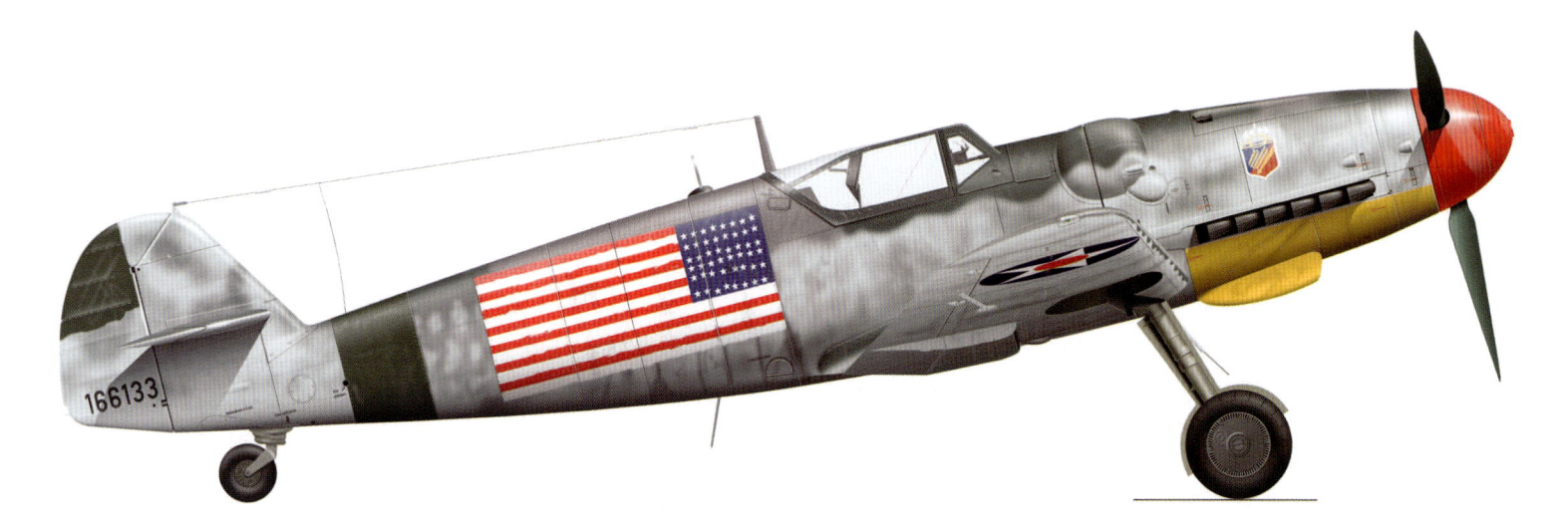

Messerschmitt Bf 109 G-6, W.Nr. 166133, previuosly 'Red 31' of Grupul 9 vânãtoare, San Giovanni, Italy, 27 August 1944

When Rumania declared war on its German ally on 25 August 1944, there were more than 1,000 Allied PoWs detained in the country. To avoid these prisoners falling into the hands of the Soviet Army, the senior US PoW, Lt. Col. James A. Gunn, was granted permission by the new Rumanian government to radio the Fifteenth Air Force in Italy to arrange their repatriation. However, the Fifteenth Air Force refused to discuss the matter by radio and Gunn was requested to report personally to Italy. His first attempt failed as his aircraft lacked adequate range, but as Captain Prince Constantin Cantacuzino, a well-known Rumanian civil and military pilot, was also flying to Italy to convey the Rumanian peace terms, he offered to take Gunn with him in his Regensburg-built Bf 109 G-6. With the Rumanian national markings overpainted and replaced with crude US insignia, the flight was made on the 27th with Cantacuzino flying and Gunn in the radio compartment in the rear fuselage.

Some of the Bf 109 G-6s that had been manufactured in Regensburg survived the war and are currently in museums all over the world. One, W.Nr. 163824, is in the Australian War Memorial, Canberra (Australia); another, W.Nr. 160756 (KT+LL) rolled-out in November 1943, is in the NASM Washington (USA). Of two others in Finland, W.Nr. 165227 (MT 452) is at Uti Air Force Base, whilst W.Nr. 167271 (MT 507) is at the Rissala Air Force base. The latter was delivered to Finland on 26 August 1944 and was only retired from service on 13 March 1956.

The successor models to the G-6, the Bf 109 G-14 and G-14/AS with full-vision canopy, entered series production in July and August 1944, and documents confirm that the G-6 continued in production in small numbers in parallel with the G-14 until January 1945. Several variants of the G-14 were built with the most diverse differences, in particular to the armament and empennages, and because of the problems encountered with the wooden empennages, reverted to ones of all-metal construction, the G-14/AS having the modified fin and rudder because of its higher-performance engine. In Regensburg in 1944, 479 G-14s were rolled out of the final assembly halls, and 1,373 G-14/AS. The G-14/AS was also produced in Cham until mid-March 1945 (Source: Logbook of Works test pilot Paul Bergmann). As a transition from the G- to the K-series, 118 G-10s were manufactued by Regensburg in November 1944, and documents record that production continued there from that month until January 1945.

Because of continual bombing raids on the German armaments industry and the transport system, aircraft production was seriously affected by the end of 1944, so that important parts ranging from tailwheels to fuel tanks were lacking and this explains why there were several variants of the G-10, such as those fitted with the DB 605 AS or DB 605 N, or with the wing of the G-6 or K-4 – depending on what wing variant was available at the time; short or long tailwheel; 660 x 160 mm mainwheels from the G-6 or 660 x 190 mm mainwheels from the K-4; and with or without MW-50. Armament comprised either the MG 151 or MK 108, depending on what happened to be on hand. The main demand was on the quantity of aircraft, and in the various final assembly lines that were spread over eastern Bavaria, no value was placed on maintaining series details, and even from the K-4 numerous production variants are known to have existed.

Production of the Bf 109 K-4 began at Regensburg in September 1944, but the planned monthly output for that month could not be achieved because design errors affecting the horizontal and vertical tail surfaces had first to be eliminated. With a few exceptions, all completed K-4s came from Regensburg, and this was the last version to be manufactured during the war. In some respects, the K-4 differed from the previously-produced G variants, in that it featured fully-covered main undercarriage wheels, a retractable high tailwheel leg and an even larger oil cooler that became necessary because of the DB 605 D engine. The hinged radio maintenance panel was moved forward by one fuselage frame, the fuel tank supports likewise. The oxygen bottles were housed in the starboard wing, and the MK 108 was standard in this series. With its MW-50, the K-4 as well as the G-10 and G-10/AS were easily able to keep pace with American P-47 Thunderbolt and P-51 Mustang fighters. When it accelerated, the K-4 could be difficult to catch. In 1944, Regensburg built a total of 857 K-4s.

That Bf 109 production suffered as a result of the employment of PoWs, foreign workers and concentration camp inmates, is evident from a report at the beginning of September 1944 in which it was stated that Erprobungsstelle Tarnewitz, the weapons-testing centre, received one of the few K-2s – W.Nr. 600056. On flying the aircraft over from Obertraubling, the ferry pilot established that the elevator bolts had not been secured, and on the second take-off, an elevator blockage occurred. In K-4 W.Nr. 330112, handed over to Tarnewitz from the Industry airfield at Suchhof, the rudder controls and pedals chafed and jammed. The wing leading-edge slats were markedly deformed and jammed on extension and retraction, and a 2 mm gap existed at the separation point between the mass-balance and the wooden skin on the elevator, and on top of that, the brakes did not function properly. On the subsequent ferry flight from the plant to the E-Stelle, an emergency landing had to be made due to loss of coolant. In 1944 alone, up to 14 October, a total of 82 Bf 109s on ferry flights from Regensburg to front line units either crashed or made emergency landings. In Bf 109 K-4, W.Nr 330112, at Tarnewitz for weapons trials, an MG 151 was installed instead of the MK 108, whilst the other K-4 had an MK 108 in each wing.

Even the front line units had their problems with aircraft that arrived, since for Bf 109 flight trials, only sufficient fuel was available for a 15-minute test-flight from mid-1944, and it was naturally not possible to conduct a comprehensive test-flight within 15 minutes. In a report of experiences dated 18 March 1945, the Technical Officer of JG 6 had this to say of the Bf 109:

'Newly-delivered aircraft were very prone to faults in the first 5 to 10 flying hours. Almost the same complaints repeat themselves which burden the unit technically and which reduce its operational readiness. The following faults were almost continually met: elevator free-play in the position lever; loose distance-pieces on the elevator control cables; too-long anchoring bolts on the suspension lever of the sprung undercarriage legs; missing range-of-travel markings on the wheel; leaky or

A newly-built Bf 109 G-14 photographed having overshot the runway due to defective brakes at Schafhof bei Amberg in August 1944. Just visible is a part of the aircraft's Werknummer applied crudely on the fuselage aft of the Balkenkreuz. The aircraft is fiitted with the improved vision canopy ('Erla' hood). (Photo: Gattinger)

Test flying newly built aircraft always has its hazards and on 17 March 1944, test pilot Peter Heller was killed flying this Bf 109 G-6, W.Nr. 162601, coded RU+GS on a flight due to engine failure whilst flying over Obertraubling airfield. (Obermeier)

NEST OF EAGLES

Messerschmitt Bf 109 K-4, W.Nr. 330204, 'White 1' of 9./JG 77, Neuruppen, November 1944

This Regensburg-built Bf 109 K-4 of 9./JG 77 is pictured at Neuruppen in November 1944 when the III. Gruppe was converting to the K-4. This particular machine is thought to have been W.Nr. 330204, and although shown here as 'White 1' with Hptm. Menzel in the cockpit preparing for a familiarisation flight, it is believed later to have been renumbered 'White 13'. With this later tactical number it is thought that this aircraft was shot down during the Bodenplatte operation mounted against Allied airfields in north-west Europe on 1 January 1945, with Lt. Herbert Abendroth at the controls.

A Bf 109 G-14/AS of 7./JG 27 seen at Finsterwalde in September 1944 commences its taxi run as a mechanic waves off the pilot. Seen clearly here is the aircraft's 'Erla' hood and the redesigned cowling profile as well as the large oil cooler. (Photo: BA Koblenz 680/8264/16)

The Hardest Years: 1944-1945

Regensburg-built Bf 109 G-14/AS, W.Nr. 784930, was found by Allied forces in 1945 at Twente in Holland. It had the tactical number 'Green 1' and the green and white unit identification bands allocated to JG 77. The lack of a Gruppe bar on the rear fuselage indicates this machine was probably flown by JG 77's I. Gruppe.

Messerschmitt Bf 109 G-14/AS, W.Nr. 784930, 'Green 1' of 1./JG 77, Twente, Holland, 1945

blocked conduits in the MW-50 system; faults in the electrical system; bad coolant mixture; almost always too-little frost-protection fluid and almost no Korrisionschutzöl (corrosion-protection oil) 39 mixed with it; chafing lubrication-return conduits on the starboard valve sump; oiling of the engine through leaky flange couplings; weapons badly centred, and the aircraft not free of W/T problems especially in the installation set. With some of the Bf 109 Ks, the ammunition belt-feed guides in the airframe were displaced by 3 to 5 mm vis-à-vis the weapons, so that the ammunition belt could not be correctly retracted and belt-jamming was pre-programmed. After only a few rounds had been fired, the MK 108s regularly failed due to an unsuitable volume of insulation for the projectile fuse. In the procurement of replacement parts, difficulties were continually encountered in receiving the Fl 8/2926 E-5 AD component for the high tailwheel.'

It is safe to assume that sabotage was deliberately practiced during production by the PoWs, foreign workers and concentration camp workers engaged in manufacture, in the form of loose screw anchorings of all kinds, incorrect electrical connections, non-adherence to correct coolant mixture ratios, improperly screwed spark plugs etc. The frost-protection fluid that was on hand was often spirited away by the Russian PoWs and drunk as an alcohol substitute, and numerous deaths of PoWs dying of alcohol poisoning are documented in lists of losses.

Arno Mittman, a pilot with JG 27, said of the Bf 109 K-4: 'At the end of October 1944, III./JG 27 was based in Großenhain near Leipzig and on 20 October, the Gruppe began conversion to the K-4. At that time, I was in 11.Staffel and each pilot was allowed only one take-off for conversion-training on this model, as fuel for more was not available. With the K-4 model, we again had an aircraft available that performance-wise, was able to hold its own against the P-47s and P-51s, were it not for the numerical superiority of the US fighters. The K-4 was faster and had a better climb rate than the G-6, and the

A line of unfinished Bf 109 Ks in one of the assembly halls at Messerschmitt Regensburg after the surrender in 1945. Note the instrument panels in boxes on the ground in front of the first aircraft. (Photo Steve Sheflin)

field of vision from the cockpit was much better. Our first sortie with the new K-4 was on 2 November 1944 to defend the Leuna [oil refinery] plant. We wound up in an overwhelming formation of P-51 Mustangs which pounced from above on to our formation. I was only able to shoot down one Mustang, but was subsequently chased by four of them and had no chance to escape. Wounded, I had to bale out of my heavily shot-up K-4. It was a black day for our III. Gruppe, and we lost five pilots killed plus four wounded.'

Volume III of the chronicle of JG 53, by aviation historian Dr. Jochen Prien, describes how the Jagdverbände themselves took care of obtaining the necessary supplies of aircraft. On 3 January 1945, 'qbi' (bad weather) prevailed, so that the Geschwader was not able to conduct any sorties. In all three Gruppen, aircraft ferry detachments were pulled together which were set in motion to go to the Messerschmitt-Werken in the southern region and to the Front depots to fly over new aircraft for the Geschwader. Helmut Ballewski wrote: 'For this purpose, a ferry detachment under my leadership, strengthened by pilots of II. Gruppe, were dispatched to the Messerschmitt factories. Regensburg, Cham, Augsburg and Ingolstadt were well-known points on this begging trip.' The III. Gruppe was finally 'successful' in Regensburg and Herzogenaurach. They were able to take charge of several brand new Bf 109 K-4s which, in the weeks to come, also formed the main equipment of III./JG 3 and which would almost completely oust the remaining G-14s. Hermann Heck, who belonged to the III. Gruppe's ferry detachment, recalled the K-4 as a 'bullish and strong aircraft' which he very much liked to fly. On the afternoon of 4 January 1945, the Ferry Detachment again assembled in Kirrlach. Production of the K-4 ran from September 1944 until well into April 1945. A handwritten note dated 11 April from the Luftwaffe Quartermaster-General mentions at least 50 Bf 109s that were taken over by the Luftwaffe in April 1945. The majority of these must have been the K-4 model.

According to RLM Lieferplan 226/2, the status as of 30 June 1944 saw the following aircraft manufactured by Messerschmitt GmbH Regensburg: 2,215 Bf 109 G-6, plus 211 of the Bf 109 G-6/AS = 2,246 aircraft. Thus, from Regensburg came the first Bf 109 Gs with the more powerful DB 605 AS engine. The total number of G-6s produced up till then – 1943/44 – were 3,176 aircraft, divided into 1,119 G-4/Trop, 1,846 G-6 and 211 G-6/AS variants. The overall Bf 109 G-6 total delivered from Regensburg to the Luftwaffe according to Lieferplan 227/2 to 30 November 1944 was 4,120 aircraft. In the second half of that year production reached its absolute zenith, with a maximum monthly production of 755 Bf 109s of various models delivered in October. During that half-year, the 3,890 Bf 109s produced were comprised as follows: G-6: 950, G-6/AS: 114, G-14: 479, G-14/AS: 1,373, G-10: 118, and K-4: 856. During the entire year 1944, Bf 109 production totalled 6,316 aircraft, which was less than the originally planned output of 7,760 aircraft, as a result of the continual bombing raids on the aircraft factories and the transportation networks. (Sources: Eisenbeiß documents, Stadtarchiv Regensburg and RLM Lieferplan 226/2 and 227/2)

Despite events, Bf 109s continued to be delivered to the Air Forces of Axis countries. Up until August 1944, Finland received 81 aircraft from Regensburg, and deliveries were also made to Italy, Hungary and Croatia. In 1944, not only was the Bf 109 produced, but from January, Me 262 fuselages were manufactured and in September, Me 262 final assembly as well. Me 323 production in Regensburg-Obertraubling ended in January 1944 with one aircraft.

Overall Production in Regensburg in 1944

	Bf 109	Me 262	Me 262 (fuselages)
January	434		7
February	305		9
March	135		8
April	343		16
May	550		33
June	659		52
July	650		72
August	704		73
September	701	2	104
October	755	10	184
November	543	14	216
December	537	23	255
Totals:	**6,316**	**49**	**1,027**

That a considerable number of Bf 109s sub-types were still being produced at the end of 1944 can be seen from the documented production figures for November, where these comprised G-6: 53, G-10: 108, G-14: 59, G-14/AS: 101 and K-4: 221. Corresponding figures for these models for December were: 1, 5, 4, 202 and 325 respectively.

The overall total of the Regensburg workforce rose from 12,824 on 30 June 44 to 14,508 on 31 December 1944. Around one-third of overall production in 1944 came from the Flossenburg and Mauthausen concentration camps. From 1939 to 1944, 9,816 Bf 109s of various models were manufactured and represented more than 35 per cent of all the Bf 109 series that were built, so that Regensburg manufactured more Bf 109s than all the other aircraft firms.

CHAPTER 6

'Zero Hour': The end in Regensburg

FORMER Messerschmitt aircraft fitter, Martin Gattinger of Regensburg, recalled the last weeks of the war in Schafhof: 'From the middle of 1944 I was engaged as a fitter at Messerschmitt in Schafhof near Amberg preparing the Bf 109s coming out of Vilseck for for their acceptance flights. We carefully checked the aircraft on arrival, fuelled them up fully and then declared them as ready for flight. We had more work to do than we wished, as the aircraft, of course, suffered to some extent from serious defects when they came to us. These consisted mostly of engine leakages or leaks from the cooling and hydraulic systems. The aircraft were distributed far and wide in Schafhof and well camouflaged in the forests, and after an engine test run, we maintenance crews had to roll the aircraft to the airfield and sometimes over the entire runway with engine running, in order to hand them over to the waiting pilots. When I became ever more proficient at handling the Bf 109, I pushed the throttle so far forward that the tailplane almost rose from the ground. We experienced no problems with the airfield personnel, as we fitters wore pilots' clothing and were indistinguishable from the real pilots. The reason for my take-off tests with the Bf 109 was the continually worsening news from all Fronts. I was particularly perturbed by the rapid advance of the Russians. Many of my comrades were greatly afraid that the Russians would advance as far as our location. We were constantly kept informed of the situation at the Front by the ferry pilots, since one could almost no longer believe our own news which was almost always propaganda that we were winning in the midst of our downfall. A few weeks before the end of the war, the situation came ever more dramatically to a head, and on no account did I want to be captured by the Russians. I therefore continued my take-off tests until just before the aircraft left the ground, but I had to be hellishly careful that nothing happened to them. I had a fully tanked-up Bf 109 constantly ready in April 1945 in reserve for Zero Hour, and if the Russians were to have advanced any further, I would have fetched my Bf 109 out of the forest and would have flown with it to the Americans. I would have trusted myself to make a belly landing with it on an airfield. Fortunately, the Americans were quicker than the Russians, hence I left my Bf 109 in the forest at Schafhof and made my way back to Regensburg when the war ended.'

Another little known action shortly before the end of the war was related to the author by Ludwig Groß: 'About two weeks before the Americans reached Regensburg, we received the order to remove the electromotors from the tooling machines or other important component parts and to pack them in crates. Special tools and precision instruments were wrapped in oilpaper and likewise packed in crates. Drawings and important construction gear were treated the same way. There were at least a few hundred crates, all of them numbered, and hidden in farms according to plan. The aim of it all was to bring Me 262 production temporarily to a standstill. We all still hoped to fight against the Russians together with the Americans, and it would then have been no problem to once again start up Me 262 production in the shortest possible time. But things did not get that far, and the crates remained where we had hidden them. Thus, after the war, many a farmer came into possession of almost priceless special tools and measuring instruments which he was able to do little with.'

'We experienced no problems with the airfield personnel, as we fitters wore pilots' clothing and were indistinguishable from the real pilots.' Martin Gattinger standing by Bf 109 K-4 W.Nr. 334161. Clearly visible are the retractable tailwheel and fuselage camouflage. The last three numerals of the Werknummer were also painted crudely on the fuselage. (Photo Gattinger)

81

NEST OF EAGLES

One of the many Bf 109 K-4s that stood around in May 1945 on the airfield at München-Riem. This aircraft carries the upper engine cowling from another Bf 109, with earlier style camouflage and possible fuselage components from a G-14. This aircraft could very well be in the serial batch of the last K-4s built. (Photo Didier Waelkens via Kees Mol)

A US serviceman looks into the cockpit of a virtually complete Bf 109 K in one of the assembly halls at Messerschmitt Regensburg, after the surrender in 1945. Due to the state of the aircraft industry prior to the surrender, large sub-assembles of these aircraft were left unpainted as seen on these Ks. (Photo Jim Crow)

On 25 April 1945, American troops reached the Danube at Regensburg. Heavy fighting took place at Bad Abbach following the crossing of the Danube, and the town was taken two days later from the south. The aircraft plants at Prüfening and Obertraubling were immediately inspected by the Americans, who discovered totally bombed-out installations. Their amazement was much the greater when the two Waldwerke 'Gauting' and 'Stauffen' were discovered, which had – literally up to the very last minute – produced aircraft for Hitler's 'Thousand-Year Reich'. Thousands of concentration camp inmates, PoWs and forced-labourers were freed, and highly welcome to the Americans was the technical booty that fell into their hands, especially the technical knowledge gained with the Me 262. Most of the old town of Regensburg had been spared from air attacks, but the main railway station and quayside as well as entire industrial communities had been bombed-out. Thousands of refugees were housed in improvised barracks, and an indescribable misery and distress prevailed. Across the Third Reich, everything came to a standstill at 'Zero Hour'.

Today, almost nothing remains of the Messerschmitt-Werke in Regensburg. It is as if it was all a bad dream. And even now, with all its problems, the town still has to overcome and come to terms with its recent past, but in this respect, Regensburg does not stand alone. In Prüfening, there remain only two buildings that have been subject to considerable alteration: the administration building, which at the time of writing is the Commercial Trade School, and the Flight Acceptance Halle used by the Siemens firm. On the former airfield grounds is now the Westpark. All other buildings have, over the years, been demolished. After the war, the damaged and partly destroyed barracks buildings on the Fliegerhorst Obertraubling were either repaired or re-erected and today form the eastern core of Neutraubling. Many refugee families found a new home here in the post-war years. From the large aircraft Hallen there still exist only the Werfthalle which has likewise been altered. The former flight operations building was been pulled down some years ago, and on the former airfield grounds, new housing areas and an industrial sector have been built. Following the closure of the Prüfening and Obertraubling airfields, the town of Regensburg no longer has an airfield. But, at the time of writing, there still exists a samll circle of people who keep open the memory of the Messerschmitt-Werke. The former apprentices gather together each year on 17 August in Regensburg at the Upper Catholic Cemetery and at 1200 hrs on the old plant grounds in Prüfening, remember their comrades who lost their lives in the bombing raid of 1943. The author hopes that this narrative will maintain as a testimony to that part of the industial history of Regensburg, which also foms a major part of German aviation history.

PART II

The Fliegerhorst Obertraubling and the Me 262

CHAPTER 7

Building the Fliegerhorst Obertraubling

The Fliegerhorst Obertraubling Garrison headquarters building. During the 'Big Week' bombing raid of 25 February 1944, the building was badly hit. Of the circular arches on the west side, three remain today and form the entrance to the Catholic parish church. (Photo Stadtverwaltung Neutraubling)

INITIAL planning for the construction of a Fliegerhorst (Air Base) near Regensburg began in 1935. It was originally to have been located directly north of Obertraubling, but the leaders of the local farmers at that time intervened against it with the argument that, in the event of air raids, the locality could be directly affected. A determining factor for a relocation of the airfield grounds to the north-east was the apparently better soil quality for farming near Obertraubling. The Fliegerhorst was thus erected in a less valuable pastureland area. In 1936, the first planning and construction work was put in train, and on an area of around 250 Hectares (2,500,000 m² = 26,909,125 ft²) north-east of the town, the Fliegerhorst Obertraubling was erected. The Principality of Thurn & Taxis had to relinquish 89 Hectars and the Kirsch-Puricelli family 80 Hectars of estate to the German Reich.

A large barracks for housing the construction workers was laid down and in the surrounding villages the families of the construction engineers and Wehrmacht relatives were accommodated. These were followed by construction measures taken for the required infrastructure where conduits for drinking water, electric power, telephone lines, drainage, and a road system were laid down. Railway lines from Obertraubling station were laid to the Fliegerhorst and a small station in the south-western part of it were built which led to the fuel filling stations that were located in front of Halle 4. The connecting road between Obertraubling and the Fliegerhorst was extended and tarred. Local construction firms participated in this project and delivered construction materials in the form of bricks and tiles.

What was for that time a huge barracks complex rose in its raw state within the space of one year, in 1937. On lush grassland there thus arose a new 'town' and for housing the construction crews, a so-called Schlangenbau (snake construction) was erected - barrack buildings that occupied a length of 380 m (1,247 ft). The main guard office with the Garrison headquarters, the angular stepped building for housing the flight personnel, the houses for the officers, garages, the air traffic control with its fire brigade and the giant aircraft hangars, were all completed by the end of 1938. The aircraft hangars were prefabricated of steel sections and erected using hydraulic pistons. The walls were of brick, and four different types of Hallen were erected. These consisted of the Werfthalle or workshop (Halle 1) measuring 121 x 50 m (397 x 164 ft); Hallen 2, 4, 6 and 8, each having a saddle-roof and measuring 105 x 35 m (344 x 115 ft), with Hallen 3, 5 and 7 each measuring 99 x 48 m (325 x 157 ft) and being the finest, having arched roofing. Hallen 9 and 10 with sloping roofs, added in 1943, measured 105 x 35 m (344 x 115 ft) and were of the most simple construction.

The landing runway, running in a north-south direction, was hardly ever used and served primarily as a parking area in front of the aircraft Hallen. The east-west take-off runway soon proved to be too short and was lengthened to a total of around 1,200 m (3,940 ft). To do this, a few farmsteads on the eastern perimeter of the airfield had to be vacated. Although planning for a concrete runway to the same length had been concluded, it was only in April 1945 that a start was made on levelling work, but this could not be completed because of the turn of the war's events. (For the layout of the Fliegerhorst Obertraubling, see Appendix 11)

From the Stuka-Fliegerschule 1 to Kommando 'Warschau-Süd'

During the pre-war years, a Luftwaffe bomber Gruppe consisted of three Staffeln with about 35 bombers, several communications aircraft and around 250 flying personnel. In addition to these, there were further units including a Gruppenstab, workshops, storage, signals, weather and medical personnel. The ground organisation encompassed a Flughafenbetriebskompanie (Airfield Operating Company), or FBK, functioning as support for the aircraft and the Fliegerhorst. An FBK had a personnel strength of around 175 men and had at its disposal the entire technical equipment ranging from fuel bowsers to cranes, which were indispensable for maintaining flight operations. In addition there were Construction Company personnel and the Airfield Administration, so that around 1,000-1,200 men were stationed at a Fliegerhorst with a corresponding number of accommodation barracks, while aircraft were housed in large hangars. As mentioned, at Obertraubling in 1941 there was a large workshop hangar and eight Hallen, to which Hallen 9 and 10 were added in 1943.

It had originally been planned to relocate I./KG 355 (later to become I./KG 53 'Legion Condor') to Obertraubling. This unit, however, was transferred to Ansbach. The Luftwaffe used Obertraubling for other units and in November 1938, the newly-formed III. Abteilung of Flakregiment 9 was stationed there. Airfield protection with heavy machine guns and light Flak was handled by airfield defence personnel. During this time, Obertraubling was a Leithorst (Main Air Base) within Luftgau (Air District) XIII and was responsible for the Cham operational base. Bomber Staffeln and other flying units made numerous interim landings at Obertraubling during the course of training flights, but as early as 1940, it had lost its status as a Leithorst and from then on was regarded as an auxiliary Fliegerhorst to the Ansbach airfield region.

'Unternehmen Winterübung 1939' (Operation Winter Exercise 1939) was started on 14 March 1939, in the course of which the remaining areas of Czechoslovakia were occupied, and I./KG 355 relocated from Ansbach to Obertraubling from where the Gruppe flew leaflet sorties on 16 and 17 March 1939 via Pilsen to Prague. On 18 March, the unit returned to Ansbach and after this brief spell of operations, all once more became quiet at Obertraubling, so that the Fliegerhorst was used only by Stukaschule 1. At this school, future Stuka pilots were trained for operations on the Henschel Hs 123 and on the Junkers Ju 87 A and B, the unit having a total of 120 training aircraft. Aircraft would take off on their training flights in quick succession and diving practice was conducted using dummy concrete bombs dropped onto the 'targets'. To make room for the Me 321 glider to make its test and acceptance flights at the Fliegerhorst,

The Flugleitung (Air Traffic Control) building with its control tower and D/F equipment. The building housed the meteorological service and to the right of the picture, the fire brigade. (Photo Stadt Neutraubling)

A 1939 view from the control tower looking in a northerly direction onto the apron, where a collection of various aircraft (Bü 131, He 46, Hs 123, Fw 44, Ju 87 A, Bf 108 and Bf 110) are visible. At centre, on the concrete apron are two fuelling trailers and a Hanomag SS 100 towing vehicle in front of Halle 3. (Photo Emmerle)

A Henschel Hs 123 of Stukaschule 1 in Obertraubling. The Hs 123 was used as a Schlachtflugzeug and was the predecessor of the Ju 87. To the right in the photograph is a Junkers W 34 with a damaged tailplane. (Photo Binder)

however, Stukaschule 1 was transferred in May 1941 to Wertheim.

Shortly after the commencement of production of the Me 321 Gigant (Giant) at Messerschmitt AG in Leipheim, in November 1940 the first contingents of detachment 'Warschau-Süd' (Warsaw-South), made up of Luftwaffe and Messerschmitt personnel, were relocated as an advance detachment to Obertraubling in order to make preparations for its assembly there. On 4 December, a Wehrmacht detachment overseeing 2,200 prisoners was relocated to the Fliegerhorst. They were tasked to work for Messerschmitt and immediately began final assembly of the aircraft, whose construction, in one blow, altered the whole daily routine and significance of the Fliegerhorst.

A Ju 87 A of Stukaschule 1. It was with this variant that the first sorties by the Legion Condor were flown in the Spanish Civil War. (Photo Schmoll)

A Kampfflugzeugstaffel equipped with the Do 17 E made an interim landing on the Fliegerhorst in the winter of 1938/39 and parked its aircraft on the east side of the airfield. (Photo Schmoll)

Two Ju 87 Bs of Stukaschule 1 at Obertraubling in 1941. (Photo Binder)

Seen here is a Ju 52 anchored by underwing cables at Obertraubling. (Photo Binder)

Building the Fliegerhorst Obertraubling

A Bf 109 D of Luftkriegsschule 1. In the background is a Ju 87 A. (Photo Binder)

Even the exotic Blohm und Voss BV 141 was stationed for a brief period at the Fliegerhorst. On 27 August 1941, a flight was made from Obertraubling to Manching and back. Although designed as an Aufklärer (reconnaissance aircraft) with its offset crew compartment, it did not go into production. (Photo Schmoll)

The Luftkriegsschule (Air War School) was relocated to Breslau in April 1941. This was the scene at the Fliegerhorst Obertraubling railway station shortly before train departure. (Photo Binder)

87

CHAPTER **8**

'The first beast is now here!': Me 321 mass production 1941-1943

ORDERED for production by the RLM, the Me 321 was developed by Messerschmitt from mid-1940 as a large Lastensegler (load-carrying glider) for the transport of heavy weaponry intended for 'Unternehmen Seelöwe' (Operation Sea-Lion), the invasion of England. Prof. Messerschmitt had outlined the first sketches for this aircraft on a table napkin and within a few months, design work was begun on it. The Junkerswerke in Dessau built and flew one prototype of the competitive Ju 322 Mammut (Mammoth) glider under the codename 'Warschau-Ost' (Warsaw East) to meet the same requirements but it was unsuccessful, and series production of further examples of it were stopped in May 1941. Despite the invasion plans having been broken off in October 1940, work on the Me 321 continued with the aim of mass production. Due to its imposing dimensions – the wingspan was 55 m (180.5 ft) and it had a wing area of 300 m² (3,229 ft²), 200 examples of this monster were to have been built, of which 100 would be produced in Obertraubling, although no suitable towing aircraft for it was available. After the arrival of the workforce, at least three of the Hallen were cleared for production. Fuselage final assembly probably took place in Hallen 4 and 6, the others being used for the wings. Only the Werfthalle was dimensionally large enough to enable the wing centre section to be attached to the fuselage, the outer wings having to be completed in the open. Technical details of this aircraft are given in the Appendices.

Delivery of the first steel tube components for the wings and fuselages, although attempted under the strict secrecy in January 1941, did not go unnoticed by the local population who circulated the rumour that high-tension masts were being built. When the first 'high-tension mast' took to the air, even the most ignorant became aware of what really was going on at the Fliegerhorst. In the Hallen, the load-bearing steel-tube airframe components were attached to the wooden ribs and stiffeners onto which the fabric skinning was affixed. After that, the control cables and cockpit were installed. The fuselage with its wooden flooring was then attached to the empennage surfaces. When this was completed, the ailerons and flaps were added, and hundreds of workers were active on high scaffolding to accomplish the work, the all-wood tail surfaces being the last to be attached. The aircraft's cavernous loading bay, whose volume corresponded to a covered heavy railway freight van, was accessed by two outward-opening doors which formed the fuselage and fabric-covered nose, and which enabled trucks, tanks, or other vehicles to be loaded via a ramp.

Three-tonne Opel Blitz trucks towing Me 321 fuselage components on the Fliegerhorst in January 1941. The hollow outer wing spars have been slid into the fuselage framework. Such transports could naturally not be kept secret, and for deception reasons, the rumour was spread that these were for high-tension masts. When the first Me 321 took to the air, the secrecy bubble burst. In any case, through conversations with military personnel quartered there, the local population were generally kept well informed about activities at the Fliegerhorst. (Photo Croneiß)

88

'The first beast is now here!' Me 321 mass production 1941-1943

The first wing spars for the Me 321 were delivered to the Fliegerhorst in January 1941. In this picture, the enormous size of the glider can be seen in comparison with the Luftwaffe personnel, where the upper side of the spar is supported on the transport trailer. The wing was later turned over and attached by the upper protruding struts to the fuselage sides. (Photo Croneiß)

A view inside the Me 321 wing main spar during assembly. (Photo Croneiß)

The Me 321 wing centre section during assembly. The hollow steel-tube main spar can be clearly seen here beneath the wooden wing ribs. (Photo Croneiß)

Prior to the maiden flight of the first Me 321A built in Obertraubling, Stukaschule 1 was ordered to vacate the Fliegerhorst, and on 1 May 1941 it began to relocate with its 121 aircraft to Wertheim. On 18 April, two of its Ju 87s collided in the air, and whereas one aircraft made an emergency landing near Hausen, the other crashed in Luckenpaint and Feldwebel Hildebrandt was killed as he was not able to leave the stricken aircraft in time. He was found with his unopened parachute in a stretch of forest quite close to the wreck. At 2000 hrs on 2 May 1941, except for the contents of the bomb storage area, the last transports of Stukaschule 1 left for Wertheim. One further unit, 9. Staffel of KG 51 'Edelweiss' was located in Obertraubling from February to April 1941 and converted from He 111s to Ju 88s there.

Following the withdrawal of all the Luftwaffe units, the Fliegerhorst became largely available for use by the Messerschmitt firm. As more and more workers became needed for production, the Luftwaffe transferred a punishment battalion to Obertraubling and a short while later, the first of 2,200 Russian Officer PoWs were brought in, housed in a camp opposite the Commandant's office.

Meanwhile, the first flight of the first Me 321 series-built aircraft took place on 7 May 1941. Initially, the Me 321 was towed-off by three Bf 110s whose engines delivered a total of 6,600 hp. The next take-off was on the following day, when a mishap occurred with a He 111 that made a crash-landing at Obertraubling and was 25% damaged. In the days that followed, the Me 321s took-off without noticeable problems on test flights. It was an imposing sight when the tow combination rose into the air. According to eyewitnesses, assembly work stopped at these moments and everyone looked towards what the runway at the three Bf 110s with their engines running at full power, behind which was the Me 321 with its thundering and smoking underwing rocket motors. Shortly after lift-off, the Me 321 released its large, 1,200 kg (2,646 lb) heavy undercarriage dolly and weaved about in wild undulations above the runway. Like the Walter HWK RI-202b RATO units, the undercarriage descended on parachutes. Since the Me 321 landed on skids, it thus stood immobile on the airfield. At first, a Sonderkommando (Special Detachment), equipped with vehicles, hydraulic hoists, and other equipment was necessary to heave the aircraft onto its undercarriage dolly, and it was an extremely tedious job until the aircraft again perched on its

89

NEST OF EAGLES

Seen here during his pilot training in 1938 at Munich-Oberwiesenfield airfield is Josef Sachsenhauser. A Regensburger, Sachsenhauser flew the Me 321 with Sonderstaffeln (GS [Gigant Staffel]) 1 and 4. (Photo Dr. J. Weißmüller)

mainwheels. A little later, manually-operated cranes mounted on Opel Blitz (Lightning) trucks were employed that raised the gliders by the fuselage nose so that they could be dropped down onto the wheels. By means of a Praga tracked vehicle, the Me 321 was subsequently towed to its parking place at Obertraubling.

Leutnant Josef Sachsenhauser of Regensburg was a Me 321 pilot; he recalled the precarious flights with these aircraft: 'Flights with the Me 321 at Obertraubling were conducted under the greatest of secrecy, although these enormous aircraft stood around in scores on the apron and could hardly be missed. Beneath each wing were up to four Walter liquid-propellant RATO units that provided a total thrust of 2,000 kg (8,818 lb) on each side. The big question at that time was: Who is to fly these giants? The Me 321 was not easy to fly as the control forces were enormous. For the large control surfaces on this glider, there was of course no hydraulic assistance and all movements were via the control levers.

The Me 321 A only had a single-seater cockpit, and it was the B-version that first had a crew of two. One had to really get used to flying that giant. Although the pilot sat above the fuselage, there was hardly any nose in front of him to indicate the attitude of the aircraft to the horizon. The cockpit was some 5 m (16 ft) above the ground and this did not make landing it an easy matter. The landing approach called for absolute precision, as going around again was not possible. For that reason, the RLM decided that in operational use, older and experienced glider pilots would be selected instead of those accustomed to motorized flight. After the first test flights, it became apparent that experienced glider pilots were doubtless in a position to master these giants in the air. In addition to a clean tow-off, a steady tow in flight and above all, a precision landing was needed, upon which the success of a mission depended.

'One difficult problem that was only solved at a relatively late date was to find aircraft that were suitable as towcraft for the Me 321. The Ju 90 could only be used for towing Me 321s that carried no payload, and we did not have a more powerful towcraft at that time. For this reason, several aircraft had to be used for a tow-off. After various trial flights, it was decided to use three Bf 110s in a 'Troikaschlepp' (three-finger tow), in which each had roughly a 120 m (400 ft)-long steel towing cable that pulled the Me 321 along for take-off. As it was, the take-off was anything other than normal. Although the three Bf 110s flew close to each other, there was still a tendency at full power for the two outside aircraft to veer outwards.

'When such a combination started to move, it was a quite ticklish situation as it demanded absolutely top performance from all the pilots involved. The Me 321 was the first to lift off, followed by the two outer towcraft and finally the leader of the trio in the centre. The towcraft retracted their mainwheels simultaneously, while the Me 321 dropped its own as soon as possible in

The first Me 321 A in front of Halle 8 at Obertraubling. The guard appears very small in comparison to the aircraft's large fuselage and 55 m wingspan. To maintain it in a level position, the tailskid is supported on a jack. In the background are further Me 321 wing sections. At this time, in the summer of 1941, Hallen 9 and 10 had not yet been erected. (Photo Croneiß)

'The first beast is now here!' Me 321 mass production 1941-1943

Below: Me 312 W1+SY is made ready for flight after an off-field landing. The Praga tracked vehicle served as a workhorse at the Obertraubling Fliegerhorst. (Photo Hübsch)

The Me 321 A (W2+SC) seen here is being jacked up by two Opel Blitz 3-ton trucks so that it can be mounted on to its main undercarriage which lies close by. (Photo Hübsch)

The Praga tracked vehicle in action. On the ground, the Me 321 nosewheels had to be directionally guided by a man holding a metal bar extension. (Photo Hübsch)

A Me 321 A wing centre section, showing the small cut-out for the single-man cockpit. It needed hundreds of men from a Luftwaffe punishment battalion to assemble the giant glider. At centre can be seen the plywood wing leading-edge profile that was attached to the wooden ribs being worked upon in the foreground. Cranes then raised the wings into the vertical position, where the canvas wing skinning was attached. The large Hallen at the Fliegerhorst were just about large enough to enable the wing centre sections to be assembled. (Photo Croneiß)

order to reduce drag. Lift-off was accomplished at around 85 km/h (53 mph). At this speed the Bf 110 hardly reacted to control movements, and it practically hung on its propellers and the tow cable. Climbing speed was around 130 km/h (81 mph) and level flight speed around 190-210 km/h (118-130 mph). Then began the dance of the towcraft, and one cable jerk after another had to be overcome. A steady flight was a rare event. If it happened to be gusty weather, the tow combination never settled down. The towing cable jerks were at times so strong that the two outside towcraft, whose cables were 10 m (33 ft) shorter than the lead aircraft, shot up to the lead's height and then with enormously strong force, were pulled back again. This pull-back resulted in

91

The wing leading edge outer skin of the Me 321 was carefully attached to the wing ribs, the remainder of the wing being canvas covered. (Photo Croneiß)

A view during fuselage assembly. The freight floor inside the fuselage of the Me 321 was built of thick wooden planks, the fuselage sides being covered with canvas. The fuselages to the rear already have their nose doors attached. (Photo Croneiß)

a loss of height which had to be regained with much 'feel'. Reacting too quickly would have led to a whole series of cable jerks. It sometimes happened that the wingtips of the left or right towcraft came into contact with the lead aircraft, and nerves of steel were required.

'When Ernst Udet observed this towing method on one occasion he said: "Listen, it can't go on like this, this is pure acrobatics." As a consequence, development of the He 111 Z was begun, with which a much better flight with the Me 321 became possible.

'In acceptance flights with the Me 321, mishaps always occurred. I can still remember well when on one Troika take-off in Obertraubling - the Me 321 had already lifted-off - the towing trio suddenly split apart, which means that one of the Bf 110s had veered off the runway and with a shorn-off undercarriage came to a standstill in a great cloud of dust. The Me 321 pilot released the cables of the towcraft and with the aid of his already-ignited RATO units, went into a left turn. An indescribable thundering of the rockets filled the air and the Me 321 continued to turn towards the airfield. Everyone waited for the moment when the rocket thrust stopped, since they worked for about 30 seconds. In an excellent piece of flying, the pilot turned and, almost grazing the ground with his wingtips, circled back to the runway. When the Me 321 was again flying level, the RATO units cut out and a few moments later, it stood undamaged in the middle of the grass landing strip. He certainly had luck! The pilot was Alfred Röhm. But this type of event did not always turn out happily, and crashes by towcraft and Me 321s that resulted in total losses with several deaths also occurred.'[1]

On 25 May 1941, a heavy four-engined aircraft droned over the Obertraubling Fliegerhorst and turned into its final approach. It was the Ju 90 Z-3 W.Nr. 900002 (KB+LA) which had a span of 35.30 m (115 ft 9.8 in). It was 1307 hrs when Flugkapitän Peter Hesselbach set the Ju 90 down for landing. The Junkers was powered by four Pratt & Whitney Twin-Wasp SC-G two-row engines each of 1,250 hp, and at that time was the most powerful of its type.[2] It was stationed for one year as a Me 321 towcraft at Obertraubling until the arrival of the He 111 Z and carried out at least 181 take-offs in towing and transport flights. On four occasions it had to land on open fields by Niederleierndorf, Burgweinting, Wolkering and Langenerling to tow Me 321s back to Obertraubling that had made emergency landings. On the day of its arrival, three take-offs each with an Me 321 in tow, were effected: at 1525 hrs with the Me 321 W1+SD; at 1653 hrs with W1+SG and at 1812 hrs, again with W1+SD. In all, Hesselbach carried out 19 towing flights up to 14 July 1941 with various Me 321s at Obertraubling, plus one in Bayreuth for the off-field landing of Me 321 W2+SB, and one in Leipheim with

---

[1.] Leutnant Josef Sachsenhauser has a flight logbook recording several operational flights he made with the Me 321 (W2+SY) on the Eastern Front, among them, carrying supplies to Bagerovo and Slavianskaya on 15 and 16 February 1942. In August 1941, Alfred Röhm flew supplies missions with the Me 321 (W2+SH) to Terespol, Orsha and Shatalovka. The lead pilot of the Bf 110 Troika was Leutnant Schalkhäuser. As a rule, an explosive mixture of petrol containers and/or ammunition crates were transported for the advanced units of German Panzer columns that were far into Russian territory.)

[2.] Editor's note: This prototype, as well as Werknr 900004 (KB+LB) had originally been scheduled for delivery to South African Airways as ZS-ANG and ZS-ANH respectively, but both were handed over on 7 April 1940 to 4./KGr. zbV 107 - *Translator*

'The first beast is now here!' Me 321 mass production 1941-1943

Final assembly of a Me 321 A at Obertraubling. The wing centre section is being mated to the fuselage which is already perched on its mainwheels. The nosewheels have already been attached. (Photo Croneiß)

Below: Traversible cranes were an essential aid for production of the giant aircraft. Here, an outer wing section is being moved into position on Me 321 A W2+SM and behind it is Halle 7. (Photo Croneiß)

With the help of two traversible cranes, the Me 321 A wing centre section is moved into position above a fuselage in front of the camouflaged Halle 6 at Obertraubling. (Photo Croneiß)

A view beneath the wing of W2+SA, the first Me 321 A to leave the Obertraubling production line. The underwing suspension points for the four Walter RATO units are clearly visible. (Photo Croneiß)

93

NEST OF EAGLES

From left to right: Messrs Wendland, Croneiß, Schmid and Hentzen inspecting production of the Me 321 A at Obertraubling in January 1941. (Photo Croneiß)

A Troika tow with three Bf 110s 'pulling' a Ju 52. (Photo Geisbe).

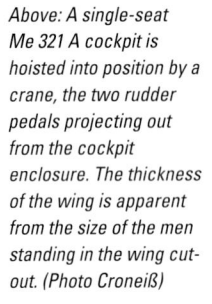

Above: A single-seat Me 321 A cockpit is hoisted into position by a crane, the two rudder pedals projecting out from the cockpit enclosure. The thickness of the wing is apparent from the size of the men standing in the wing cut-out. (Photo Croneiß)

From May 1941 until April 1942, the Ju 90 (KB+LA) was used as towcraft for the Me 321 at Obertraubling. Powered by four Pratt & Whitney Twin-Wasp SC-G radials, it was possible to safely tow a Me 321 carrying a 3-tonne payload. Only one Ju 90 of this type, however, was available. Second from left is Flugkapitän Alfried Gymnich who piloted the Ju 90. (Photo Schmid)

Me 321 W3+SB. He took-off on 16 transport flights, mostly to Leipheim, but also to Gablingen and to Schroda. Since Hesselbach had been assigned to conduct flight trials for the Junkerswerke at Dessau, on 13 and 14 July 1941, Flugkapitän Alfried Gymnich took over the Ju 90 KB+LA, with which he was occupied uninterruptedly from August 1941 until 24 April 1942 until the arrival of the He 111 Z, and according to his flight logbook, he conducted 143 take-offs and landings with it. Flights were also undertaken to the Eastern Front to tow back Me 321s that had made emergency landings.

On 27 May 1941 the Workshop Company at Leipheim, consisting of 10 officers and 120 men, moved to Obertraubling to the 'Warschau-Süd' Detachment. One day later, a Me 321 crashed near to Obertraubling. It was being towed from Leipheim on a ferry flight by three Bf 110s and made a smooth landing at Obertraubling on its skids. After it landed, the three 5,000-litre tanks it had on board were filled with water. It was then towed-off by the towcraft trio from the 1,200 m (3,940 ft) grass runway with the aid of its RATO units and absolved its planned flight programme. On landing at Obertraubling, the Me 321 suddenly encountered

At 0720 hrs on 20 June 1941, piloted by Flugkapitän Hesselbach, Ju 90 KB+LA towed the Me 321 W2+SG, that had made an off-field emergency landing near Niederleierndorf, to Obertraubling. (Photo Schmid)

stormy gusts. The weather service had measured a windspeed of 40 m/sec (89 mph), whch presumably led to the tailplane breaking off. It crashed from a height of about 120 m and smashed to pieces on the ground between Barbing and the Fliegerhorst. According to the latest information, parts of a landing flap had broken away, hit the tailplane and damaged it so severely that it led to the crash. The crew, comprising the pilot Leutnant Otto Bräutigam, co-pilot Ing. Bernhard Flinsch of the Erprobungsstelle Rechlin, Leutnant Fritz Schwarz, Gefreiter Adolf Engel and Messerschmitt's engineer Josef Sinz, all perished at 2055 hrs in the crash. Hanna Reitsch fortunately survived the crash, for shortly before take-off, she had to pay a visit to the toilet. Because the delay was too long for Otto Bräutigam, he had taken off without her. An investigation committee consisting of Prof. Messerschmitt, Dipl.-Ing. Fuchs of the RLM and Hauptmann Bachmeier of the military security service in Nuremberg was instituted to determine the cause of the crash.

On 2 June 1941, the Sonderkommando was strengthened once more by 30 men, and further personnel followed on 16 June. Several eyewitnesses reported that among the punishment detachment that had been engaged on Me 321 production in Obertraubling, was an almost complete U-boat crew. Test-flying resumed on 16 June, and at the very first take-off with the Troika, one Bf 110 did not lift-off and was destroyed just beyond the airfield fence. The crew miraculously escaped but were suffered shock. The two other Bf 110s just about managed to get the Me 321 airborne. With their engines running hot, they towed it aloft, but at a height of some 150 m (490 ft) had to release the tow cables. The Me 321 had no choice but to make an emergency landing in a field west of Barbing, but no damage was inflicted to the aircraft. On 17 June, the tow cables broke between three Bf 110s and Me 321 W1+SG, which managed to make an emergency landing at Niederleierndorf. The following day, another Me 321 emergency landing ocurred at 2200 hrs at Rosenhof, east of the Fliegerhorst, and the ground services had their hands full to get the aircraft back to the airfield.

Me 321 W1+SG at Niederleierdorf was flown back to Obertraubling under spectacular circumstances. First of all, it was heaved onto its undercarriage, the eight underwing RATO units were mounted in place, and between the road that connected Niederleierndorf and Schierling and the deeper-lying road, a take-off stretch was steamrollered flat and supported by wooden bracing. After three days, preparations had been completed, and in the early morning hours of 20 June 1941, Ju 90 KB+LA with Flugkapitän Hesselbach at the controls landed on the rollered stretch. The towing cable was attached and at 0720 hrs the Ju 90's engines were run-up to full power and Hesselbach released the brakes. The Ju 90 continually picked up speed and what then happened caused the hair of all those watching to stand on end. The Ju 90 droned along the take-off run and at the ramp which ran over the road, it was literally catapulted into the air. The Me 321, which stood at its forward end on its landing skids and on its wheels, had ignited all of its eight RATO units whilst on the move and thundered on behind. Roughly 200 m (660 ft) behind the road, the Ju 90 stalled, and the pilot was only able to get it under control again just a few metres above the ground. It only needed a little less clearance and the propellers would have made contact with the ground. It was an absolute masterpiece of flying ability and also involved much good fortune. The take-off was filmed by Theo Croneiß and even today shows the drama of the event. When the tow combination slowly gained height, a huge weight fell from the hearts of the observers.

The incidents in Me 321 acceptance flights did not tail off. In a field landing west of Harting on 23 June 1941, the tailplane of one was damaged. On the following day, there was a serious accident. A Bf 110 of a

A Troika tow above Obertraubling, with three Bf 110s towing an Me 321 with its mainwheels still attached but with both nosewheels already jettisoned. The Me 321 was nevertheless able to make a smooth landing at the Fliegerhorst, as documented in a film record of the event. The three tow cables had lengths of – on the right, 140 m (459.3 ft); at centre, 155 m (508.5 ft); and on the left, 130 m (426.5 ft). (Photo F. Müller-Romminger)

A motor vehicle parked in front of towcraft Bf 110 E, W.Nr. 3623, stationed at Obertraubling. Such aircraft had a large white S on their noses and featured the larger oil coolers of the later F- and G-series. In the background is Me 321 W2+SN. (Photo Hübsch)

NEST OF EAGLES

This Bf 110 which was converted for towing purposes, shows that the wing root fairing had been removed in order that the towing cable could be fed into the fuselage and down to the tail before being attached to a towing hook. (Hübsch)

A crashed Bf 110 towcraft lies inverted in a field. The crew – pilot Unteroffizier Erhardt and radioman, Gefreiter Greiner – died in the wreckage. (Photo Geisbe)

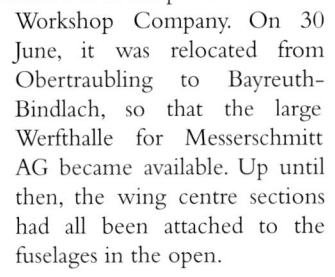

Seen here is Me 321 W2+SA on its skids. In the picture are two more Me 321s and a Bf 110 towcraft. The W2+SA was first flown from Obertraubling to Merseburg and then ferried to the Eastern Front by Unteroffizier Heinz Powilleit. (Photo Emmerle).

W2+SA is towed on the east side of the airfield to its take-off point for its flight to Merseburg. (Photo Hübsch)

towing trio veered away and crashed onto the Fliegerhorst motor transport shedne parachute hung in the sky. The radio operator, Gefreiter Dörfl, was burned beyond recognition in the wreck, but the fire brigade quickly had the fire under control.

In a ceremony in the Welfare Building on 16 June 1941, the airfield Kommandant, Major Weinlich, and Hauptmann Weigert said farewell to the personnel of the Workshop Company. On 30 June, it was relocated from Obertraubling to Bayreuth-Bindlach, so that the large Werfthalle for Messerschmitt AG became available. Up until then, the wing centre sections had all been attached to the fuselages in the open.

On 11 July, an Me 321 made an emergency landing at Wolkering; on 22 July, at Langenerling, and on 25 July, one landed at 1130 hrs near the railway station in Obertraubling, followed that same day at 1902 hrs by an emergency landing at Harting, while a Bf 110 landed on the road between the Fliegerhorst and Obertraubling. The Bf 110 pilot and his radio opeartor were slightly injured, but the aircraft 50% damaged. An emergency landing by a Me 321 also took place on 27 July at 2100 hrs near Obertraubling.

During the month of July, the first Me 321s were ferried to the Eastern Front by Sonderstaffel (GS ['Gigant Staffel']) 4. From Obertraubling, and after Merseburg, the route taken by 'Gigant Staffel' (GS) 4 was via Bednary, Jasionka, Hranovka, Vinnitsa and Nikolayev to the southern sector of the Eastern Front. The northern route was via Schroda, Warsaw, and Terespol to Orsha. Unteroffizier Heinz Powilleit recorded: 'On 3 July 1941, I was to ferry the first Me 321 from Obertraubling to Merseburg. The Me 321 W2+SB already stood on the runway, when just a few minutes before take-off, an Oberfeldwebel suddenly appeared who claimed this ferry flight for himself. Since his 'Ober' rank was above my 'Unter', I had to give in, and in place of that, was assigned the task of ferrying the second Me 321 W2+SA to Merseburg. However, the ambitious Oberfeldwebel only got as far as Bayreuth where he made an off-field landing. We took off with W2+SA towed by three He 111s led by Leutnant Hammon at 1915 hrs from Obertraubling and landed safely at 2045 hrs in Merseburg, and so it came about that the crew of Powilleit and Jung was the first to master an official ferry flight over a distance of 280 km (174 mls) without any major problems. But we did have one problem during the flight. From the very beginning, the aircraft flew with its port wing constantly hanging low. Although Ernst Jung corrected the aileron trim, it did not change anything, because it kept going back to the old position. Since I continually steered against this, I was soon bathed in sweat. These Me 321s only had the one-man cockpit, and Ernst Jung was unable to help me here. It was only when he hung on to the aileron control rod that I was somewhat relieved. He now became bathed in sweat, because he had to exert a fair amount of effort. But together we succeeded in bringing the Me 321 safely through. When we landed at Merseburg, Oberst Fritz Morzik greeted us with the words: "The first beast is now here!" A short while later, I suffered from severe angina which put me out of action.'[3]

Feldwebel Fritz Hübsch of Augsburg, recalled his experiences with the Me 321: 'In 1939, I qualified for the Instructors' Licence for Gliders and was assigned to the airfield at Königsberg-Neuhausen. It was there that I received the first training on the DFS 230 troop-carrying glider and acquired my (L) Glider Pilot's Licence. At the beginning of 1941, I received orders to ferry a two-seater DFS Kranich (Crane) glider to Stuttgart-Echterdingen and to report there to a Sonderkommando. Several glider pilots were assembled in Stuttgart and trained in towing flights in a Ju 52. For this purpose, the propeller of the central engine was removed and a towline firmly attached to it. The Ju 52 was towed by three Bf 110s to altitude. At around 400 m (1,320 ft) it was released and the 'Tante Ju' then glided with its other engines at idling revs for the landing. After two take-offs and landings, I switched to the pilot's seat and steered the Junkers and brought it in to land. It touched down gently at around 80 km/h (50 mph). We were told that the reason for this type of training was that we were to fly a large load-carrying glider and that with the Ju 52 we should familiarize ourselves with the high seating position. This preliminary training ended with a cross-country tow to Gablingen and back. I was subsequently assigned to go to Obertraubling to the 'Kommando Warschau-Süd.' Until then I had not yet seen an Me 321, not to mention ever having heard anything of this Kommando. Everything was surrounded by a veil of secrecy. I travelled by rail from Stuttgart via Regensburg to Obertraubling. Shortly before the train arrived at the station, I saw the first Me 321 standing in a field. On the way to the Fliegerhorst, I was able to recognise numerous other aircraft parked on the airfield grounds. After I had reported to my Staffelführer, Leutnant Sachsenhauser, we went out to the airfield. I now stood before this giant glider and thought to myself: "Wow - and you're supposed to fly this big bluebottle?" On looking closer at the enormous wings and their thick profile, it became clear to me that it could not fly fast, and with its massive fuselage, was not exactly sleek-looking.

'On my first flight with the Me 321, I had to jettison both nosewheels. On the second take-off, I sat in the co-pilot's seat and was allowed to get a feel of the controls. Looking out of the window, it felt like being on the second floor of a building. I had in my hands a control wheel that was typical for the Me 321, mounted on a control column, and already on the third take-off I sat at the controls. The take-off went without a hitch and after flying a wide circuit of the airfield, I floated in the Me 321 ready for the landing in Obertraubling. What a feeling it was to make a point-landing with this enormous ship!

'After the landing, it was extremely tedious and time-consuming to have the Me 321 heaved onto its undercarriage, for which reason it was not released on all subsequent flights. After landing, the aircraft was towed by a tracked vehicle to its take-off position, and the next flight could commence. In one of the next flights, because of technical problems, one of the Bf 110s had to drop out of the towing trio. Both aircraft released their tow cables, which fell onto an overhead railway electricity line near the Ostbahnhof (east railway station) and caused a short-circuit. The resulting power loss caused the entire rail traffic to come to a standstill. After five take-offs and landings, my conversion training was concluded. For another reason too, Obertraubling still well remains in my memory. In a DFS Kranich glider, I obtained my Silver C Certificate.

Fritz Hübsch as an Unteroffizier in the Luftwaffe. (Photo Hübsch)

'I made further take-offs with the Me 321 at Leipheim and ferried the aircraft in Troika tows to Reims, Dijon and Marseilles. In 1942, in the neighbourhood of Marseilles, some Me 321s stood ready for the planned invasion of Malta, but that did not take place. We then received the He 111 Z towcraft which made flying considerably easier, but only 12 aircraft of this model were built.'

In a conference on 24 July 1941, it was decided to tar the Fliegerhorst roads, erect additional barracks for the extra personnel and to pave the aircraft fuel filling-stations. On 1 August 1941, a discussion was held with the administrator of the Lerchenfeld estate, as the runway in the direction of Lerchenfeld had to be lengthened.

Strong nerves were still needed in making Me 321 acceptance flights, as the series of accidents did not tail off. At 1905 hrs on 2 August 1941, an Me 321 was able to make a smooth emergency landing near Lerchenfeld. On the same day however, a Bf 110 crashed and burned on impact near Schwaighof (Geisling) and both crew members were killed. On 18 August, a Bf 110 veered on take-off. When it ran on only one mainwheel, its pilot released the towline. Following a turn-around, the Bf 110 came to a standstill in a huge cloud of dust. Since the tow combination had already attained a speed of 120 km/h (75 mph) when the Bf 110 released the cable, the two other towcraft just about managed to take off. In a flat turn to port, both Bf 110s brought the Me 321 from a height of some 400 m (1,320 ft) back to the airfield.

Acceptance pilot Walter Starbati recalled a hair-raising incident during towing trials of the Me 321 with the He 111 : 'On 22 August 1941, the first take-off took place with Me 321 W4+SJ in tow by three He 111 H-6s (DF+OQ, DF+OR and DF+OS). Their pilots were Kurt Oppitz, Karl Schieferstein and Hermann Zitter.

This Ju 52 (H4+AR) served to instruct future Me 321 pilots by making them accustomed to a high seating position. For this purpose, the propeller of the centre engine was removed and a coupling installed for the tow cable. (Photo Geisbe)

[3.] The first Me 321 (W2+SB) that took off on 3 July and landed near Bayreuth, had to be towed back to Obertraubling by the Ju 90 (KB+LA) on 11 July as it had become slightly damaged on landing.)

The He 111 also served as towcraft. At first, three such aircraft were used, but this was later reduced to only two. Even when flown by an experienced pilot, it was very difficult to hold the port aircraft in the tow in position. (Photo Geisbe)

A photograph taken from the wing of an Me 321 showing four other aircraft lined up ready for acceptance flight trials at Obertraubling. The one at extreme left is W2+SO. (Photo Hübsch)

On take-off, the port He 111 H-6 veered off course. The two remaining aircraft continued the tow. At 400 m altitude over the airfield, I released the tow cables to both aircraft and all of us landed in Obertraubling without mishap. The subsequent discussion indicated that no further take-offs could be made with the normal towing cables, so they were lengthened by another 75 m (246 ft).

'The second take-off took place the next day. For unexplained reasons, the cable of the port He 111 got caught behind the Me 321 nosewheel and ripped the cable attachment ring. Again, only two He 111s towed it off. The flight went off normally and showed that the power of the two He 111s was fully adequate for conducting an acceptance flight with an unloaded Me 321. The average climb rate was 2.5-3.0 m/sec (8.2-9.8 ft/sec) and the Me 321 indicated airspeed 170-180 km/h (106-112 mph). At 600 m (1,970 ft) above the airfield, the starboard He 111 was released, the remaining He 111s continuing the tow for a normal circuit of the airfield for about 3 to 5 minutes at a height of 700 m (2,300 ft). The climbing performance of the He 111 was much more favourable than with the Me 110. Because of the long tow cable, the towcraft needed a considerably longer take-off run, with a cable length of 220 and 225 m (721 and 738 ft). As the cable friction on the ground was very unfavourable, it was decided to shorten the cable by 40 m (131 ft).

'The third take-off took place on 25 August 1941. At first, all went normally, and even the tow presented no problems, with no cable jerks, and available power was favourable. In 18 minutes, the three He 111s had reached an altitude of 2,000 m (6,560 ft) with the unloaded Me 321. A fourth take-off was made on 26 August as a practise flight and went off normally.'

At 2010 hrs on 25 August 1941, an Me 321 made an emergency landing west of the Walhalla Straße at the junction to the Hartinger Straße. A Bf 110 had released the towing cable too early, which impacted on a high-tension line at the Ostbahnhof. On 27 August, another Me 321 made an emergency landing south of Harting and suffered damage. On the subject of this emergency landing, Walter Starbati recalled: 'The first test on 27 August 1941 with the container-equipped Me 321 (W3+SK) was to take place, and adequate preparations had been carefully made. Two of the containers were filled, the centre one remaining empty. Take-off was with the aid of eight RATO units, and trim was set at 0°. Right after the take-off run had started, after a distance of about 150 m (500 ft), the port He 111 veered. The other two He 111s nevertheless attempted to continue the take-off. It was only by my pulling the nose up with all my strength that just after reaching the edge of the airfield I rose from the runway. The He 111s were at that point some 10-12 m (33-39 ft) higher than the Me 321. After I had got the Me 321 into the air and attempted slowly to gain height, the starboard He 111 released the tow cable whilst the remaining He 111 broke out to port. It looked as though it was going to crash and I immediately released the tow. Even with a rapid change of trim the Me 321 could not be held, and only with the greatest of effort was I able to right it, and hopefully, to force it to make a smooth landing. I had to circumvent a tree-topped hill and let the aircraft turn away to starboard. That explains the reason why, on impact with the ground, the aircraft executed a 180-degree turn and became damaged.

'On 28 August, another take-off was conducted, when an unloaded Me 321 was towed off. Dipl-Ing. Werner Altrogge from the Erprobungsstelle Rechlin flew the port He 111. But he was unable to remain with the combination and at a height of about 20 m (66 ft) he broke away to port and then disengaged the tow. Trials had shown that the port He 111 was only able to remain in the tow with the greatest of exertions. The risk was too great as a problem-free take-off and tow could not be guaranteed.'

At 1700 hrs on 15 September 1941, a Bf 110 and an Me 321 made an emergency landing near Harting. There were no injuries to the crews, but the Bf 110 suffered 30% damage. On the following day, an Me 321 made an emergency landing near Wolkering.

Walter Starbati remembered: 'On 16 September 1941, another flight test was made from Obertraubling with the He 111s and Me 321. For the continuation of trials, we installed two wing couplings in the Me 321 W6+SF. The take-off that day with four RATO units went off normally, even though an unequal pull between the towing aircraft led the glider to deviate from its take-off direction. With only a small initial speed, it could not be held on course with the rudder. At a height of about 180 m (600 ft), the starboard aircraft veered strongly to the right, but attempted to again come back on course. This was accomplished successfully, but resulted in a

'The first beast is now here!' Me 321 mass production 1941-1943

The huge fin and rudder of the Me 321. (Photo Geisbe)

A view of the front end of the powerful Ju 90 (KB+LA) W.Nr. 900002. Noteworthy are the almost man-sized mainwheels and the rear-view mirror outside the cockpit, by means of which the pilot had visual contact with the towed glider. (Photo Kössler)

This Me 321 A (W1+SN) from the first series built in Leipheim rests on its skids in front of one of the production halls in Obertraubling, where many of these aircraft were to be found. As confirmed in his flight logbook, Unteroffizier Heinz Powilleit flew this aircraft on a mission on 28 September 1941 from Vinnitsa-South airfield to Nikolayev-East. (Photo Schmid).

seemingly strong pull on the starboard wing [of the glider] which was suddenly pulled forward. The port He 111 thus received a strong jerk to the rear and was immediately torn 50 degrees to the left and out of the formation, and had to disengage. I was therefore compelled to release the tow cables that had been coupled to the wing to the left and right. The cable on the left only detached from the main coupling but not, however, from the wing coupling at outer left. Since both wing couplings were operated by a joint coupling, the right cable fell out of the starboard side wing. The 5 cm (2 in)-thick capture-cable broke, and the approximately 20 m (66 ft) long cable slipped out of the wing coupling and wound itself some six to eight times around the tow cable of the towing aircraft and around the cable of the starboard He 111 which, after release of the wing coupling, towed only on the main coupling at outer right. The entanglement of the cable was noticed by the towing aircraft and we all released our cables almost simultaneously.

'In the off-field landing that followed, with the cable hanging beneath the left wing coupling, I destroyed a high-tension cable and as a result, ripped the wing coupling out of the wing, but I landed without any problems or damage. Because of this incident and after checking with the pilots and with Flugkapitän Altrogge, further take-offs with the wing tow method were abandoned. The He 111 trials were continued when Heinkel-Rostock readied a He 111 with the work already done on the outriggers.'

The problems encountered on take-offs with the Me 321 in Obertraubling naturally occurred in front line operations, and Heinz Powilleit reported on his first such experience: 'With the Me 321 W1+SH and the Bf 110 towing trio piloted by Drewes, Freitag and Kandzia, we took off on 17 August 1941 in Jasionka and flew to Hranovka, where our unit was first based. We camped out in the open near to the village. On 5 September, we proceeded further to Vinnitsa-South, where the Me 321 was loaded with 80 canisters each holding 200 litres of petrol. An engineer supervised the loading and the orderly fastening of the canisters. The tailplane incidence angle was also corrected for the load. On 20 September, we were to fly to Nikolayev-East. In order to get into the cockpit, I had to laboriously clamber over the canisters. In this fully-loaded take-off, the starboard cable anchoring broke shortly before lift-off. Although the RATO units had been ignited, I cut the tow connections, whereupon the three Bf 110s were able to ascend unattached. I myself rolled on with my Me 321 and slid further along the ground toward an overhead power line. The power lines ripped apart, and although a mast broke in two, there were no sparks! Thank goodness there was only a power cut. The fastening of the containers held. We were certainly lucky! The Me 321 suffered only minor damage. On 28 September, the 80 canisters were loaded into Me 321 W1+SN and once more, three Bf 110s stood ready for take-off, led this time by Leutnant Szia.

The take-off at 0800 hrs went without a hitch. The towcraft brought us to an altitude of 3,000 m (9,840 ft) and visibility was good. At about 15 km (9 mls) away from our destination I released the tow cables and after a flying distance of 310 km (193 mls), we landed safely at 0950 hrs at Nikolayev-East. On the following day we returned to Vinnitsa. After some 190 km (118 mls), the starboard cable fastening again broke and I had to release the tow. I was able to make a smooth landing near to a small village by the name of Krivoye Osero. On 5 October, we were then able to be towed back by the Ju 90 (KB+LA) to Vinnitsa. During that time, we became familiar with the simple life of the Ukrainian peasants. The populace were friendly towards us and took good care of us. The only thing that caused us problems were the lice. In Vinnitsa, the bad weather slowly made itself felt. At first, the entire airfield became a morass, and then came the first frost. In December we relocated to Posen, where we went into quarantine and were thoroughly de-loused. This was followed by Christmas leave.'

In Obertraubling meanwhile, acceptance flights continued, but not without mishaps. At 1800 hrs on 19 September 1941, an Me 321 crashed on Obertraubling airfield, and the aircraft was 80% destroyed. An emergency landing was made by a Bf 110 of the Tow Detachment near Diesenhofen, in which the pilot, Unteroffizier Lohmann, was heavily injured and the aircraft 90% destroyed. The Me 321s that had made off-field landings on 17 September at Burgweinting, the one on 18 September at Langenerling and the one on 22 September at Wolkering, were each towed back to Obertraubling by Flugkapitän Gymnich who piloted the Ju 90 KB+LA.

Trials with the He 111 as a towcraft for the Me 321 were resumed at Obertraubling on 28 September 1941, but this time only two He 111s towed the glider. Walter Starbati recalls: 'Take-off took place with four RATO units and passed off normally. At a height of some 150 m (490 ft), the starboard aircraft veered inwards and with its wing, touched the He 111 alongside on its fuselage and tailplane. After that, both pilots released their tow cables, whereupon I released the cables from the glider. The off-field landing that followed went off smoothly. The Me 321 was probably capable of being transported back to Wolkering, where quite nearby, I was to take off with a Me 321 that had recently made an off-field landing. The take-off stretch was still in good condition, so that a lift-off was therefore possible. The reason for this was as follows: in throttling back from take-off to cruising power, the aircraft mechanic had set the propeller revs at unequal speeds. The starboard engine thus had too much power and the leading aircraft had turned to port. When the towing cable made contact, the taiplane of the starboard He 111 became damaged and had to be replaced. Acceptance trials with two He 111s were pursued further.'

At 1203 hrs on 9 November 1941, a Bf 110 and a Me 321 made an emergency landing at Harting. Three days later, a successful attempt was made to land an Me 321 with the aid of a brake parachute at the airfield. On ferry flights, one Me 321 made an emergency landing at Monheim, another between Neuburg/Danube and Öttingen, and a further machine at Nördlingen. On 7 December, five storm damaged Me 321s at Obertraubling tore away from their moorings. A working party of 120 soldiers was eventually able, with great effort, to properly re-anchor the aircraft.

In the afternoon of 10 December 1941, take-off preparations were begun at Obertraubling for the ferry flight of Me 321 W4+SB to Leipheim. The aircraft was loaded with only a crate of ballast. The towcraft was to be the Ju 90 KB+LA piloted by the very experienced Flugkapitän Gymnich. The Me 321 crew with Feldwebel Riek as pilot, accompanied by Halbig and Walz, climbed aboard W4+SB which had been parked in front of the 100 m (328 ft)-long Halle 5 and once more checked out the aircraft. Two RATO units that were to have been dropped by parachute after take-off were hung beneath the wings. A towing vehicle then rolled in front of the Me 321 and slowly towed it to the eastern end of the runway. Gymnich and Riek both contacted the airfield control tower and obtained the latest weather forecast data. Weather conditions for the prospective flight were anything other than ideal. A strong west wind was blowing over the countryside with gusts up to Strength 8, in addition to some scattered rain showers. The cloudbase lay at around 1,000 m (3,280 ft). It would certainly be no easy task as the Ju 90 would have to perform sterling work to get the glider over to Leipheim. Above all, Feldwebel Riek in the Me 321 would have a strenuous flight ahead of him, for the glider's controls could only be moved in such weather with very great effort. Gymnich boarded the Ju 90 parked in front of the control tower and started the first engine. After all four engines had run up and the oil and temperature gauges had reached their usual values, he released the brakes and rolled down the runway. The Ju 90 taxied to some 100 metres in front of the Me 321 in the direction of take-off, the 120 m (394 ft)-long towing cable was attached to both aircraft and the ground crew gave the starting signal. The Ju 90 rolled carefully forward and the tow cable became taut. There now began a flight that was to end in catastrophy. Gymnich brought all four engines to full throttle, so that the Ju 90 vibrated all over. Its brakes were released and the towing cable began to move. At that moment, Riek ignited the RATO units which burned for 30 seconds. It must have been an imposing sight when the Ju 90 lifted off at 1337 hrs with the thundering rocket-assisted Me 321 behind it. Take-off was accomplished without any problem, and after the Me 321 had jettisoned its rockets, the Ju 90 took up a 250-degree course and climbed to around 450 m (1,475 ft) altitude. As was to be expected, the combination progressed only slowly as conditions were very gusty. Both aircraft were thoroughly shaken about and bobbed up and down. An important navigational point on the route was the Befreiungshalle (Liberation Hall) and Gymnich steered precisely over it. The time was 1345 hrs. The combination was about 1 km ahead of Kelheim when hefty gusts once more rattled through the frames of both aircraft. According to the Ju 90 crew, the Me 321 suddenly made a rolling movement and then nosed steeply downwards. None of the crew succeeded in baling out. The glider impacted in the forest behind the foresters' school in Goldberg. Only a few seconds later, it would have been in the middle of Kelheim and would have crashed into the town, with conceivably catastrophic results. After the towing cable snapped, the Ju 90 turned about to the Befreiungshalle and in the direction of Regensburg, flew over the Me 321 crash site that had killed all on board. At 1359 hrs, Gymnich

Above left: On 27 October 1941, the Ju 90 V7 (GF+GH) piloted by Flugkapitän Pancherz became available as a towcraft for the Me 321 at Obertraubling. Whereas the Ju 90 has started to retract its mainwheels, the Me 321 is following along behind it with its four RATO units in operation. In the background is the Flight Control building, in front of which are three He 111s and at least nine Me 321s. (Photo EADS)

A Me 321 being towed by the Ju 90. (Photo Müller-Romminger)

touched down at Obertraubling and an hour later stood at the scene of the crash, where soldiers from the Fliegerhorst immediately cordoned everything off.

Ulrich Huber of Ihrlerstein recalled the crash: 'It was in the early afternoon of 10 December 1941. I had already left school and was at home when I became aware of the typical sound of aircraft engines. I had always had a great interest in aircraft and was quite familiar with almost all types. I immediately ran out of the house in the direction of Brand. From there, I had a very good all-round view of the Danube and Altmühl valleys. To the [north]-east, in the direction of Regensburg, I could make out a large four-engined aircraft that was towing a large glider. Since a strong west wind was blowing, the tow combination made slow progress. At a height of around 500 m (1,640 m), they approached Kelheim. I had sufficient time to be able to observe the impressive size of these aircraft. From the sound of the engines, they were running at full power. Despite the hefty wind, both aircraft appeared to be peacefully on their way towards the [south]-west. Shortly before Kelheim, the aircraft had almost reached the spot where I was, when movement suddenly appeared in the tow. The Me 321 began to oscillate like a ship in a storm and I could hear the towing cable snap. The glider immediately went into a dive and the four-engined aircraft literally shot on ahead as if released from a heavy load, but the Me 321 continued to dive at an ever steeper angle. Everything happened so very quickly and only lasted a few seconds. If the towing cable had snapped a little later, the glider would have crashed into the town… The Me 321 had crashed in the forest behind the foresters' school on the Goldberg. No parachutes were to be seen and all of the crew of the Me 321 must have perished. I immediatly set off from Ihrlerstein across the fields to the crash site. It was a picture of destruction, for the Me 321 was totally shattered on impact and a deathly silence reigned over the forest. Three bodies were later recovered. It was about an hour after the crash when the crew of the four-engined aircraft and numerous other soldiers arrived. All civilians had to leave the site. For me, the whole event had a sequel. On scouting for the crash site, I ruined my new shoes. What it meant in wartime to obtain new shoes, one just cannot imagine today. Anyway, the greeting I got at home from my mother was a corresponding one.'

Josef Wagner of Kelheimwinzer, at that time 14 years old, also recalled: 'That afternoon my brother and I became aware of the droning of hardworking aircraft engines. We looked in a northerly direction towards the Winzer heights, when a large four-engined aircraft appeared that was towing an even bigger aircraft… The engine noise of the towing aircraft was so loud - a loudness that I had never until then heard from an aircraft. We observed them from behind to the left, and despite the growling engine noise, we could hear how the towing cable snapped like the crack of a whip. The glider first put its nose up briefly and then dived to the ground in a rolling movement over its right wing. With an enormous noise the aircraft impacted above the Winzer heights into the forest. My brother and I immediately ran to the crash site and met up with the first people [who had got there]. Two crew were still in the aircraft, but showed no sign of life. A third crew member, also lifeless, lay about 10 metres away from the aircraft, on the floor of the forest. A half hour later, the police appeared, and after a further half hour, the first military personnel appeared and cordoned off the whole area. All civilians were ordered to leave the crash site, as the area was declared a military zone.'

In the winter of 1941-42, about 50 flight-cleared Me 321s stood at Leipheim and Obertraubling ready to be collected. To protect the aircraft from the weather, protective roofing was intended to be built. Except for the erection of a few initial roofs, the project failed due to the lack of materials and manpower just as much as the intention to tow Me 321s to France, because the Bf 110 towcraft had been put to other uses by the Luftwaffe. The elevators and flaps of all the parked Me 321s had been removed and stored inside the aircraft. Up until 3 February 1942, only four protective roofs had been completed. Eleven others were in a more or less advanced state of construction. Luftwaffe personnel carried out necessary repairs to the parked Me 321s in the spring of 1942 so that these could be cleared for flight once more. On Christmas Day 1941, several Me 321s were damaged in a storm at Obertraubling.

In the meantime, the Sonderstaffeln (GS) 1, 2, 4 and 22 had been established. These units each had 5 Me 321s and 12 to 15 Bf 110s as towcraft. In addition to that, there were sufficient personnel to manage the RATO units, special vehicles and ground instruments. In view of the war situation in 1941-42, an extremely large outlay in terms of personnel and materials was employed to bring the Me 321 to a state of operational readiness. On a few critical battlefronts in the East, some successes

NEST OF EAGLES

From April 1942, the first He 111 Z (Zwilling - 'twins') became available as air tugs for the Me 321. Only 12 examples of the He 111 Z were built, which consisted of two He 111 H-6s joined by a centre section having a fifth engine. Powered by five Jumo 211 F motors delivering a total of 6,700 hp, it was capable of towing off a fully-loaded Me 321 without problem. To increase towing range, it could be fitted with two 900-litre underwing droptanks. Seen here are two He 111 Zs parked in front of the Flight Control building at Obertraubling. (Photo Hübsch)

The crew of an He 111 Z tug snatch an opportunity for a rest in between flights. (Photo Geisbe)

Unteroffizier Karl Geisbe at the controls of an Me 321. Note the chain drive which operated the ailerons. (Photo Geisbe)

were achieved with the Me 321 supplying ground forces with urgently-needed supplies and fuel. In the long term, however, in view of the ever-worsening war situation, this type of effort could hardly be maintained. A suitable towcraft only first became available in April 1942 with the He 111 Z. On 13 April 1942, the day that the first take-off of a He 111 Z ('Zwilling') tug and Me 321 in tow took place at Obertraubling, production of the Me 321 in Leipheim and Obertraubling, was terminated. A total of 175 machines had been built. With the arrival of the He 111 Z, Sonderstaffel (GS) 3 was additionally established.

In October 1942, a number of Me 321s were ferried from Obertraubling to Leipheim including W6+SJ, W6+SU, W6+SW, W6+SX, W6+SZ and W8+SS. Further aircraft were ferried from Obertraubling to Dijon in France in November.

A barbaric act of another kind took place on 23 October 1942. Three Russian PoWs were caught stealing some cabbages. The guards immediately opened fire and two of the PoWs were shot on the spot. The third PoW survived heavily wounded.

Unteroffizier Karl Geisbe recalled another misadventure with an Me 321: 'Towed by a He 111 Z, on 30 October 1942 we took-off at 1747 hrs in the Me 321 (W6+SP) from Obertraubling on a ferry flight to Lechfeld. It was agreed that we would fly at 400 m (1,310 ft). The take-off went off well. After jettisoning the undercarriage and making a circuit of the airfield, we headed in a westerly direction. A short while later, the He 111 Z suddenly waggled its wings and released the towline - and that, at a height of only 200 m (660 ft). *Damn it*, I thought, *this can't be true*; we were already west of the Regensburg-Munich railway line. There remained no time to ponder it. I made a quick decision: back to the airfield. I began a circle to port and descended ever more steeply towards the Fliegerhorst. I very soon came to realize that we would not make it to the airfield. However, I wanted to pass over the railtracks, as this would certainly ease bringing back the Me 321 to the airfield. On flying low over the tracks, we saw a shocked railway-crossing signalman who hastily fled from his post. We were already pretty low; our height was at the most 10 m (33 ft). Ahead of the railtrack I again rose up and flew over it. Suddenly, a terrible crack was felt at the rear, but I was able to subsequently land the aircraft on an adjacent open field. What had happened? We had flown so low that we had caught the overhead railway cabling with our tailskid and had rent the power line. The Me 321 suffered slight damage to the tailplane. At 1805 hrs, we were on the ground once more.'

According to the Daily War Diary, on 27 December 1942 – a Sunday, the next total loss of a Me 321 occurred at Obertraubling. Unteroffizier Helmut Sachse crashed in one in a landing approach between Harting and the runway. The landing was supposed to be a point-target one using the brake parachute to shorten the landing run. Helmut Sachse, Detlef Willekins and a further crew member were killed in the crash. Unteroffizier Helmut Scholz recalled: 'I shall never forget that on this third day of Christmas 1942 flying was ordered by Leutnant Knippel. Everything was covered in deep snow, with a clear blue sky. We wished that the Leutnant would be plagued by the pest. For the take-off, my friend Helmut Sachse came with the order to carry out a point-landing with a Me 321 using the brake chute. I got on board, but our Leutnant Knippel caught me doing so and said: 'Scholz, you have flown already.' There remained nothing else for me to do than to leave the aircraft again. That, however, saved my life. The Me 321 was towed by a He 111 Z. The take-off was successful, and at about 600 m (1,970 ft) over the airfield, the glider was released. Helmut Sachse went over into the landing approach; he turned far to the west and then flew heading east towards the airfield. At about 600 m away from it and at a height of some 180 m (590 ft), he streamed the brake chute. I was standing opposite Flight Control with a view to the Walhalla and observed Sachse making his landing approach. Suddenly, I was able to recognise from the starboard landing flap, how at first came a small, then gradually increasing, element detached itself and struck the tailplane. Only fractions of a second later, the tailplane broke away and the Me 321 dived to the ground. It was all over: there was no chance of survival! I stood as if struck by lightning, incapable of any reaction. How could such a thing happen? The way I figured, there were only three possibilities. Either the maximum permissible speed for letting down the flaps had been exceeded, or it was due to material failure, or sabotage. Hardly had the snow and dust clouds settled over the crash site, when we rushed over in the hope that we could render assistance to our comrades, but we were only able to retrieve them as dead bodies.'

Hermann Vilsmeier of Obertraubling witnessed the accident at close quarters: 'On Sundays and days of rest, we children always had to accompany our parents for a walk. On 26 or 27 December 1942, we went to the Walhalla Allee in the direction of the Fliegerhorst. On this day, there was bright and fine winter weather and the countryside was covered in a thick layer of snow. We had roughly reached the area of the Allee where all the trees had been cut down, when we saw an Me 321 coming from Regensburg flying in our direction. The aircraft entered the landing approach-path somewhat steeply and was only about 150 m (490 ft) up when a brake chute streamed out. Hardly had it opened when something on the aircraft broke off. The Me 321 then dived steeply downwards and impacted about 400 m (1,310 ft) in front of the airfield. It did not take long before several soldiers came running up in an attempt to rescue their comrades. Later on, we learned that all three of the crew had perished.'

At the beginning of January 1943, the situation for the 6. Armee in Stalingrad took a dramatic turn.

Gigant pilots from left: Karl Geisbe and Rockstroh, and from the right: Heinz Powilleit and Fritz Hübsch. (Photo Geisbe)

Despite its superior engine power, the He 111 Z was frequently taxed to the limits of its capabilities. Here engine No. 1 is filled with engine oil from a bowser. In the foreground is a crane mounted on an Opel Blitz 3-tonne truck; two such vehicles – used by field workshop and airfield operating detachments – could lift an Me 321 so that it could be heaved onto its wheeled undercarriage. (Photo Hübsch)

A Me 321 in tow by a He 111 Z. (Photo Geisbe)

NEST OF EAGLES

The end of the first Obertraubling-built Me 321 (W2+SA). After the Bf 110 towcraft crashed during take-off in Orsha, the glider suffered damage when it hit the anti-shrapnel protective wall of an aircraft revetment. Note the Walter RATO units still hanging beneath the wings. (Photo Hübsch)

A view from the cockpit of a two-seater Me 321 B of a He 111 Z towcraft. Both pilots have a firm grip on the steering wheel, with which the ailerons were operated. (Photo Hübsch)

A He 111 Z, TM+KU, in 1942/43 winter camouflage. (Photo Geisbe)

This He 111 Z is also finished in a winter camouflage, rather tarnished here, for its use on the Eastern Front. On flights at the front line, the aircraft carried armament, as seen here, with a 20 mm MG/FF-M in the nearest cockpit. (Photo Hübsch)

Surrounded by the Russians, cut off and without sufficient supplies, the half-starved soldiers could no longer put up any resistance. However, for the Stalingrad operation, a number of Me 321s had stood ready at the Fliegerhorsts in Regensburg, Obertraubling, and in Lechfeld. Already on 12 January, two Me 321s had been towed to Stalino as a forward unit; two more followed on the 22nd, and on the 24th, five He 111 Zs returned from the Eastern Front and landed at Obertraubling in order that further Me 321s could carry supplies from Stalingrad via Jasionka and Zhitomir to Stalino. This concentrated transport capacity, however, arrived too late at the Front, for the great misery had already begun at Stalingrad, and the weather had turned so bad that no more flights could be made. Fritz Hübsch recalled his flights with the Me 321 in 1943: 'On 10 January 1943, I piloted Me 321 (W8+SK) in tow behind a He 111 Z on an extremely risky mission from Lechfeld to Stalingrad. Loaded with 20 tonnes (44,090 lb) of supplies, the journey covered over 1,000 km (621 mls) to Minsk and from there to Zhitomir. Because of bad weather, we could not fly on to Stalingrad. By the time the weather improved, the battle for Stalingrad was over - in some ways fortunately, otherwise for my crew and myself it would certainly have been a flight with no return. But one crisis after another followed in the East and the Russians exerted immense pressure on the southern sector of our Front. After Stalingrad, they thrust further forward and occupied Rostov on Lake Azov. In doing so, they cut off the German troops who had to pull out of the Caucasus. Those troops that did not escape at Rostov now sat firmly in the Kuban bridgehead, crying out for supplies, and hoped to be rescued.

'We relocated further, to the Crimea, to be exact, to the Kertsch peninsula to provide supplies to the Kuban bridgehead. On the outbound flight, we transported everything that the troops needed there - even hay for the horses of the mountain troops who had fought their way back out of the Caucasus right up to the Kuban. On the return flight we as a rule carried wounded soldiers, and up to 80 men could be transported in the Me 321. At the bridgehead, more and more exhausted German troops continued to pile up, desperately attempting to defend themselves against the stubborn and oppressive enemy. We even flew in the worst weather conditions, for we knew that our Army comrades urgently needed supplies in order to be able to withstand the Russian pressure. For this purpose, the aircraft were loaded to the limits of their performance.

'I came to feel this load in the true sense of the word, on my own body. We had already flown a number of missions partly under fire from the Russians in the Kuban bridgehead and relocated via Saki back to Zhitomir, where my Me 321 was loaded with 50 oil and fuel containers and was to take-off for Kertsch. We were towed by a He 111 Z and had not even jettisoned the undercarriage, when it happened at a height of 10 m (33 ft) or so. The starboard aileron broke off and flew away. Everything then happened like lightning - the Me 321 dipped downwards over its starboard wing and could not be held any longer. The wing rammed into the ground; my co-pilot and I, complete with our seatbelts, were catapulted out of the cockpit and we wound up in the snow. Other than scrapes and bruises, we suffered no earnest injuries, although for over a week I felt pain to every bone in my body. Our aircraft mechanic, however, who was in the freight compartment and responsible for jettisoning the two nosewheels, had no chance. He was hit by the containers and his lifeless body was retrieved

A fine view of a Fw 200 C-3 of KG 40 at Obertraubling in January 1943. Above it, a He 111 Zwilling is towing two Go 242s. (Photo BA Koblenz 272/2584/31)

The same Fw 200 has unloaded its passengers at Obertraubling. A few of these aircraft were used on supply missions to the 6. Armee in Stalingrad. (Photo BA 272/2584/26)

from the wreckage. Why the aileron flew away, was something that could no longer be determined. For me, only three things could possibly have been the cause. It was either material fatigue as a result of being overstressed, a bad welding joint on one of the aileron supports, or damage due to enemy fire that had not been suspected to exist.'

A surviving Flying Order (see Appendix 12), documents a flight made on 12 January 1943 by Sonderstaffel (GS) 4 with Me 321 W8+SV from Obertraubling via Jasionka and Zhitomir-South to Stalino. The tug was a He 111 Z and the Me 321 pilot was Unteroffizier Geisbe, who later recorded: 'The aircraft that I was originally scheduled to fly, I ferried over from Öttingen to Obertraubling. On arrival there, Leutnant Sachsenhauser asked me what this giant was like to fly, and I said to him that up to now, it was the best Me 321 that I had flown. I thereupon had to relinquish the aircraft to Sachsenhauser. After it was loaded, it was this Me 321 that was rammed by a He 111 and went up in flames. I was then assigned W8+SV which was loaded with equipment that was necessary for Me 321 flying operations on the Eastern Front: undercarriages, ramps, RATO units, etc. In tow behind a He 111 Z, we took off at 1145 hrs from Obertraubling. We flew for some 90 minutes without any view of the ground. On reaching the Riesengebirge area, we were able to see the ground again and flew alongside a multi-track railway stretch towards Krakau. Without any visible reason, the He 111 Z deviated some 15 degrees off course to the north-east. By waving continually, we tried to make the radio operator aware of the course deviation. I thereupon swerved several times sharply to port in order to turn the He 111 Z to starboard and bring it back on course. The pilot in it, however, showed no reaction at all, and we thought to ourselves: "Are they all asleep?"

'Through continuous flight in a slight climb, we came to around 2,200 m (7,220 ft). It must have been in the neighbourhood of Kamienz when signs of life set in ahead of us. The crew had apparently become aware that they were off course. They turned their crate onto the opposite course and with ever increasing speed we started to descend so much so that we became anxious and alarmed. I had the feeling that they flew so fast in order to force us to release the towing cable. My comrade Brixa was of the opinion that the Heinkel would now tow us to Gleiwitz. It now began to get darker. At about 150 m altitude, we flew over a small town that had a railway station and banked over a high water tower. After flying over the little town a second time, the towline was released. Thanks to the high speed, by flying an opposite course we were able to reach the perimeter of the town. We broke two telephone poles before we set down on the snow. On gliding to a stop, the forward port skid hit a large rock. The aircraft was turned sideways by 30 degrees and the fuselage fabric

105

NEST OF EAGLES

Two photographs of Me 321 B, W6+SW, in factory-fresh winter camouflage, being loaded at Obertraubling for a mission to Stalingrad in January 1943. Note the non-winter camouflaged Me 321 in the photograph lower right. (Photo BA Koblenz 372/2584/20 and Koblenz 372/2548/27)

Messerschmitt Me 321 B, W6+SW, Obertraubling, January 1943

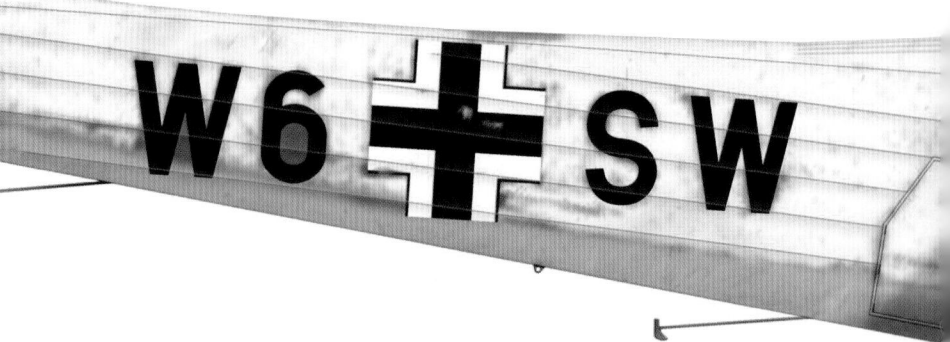

'The first beast is now here!' Me 321 mass production 1941-1943

The take-off position of Me 321, W8+SV, in winter camouflage with its He 111 Z tug photographed on 10 January 1943 for the flight from Obertraubling to Stalino. Due to bad weather, the mission to Stalingrad could not be carried out. This view gives great scale to the large wingspan of these gliders. (Photo Powilleit)

was ripped apart. Heavily damaged, the Me 321 came to a standstill in the deeply snowed-in landscape near Tarnowitz and had to be scrapped. The He 111 Z landed some 1,000 m (3,280 ft) to the side of us in deep snow. After it was refuelled, it took-off for Posen. On landing, it broke an undercarriage leg.

'On looking back, I must say that flying those giants called for an enormous amount of effort, but only brought little success. All the measures taken for the support of Stalingrad came too late, as our higher-ups should have started it all at least four weeks earlier. The reasons for the meagre success with the Me 321 were multifarious. For towing, for example, we needed experienced pilots and not those who had just come straight from training school and had only mastered

The remains of an Me 321 in which Fritz Hübsch crashed at Zhitomir in 1943. The undercarriage wheels are recognizable in the wreckage. (Photo Hübsch)

NEST OF EAGLES

Me 321 B W8+SK at Zhitomir in January 1943. Noteworthy in this photograph is that the winter camouflage has not been applied to the fuselage sides. (Photo Hübsch)

flying in a straight line. They were many young Leutnants who imagined that they had invented flying, and didn't believe anything we old hands told them. To my satisfaction, I experienced one who became rather meek after he forgot to lock the cockpit hood of his Me 110, which flew away during the take-off and shattered his radio mast. Quite shocked, he disengaged the tow line, his aircraft veered off to the side and came to a standstill with a broken undercarriage. The take-off of the entire combination was thus a failure, since I disengaged the towlines to the other two towcraft and just about came to a stop at the edge of the airfield. When he thereafter asked me how much I had been able to observe, I described my observations to him and remarked that I would not make any report on the matter.

'A further mission took place on 26 January 1943 with Me 321, W6+ST, piloted by Unteroffizier Geisbe, with Gefreiter Michels as second pilot. Take-off was at 1030 hrs behind a He 111 Z from the wintry Obertraubling Fliegerhorst, with landing at 1405 hrs in Jasionka. On 28 January, a further relocation took place towards the Front. The day ended with a take-off at Jasionka at 0830 hrs and a smooth landing at Zhitomir at 1110 hrs. On the next day, we flew on in the direction of Stalino. The runway in Zhitomir was covered in thick snow, and parallel to it lay a high wall of snow. Under these ground conditions, it was very difficult for the He 111 Z to gain momentum. At the end of the runway, a strong side wind made us fly at an angle. At a height of some 5 m (16.5 ft) from the ground, the undercarriage smashed into the tailplane and damaged it heavily. The radioman in the Heinkel had seen this and immediately disengaged the tow. At a height of 2 to 3 metres and lower, and at low speed, the Me 321 turned with the wind into a sloping valley with no possibility of landing. We smashed head-on into a strong wooden mast which we could not avoid, and from the force of the impact, the nose loading doors were wrenched off. Snow was rammed into the fuselage and brought it to a standstill at the edge of a village. On becoming aware in Obertraubling of our flight orders, we immediately had misgivings about Obergefreiter Schöchle being assigned to our crew and tasked to jettison the undercarriage, as he was unsuitable to perform this duty. He was an ass who could not be taken seriously and in the Staffel, served only as a dogsbody for the officers. The responsibility for this accident lay clearly with our superiors.'

The next step was motorizing the giants. At least 68 Me 321s underwent final assembly and acceptance flying at Obertraubling. Some of these found themselves in operation at focal points on the Eastern Front. For full details of Me 321s produced at Obertraubling and their various subsequent locations, see Appendix 12.

Me 321 W6+ST seen after making an emergency landing in a Russian village. The undercarriage was jettisoned too early on take-off and struck the tailplane, so that the entire empennage surfaces twisted. (Photo Geisbe)

A Gotha Go 242, a smaller sister to the Me 321, on its landing approach. A ferry flight was made on 4 March 1942 by the Ju 90 (KB+LA) that towed two Go 242s from Obertraubling to Langendiebach. (Photo Geisbe)

An Opel Blitz 3-tonne truck behind a Go 242. The Me 321 could carry with ease two of these trucks. (Photo Geisbe)

108

CHAPTER 9

The Me 163 B at Obertraubling: 1942-1944

FROM 1 January 1942, the Fliegerhorst Obertraubling was officially taken over by Messerschmitt GmbH Regensburg from Messerschmitt AG Augsburg. From June 1942, Obertraubling belonged to the Fürth airfield region. Since the Messerschmitt-Werke had taken over the Fliegerhorst, the Obertraubling airfield Garrison HQ was reduced to the status of a simple Airfield Detachment. A further Special Detachment was established there in 1942. Erprobungskommando (EK) 16, led by Hauptmann Wolfgang Späte and Oberleutnant Rudolf Opitz, tested the world's first - and to date, only operational – rocket-powered interceptor at the base. Some civilian test pilots engaged in this activity including Hanna Reitsch and Heini Dittmar.

The Me 163 was the first aircraft in aviation history to exceed a speed of 1,000 km/h (621 mph) in level flight. This took place on 2 October 1941, when Heini Dittmar took off on his record flight from Peenemünde-West. However, this hitherto unattained speed record was kept secret throughout the war. Its designer, Alexander Lippisch, had for years designed and built tailless aircraft with remarkable flying characteristics. To preserve secrecy, it was designated 'Me 163', although Prof. Messerschmitt played no part in its design. As the type number had originally been accorded to the Bf 163 that had been designed to meet the same RLM specification (of which three prototypes, the Bf 163 V1 to V3, had been ordered for trials) and resulted in the competitive Fieseler Fi 156 Storch short take-off and landing communications aircraft winning the competition, the first prototype Me 163 A was therefore designated the V4 (KE+SW). When Lippisch and his team of specialists left the DFS and joined Messerschmitt on 2 January 1939, preparations were made at Abteilung L (for Lippisch) for series production to be undertaken in Augsburg and Regensburg.

Whereas the unarmed Me 163 A was used for training purposes, the armed Me 163 B version climbed to its interception altitude of 12,000 m (39,370 ft) in 3.45 minutes, and after firing at its bomber targets, landed in gliding flight with empty fuel tanks on its hydraulically-sprung extended fuselage skid. Because of its limited range and lack of protection from attack by enemy fighters during the landing phase, another circuit of the airfield was not possible, and in view of the overall effort involved, its successes against American bomber formations was very low. From the technical aspect, however, it represented a milestone in aviation history. The pilots who flew the aircraft on operations deserved the highest respect, as each flight in it was akin to riding a bomb. The two components of its propellants, codenamed T-Stoff (80%-strength hydrogen peroxide) and C-Stoff (a mixture of 57% hydrazine hydrate, 30% methanol and 13% water), ignited spontaneously on contact with each other in the rocket combustion chamber. T-Stoff would decompose all organic materials, including a pilot, who would wear a special flying suit made of PVC and at take-off, he breathed oxygen beneath enclosing protective headgear. The pilot sat between two T-Stoff tanks in the cockpit, and at the slightest leakage, would have had to exit the aircraft or else would have suffered extensive injuries were it not for his protective clothing and oxygen supply. Accidents were a common everyday occurrence at Obertraubling, where on occasion a fully-fuelled aircraft exploded on take-off, or propellant residue in the fuel tanks either exploded on an aircraft setting down too hard on its landing skid, or because an aircraft mechanic had inadvertantly filled both propellants into the same collector tank which led to immediate explosive combustion. To avoid the latter circumstance, the propellant tanks were later distinguished by being marked in different colours. Also, if the aircraft happened to overturn on landing, the pilot was likely to become dissolved by leaking T-Stoff. The Me 163 B, however, entered operational service only in mid-1944, at a time when the Allies already held air

NEST OF EAGLES

Me 163 BV2, VD-EL, was produced by Messerschmitt GmbH at Regensburg and assembled at Obertraubling. It was afterwards sent to Augsburg for the installation of guns and radio equipment. Note the fairing over the rocket exhaust, black patch on rudder and tail skid. In September 1942, Dittmar proposed raising the tail of the Me 163 to improve the aircraft's attitude on take off by increasing the height of the rear fuselage structure below the rocket nozzle. This modification was successfully tested on BV1, which was produced at Augsburg. These photographs of BV2 were taken at Augsburg in September before four 20 mm MG 151 machine guns had been installed, two in the wing roots and two in gondolas to the underside of the wing. The guns were fired for the first time at Augsburg on 6 October 1942. (Stephen Ransom)

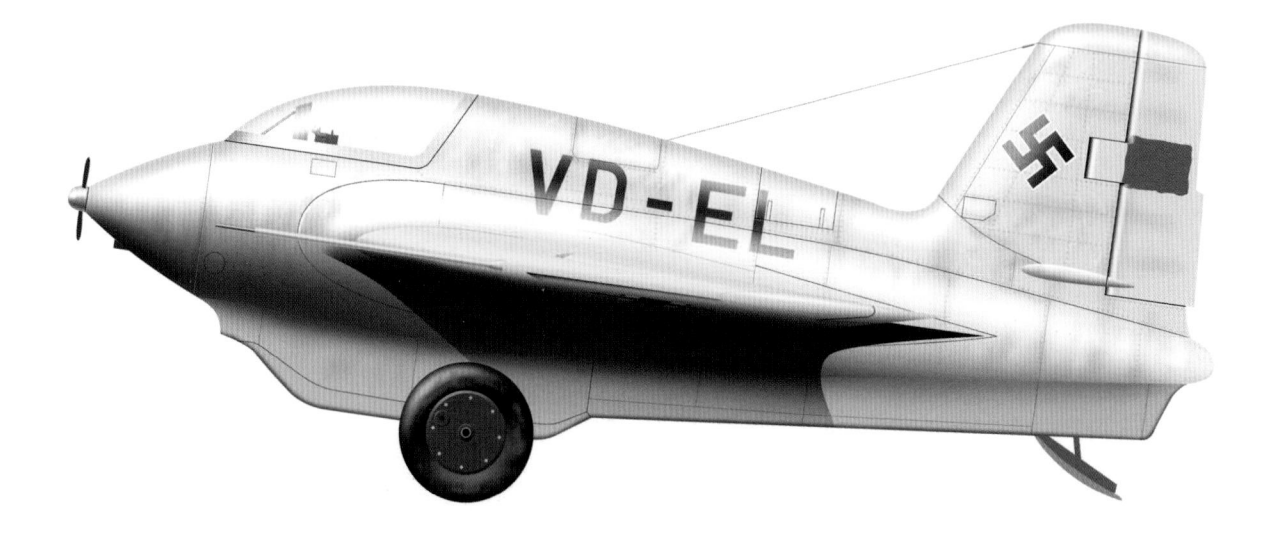

Messerschmitt Me 163 BV2, VD+EL, W.Nr. 163 100 11, Messerschmitt AG, Lechfeld, October 1942

supremacy over the Reich and as a result, it was of little military use.

At the beginning of April 1942, a team from Abteilung L installed itself in three buildings in the north-east section of the plant grounds in Prüfening. Entry to this area of the works was permitted only with special identification, and series manufacture of the Me 163 B commenced with the necessary tooling, jigs and works installations for the fuselage and fin and rudder. It was here that the Me 163 B V2 to V4 underwent final assembly, the V2 having been test-flown under tow as a glider on 4 and 5 August 1942 from

Obertraubling. On the latter date, the V2 was ferried at 1625 hrs from Obertraubling to Augsburg.

Final assembly of the Me 163 B V5 and acceptance flights, conducted at Obertraubling, necessitated additional personnel – 15 production checkers, 6 work preparers, 10 construction jig fitters and 300 workers for final assembly. Within the scope of the RLM production programme, 66 Me 163 Bs were to have been built in 1942, but due to continual design changes, only 8 airframes were completed that year. The wooden wings were manufactured by a plant in Zeulenroda, and in a Works examination of the first 70 airframes, 2 mm of play was established in the main bolts of the wing attachment joints. At high speeds, this could have led to wing breakage. Even the V5 prototype flown by Flugkapitän Hanna Reitsch had this impermissably high play in the wings. Fortunately for her, because the undercarriage dolly did not jettison on her last flight with it, it did not attain high speed, and it was only through an enormous amount of effort that this error was able to be eliminated. A further problem was caused by the Plexiglas canopy which developed flaws and distortions, and it was only when the glass thickness was reduced from 8 mm to 6 mm that these provided undistorted vision. In January 1943 alone, Me 163 production was six aircraft less than planned. As a result of further structural alterations, for example to the skid hydraulics, not a single airframe was delivered during the following month. In all, Me 163 Bs delivered in 1943 from Obertraubling totalled 62 aircraft.

Since the Walter 109-509A 'hot' rocket motor was not yet available for the Me 163 B V5, it was towed aloft by a Bf 110 piloted by Kurt Opitz, accompanied by Werkmeister Willy Elias who sat in the rear cockpit in the Bf 110. On 30 October 1942, Reitsch made her fifth flight in the V5 which had been fully equipped with two 20 mm MG 151 cannon with 80 rounds per gun, radio aids and the Revi 16 B gunsight. After lift-off Reitsch wanted to release the two-wheel undercarriage dolly at a height of some 8 m (26 ft) above the runway, but noticed that something was not in order. The entire aircraft hummed and vibrated noticeably as if a strong vortex was the cause. From below, she saw red signal flares climbing towards her. She tried to establish contact with the Bf 110 through the head microphone but was unsuccessful. Instead, she saw an excited Elias waving with a white cloth, whilst the towcraft began to repeatedly extend and retract its own main undercarriage, clearly indicating that the fault lay with her own dolly. The Bf 110 made a number of circuits of the airfield with her still in tow. Her sole wish was to gain sufficient height so as to release the towline and check whether the Me 163 could be steered without danger. But since the tow connection did not release, Opitz realized what she wanted to do and took her up as far as the cloudbase allowed. At 3,500 m (11,500 ft), she disengaged the towline and attempted with abrupt movements to shake off the dolly. Continual vibrations, however, made her aware that it still hung in place, so that she tried to ascertain whether the aircraft was undamaged and remained fully controllable. As no test pilot likes to abandon a valuable aircraft as long as the slenderest chance exists of bringing it down to earth safely, she descended, as planned, to a height of 80 m (260 ft), where she intended to sideslip onto the edge of the airfield. But despite sufficient airspeed, the aircraft suddenly sank and no longer reacted to any control movements, especially the rudder, which lay in the region of turbulence caused by the suspended dolly. It all happened so suddenly that little time remained for further exertions, and compressing her body as much as possible, braced herself for the crash-landing in a ploughed field. On impact, she was accelerated forwards and hit her head against the Revi 16 B. When the aircraft stopped, she automatically raised her right hand and ejected the undamaged canopy. She carefully felt herself all over with her other hand, and established that she was still in one piece and able to move her limbs. The feeling was one of numbness but without pain. But all at once, she became aware of streaming blood, and when her fingers touched her face, where there would normally have been her nose, there was only a wide open cleft, and her nostrils formed bloody bubbles on breathing. She held her head quite still, otherwise she would have had a blackout, and from a pocket, took out paper and pencil to record the cause and circumstances of the crash. She held a handerkerchief in front of her nose to prevent her badly injured face from being seen by her rescuers. The aircraft itself was only slightly damaged. On arrival, Elias lifted her carefully out of the cockpit, but she refused to be taken to the airfield by ambulance and under her own efforts, accompanied by the others, made her way to the Fliegerhorst sickbay to have her injuries bandaged up. Seated next to the driver, she was then driven by car to the New Hospital in Regensburg, where she refused to enter the building by the main entrance as she did not want to attract any attention. The party thus went inside up some steps via the rear entrance into the medical room, where an immediate examination revealed that she had suffered a fractured skull.

An immediate detailed investigation into the accident was begun, which resulted in the conclusions that the reason the dolly did not release was due to an undercarriage design error that was eliminated

In 1941/42, Flugkapitän Hanna Reitsch was a permanent guest at the Fliegerhorst Obertraubling when she was engaged in the acceptance flights of the Me 163 as well as the Me 321. (Photo Radinger)

Flugkapitän Hanna Reitsch discusses the Me 163 with Messerschmitt design staff and Alexander Lippisch (on right in photograph below right). The photographs may have been taken at Obertraubling, the airfield adjoining Messerschmitt's factory at Regensburg, where Hanna Reitsch was seriously injured while flying Me 163 BV5 on 30 October 1942.

NEST OF EAGLES

Me 163s of I./JG 400 on the apron at the east end of the runway at Brandis in the late summer of 1944. The aircraft are covered with tarpaulins to protect them from rain.

Me 163 Bs 'Yellow 2' and 'Yellow 13' of 7./JG 400 on the apron at Husum. Note the camouflage markings of Yellow 13.

immediately by Dipl.-Ing. Armbrust, but which was not the primary cause of the accident. Flight trials with suspended dolly and smooth landings confirmed this assumption and as always with accidents, it was due to a combination of several factors. Because of her small stature, Reitsch had not secured herself with the cockpit shoulder straps, as she would not have been able to move the control column forward fully. A large cushion had been placed on the seat to enable her to reach the rudder pedals, and in order to press these down to the full extent, wooden chocks had to be screwed to them, but they were not installed in the V5. Without the chocks, Hanna was able only to exert sufficient pressure on the pedals by twisting her whole body. In addition, the Revi 16 B reflector gunsight had not been folded to one side on landing, and had caused the severe head injuries. Hauptmann Späte, responsible for flight operations and who was in Peenemünde on the day the accident occurred, could not hold any individual responsible for the accident. It thus remained a conglomeration of unfortunate circumstances that caused the mishap, for which even Reitsch was partially the cause, as she had insisted on taking off without the wooden rudder-pedal chocks.

In a medical report, Reitsch had suffered the following injuries: basal skull fracture, brain compression, brain concussion, wounds to and shattering of the nasal bone, numerous bruises, and skin abrasions to the whole body. Up to 27 March 1943, and hence for almost five months, Reitsch was under medical attention in the women's hospital at Regensburg. Following this accident with the V5, no further works flight trials took place with the Me 163 B. Final assembly of 70 aircraft at Obertraubling was terminated, insofar as they were not used as test aircraft. When the production buildings in Prüfening became heavily damaged in the bombing raid on 17 August 1943, a portion of Bf 109 final assembly was transferred to Obertraubling, where this work and works flight-testing of the Me 323 also took place. Because available space in the Hallen was needed for fighter production, Me 163 B final assembly was undertaken in the autumn of 1943 by the Klemm Flugzeugbau, with flight trials performed in Lechfeld. Due to constant modifications to production aircraft, such as the incorporation of a brake chute, pressure cabin and airbrakes that had not been intended in its original concept, its service introduction became delayed. The powerplant also turned out to be heavier than planned and additional fuel tank protection drove the weight up, so that the aircraft eventually weighed around 1,000 kg (2,200 lb) more than intended. For details of Me 163 B dimensions, weights and performance, see Appendix 13.

After all the problems experienced with it, the conclusion was drawn that only a technically refined version would allow its fastest possible introduction to operational service. Despite this, it took until mid-1944 until JG 400 formed out of the former EK 16, commenced operations with the Me 163 B from airfields at Zwischenahn, Brandis near Leipzig, and Venlo. Its employment within the framework of Reichsverteidigung as a defence against enemy bombers was not anywhere near as sucessful as was hoped. A decisive factor was far too short range and its landing approach in a glider configuration, in which some fell victim to enemy fighters. Added to that was the lack of fuel at the end of 1944, as the factories that produced the propellants were destroyed by enemy action. In a similar manner to the early Me 321 gliders, the Me 163 B stood around helpless and vulnerable after landing until lifted and towed away by special vehicles. For operational use, it called for a comprehensive logistics system with corresponding special equipment ranging from fuel bowsers to powerplant test stands, which were only available at a few airfields. It should also be mentioned here that following considerable differences of opinion with Prof. Messerschmitt, Alexander Lippisch and most of his team left the firm in 1943. The last confirmed sortie with the Me 163 B by JG 400 took place on 10 April 1945. After the war, a number of intact Me 163 Bs were captured by the Allies who carried out flight trials with the aircraft, but not under rocket power.

CHAPTER 10

Me 323 Production at Obertraubling: 1942-1944

THE Me 321 was modified by Prof. Dr.-Ing. Willy Messerschmitt into the powered Me 323. The Me 323 possessed a number of innovative structural features which still hold valid for today's transport aircraft development. A comparison of modern transport aircraft with the Me 323 shows that they have the following in common: a shoulder wing; a large loading bay of almost rectangular cross-section; large freight doors, and tandem sets of wheels in external bays beside the fuselage, and in this sphere, Messerschmitt carried out pioneering work.

An analysis conducted on operations with the Me 321 revealed the following: the poor operational experiences with it were based not so much on its design, but primarily on the towing method as well as the tiresome and time-consuming take-off preparations. As early as the autumn of 1941, Prof. Messerschmitt himself drew up plans for a motorized version of the Me 321 and submitted them to the RLM. In the Technisches Amt (Technical office), immediate measures were instituted to find a suitable powerplant for this project. When France was occupied in 1940, a large number of two-row 14-cylinder Gnôme-Rhone 14 N 48/49 radial engines were captured that had been earmarked to power the Bloch 175 and Loiré-et-Olivier LeO 451 twin-engined bombers. Messerschmitt thereupon received the RLM order to modify an Me 321 as an appropriate experimental carrier for these engines, and the resultant Me 321 B was powered by four Gnôme-Rhone 14s. This made structural strengthening necessary, particularly to the fuselage and wing centre-section, but it also influenced the flight trials. With a load of 10 tonnes (22,050 lb), the Me 321 B was unable to take off. Since more powerful engines were not available, it was decided at Messerschmitt to equip it with six engines, the resulting aircraft known as the Me 323. The initially planned 8-wheel undercarriage had to be increased to 10 wheels, of which 5 were mounted on either side of the fuselage in enclosed bays. The two forward pairs of wheels each measured 935 x 320 mm (36.8 x 12.6 in) and the three rear rows, 1,200 x 420 mm (47.2 x 16.5 in), which were suspended on springs. With this undercarriage, it was possible to land on almost every temporary forward airfield near to the front line. Initial flight trials with the aircraft turned out to be so favourable that the RLM ordered a pre-series of 10 aircraft. Me 323 series manufacture thus began in the summer of 1942 at Leipheim and Obertraubling, the RLM placing an order for 200 aircraft. At first, production commenced on available Me 321 airframes that were modified, and deliveries of major components were assigned to individual industrial concerns. Whereas the Mannesmann plant at Rath near Düsseldorf supplied the fuselage mesh frames, the wing spars were completed at its Komotau factory. Undercarriage frames and wheel forks were produced by Skoda in Pilsen, whilst the wing nose and end ribs were furnished by the Möbelfabrik May furniture firm in Stuttgart, the Hirth firm in Nabern/Teck producing the complete empennages.

In studying documents concerning production of the Me 323, a unique obstacle run becomes apparent in the armaments industry, and above all on the part of the RLM, which at that time did not appear able to coordinate manufacture of its various structural components. First and foremost, there were an insufficient number of large Hallen suitable for final assembly, so that Messerschmitt was forced to carry out final assembly partly in the open. Some of the problems that played a significant role in delaying production of the Me 323 were as follows: the manufacturing programme calling for additional Hallen in Obertraubling lay far behind the firmly established plan due to lack of materials and labour, so that RLM Programme 222 for Me 323 production could not be maintained. In February 1942, only 30 per cent of the required quantity of fuel was allocated for delivery of the airframe components, and for transportation of the fuselage frames to Obertraubling, the Mannesmann-Werke in Düsseldorf was to have utilized trucks driven

113

This overhead view of Obertraubling, taken at the beginning of 1943, shows three Me 323s and several Me 321s (one in white winter camouflage) parked in front of the various Hallen. At lower centre is a He 111 Z. It can be assumed that at least some of the Me 321s that had been towed back from the Eastern Front, following a thorough examination and structural strengthening, were converted into Me 323s. (Photo USAF)

A group of the Obertraubling Works management. From left to right: Flugkapitän Trenkle, Technical Director Linder, Betriebsleiter Schmid and Administration head Wendland. (Photo Schmid)

by wood-produced gas. These, however, were not powerful enough to transport the fuselage mesh frames over motorway inclines. Subsequently, preparations were made to transport the fuselage frames by barge on the Rhine from Düsseldorf to Mannheim, but resulted in further delays due to the onset of ice in the winter of 1941-42 and high water in spring 1942. The completed fuselage frames thus piled up at Mannesmann and hindered further production. A constant problem was also the lack of manpower. For Obertraubling, 4,100 Russian PoWs were requested but until 16 March 1942, no binding agreement followed, so that 1,000 Russian Officer PoWs that had been scheduled for Augsburg had to be diverted to Obertraubling.

On 26 September 1942, manufacture of the Me 323 came to a total standstill at Leipheim because all of the Wehrmacht prisoners had been withdrawn and the 1,307 camp inmates requested by Messerschmitt AG had not yet arrived. Strangely enough, the Wehrmacht prisoners who had been employed previously in aircraft construction and as had been intended in a Führer directive, were not used in support of the front line, but were sent to do spadework on parade grounds in Wildflecken or Klagenfurt!

Due to the aforementioned lack of Hallen in Regensburg, RLM Programme 222 could not be maintained (according to a letter dated 22 November 1942 to Oberst i.G. Vorwald), so that for Obertraubling, a maximum of 12 Me 323s per month was envisaged from May 1943, assuming a sufficient number of German skilled workers would be available.

In December 1941, two four-engined Me 323s were to have been ready to fly at Obertraubling, followed by two six-engined examples. Both the former and one of the latter were ready to fly in January 1942. The first take-off of the four-engined Me 323 V1 (W1+SZ) took place there on 20 January. It was followed by the second six-engined version around mid-February, but heavy snowfalls hindered flying operations, and it was only under the greatest of exertions that it became possible to clear of snow a take-off stretch 1,000 m (3,280 ft) long by 100 m (328 ft) wide. A further problem was the lack of engines for the Me 323. For the initial phase, Alfa-Romeo 135 RC 32 engines were intended for installation, but these were not delivered. As a consequence, it was planned to use Junkers Jumo 211 J engines, as installed in the Ju 88. But these engines, together with their variable-pitch propellers, were likewise not available in sufficient quantities, and resulted in further delays to the construction programme. In using the Gnôme-Rhone engines with their Ratier propellers that had been obtained from occupied France, a satisfactory solution had been found, as these became available in sufficient quantities. In 1942, seven V-models and 16 series-built Me 323s were built in Obertraubling.

For the construction programme, a further 351 Russian PoWs arrived on 8 May 1942. At the end of the year, the total number of the workforce at Obertraubling consisted of 3,811, of which 2,756 were PoWs. To accommmodate the PoWs, the erection of a large barracks next to the main guardhouse was begun at the start of 1942. It was planned to house 4,000 Russian PoWs, 100 guards, 200 supervisory personnel, 208 armaments industry soldiers and 280 specialist workers for a few months and a further 350 Messerschmitt personnel.

Although acceptance flights with the Me 323 largely went off without major mishaps, further accidents happened with the Me 321 and the tugs of the Großraumsegler (GS) Sonderstaffeln. On 2 May 1942, a He 111 Z crashed on take-off in Obertraubling and resulted in the deaths of three crew members, among them the pilot, Oberfeldwebel Grzega.

Heinrich Dienstl recalled this crash: 'As an aircraft mechanic, I was a member of Oberstleutnant Sachsenhauser's crew. My task was to ensure that the cargo was properly secured and its weight properly distributed, and in addition, I was responsible for jettisoning both nosewheel undercarriage units. On 2 May 1942, a new pilot was to make a familiarization flight in the Me 321. Since we had the He 111 Z, flying the tow combination had become relatively harmless. The new pilot was given the appropriate instructions by Sachsenhauser, who told him that when applying aileron control, he was to avoid extending it to its full deflection if possible. In the Me 321, the latter had the unpleasant characteristic at maximum extension of remaining firmly fixed, so that it was only with great physical exertion that it could again be countered. At Sachsenhauser's instruction, I flew on this works test flight with the new crew in order to instruct the aircraft mechanic. The He 111 Z rolled in front of the Me 321, the towing cable was attached, and off we went. Take-off went according to plan. But we were then caught by a gust of wind, and it became very loud inside the cockpit above me. I immediately climbed the ladder up top. The pilots there were hanging onto the control columns. We pulled the He 111 Z sideways whilst still at low speed. Everything then happened like lightning. The He 111 Z crew disengaged the towline and turned downwards at an angle. The towcraft could not be held anymore, and it dipped down over its wing. A few seconds later, we saw a ball of fire that signalled the end of the He 111 Z. We on the other hand, landed safely. None of the three crew of the He 111 Z survived the crash, so that once more, flying the Gigant had demanded victims, even though in this instance it was totally unnecessary, as the Me 321 pilot did not stick to instructions.'

A further witness to this crash was Unteroffizier Geisbe: 'On this day, our Detachment leader, Hauptmann Schäfer, was determined to make a familiarization flight with Oberfeldwebel Jödicke. Grzega's He 111 Z was the sole tug available. Although almost all of Grzega's crew were on a boat trip on the Danube, he went with his He 111 Z and two aircraft mechanics to the take-off point. Shortly after both aircraft lifted off, the Me 321 pulled its nose up unusually high and turned away from its direction of flight. At a height of 80 m (260 ft) at the most, it pulled the He 111 Z sideways, with the result that it dived over its port wing, touched the ground, and exploded. The fault this time lay squarely on both pilots in the Me 321.'

On 11 May 1942, due to an engine defect, a Bf 110 of GS 2 made an emergency landing at Obertraubling, in which the pilot was injured.

In the late summer of 1942, the first series-built Me 323 arrived from final assembly in Obertraubling. In one of the technical and instructional flights, an Me 323 was destroyed when it crashed. Unteroffizier Heinz Powilleit recalled the event: 'In the spring of 1942, most of the Giganten pilots were attending a navigation course in Leipheim which had the aim of elevating us to Me 323 pilots. Our military grades, apparently, were too low to fly a motorized aircraft. That the powered aircraft pilots had their problems with the flying characteristics of a motorized cargo glider is something that I experienced in Obertraubling. It was a fantastic summer day, and for us Me 321 pilots, performance flights with small gliders were lined up for us, and was a military matter. In this connection, we also had time to observe the works flight tests undertaken by Messerschmitt personnel. One Me 323 was prepared for a works flight and stood ready not far from the runway. From the control tower, we saw a middle-aged Major in full dress with all his medals approaching. He rushed up to the Me 323, which in the meantime had been rolled to the take-off point. He clambered into the pilot's seat and took-off without any problems. Whether he wanted to make a test flight or whether he wanted to take over the aircraft perhaps only for a trial, was not known to us. After a circuit of the airfield, he set down for the landing. On the approach, the Me 323 was too high and drifted far over the the marked-out landing cross. There was still sufficient room to make a landing on the airfield. However, his ambition seemed to have got the better of him in that he wanted to land the aircraft on the cross. He put on the power and flew another, rather tighter circuit of the airfield. As he again wandered too high, he started yet another circuit. He wanted to be precise, flew another round and set down for the third time. But even on this approach, he still flew too high. His decision to go round again was taken too late. The Me 323 was already flying too slowly and too low. Despite that, the Major revved up to full power. As a result of the pull of the propellers and because of the deteriorating effect of the elevators caused by the low forward speed, the aircraft became nose heavy and the nose touched the ground, but sprang into the air again. The Major once more gave full power to all six engines, but his speed was gone. The aircraft now hit the ground at a steep angle but rose up once more. At the third brutal impact, the Me 323 was shattered. Its end was ghastly! The Major, bloody and heavily injured, was pulled out of the wreck. Ambulance personnel were there immediately, laid him on a stretcher and took him to the field hospital. The whole sequence, from leaving the control tower at a daredevil pace up to the stretcher, lasted 20 minutes at the most. It was very macabre! Because of his ambition to land the crate on the landing cross, a powered Me 323 was flown to nothing more than scrap. The event put us Me 321 pilots into a dark mood. The Me 323 of course, was a motorized glider, and on the landing approach, floated much further in the air than a normal motorized aircraft.'[1]

An impressive photograph of an Me 323 on its landing approach. (Photo Schmoll)

In December 1942, Messerschmitt GmbH Regensburg received a direct order from Reichsmarschall Göring to have 15 Me 323s ready by 31 January 1943 for immediate use in the Stalingrad campaign. The firm managed to do so, through Flugkapitän Heinrich Obermeier, who not only performed all acceptance flights with the 15 Me 323s, but also the necessary works flights with eight other examples. For his engagement, Obermeier received from the Regensburg Works Chief, Merkel, a personal written acknowledgement of thanks.

Former Oberfeldwebel Ludwig Kandler of Saal recalled in regard to the Me 323: 'In 1938, I joined the Luftwaffe as a skilled vehicle mechanic and was posted to Fürth. After basic training at Fürth, I was transferred for a few weeks to a Sonderkommando (Special Detachment) which supported the Horten brothers on the Wasserkuppe in flight trials of their gliders. There was also a motorized Focke-Wulf Fw 56 towcraft there for this purpose. During these weeks at the Wasserkuppe, the decision ripened within me to apply to become a pilot in the Luftwaffe. Upon my return to Fürth, I filled out an appropriate application. Almost a year went by, and then I received a rejection. Because of my technical training in armament and aero-engines, I was not released. In the meantime, I had become an Unteroffizier and in 1940 was posted to Obertraubling. The Fliegerhorst there was laid out very generously. What impressed me most, however, were the many large trees that had been planted immediately after completion of the buildings. In Obertraubling, I led a small Detachment and we equipped He 111 bombers with deflectors in the bomb-bays. Flights with the Gigant aircraft then began. At first,

---

[1] The Me 323 was W.Nr. 1258 (VM+IF) which was 90% damaged. The crash-landing resulted in one dead and two heavily injured, among them Major Markus Zeidler. When one views the reports of losses sustained by the Me 323 units, it is apparent that several accidents occured during landings, such as parked Me 323s being rammed, because they were obviously set down too late on the runway.

NEST OF EAGLES

On 21 April 1943, Reichsstatthalter (Governor) Ritter von Epp visited the Messerschmitt-Werke. At right of the picture is Messerschmitt Technical Director, Dipl.-Ing. Linder. (Photo Willbold, EADS)

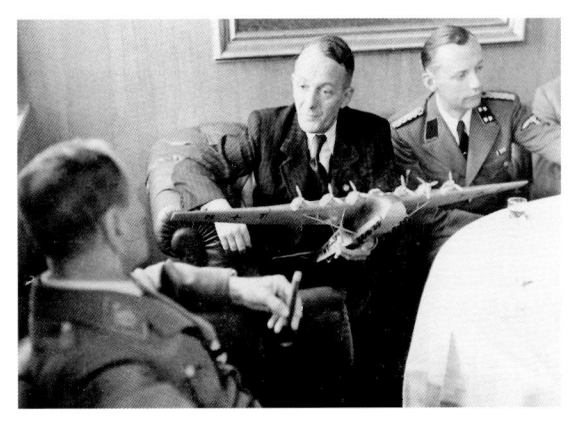

In conversation with (at left) Ritter von Epp, Technical Director Linder holds a superb model of the Me 323 and explains its design details. (Photo Willbold, EADS)

I had nothing to do with this, as I was engaged in the workshop.

'It was, nevertheless, a breathtaking sight when a tow combination rose into the air. When the first Me 323s stood on the airfield around the beginning of 1942, I was detailed to install the weapons in them. Initially, these were only MG 15s and MG 131s, but were followed later by 20 mm MG 151s in turrets. My commander proposed that I should apply for air-gunner training, as I had good chances of being accepted, for due to my small stature, I would have fitted well in the Me 323 wing-mounted rotatable turrets. Additionally, I understood much about aero-engines and could have been a flight mechanic, as they sat in the wings. However, at the time, I thought it all over very carefully. On the one hand, it was tempting to be a member of an aircrew with all its advantages, but on the other hand, I was aware that such a transfer could be a suicidal one. I can't exactly say today what had caused me at the time to turn it down. Perhaps it was an obstinate reaction because I had been rejected as a pilot. On my side, however, this rejection presumably saved my life. But as had happened with Barras, I was posted away. Having meanwhile become a Feldwebel, I wound up in the aircraft depot in Erding and was immediately sent to Sicily to the airfield at Trapani. It could have been even worse; I could have found myself on the Eastern Front. At the beginning of 1943, there were numerous bomber and fighter units in Sicily, which needed replacement parts, and above all, aero-engines. At Trapani, we were a branch of the aircraft depot and coordinated supplies through Bari and Naples. At that time also, I saw Me 323s on their way to Tunisia. Among them were certainly

Messerschmitt Me 323 E-2, W.Nr. 1282, SL+HD, Obertraubling, summer 1943

Me 323 Production at Obertraubling: 1942-1944

aircraft from Obertraubling in which I had installed the weapons. Whereas I had initially yearned to be on an Me 323s, their losses became increasingly greater. We even counted that from seven aircraft, only five returned. When it all ended in Tunisia and many of the Giganten had been shot down over the Mediterranean, I thought to myself that I had made the right decision that time in Obertraubling.'

That the situation had certainly been quite rightly assessed by Kandler, is borne out by the following losses by KG 323 zbV in the Mediterranean theatre in the space of only five months of operations:

Status as of 30 April 1943:

Personnel		Me 323	
Killed	42	Destroyed	39
Missing	204	Missing	29
Heavily injured	28	Heavily damaged	21
Lightly injured	52	Lightly damaged	12
Total	**326**	**Total**	**101**

The figure of 101 lost or damaged Me 323s in less than six months of operations corresponds to the number of series-built aircraft that had been produced in Obertraubling from 1942 to 1944. Such losses suffered by a transport unit, it should be noted, were quite clearly due to the greatly strengthened Allied flying units. The few German fighter units were no longer capable of securing air superiority over the front line nor over the supply routes. For the German troops, it was simply a sacrifice.

At this time (1943), Me 323 production at Obertraubling was in full swing. From 1 January 1942, Dipl-Ing. Karl Schmid of Messerschmitt Regensburg was responsible for Me 323 production at the base and was quickly confronted with its deficiencies. But instead of requesting additional personnel, which he would not have received in any case, Schmid adopted a quite different course of action. He analysed all the

Me 323 E-2, W.Nr. 1282, SL+HD, photographed at Obertraubling in the summer of 1943. (Photo DM Munich)

117

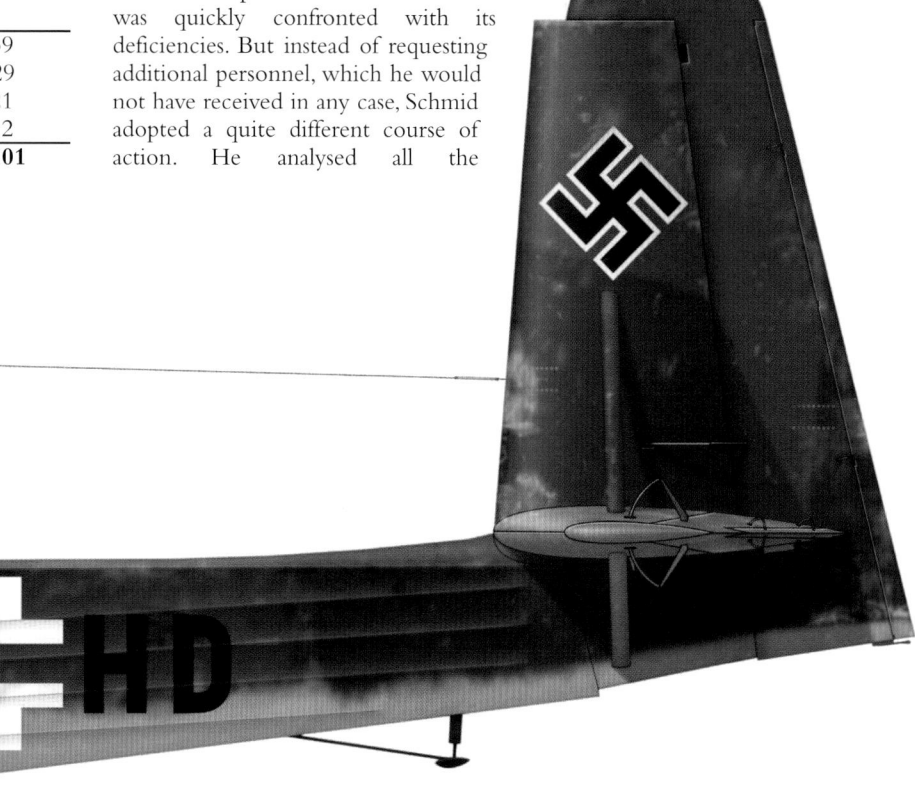

Factory-fresh Me 323, W9+SA, photographed shortly after roll-out.

Seen here is Me 323 RL+UJ resting on its rear mainwheels and tailskid. (Photo Schmoll)

manufacturing steps and reorganized the production run. As a result, he achieved a five-fold increase in monthly production with the available personnel than hitherto and for this performance, he became the only member of the aviation industry sphere to be awarded the Ritterkreuz (Knight's Cross) to the Kriegsverdienstkreuz (War Service Cross) for his work connected to the Me 323 while at the RLM in Berlin. Following his return from Berlin, a great celebration (Works assembly) took place on 19 June 1943 in the Werfthalle at the Fliegerhorst. Under his leadership, until 31 March 1943, a total of 49 Me 323 Ds were built, whilst from final assembly in Leipheim during the same period, only 23 Me 323 Ds were built. A few weeks later, Schmid fell from the wing of an Me 323 and was heavily injured. It was only after months of recuperation that, in 1944, he took on a new task in the realm of wireless instrument manufacture at the Regensburger Leichtmetall GmbH in Marienbad.

Together with Linder, Schmid, Wrede, Widmann and Dr. Wedemeyer - to name only a few - Regensburg had an extremely capable and competent team possessing a strong organizationally-talented corps of engineers, without which aircraft production would have fallen apart during the hail of bombs that fell on it from 1943 to 1945.

In 1943, with 86 aircraft produced, Me 323 production reached its peak. Following the devastating

With the aid of a model Halle, Karl Schmid explains to his colleagues the newly-agreed production run which enabled a significant increase in production without the need for additional personnel. It was a general measure adopted that the Messerschmitt engineers verified and laid down the manufacturing process with the aid of models. In this way, it could be very reliably determined to what extent the need for space was satisfied in the Hallen (Photo Schmid)

The Fliegerhorst Obertraubling in summer 1943, seen from the south-west. In the foreground is the road from Obertraubling to the Fliegerhorst. A total of eight Me 323s are parked in front the Werfthalle and Halle 2 with the Flight Traffic Control building visible at right. This photograph was taken secretly after passing one of the guardposts. (Photo Illenberger)

Me 323 Production at Obertraubling: 1942-1944

Karl Schmid (in dark suit) in conversation with two Messerschmitt mechanics on the wing of an Me 323. A few weeks after this picture was taken, Schmid fell from one such wing and was seriously injured. (Photo Schmid)

Karl Schmid (at centre) in discussion with members of the plant workforce in front of an Me 323 at Obertraubling. (Photo Schmid)

Far left: A Works assembly on 19 June 1943 in the Werfthalle in front of an Me 323 E on the occasion of the award of the Ritterkreuz to the Kriegsverdienstkreuz to Betriebsleiter (Works head) Karl Schmid. (Photo Schmid)

Above right: After the ceremony, completed Me 323s were inspected. From right to left: RLM Generaling. Lucht, Gauleiter Wächtler, and Director Seiler. Behind them (with hat) are Prof. Messerschmitt in conversation with Directors Kokothaki and Merkel. Noteworthy on this Me 323 E is that the nose MG 131s have not yet been installed. (Photo Schmid)

An overhead view of the Fliegerhorst Obertraubling in the summer of 1943, where no fewer than 20 Me 323s can be seen parked outside the various Hallen. Beyond the boundary of the Fiegerhorst at left is the PoW camp. (Photo USAF)

119

NEST OF EAGLES

Final assembly of an Me 323 E-2 wing in the large Werfthalle (Halle 1) at Obertraubling in the summer of 1943. Note the EDL 151 wing turrets in each outer wing. (Photo BA Koblenz 78/106/26)

A factory-fresh Me 323 E at Obertraubling in June 1943. As visible in the photograph, a large number of traversible raised platforms were necessary for engine maintenance. The cockpit canopy is raised, and in the starboard nose door can be seen the MG 131 weapon Stand. (Photo Schmid)

bombing raid on 17 August 1943 on the Messerschmitt Werk I in Prüfening, six Hallen were freed for Bf 109 G production in Obertraubling. This resulted in a drop in Me 323 output to eight aircraft per month. In the Obertraubling Hallen, production of Me 262 fuselages commenced in January 1944, so that it now became a focal point of fighter production.

One further Me 323 was completed in January 1944, and with it ended production of the first war zone transport and of one of the world's largest aircraft at the time. According to the USSBS, 101 Me 323 D and E versions as well as seven pre-production aircraft were produced. All construction jigs and special equipment for Me 323 assembly were dismantled and with termination of production, a notable era came to an end. None of the flying giants survived the war. Up to the mid-1960s, a fuselage segment of one served as a jumping tower on the dredging lake in Neutraubling. But even this last Gigant relic has disappeared, and the only thing that remains is a vague memory of an aviation epoch that resulted in several victims.

To what extent its transport capabilities and to what extent it provided supplies to all Fronts is demonstrated by the following figures: the majority of the 213 examples built consisted of the Me 323 D-6 variant powered by six Gnôme-Rhone 14 N 48/49 engines that delivered a total of 6,600 hp at take-off. Its range was around 750 km (466 mls) and with auxiliary fuselage tanks, could be extended to 1,100 km (683 mls). As a result of the weight of the powerplants, armament, undercarriage and diverse equipment, useful payload sank to 11 tonnes (24,250 lb). With the aid of RATO units, it could carry payloads up to 16 tonnes (35,275 lb) in the overload condition. Its normal load consisted of either two medium trucks inclusive of their 2-tonne

In this photograph of Me 323 SL+SJ taken at München-Riem in 1943, a test run is being made on engine No.3. In service, the engines had to continually give maximum performance and needed very good maintenance. Photo Schmoll)

120

An Me 323 is fuelled from a bowser which has ample room beneath the wings. The Me 323 D version held a total of 5,340 litres of fuel. (Photo Hübsch)

A loading exercise involving an Me 323 with 'LeO' engines mounted on an Opel Blitz 3-tonner at Obertraubling in 1943 (Photo Croneiß)

Above left: This scene shows the capacious Me 323 freight bay, which corresponded to that of a railway goods wagon.

(4,410 lb) loads; one 88 mm Flak gun together with its crew and a large supply of ammunition; more than 50 petrol canisters each holding 200 litres; almost 9,000 loaves of bread; 130 fully-equipped troops, or 60 wounded on stretchers. This payload corresponded to the loading capacity of six Ju 52s and 18 aircrew, or only nine aircrew for the Me 323. Quite apart from that, the Ju 52 was not able to carry large vehicles. Whereas the Ju 52 needed 1 litre per ton of payload and flying kilometre, the Me 323 only needed 0.57 litres/km. The technical description of the Me 323 D variants and Werknummern are listed in Appendix 14.

In October 1942, I./KG zbV 323 was established at Leipheim, which from 15 May 1943 was renamed Transportgeschwader TG 5, to which II. Gruppe was added a short while later. The first operational use of the Me 323 was to carry supplies to the island of Crete in November 1942, where each flight from Athens to Thymbakion on the southern part of the island brought up to 13 tonnes (28,660 lb) of fuel and motor oil. For supplying the Afrika Korps in Tunisia, the aircraft were stationed in Naples-Pomigliano, and transported anti-tank, Flak and artillery weapons, armoured cars, trucks and armoured self-drive gun mounts. Whereas transport flights to Tunisia were relatively safe at the end of 1942, this changed drastically in the spring of 1943. Increasing numbers of Me 323s were shot down on the way to Tunis or Bizerta or, shortly after landing there, were damaged or destroyed by low-flying enemy aircraft. Even on the airfields in Naples or in Sicily, the aircraft were endangered by bombing raids. Against the increasingly overwhelming number of Allied fighters, the Gigants were like cumbersome flying dinosaurs which, despite their improved defensive armament, had no chance of survival. What it meant to be in a slow-flying transport made up of steel tube and fabric covering, fully packed with munitions and fuel canisters, almost defenceless against attack by enemy fighters, one can hardly imagine at the present time.

At the urgent appeal of the Afrika Korps, whose fuel reserves had come to an end, the last mission of 14 aircraft of Transportgeschwader Me 323 was flown on 22 April 1943 as a replenishment flight to Tunis. Each of the Me 323s was loaded with 13 tonnes of petrol, and in all, carried 700 canisters. Within sight of the North African coast and just a few minutes away from their destination, Allied fighters pounced. Agents on Sicily had radioed their flight to Allied headquarters in North Africa, and all

NEST OF EAGLES

Two photographs of lorries being unloaded from the same Me 323 during a loading exercise at Obertraubling with a Mercedes-Benz Type 3000 A lorry (top) and an Opel Blitz (right). The Blitz can just be seen behind the Mercedes-Benz lorry inside the fuselage in the top photograph. Trials of this nature were necessary to determine the c.g. of the aircraft and for the lash-down positions for the vehicles. (Photo Willbold, EADS)

14 Me 323s were shot down: six belonging to I.Gruppe and eight of II./KG 323 zbV. Of their crews consisting of 138 men, only 19 survived and about 170 tonnes of fuel that was so urgently needed in Tunisia sank in the Mediterranean. Of the aircraft shot down, eight came from the production line in Obertraubling. From the end of November 1942 until that ill-fated day in 1943, a total of 1,200 sorties and around 15,000 tonnes (33,070 lb) of supplies were flown over to Tunisia. These transported 309 trucks, 51 medium-sized vehicles, 200 artillery pieces up to 15 cm calibre, 324 light field guns, 83 Pak and Flak guns, 42 radar sets and 96 armoured personnel vehicles and self-drive gun mounts.

As a result of enemy action, 21 Me 323s were lost in April 1943 and a further seven due to other causes the same month. On 30 April, 35 Me 323s were still available in the Mediterranean but II./KG 323 zbV was withdrawn from the theatre and re-equipped in Leipheim. The few Me 323s that were still on hand with I. Gruppe were flown on supply missions from Naples to Sardinia and Corsica and suffered severe losses. At the end of September 1943, the renamed TG 5 relocated to take over new Me 323s in Leipheim, a number of its crews drawn from Obertraubling. It was subsequently sent to the Eastern Front and made transport flights from Warsaw to the front line.

War reporter Kurt Dürpisch recorded Me 323 operations from Warsaw at the end of 1943: 'It is still early afternoon, but it already begins to get dim. On the large airfield at Warsaw, the first red flickers of lighting rise from the aircraft hangars and chimneys, and runway lighting is also switched on. A distant droning of aircraft engines signalled that landings are soon to be expected. These are the Me 323s of TG 5, which this morning took off with supplies to the Eastern Front and are now on their way back. In low-level flight, they thunder over the airfield. Five of them took off, and five are returning. Some of them fire off red flares as a signal to those on the ground: "We have wounded on board, and will be the first to land!" One after another, they line up for the landing approach. The first one comes in to land, sets down, and is immediately waved from the runway to its parking position. An indescribable noise reigns on the airfield, as the aircraft with their droning engines roll to their parking spots. At the flight operations centre, a long column of waiting ambulances begin to move in the direction of the parked aircraft. Returning from the Front, these aircraft have a number of severely wounded

Me 323 Production at Obertraubling: 1942-1944

One of the first Me 323 Ds produced at Obertraubling. The rudder markings 'X1 B' indicate that this machine belonged to I./KG zbV 323 (renamed I./TG 5 from May 1943). (Photo Obermeier)

On the ground in front of the large nose doors of this Me 323, a bomb is waiting to be loaded. (Photo Hübsch)

men on board. Shortly after the engines have been switched off, the large nose doors are opened and swung to the sides. The view falls upon the aircraft's enormous loading bay, where the whole misery of war unfolds. On the floor, lying on straw sacks and covered with woollen blankets lie the wounded soldiers, who just a few days and hours before, were sent to fight on the Dniepr. They are removed carefully by the medical orderlies and laid on stretchers. A doctor on the spot tends to the most urgent cases. One by one the ambulances drive off and return to fetch the next ones to transport them to the field hospital.

'The crews are affected by the continually strenuous daily operations. Hardly have the wounded been taken off, when the ground personnel begin to tank-up the Me 323s. A brief check of the engines and the elimination of any damage, and the aircraft are made ready for loading for operations the next day. On such days, ammunition and fuel are needed at the Front more than anything else, and on each flight the Me 323s carry some 10 to 12 tonnes to the focal points of the great

Field artillery, such as this Type 37 Flak 8.8, was transported by the Me 323. Because of its accurate and rapid rate of fire, the 8.8 was an extremely feared weapon, both when aimed at airborne and at ground targets, and especially as an anti-tank weapon. Behind it is a Hanomag Sonderkraftfahrtzeug 7 half-tracked vehicle. (Photo Willbold, EADS)

NEST OF EAGLES

At the beginning of March 1943, Me 323s landed in Bizerta (Tunisia) and brought urgently-needed supplies for the Afrika Korps.
(Photo Fischer)

battlefields on the Eastern Front. As described above, they return with wounded. Some of those heavily wounded, however, do not survive the return flight and die on board. But by means of this air bridge, hundreds are soon placed under medical care and thank their survival to the Me 323.'

I./TG 5 flew to the southern sector of the front to Odessa and Focsani, whilst II./TG 5 flew to the northern sector to Kirovograd and Riga.

The last available Me 323s flew far beyond the limits of their capabilities and once more suffered heavy losses, partly caused by enemy action and partly through technical defects. It so happened that on 16 March 1944, an Me 323 crashed near Odessa with 70 men on board and resulted in 63 fatalities. At Riga, an Me 323 was shot down by four Russian fighters. But there were also successes, and on one occasion an Me 323, while on a nocturnal mission, was able to evacuate 100 soldiers encircled in the Crimea and 140 female signals assistants from Rumania. Ahead of the advancing Soviet armies, several Me 323s had to be blown up on their airfields because airfield conditions were such that a take-off was not possible or because of technical defects, were no longer operational. Relocations were constantly made westwards. A last gathering point in June 1944 for TG 5 was the airfield at Kecskemet in Hungary. On 23 August 1944 TG 5 was disbanded, and the 'giants' disappeared forever from the skies.

Special versions of the Me 323 existed. At least on was fitted out as a flying workshop in 1943. On board were firmly-fixed cupboards, work benches, turning and milling machines, air compressors and electricity generators as well as workshop tents and a truck. Besides appropriate substitute parts, the crew comprised 18 to 20 men: engine fitters, electricians, welders, aircraft mechanics, a carpenter and a sail-maker - the latter to make repairs to the fabric skinning. By using such aircraft, damaged Me 323s near the front line could be repaired or else made airworthy enough to be flown to larger airfields in the rear for more thorough overhaul.

Another special version was the WT = Waffenträger (weapons carrier), of which at least five examples are known to have been built – W.Nr. 1272 (VM+IT), W.Nr. 1298 (SL+HT), W.Nr. 330004 (C8+GC) and two others whose Werknummern are unknown (DU+PP and RL+UE). Erwin Walter recalled: 'The Me 323 WT was full of airborne weapons and looked like a porcupine. The task of this WT was to act as escort to the normal Me 323 transports. As a result of operational experience and above all, because of losses suffered in the Mediterranean, it was believed that the Me 323 units would thereby be able to protect themselves from attacks by enemy fighters. As far as I am aware, only two such WT examples were completed; I flew as aircraft mechanic in RL+UE. On board the Me 323 were two mechanics. One sat in the port wing between engines 2 and 3, with the second in the starboard wing between engines 4 and 5. These two were responsible for starting the engines and their constant supervision in flight. Once the engines were running and the pilots rolled to the take-off point, they then reported via the aircraft radio: 'We are taking over' and from then on, we merely had a purely supervisory function to perform for each of the three engines on our side. We had to pay special

Me 323 Production at Obertraubling: 1942-1944

An Me 323 E of I./TG 5 brings wounded soldiers back from the Eastern Front. Waiting beside it are two Phänomen Granit medical trucks to transport the wounded to the nearest field hospital.
(Photo DM Munich)

attention to boost pressure, engine revs, oil temperature and oil pressure. In the event of an engine failing, we had to feather the propeller. Being right behind the engines it was naturally very loud, and communication was only possible over the intercom. For this purpose we had the usual network headgear with a built-in throat-type microphone and headphones which dampened the noise. On the wing leading edge was a small window to provide vision forwards and downwards, and a further window was built into the emergency escape hatch that was located on the upper surface of the wing. The emergency escape hatch, however, was dimensioned so small that one could hardly pass through with a

Me 323 E-2, W.Nr. 1269, C8+CB of 1./TG 5 photographed in Russia in 1944. The E-2, differed from the E-1, in having two upper wing-mounted, electrically-powered turrets, each armed with an MG 151 machine gun. The barrel of one of these weapons can be seen to the rear of the outer starboard engine. Although shown here on the Eastern Front in 1944, this aircraft may earlier have flown in Italy until the Gruppe transferred to the East in 1943.
On 23 February 1944, C8+CB hit an obstacle after an engine failure and was 50 % damaged.

Messerschmitt Me 323 E-2, W.Nr. 1269, C8+CB, Stab 1./TG 5, Russia, 1944

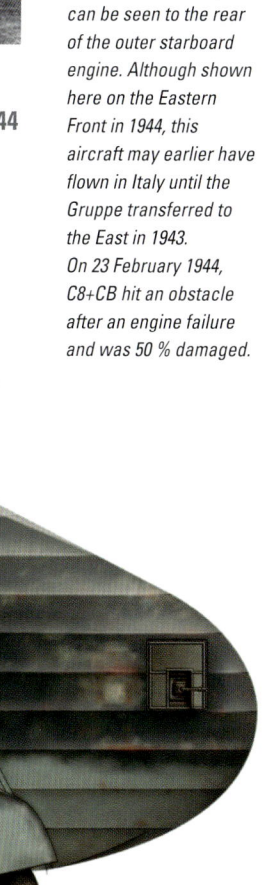

125

NEST OF EAGLES

The Me 323 WT – a heavily armed weapons carrier – RL+UE, one of the few such aircraft built. According to the testimony of an eyewitness, RL+UE was used several times for carrying out technical modifications in Obertraubling. This model was put forward as a result of experiences in the Mediterannean theatre and was armed with nine MG 151/20s and three MG 131s. It was to act as escort to ward off fighter attacks on the giant transports, but from available knowledge, was hardly used in this role. (Photo Dabrowski)

This Me 323 was a total write-off. Quite often, structural breaks resulted form overstressing. (Photo Obermeier)

The Me 323 also suffered losses. Here, the empennage has broken off. (Photo Obermeier)

parachute. The mechanic therefore had a breast parachute which always lay within his reach. In the event of needing to bale out, the following procedure was applied: the hood above the head was unlatched, the exit hatch ejected, and then you climbed half out of the emergency hatch. With the upper part of the body, one was thus suspended in the airflow over the wing. Your parachute had now to be pulled in and attached in order to now clamber out over the wing. To my good luck, I never had the occasion to make use of this procedure.

'Besides the regular crew, the Me 323 WT had a Kampfkommandant (Battle Commander) and eleven air gunners as well as two weapons mechanics. As a rule, the crew numbered around 18 to 20 men. The Kampfkommandant of my aircraft was Oberleutnant Römer. During the flight, he sat in the cockpit beside the radioman and from here, directed the air gunners over the intercom. Armament consisted of two HDL 151 weapon stands equipped with MG 151/20s on each wing, with a rotatable fifth stand in the fuselage nose.

On the sides near the nose were two MG 131s and on the forward third of the fuselage was a MG 151 ball turret on each side. At the fuselage centre was a MG 151 lateral stand on each side, plus a further MG 131 in a C-Stand in the fuselage that fired downwards. In all, this meant nine 20 mm and three 13 mm guns. We were some weeks with RL+UE at Tarnewitz, the Luftwaffe E-Stelle for weapons testing, and we tested our weapons. When the wing gunners were commanded to open fire, the whole aircraft trembled. The noise from the rounds fired from the four MG 151s even drowned out the drone of the engines. The Me 323 WT could not transport any freight, as it carried a large power generator in the freight compartment that was necessary to steer the weapon stands and electrical triggering of the MG 151s. I was on several occasions at Fliegerhorst Obertraubling with this Me 323, for it was here that the requisite replenishments for the aircraft could be made.

'With a normal Me 323, I was on operations in the Mediterranean theatre and flew about six times to Tunisia with some fifty 200-litre petrol canisters on board. The Afrika Korps needed fuel and ammunition. We flew until we were exhausted and our aircraft were shot down in droves by Allied fighters. It is more than a small miracle that I survived this period. The Waffenträger were not used in the Mediterranean theatre, but I can very well remember one of our last flights with it. When the Rumanians changed sides and went over to the Russians, we received the order in August 1944 to fetch out encircled Wehrmacht and female signals personnel that were trapped in the neighbourhood of Bucharest. We took off with the last operational Giganten from Kecskemet to Bucharest, and four transports and our Waffenträger droned towards the East. It was planned that the four transports would land there whilst we circled the airfield to ensure safe loading. As we arrived there, the Russians were already at the airfield and we had to watch helplessly as they goaded our people into vehicles and took them away to the East. We would have loved to have gone in there with our aircraft cannon, but would only have endangered our own people. Since we were the leading aircraft of the formation, a decision had to be taken. One possibility was to land and with all the weapons on our aircraft in action, secure the area and enable some of the personnel to be transported out, but on the other hand, the aircraft would have been extremely endangered, for on the ground, they presented excellent targets. We did not find it an easy matter to simply fly back. Our air gunners sent out a radio message and as an answer, we were given the order to break off the action and return. With heavy hearts and anxious misgivings, we started the return flight. How was this war to come to an end for us? The way the situation presented itself, surely in catastrophe.'

Seen here in January 1943 is Me 323 D (DT+IT) W.Nr. 1220 of I./TG 5 on the Eastern Front, probably photographed at Lemberg. Its enormous size compared with the two Ju 52s is evident. (Photo Emmerle)

Left and below: The Me 323 VM+IZ was equipped as a flying workshop that could repair damaged or technically defective Me 323s to make them operational once more, the tents and the Opel Blitz truck forming part of its on-board equipment. In the background (left) at right is a Me 321 B. In the background (below) at right are Hallen 6 and 7 and behind them can be seen the Staffelbau (stepped-type) apartments. (Photo Willbold, EADS)

NEST OF EAGLES

*Above: A view inside the Me 323 workshop area. The compressor and generator are visible in the foreground at left and right. On the workbench at left is a lathe, and numerous workbenches, cupboards and drawers for replacement parts complete the inventory. On the fuselage horizontal steel-tube framework at left and right are attachment lugs to fix various types of loads.
(Photo Willbold, EADS)*

Compressors, electricity generators and the workshop tent seen here were part of the Me 323 flying workshop's equipment. In the background is the Fliegerhorst Obertraubling Halle 6. (Photo Willbold, EADS)

The engines of this unmarked Me 323 D are covered over with tarpaulins for protection against the weather. (Photo Hübsch)

CHAPTER 11

Bombing

An attempted escape by two Russians in a Bf 109 G-6

IN January 1944, series production of Me 262 fuselages began at Obertraubling. Due to lack of space, final assembly of the Me 323 was relocated to the Zeppelinwerke in Friedrichshafen after one last example was completed that month. The RLM Lieferplan 223, Alteration Status B, envisaged that in January 1944, 400 Bf 109 G-6 and 20 G-6/Trop would be produced, followed in February by 500 G-6s. Actual production, however, was 434 Bf 109 G-6s. Since reconnaissance by Allied aircraft confirmed that Bf 109 production was in full swing, it was not long before the first bombing raids were to follow.

Prior to the first bombing raid on Obertraubling by the USAAF on 22 February 1944, an event of another kind took place there. According to eyewitnesses, it must have been around mid-February 1944, when two Russian officer PoWs employed in flight-test operations attempted to escape in a Bf 109 G-6. As related by Meister Ludwig Groß who worked in this sector in Obertraubling: 'As far as I remember, it was around mid-February 1944 when we in the Einflug were taking our breakfast break when suddenly, a Bf 109 started up, began to roll, and thundered over the runway. It immediately became clear to us that something was not quite right, for although parked aircraft were ready to be collected, no take-off had been announced to us. The Bf 109 also did not ascend properly; it remained caught by its undercarriage on the airfield fence and suffered damage. Together with Zieghaus, the head of flight-test operations, I immediately drove to the accident spot. On the way there we drew our revolvers, which every Meister had on his person and at the spot, held one of the Russians captive. The second had got close to a Flak position and was held there by Flak soldiers. Both Russians were brought to the flight operations centre and were severely mishandled by the soldiers. Two or three days later, I again saw one of the pair who had a battered face as a result of beatings. As already mentioned, both were Russian officers, Leutnant Vassily Yaresh and Dimitry Utevikov - an artillery Leutnant and a Russian Air Force Leutnant who worked in our flight-test operations. They supposedly wanted to escape to Switzerland.

'The two Russians were sentenced to death and were shot, at one of the Me 109 firing ranges. For Zieghaus, it had an unpleasant sequel, as he was thoroughly questioned by the Gestapo about the incident.'

Oberleutnant Riedmeir recalled: 'On a February day in 1944, all the pilots of the flight-test unit were sitting in the operations area on the Fliegerhorst Obertraubling, for on this morning, the weather did not permit flying activity. Suddenly, an engine started up and we could distinctly hear an aircraft on the move. We all looked around rather puzzled as to who it could be in a 109, when just as abruptly the engine noise stopped. The word quickly went round that two Russians wanted to escape with a 109 and ended up crashing it. Both were taken captive, and two or three days later, a war tribunal was held and conducted corresponding questioning. As far as I recall, it was on the following day when Oberleutnant Freiherr von Falkenhorst officially appeared and asked me what was going on here. I explained the situation to him and said to him that I thought it a great performance to simply fly away with a 109. He became thoroughly amused about it and joked with me: "Just imagine all that's possible in a Luftwaffe Fliegerhorst, where one can even steal a 109. That's marvellous, Riedmeir!" Our conversation had apparently found an uninvited eavesdropper who had listened-in on our harmless exchange. In any case, we were both summoned to and questioned by the war tribunal. I was asked immediately by them why I admired the Russians for their action. I replied that from the flying aspect, it is a certainly great performance, without instruction on its flight characteristics, to take-off in a fighter aircraft. Not only that, it conformed to the code of honour of an

A Bf 109 G-6/R-6 trop line-up ready for factory check flights at Obertraubling. The aircraft display the typical local camouflage pattern on the fuselage sides, and are equipped with the R-6 Rüstsatz consisting of the MG 151/20 mounted beneath the wings. (Photo BA Koblenz 6505438/7)

officer, to make use of every opportunity to escape. To my good fortune, the war tribunal was headed by an old war tribunal councillor who as an officer in the First World War, had been taken prisoner by the Russians and was able to escape. He showed understanding for my utterances and I was gracefully dismissed. A stone fell from my heart, as it could have turned out adversely. The war tribunal sentenced the two Russian officers to death by shooting for having damaged Wehrmacht property. A few days later, at the firing stand where otherwise Bf 109 weapons would be tested, the two of them were shot. At the execution, I found the large crowd of curious onlookers disgusting, as half the Fliegerhorst was present. The take-off had only misfired because both Russians had crammed themselves into the tight 109 cockpit so that the hood could not be properly closed. During the take-off run, it leapt off at high speed, which then led to the aircraft mishap.'

Yaresh and Utevikov were shot on 14 February 1944 and were buried two days later in the Irlerhohe Special Cemetery. According to unconfirmed details, a further incident of this nature is said to have taken place at the end of 1944, involving another escape attempt with a Bf 109.

22 February 1944

Until the beginning of 1944, the Fliegerhorst was spared from bombing raids. But the numerous Flak positions gave a misleading impression of security. On 20 February 1944, a bomber formation consisting of 89 Boeing B-17 Flying Fortresses of the US Fifteenth Air Force made its approach to Regensburg. Because of cloud cover, the attack was broken off and the bombers returned to their bases. Two days later, the bombers were again on their way to the Fliegerhorst and, on this occasion, effected a deadly blow. At 1126 hrs, the bombers entered Reich territory and at 1216 hrs, the air raid warning sounded in Regensburg. Flying past Salzburg, the USAAF formation flew over Altötting in the direction of Straubing and then turned towards Regensburg. Their altitude lay between 21,000 and 23,000 ft, but an almost closed cloud layer hindered their target sighting. The bomber escort, comprising 122 P-38 Lightning fighters, had a range sufficient only to reach the Alps, from where on the bombers were on their own. Continual attacks by German fighters of II./JG 53, I./JG 301, II./ZG 1 at the beginning, and 2./JG 104 as well as 5./JG 5 directly over the target or after leaving it, resulted in 17 bomber and two fighter losses. Two bombers were shot down by the Flak and several others were heavily damaged. The damaged bombers usually sought to land in Switzerland, but were mostly shot down by fighters outside of the Flak zone.

One bomber formation, consisting of 61 B-17s, was to attack the Messerschmitt Werk I in Prüfening. Due to a navigational error – a railway bridge at Poikam was mistaken for the one at Mariaort, the bombers dropped their loads near Bad Abbach. At 1220 hrs, a total of 1,096 bombs weighing 150 tons was dropped north of Bad Abbach, mostly on open countryside. The formation, whose target was Obertraubling, reached its attack position at 1245 hrs. Up to 1312 hrs, 741 500 lb demolition bombs and 306 100 lb incendiary bombs were dropped on the Fliegerhorst, making a total of 180 tons that left a trail of destruction. It must have been an unimaginable inferno. Hundreds of bomber engines

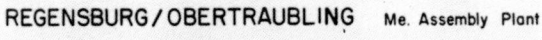

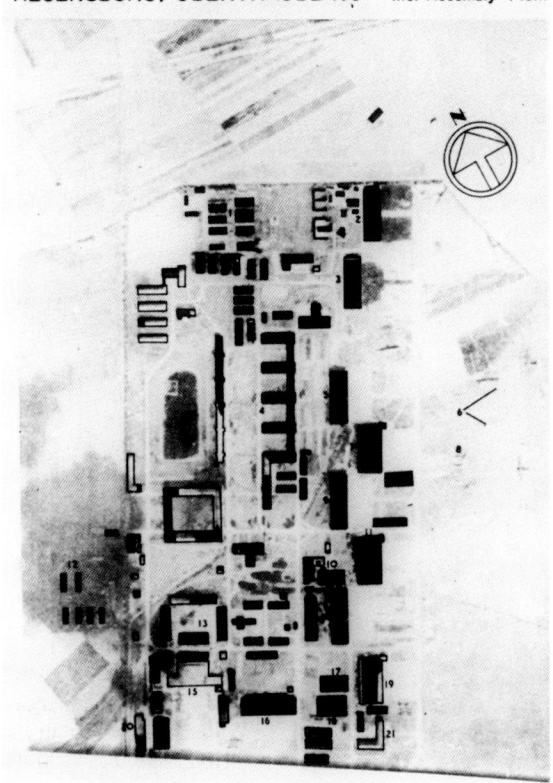

Aerial photograph of the Fliegerhorst Obertraubling of February 1944, prior to the first bombing raid (Photo USAF)

The Kommandogerät 40 at the Rosenhof Flak battery in February 1944. (Photo K. Strippel)

The crew of 2./484 Flakbatterie posing in front of the wireless communications hut near Rosenhof. (Photo K. Strippel)

To defend the Fliegerhorst, numerous Flak batteries were erected. This one shows a Russian weapon that had been captured on the Eastern Front and which had been bored out to the German 8.8 cm calibre. It is positioned west of Piesenkofen in an open field and was part of 1. Batterie of Flakabteilung 906. At the centre is the road from Piesenkofen to Oberhinkofen, and behind it are the anti-aircraft batteries of 1./484. (Photo Schmoll)

thundered above and with about 65 guns, the Flak around Regensburg and the Fliegerhorst fired their rounds in salvoes into the sky, their explosions leaving puffs of black smoke. Black is also the colour of death, which prevailed both on the ground and in the air. Bombers plummeted to earth with a screeching howl, and with rumbling impacts, black tower-high explosion clouds rising up, while the earth trembled under bomb impacts.

It was 1255 hrs over Obertraubling when a Consolidated B-24 Liberator of the 376th BG suffered a direct hit from concentrated Flak fire, exploding in the air and bringing down a second B-24 with it. According to German and American statements, both bombers ripped apart in the air. Wings, engines, empennages and fuselage debris rained down and fell in the immediate neighbourhood of the Fliegerhorst and on the communities of Barbing, Harting and Lerchenfeld. With their 10.5 cm Flak weapons, the extremely accurate Railway Flak Battery had probably fired the decisive shot.

Since the middle of February, I./JG 5 was equipping at the Fliegerhorst Obertraubling. It had originally been

Since the Walhalla was easy to recognise by enemy bombers and served as a navigational point for their Fliegerhorst Obertraubling target, it was covered over with camouflage netting. This measure, however, was ineffective as the bombers had no difficulty finding the Fliegerhorst. (Photo Illenberger)

In the background of the 1./484 Flak battery is the Obertraubling church tower (Photo Schmoll)

The accommodation barracks for 1./484 directly on the road to Oberhinkofen (Foto Schmoll)

stationed in Kirkenes in northern Norway and had flown escort flights for attacks on Murmansk. This Jagdgruppe subsequently relocated to Bulgaria to protect the Rumanian oilfields. In Sofia, it handed over its Bf 109 Gs to the Bulgarian Air Force before coming to Obertraubling to be re-equipped with newer aircraft for the Reichsverteidigung. At Obertraubling, I./JG 5 was not yet incorporated into the air raid warning system for Reich defence when the bombers were making their approach. At literally the last minute, at 1230 hrs, a few Bf 109 G-6/R-6s took-off to intercept the approaching bombers. Until the fighters reached the altitude of the bombers, these had already released their bombloads and were making their return journey. The I./JG 5 pilots took up the chase and Leutnant Heinrich Freiherr von Podewils was successful after three attacks, at 1245 hrs, in bringing down a B-17 near Schwimmbach, south-west of Straubing. Another B-17 was shot down by Oberleutnant Senoner at 1250 hrs near Zangberg, 5 km (3.1 mls) north-west of Mühldorf/Inn. Major Gerlitz also took off and chased a B-17, which at 1258 hrs, disintegrated on the ground near Oberneukirchen, south of Mühldorf. When the German fighters returned to Obertraubling, they had problems finding a landing strip on the bombed-out Fliegerhorst.

Leutnant Heinrich Freiherr von Podewils of I./JG 5 recalled: 'In January 1944, we were still stationed in Sofia/Vraschdebna. After giving brief instructions, we handed over our aircraft there to Bulgarian Air Force pilots and relocated via rail transport to Obertraubling. On 19 February, in the Fliegerhorst mess we celebrated our return from the Front. What an abstinence-rich time we had put behind us! Coming from tough but successful missions on the Eismeer (North Polar Sea) and tasked to protect the Rumanian oilfields, we were now to strengthen the defence of the Reich. That this defence of the homeland would soon result in large sacrifices, was something we suspected more than we knew at this time. Completely unfamiliar to us was the air raid alarm that

At around midday on 22 February 1944, the first demolition bombs exploded on the Fliegerhorst. Clearly visible at centre are the control tower and the flight operations building as well as Halle 3 to the right, the picture taken from the Flak emplacement of Eisenbahnflakbatterie 1./227 (E). (Photo Dr. Wedemeyer)

sounded at 1216 hrs on 22 February 1944. We were still equipping with the Bf 109 G-6/R-6, and only a few of the aircraft were operational. Everyone ran to them, as we had done a thousand times at the Front, and did all the necessary to get the engines started. We just managed to leave the airfield at 1230 hrs before the first bombs fell a few minutes later. We had no vectoring from the ground and had to first look for the bombers, as these flew over in 8/10ths cloud. With the experienced Unteroffizier Scharf at my side, we rose through a hole in the clouds to interception altitude and encountered a massed bomber formation that was already making their way back. We made three attacks on them; from behind, and then to the left and right. One can hardly imagine today what it meant to attack such a heavily-armed bomber formation. We were met with such a concentrated barrage of defensive fire that our hearts sank into our pants. It called for a competent portion of self-control to dive into that defensive fire and approach the bombers to firing distance. After the third attack, one of the bombers increasingly lost more and more parts and both of its starboard engines had stopped. The bomber went into a dive, but 3 parachutes could be seen. Some 15 km (9 mls) southwest of Straubing near Schwimmbach, the B-17 at 1250 hrs hit the ground. At 1330 hrs, we returned to Obertraubling. Already from afar, we could see the black clouds of smoke over the Fliegerhorst and suspected nothing good. We had to circle several times over the airfield before we could find a suitable landing stretch. One hour before, we had left from an intact Fliegerhorst, where now there was a heap of rubble. Several of the Hallen and buildings had been severely hit, and the mess hall in which we had celebrated on 19 February had been destroyed by a direct hit. The smell of fires lay in the air; even our accommodation area had been hit and most of the windows had been shattered.'

Heinz Birkholz of I./JG 5 also recalled this bombing raid: 'In February 1944, after missions in Rumania and Bulgaria to protect the oil refineries at Ploesti, I./JG 5 returned to Germany for Reich defence. Our first station was Obertraubling. Upon unloading our technical equipment that had arrived by rail, I injured both my feet severely when the hinged door of one of the wagons fell on them. I was taken to the Fliegerhorst field hospital that was full with casualties and had only a tiny attic room for myself.

An enormous column of smoke over the Fliegerhorst epitomises the extent of destruction by the 15th USAAF. In the foreground are the 10.5 cm Flak defences of the Eisenbahnflakbatterie 1./227. In the bombing raid on 25 February 1944, this Flakbatterie was destroyed in a carpet of bombs in which 53 of the flak crews were killed and over 40 partially heavily injured. The Batterie was located only about 800 m from the Fliegerhorst and lay in the approach path of the bombers. Even at that time, it was unfathomable how the Flakbatterie could be stationed so close to the Fliegerhorst. (Photo Wedemeyer)

'Almost daily there was an air raid alarm, but I never sought to go into the air-raid shelter as climbing the stairs was an effort for me. On 22 February, when my wounds were on the way to healing, I finally hobbled down into the fresh air and chatted with some of my comrades. Suddenly the sirens howled. Since nothing had previously ever happened, I remained calm. But we soon heard the sound of engines which kept getting louder and which turned into a dangerous roar. We then discovered the approaching four-engined bombers that were flying in tight formations past the airfield, then turned round far over the Danube and made their way back, heading directly towards our Fliegerhorst. Now,

This Bf 109 G-6/Trop from the 1943 Regensburg production batch was damaged in combat on 22 February 1944 and had to make an emergency landing near Passau. Its pilot, Oberfeldwebel Heinz Arnold of I./JG 27, was stationed in Fels, near Wagram. On 22 and 25 February 1944, I./JG 27 was tasked, with all its aircraft, to engage the bombers flying towards Regensburg. (Photo Schmid, Passau)

everything became clear to us. We were the target. It was the turn of Obertraubling and the Messerschmitt-Werke from where we were to fetch our new aircraft. When I saw how the whole formation opened their bomb doors, I could only shout out: "Run, everybody into the cellar!"

'I told one young pilot - he was at the most 18, who had been appointed as guard, to quickly seek cover in one of the one-man trenches. I had never imagined that with my foot injuries I could run so fast as on this day. Hardly was I in the cellar when the first bombs fell and all the walls of the building trembled. Dust showered down everywhere, and water pipes burst. I immediately wet my handkerchief and held it to my mouth and nose so as to be able to breathe at all.

'It lasted about half an hour. We waited for awhile and then ventured out of the cellar. I immediately searched for the young pilot, whose one-man trench had been covered with debris. We dug him out; he was still alive, but his once dark hair had turned snow-white! My comrades immediately took him to the field hospital. After I had hobbled back into my attic room, I was unable to believe my eyes. The door had blown out and I looked up into the smoke-blackened sky. A hundredweight-heavy concrete block from the perimeter had flown through the roof directly onto my bed that was broken in two at the centre. Had I – as always – remained lying there during an air raid alarm…'

The effects of the bombing raid on the Fliegerhorst were catastrophic. The B-24 formation reached Obertraubling at 1245 hrs and covered the place with 180.5 tons of bombs that were dropped from a height of 19,700-23,000 ft between 1245 and 1312 hrs. Fourteen B-24 heavy bombers were reported as lost. Around 300 demolition bombs fell directly on the Fliegerhorst installations, where two Hallen were destroyed, two heavily and six lightly damaged; 27 people were killed, 48 injured, and two reported missing. At least 120 Bf 109 G-6s parked in front of the Hallen were destroyed and many more were heavily damaged. Considerable damage was done to the final assembly area, material storage, in the workshop, sheet-metal shop, the training workshop, as well as a good deal of destruction in the barracks area. Several large fires broke out. Bombs fell in the immediate neighbourhood too, and numerous small villages had been hit. A number of important road connections and railway lines were hit badly, as for example, the Reichsstraße 16 at Bad Abbach and the Regensburg-Straubing rail line, so that rail traffic had to be diverted.

The B-17s had made a navigational error on approach to their target and at 1250 hrs dropped around 150 tons of bombs near Bad Abbach and Matting (southwest of Prüfening) on open countryside and into the Danube. Five B-17s fell victim to fighter attacks. That the bombing raid of 22 February was partly unsuccessful was soon established by a reconnaissance aircraft, because it showed that the plant in Prüfening had suffered no bomb hits at all. A second raid on Regensburg was therefore necessary, and this time, it was a coordinated mission by the Eighth and Fifteenth Air Forces on the Messerschmitt-Werke. A devastating one-time double blow was thus prepared against Regensburg that has been seldom matched in the history of air warfare.

That further bombing raids were expected by the Messerschmitt Works management was indicated by a further reconnaissance flight which Generaling. Roluf Lucht and Dr. Wedemeyer undertook on the morning of 25 February 1944 in a Fieseler Storch. The purpose of this flight was to locate wooded areas with connections to roads, suitable for dispersal production in the surroundings of Regensburg. Up until the bombing raid of 22 February, about 40 per cent of production had already been dispersed or was in the process of becoming so, with final assembly still being carried out in the two plants in Regensburg.

25 February 1944

On this superb winter day, there was a beautiful blue sky over southern Germany. One of the heaviest air battles of World War II, in terms of losses suffered, extending from

Messerschmitt Bf 109 G-6, W.Nr. 162656, Regensburg, 22 February 1944

After the bombing raid on 22 February 1944, some 200 Bf 109s, like this factory fresh, but uncamouflaged Bf 109 G-6 (which was probably W.Nr. 162656 as indicated by the number on the rear fuselage), were either destroyed or heavily damaged. Note that the later style wooden tail fin and rudder are already camouflaged - as these were subcontracted and delivered fully painted for fitment. (Photo Gattinger)

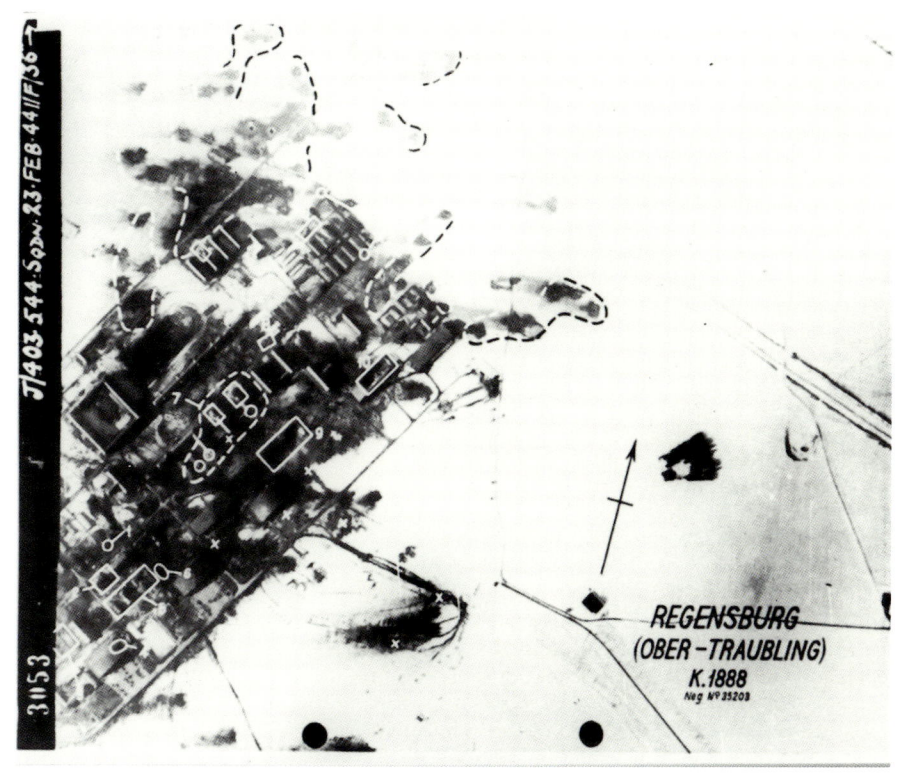

This annotated photograph taken by a U.S. reconnaissance aircraft on 23 February 1944 shows the extent of destruction at the Fliegerhorst. (Photo USAF)

NEST OF EAGLES

*The forward lower port-side fuselage of a shot-down B-24 Liberator of the US Fifteenth Air Force lies in the snow. In the coordinated fire of the Obertraubling Flak batteries, a B-24 of the 376th BG received a direct hit over the Fliegerhorst, and exploded and in doing so brought down another B-24 with it. Both bombers broke up in the air, the fragments falling widely in the neighbourhood of the Fliegerhorst. Out of the 20 crew members, only five survived.
(Photo Dr. Wedemeyer)*

*The starboard wing of one of the crashed B-24s. The Pratt & Whitney radial engines and propellers lie partially buried in the ground.
(Photo Dr. Wedemeyer)*

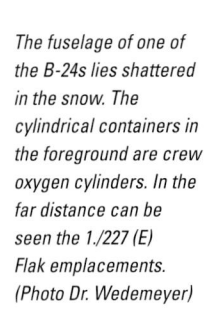

*The fuselage of one of the B-24s lies shattered in the snow. The cylindrical containers in the foreground are crew oxygen cylinders. In the far distance can be seen the 1./227 (E) Flak emplacements.
(Photo Dr. Wedemeyer)*

In the foreground is an anti-aircraft target range-finder of the 1./906 Flakbatterie. In the background at left is a captured 8.8 cm Flak gun. (Photo Schmoll)

The 2./484 Flak battery near Rosenhof, east of the Fliegerhorst Obertraubling. (Photo K. Strippel)

the Adriatic to the Atlantic coast cost the US air forces over 70 four-engined bombers and seven fighters, of which 39 came from the 15th and 31 from the Eighth Air Force. Five bombers were so badly damaged that after successful emergeny landings, they had to be scrapped. The target for the Fifteenth Air Force was the Messerschmitt plant in Prüfening. Alternate targets were the harbours in Pola and Zara, Graz airfield and the Zell am See railway station. Because of strong German fighter defences, some of the bombers broke off their operation and bombarded the alternative targets. Some 40 minutes later, the Eighth Air Force was to attack Prüfening and Obertraubling.

At 1010 hrs, the Fifteenth Air Force entered Reich territory. Taking-off from their bases in southern Italy, 176 bombers had approached from the Adriatic. Due to technical problems, 35 of them broke off their mission. For fighter protection, they had 85 P-38s whose range, however, only reached as far as the Alps, from where the bombers had to fight their way to Prüfening on their own, losing 33 B-17s and B-24s between Laubach and the target. Three P-38s and one P-47 were shot down. From 1240 to 1315 hrs, 116 bombers dropped 1,237 demolition bombs weighing some 280 tons on the installations in Prüfening, where the focal point was the large assembly halls to the north of the plant with its metalworking, pre- and final assembly halls. After their departure, four large fires became visible; an enormous column of smoke rose into the blue sky that could be seen from hundreds of kilometres away. All of the German fighter and Zerstörer Geschwader that were stationed in the south of the Reich, in Ostmark (Austria) and in northern Italy attacked the bombers both on their outbound and return flights. Successful attacks were made against the Fifteenth Air Force by III./JG 3, I./JG 5, I. and II./JG 27, I. and II./JG 53, I./JG 77, I./JG 104, I./JG 301 as well as II./ZG 1, I. and II./ZG 76 and I./ZG 101. Hardly had the fighters landed (many were also engaged in chasing the bombers heading southwards), when a further strong bomber formation was heading for Regensburg from the west. However an element of the German fighter and Zerstörer force had already been refuelled and rearmed and hence took off to engage the Eighth Air Force. On this day, aircraft from all three of the Eighth's Air Divisions had taken off from England with for the Reich. With 196 B-17s, the 1st Air Division reached Augsburg and bombed the Messerschmitt plant, and 50 of its B-17s dropped their bombs on industrial installations in Stuttgart. The main target, however, was Messerschmitt Regensburg, where 267 B-17s of the 3rd Air Division arrived and completed the destruction. They had no navigational problems as the enormous cloud of smoke from the attack by the Fifteenth Air Force over Prüfening showed them the way to the target. The 3rd Air Division was escorted by the first 40 available P-51 B Mustang fighters of the 357th Fighter Group, so that 'acceptable' bomber losses amounted to 12 B-17s destroyed and 86 damaged for the loss of two P-51s and one P-47 Thunderbolt.

After the raid by the Fifteenth Air Force, the air raid warning was still in force in Prüfening when the approaching bombers split into two formations. The 95th, 100th and 390th Bomb Groups attacked the plant with 108 B-17s and although the smoke clouds caused by the Fifteenth Air Force were still present and hindered target approach, their carpet of bombs had

137

covered the plant. From 1356 to 1406 hrs, 695 heavy demolition and 1,636 incendiary bombs fell on its installations and in the surrounding area, amounting in weight to around 230 tons of bombs.

The second bomber formation flew in the direction of Landshut and turned over Rottenburg to attack the Fliegerhorst Obertraubling from the south-west. The 94th, 96th, 385th, 388th, 447th and 452nd BGs, commencing at 1406 hrs, dropped 1,295 500 lb incendiaries and 1,028 fragmentation bombs, corresponding to a weight of 348 tons. Well-placed Flak fire (for the various Flak positions see Appendix 16) and bitterly fought air battles were unable to hinder extensive destruction of the Fliegerhorst. From what is known today, the Eisenbahn (railway) Flak Battery 227 (E) shot down two B-17s of 385th BG. This Battery found itself in the midst of carpet bombing by the 447th and 385th BGs, so that 53 Flak personnel were killed and 40 injured, with their guns either destroyed or else badly damaged. The B-17 F 42-30822, piloted by Lieutenant Delmar A. Gray of the 385th BG received direct hits from Battery 227 (E) on the starboard side of its nose and the engines on the starboard wing. The B-17 rolled over and then dived in a plume of smoke vertically over Obertraubling, breaking up in the air, its parts impacting the Fliegerhorst and the surroundings. Four of its crew were killed. Flying directly beside it, B-17 F (42-3422) 'Winnie The Pooh', piloted by Lieutenant Nelson H. Davis, had one engine shot off. After it had ejected all of its bombs, the crew attempted to fly to Switzerland but one after another, two more of its engines quit, and the bomber could not be held in level flight. Davis gave the order to bale out and when only the two pilots remained in the aircraft, a Bf 110 approached the bomber without opening fire. The B-17's co-pilot Leutnant Robert C. Clarke then parachuted out and landed near Offenburg. Davis himself jumped out near Kirchdorf but his parachute did not open due to lack of sufficient altitude. His shattered body was found in a field east of Kirchdorf. The crewless B-17 continued on course to Wildenburg, and all observers on the ground believed that it would crash into the village, when it suddenly entered a turn to port and exploded on impact in a forest only about 500 m (550 yds) away from Wildenberg and about 30 km (18.6 mls) south-west of Regensburg.

The Bf 109 G-6s of I./JG 5 likewise took off from Obertraubling to counterattack at the last minute and entered into combat with P-51 Mustangs. Oberleutnant Senoner, who had shortly before shot down two of the Fifteenth Air Force bombers, fell victim to a P-51.

Leutnant Heinrich Freiherr von Podewils of I./JG 5 recorded: 'On 25 February 1944, at midday (at 1231 hrs - author) the air raid sirens again sounded. The first American waves of bombers attacked the plant in Prüfening. As on 22 February, we arrived at the location too late. Flying diagonally over the town, we attempted to connect up with the bombers. We were successful in attacking some of the B-24s that were flying away. After landing in Obertraubling at 1230 hrs, our fighters that were returning one by one were immediately refuelled and rearmed. Our well-practiced ground crew were absolutely first-class. In innumerable sorties on the most diverse Fronts, they had performed all the necessary motions a thousand times. Oberleutnant Senoner reported two shoot-downs. Hardly were our aircraft ready for another sortie, when attacking bombers were again announced. We said to ourselves: "That just can't be!" But not even 15 minutes later, we were soon taught otherwise. They came - and how! Each one of us made a dash for his aircraft so as to be able to take off as soon as possible. My Me 109 was parked on the concrete in front of one of the large hangars at the Fliegerhorst. Quickly into the aircraft, I strapped myself in and closed the canopy. The second mechanic was already cranking the starting handle, and when the revolutions reached the maximum figure, I activated the clutch. The airscrew made three or four turns, but the engine did not start. A new attempt was then made with the power lever almost at full load. Again the same thing; the otherwise reliable DB 605 engine showed no sign of life. The other aircraft had long since taken off. Even after we had made several attempts, the engine did not turn. From the time the first alarm siren had gone off, some 10 to 12 minutes had passed when the first bombers were recognizable in the blue sky. Now there was nothing for it but to get out of my Me 109 and head for the cover! I ran right across the airfield, my flying clothing and fur boots causing me enormous difficulties. Almost too late, I became aware that I was heading for a fuel bowser, which was parked on a railway shunt line at the southern edge of the airfield. The first enemy formation had released its bombs and with an unearthly whistle, the bombs descended. Then all hell broke loose as bombs went off in a thunderous roar. High black clouds from the demolition bombs rose, and pressure waves spread over the whole area. A heavy Railway Flak Battery near the Fliegerhorst fired everything that their barrels could give. Two bombers were hit by rapid fire from the Flak, and one went down in circles directly over the airfield. The next wave of bombers scored a direct hit on the Railway Flak Battery, so that their fire was suddenly silenced.

'The entire Fliegerhorst meanwhile lay beneath a thick pall of smoke. After the last bombers had departed, I headed back to my Me 109, but it was completely destroyed. The Fliegerhorst had been badly hit in all areas and almost all of our equipment had been destroyed. Our quarters had also suffered heavy damage. We pilots were thus requartered in the Park Hotel Maximilian in Regensburg. A few days later, we relocated to Herzogenraurach, but it was only on 16 March that I./JG 5 could again report itself ready for operations.'

On this day, the Eighth Air Force lost a total of 31 four-engined bombers and 310 of its crews. A further 298 bombers headed away damaged and with four dead and 26 wounded on board. One B-17 and two B-24s were so badly shot up that they had to be scrapped in England. The Luftwaffe had won a battle and in total the US air forces lost 75 bombers and seven fighters as opposed to around 40 German aircraft, but they were unable to prevent the destruction of the aircraft plants. A total of 864 tons of bombs had fallen on both plants and had turned them into a cratered landscape. At the Messerschmitt Werk I in Prüfening, all of the Hallen were hit. Almost all buildings had been either damaged or destroyed through collapse or by being set on fire. The loss in production was temporarily assessed as 100%. At the Fliegerhorst Obertraubling, almost all the Hallen and buildings had been likewise destroyed. Of the ten largest assembly halls, only two were still undamaged. Those final and pre-assembly halls that had been hit in the 22 February 1944 raid were once more hit by heavy demolition bombs. No plans were made for reconstruction of the Fliegerhorst. On the contrary, because of the two Hallen that were still intact, further bombing raids were expected. In all, 189 tooling machines were destroyed, most of them from intense heat; an entire day's production of electrical parts had been set on fire. As a result of the raging fire with its

On 25 February 1944: B-24 Liberators of the US Fifteenth Air Force bombers head away from the Messerschmitt plant at Regensburg. The River Danube, which served as a very good marker for the bombing raids, can also be seen here. (Photo USAF).

This photograph taken by the US Eighth Air Force on 25 February 1944 shows B-17s leaving the Messerschmitt plant after the one-hour raid by the Eighth and Fifteenth Air Forces. The black column of smoke to the left of the main pall, is from a diesel fuel tank hit in the raid at a railway goods yard. (Photo USAF)

temperatures of over 1,500°C, a large portion of aircraft dural sheets were destroyed. The firefighters fought to the fullest extent and risk, but against such fires they had no chance. Drenching the fire with water was not possible because with the high temperatures, the water would have decomposed into its elements of oxygen and hydrogen and would have caused explosive combustion.

The engine storage area was also heavily damaged. In order to still enable production of the Bf 109 in any way at all at Obertraubling, pre- and final assembly was moved into the two remaining Hallen. For the month of March, completion of 150 Bf 109 G-6s was planned, even though this was numerically low. Final assembly of Me 262 fuselages was immediately transferred to Passau and once more became delayed decisively.

It again became clear to all those responsible that concentrated and unprotected aircraft manufacture at one location at this stage of the war was no longer possible. A special OKL train with Generalfeldmarschall Milch and Reichsdienstleiter Karl-Otto Saur arrived in Regensburg on 10 March 1944. There had been enormous problems getting production up to the fullest extent, or else taking the necessary decisions to relocate it. In order to carry out the necessary clearing-up and repair work to maintain production, there was insufficient manpower and materials available, as also to introduce the necessary building measures for relocation of pre- and final assembly. Chaos and lack of co-ordination in official quarters also played their part. The L VI labour battalion from the Ruhr region that had been requested, was not in agreement with its planned accommodation in a school and made its employment dependent upon better quarters. Such things still existed in 1944.

Through retraining of large elements of the workforce, the works management was able to get production up and running. At the beginning of March, Bf 109 G production started with an output of five aircraft per day. According to records, somewhat draconian measures were taken in the OKL special train. A Construction Director from Nuremberg, who was a 'Gau-Bevollmächtigter' ('District Plenipotentiary'), was arrested in the train, taken to Berlin and handed over to to Obergruppenführer Ernst Kaltenbrunner of the SD in Berlin. He had merely transferred a small number of the urgently needed workmen to Regensburg but was not able to take the decision to close other construction sites and to withdraw them for this purpose. As a consequence, the bomb damage at the Messerschmitt plant could not be repaired to the required extent, which in turn, had an effect on extremely important war

NEST OF EAGLES

Rubble surrounds the destroyed Fliegerhorst Kommandantur following the bombing raid of 25 February 1944. (Photo MZ Archiv)

A monument to destruction: a heavily damaged Bf 109 G-6 wearing no camouflage finish except areas of RLM 76, lies nose down-tail up following the devastating American air raid on Regensburg on 25 February 1944. (Photo Gattinger)

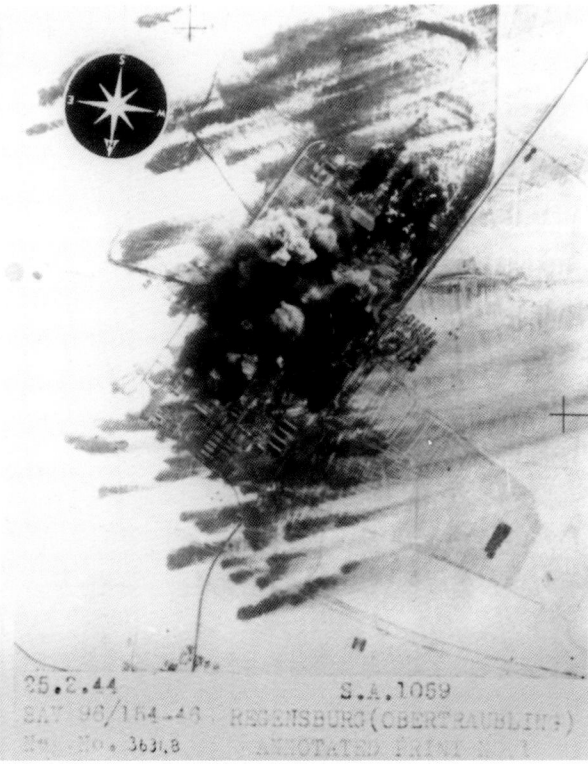

This is how the bomb carpet looked from above. There are clear signs of fires and destruction at the Fliegerhorst. In this raid, 28 were killed and 48 wounded. (Photo USAF)

Bombing

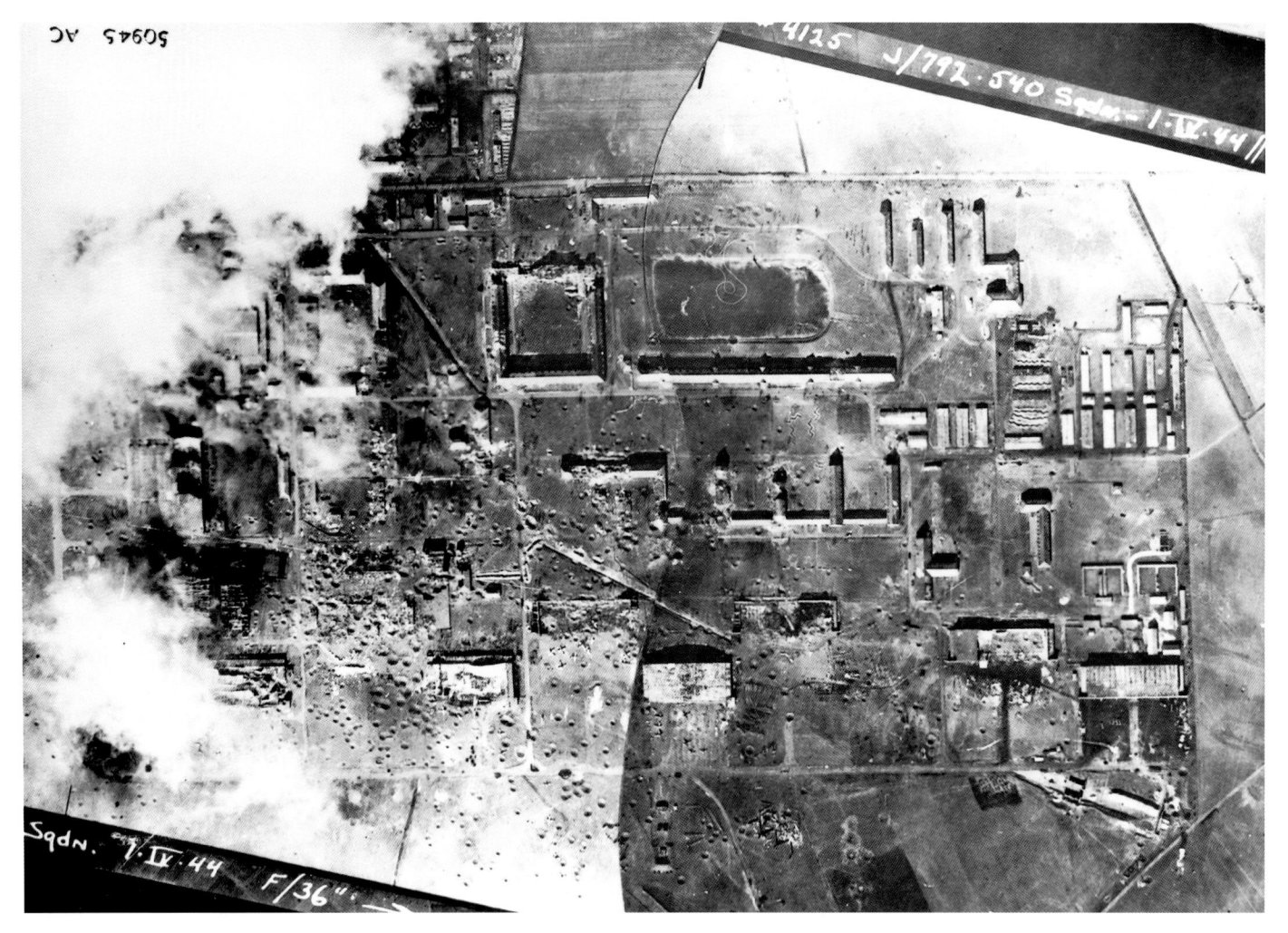

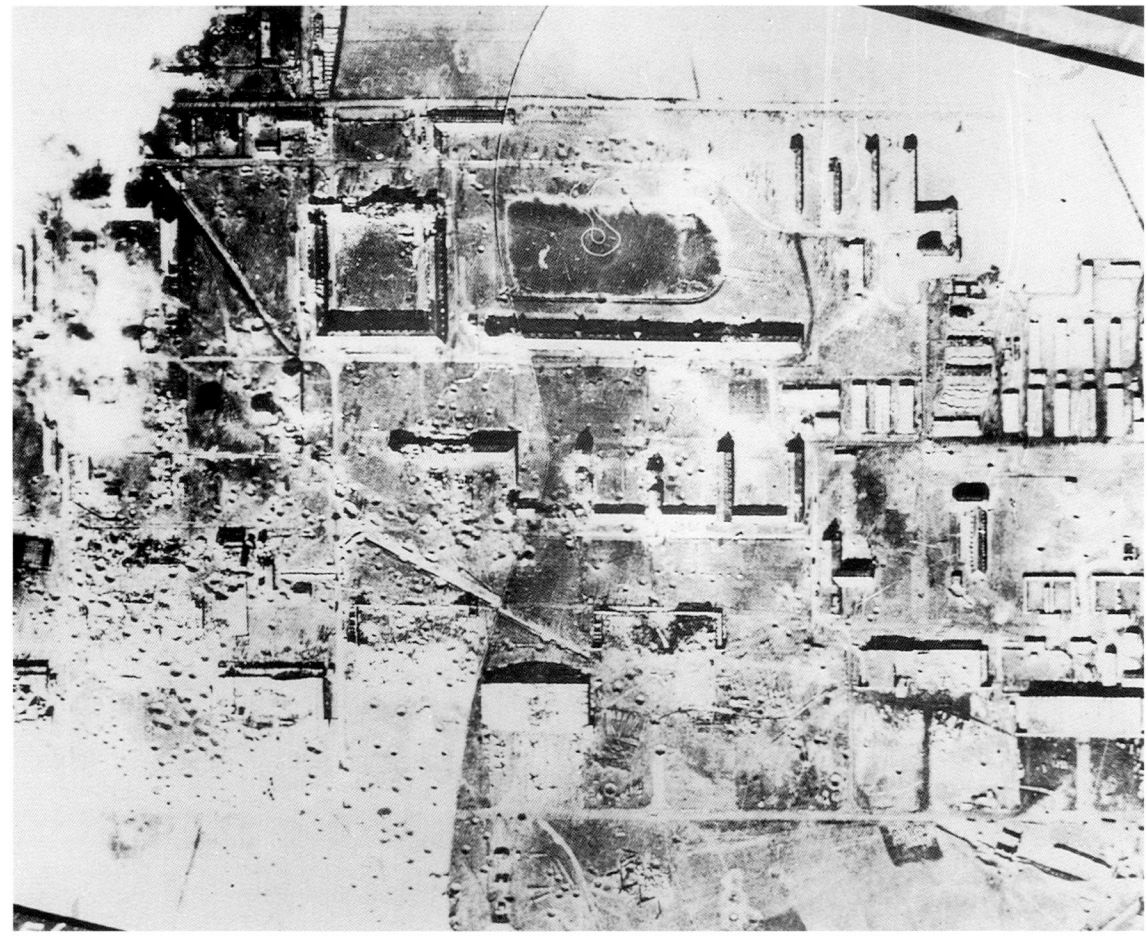

Two photographs showing the combined results of the bombing raids of 22 and 25 February 1944. The Fliegerhorst Obertraubling is pitted with bomb craters and almost all of the Hallen show strike damage. A part of the barracks buildings has also been hit. A total of 410 tons of bombs turned the Fliegerhorst into a veritable lunar landscape. (Photos USAF)

NEST OF EAGLES

Here, the effects of the third bombing raid. The Fliegerhorst lies beneath a giant impenetrable cloud of smoke and dust. On the approach road to the airfield, fire-brigade vehicles rushing to assist can be seen. (Photo Stadt Neutraubling).

On 21 July 1944, the Fliegerhorst Obertraubling was bombed and heavily hit for the third time, with a further 210 tons of bombs. (Photo USAF)

production. Out of four urgently needed production Hallen in Prüfening, only one was completed by 10 March due to a lack of glaziers and roof tilers, and a War Tribunal case was initiated against a Hauptmann of the Construction Battalion.

Of the 1,300 Russian officer PoWs who were set to work in aircraft manufacture in Obertraubling, 700 were taken to the Flossenburg concentration camp in order to perform such work there. The reason given was that the Russian PoWs could be better controlled in a concentration camp. It can be assumed that a certain degree of selection had been undertaken and that those Russians, who had made a negative impression in terms of work performance and attitude were transferred to the camp. Further measures taken included the establishment of three production groups which, independently of each other, produced Bf 109 parts. These were distributed into north, central, and east groups, and had commenced production. The production groups coordinated their output with the railway infrastructure and in the event of bottlenecks, also with trucks; this signified a total dispersal of production.

For the initial dispersal in the villages and forests around Regensburg, at least five Hallen or temporary tents became necessary. The possibility of underground production was also considered, for which purpose the Messerschmitt Works leadership wanted to lay out suitable galleries in the region of the Regensburg chalk caves (which exist today). For the construction of galleries or tunnels, however, the Jägerstab (Fighter Staff) was unable to provide any support in the way of materials. Since the plant in Regensburg had been dispersed, Flak protection of the town was reduced by a third. In a concluding conference, further measures were decided upon including weekly working time being raised from 58-60 hours to 72 hours. Fifteen new

September 1944: A Bf 109 G-14 AS is being towed from the shooting range opposite Halle 7 by a truck at Obertraubling. (Photo E. Steinbügl)

barracks were already under construction and from France, new prefabricated Hallen were earmarked for pre-assembly in Regensburg. As a temporary measure, circus and beer tents were to be requisitioned. The need for tooling equipment for the Me 262 amounted to 350 pieces, especially for presses (stamping machines), and here a bottleneck existed, but it was overcome through deliveries from Italy. Final assembly of Me 262 fuselages was dispersed from Obertraubling to Obernzell near Passau. In Regensburg there were still two presses for Bf 109 manufacture which had to be protected as only one other remained in Vienna. In the event of loss of the Regensburg press, half of Bf 109 production would have been lost. It was decided that the new location for both presses was to be in the Olympia tunnel at Eschenlohe, to where all tooling was to be dispersed. All mechanically manufactured and treated parts for the Bf 109 and for the Me 262 fuselage came from this tunnel from mid-1944.

In the months that followed, all preparations for decentralized aircraft production were in full swing such as were never before seen in modern industrial production. Production figures reached their maximum in 1944, and it was only because of air attacks on the German traffic network and the general war situation that problems affected production. The air attacks on the plants themselves had virtually no effect on decentralized production. The fact that the activities of both the plants continued to be monitored by the RAF and USAAF was demonstrated by yet more bombing raids, on Werk I at Prüfening (related in Part I of this volume) and Obertraubling on 21 July 1944, and on the Fliegerhorst again on 16 February 1945.

21 July 1944

After the Eighth and Fifteenth Air Forces had completed their raids on Messerschmitt Werk I at Prüfening, the next target was the Messerschmitt Werk II and the airfield at the Fliegerhorst Obertraubling, both of which were severely pounded. In this raid, which lasted only five minutes, between 1110 and 1115 hrs, 90 B-17s dropped 233.5 tons of bombs. Here, 30 Bf 109 G-6s that had been parked at distances of 150 m (490 ft) apart at the edge of the airfield remained undamaged. In Hallen 7 and 10, however, all of the Bf 109s under construction were destroyed and medium intensity fires broke out at the Flight Operations building. In the Werfthalle, three small fires broke out; the Halle 2 (main storage and sheetmetal shop), Halle 7 (final assembly), Halle 10 (pre-assembly) and the Heizhaus II (Works heating plant) were burnt down. Valuable materials, however, were able to be saved. The communications building was completely destroyed by a direct hit, several fires breaking out in the mess building. In the southern sector and in the eastern wing of the construction department, total destruction was caused by direct hits from high-explosive bombs. The oil storage depot was also burnt out, and 15 barrack buildings that housed the Russian PoWs were destroyed by fire. To put out the 150 fires at the Fliegerhorst, two Wehrmacht units, fire-fighting units from Regensburg and Burglengenfeld, Wehrmacht Hilfskommandos and Reichsarbeitsdienst tackled the blazes, the bombing raid resulting in 30 injured and four killed.

Numerous fragmentation and incendiary bombs also fell in the neighbouring areas of Harting and Barbing which destroyed haystacks and some 9.5 Hectares of cornfields. Following these renewed heavy blows on both locations, aircraft production was henceforth dispersed to the Waldwerke that were almost on the point of completion, so that dispersal production now took place on a scale such as had never before been undertaken by industry, let alone in wartime. According to the USSBS and Survey of Messerschmitt Factories and Functions, (Volumes I to IV), as a result of superb organisation, Messerschmitt GmbH Regensburg was turned into the most productive aircraft plant in 1944.

On the Fliegerhorst, a part of final assembly of the Bf 109 remained over an area of 2,500 m² (26,909 ft²) in the damaged yet hastily repaired Hallen as well as a reduced works flight-test operation. The Bf 109 G and K airframes that were turned out at the Waldwerk 'Gauting' were delivered to the Fliegerhorst where the wings and radio equipment were fitted and the armament calibrated and test-fired. Following successful acceptance, the aircraft were test-flown by acceptance pilots and ferried to Puchhof near Straubing. These pilots, around seven or eight in number, were brought over in an Fw 58 Weihe to collect the Bf 109s from Puchhof. The plant's airfield was cleared each day and the Bf 109s that had been parked there had to be separated from one another by large safety distances. Some of these aircraft were taken over by 3./Süd FlüG 1 at Landau/Isar and ferried to operational units. From September 1944 onwards, final acceptance and works trials of Me 262s took place at Obertraubling.

NEST OF EAGLES

In February 1945, many Me 262s ready for acceptance flights were covered with camouflage netting on Obertraubling airfield such as Me 262 A W.Nr. 170303, V303, (which became the replacement V7) seen here which was used in a series of trials to test brakes, generators, RATO units, bomb-release and cabin ventilation.
(Photo Radinger)

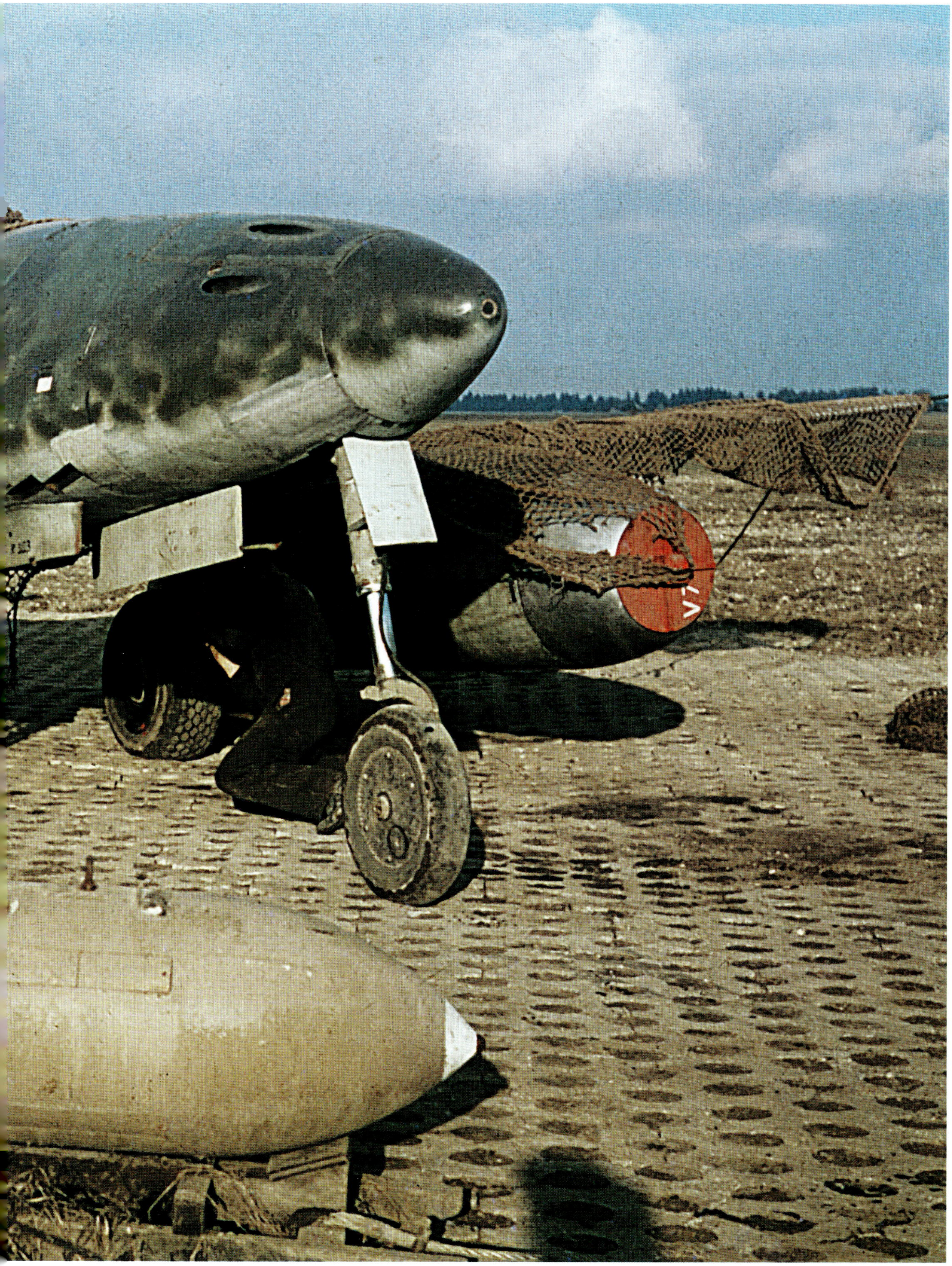
V7

NEST OF EAGLES

On 16 February 1945, Obertraubling was again subjected to a bombing raid. Besides heavy demolition bombs, thousands of small fragmentation bombs were also dropped. In this raid, some 40 Me 262s were either destroyed or heavily damaged (Photo USAF)

B-24s of the US Fifteenth Air Force seen flying off to the east after dropping their bombs on the Fliegerhorst Obertraubling. As on previous raids, the airfield once again lies under ever-increasing palls of smoke from 515 tons of bombs. It was not, however, to be the last bombing raid, for on 11 April 1945, the 2nd Air Division of the Eighth Air Force dropped 159 tons of bombst. No Luftwaffe Fliegerhorst was bombed as often as Obertraubling. (Photo USAF)

CHAPTER **12**

Messerschmitt Me 262

AT the end of 1944, residents of eastern Bavaria peered in astonishment up at the sky where, with an engine noise previously unknown to them, an aircraft travelling at high speed was leaving a condensation trail. Only a few people at that time were aware of what a giant leap in the history of aviation and technology was being played out when the first Me 262 turbojet fighter took off and landed at the Fliegerhorst at Obertraubling. For pilots too, it was an experience to fly an aircraft that no longer had propellers.

As the former Oberleutnant and works test pilot Adolf Riedmeier recalled: 'Instead of the rumbling, loud piston engine, whose vibrations disseminated over the whole aircraft, one now sat in a machine in which, during flight, only a weak whine of the engines was audible; furthermore no engine noise disturbed radio communication. For me, it was almost more of a glide than the previously usual way of flying. Because of the considerably higher speeds, control of the Me 262, and above all navigation, required a higher degree of concentration. By the time one became aware of it, one was already kilometres away from the airfield – almost twice as far away as in a Bf 109. The approach flightpath for landing for example, had to be commenced earlier, with plenty of room for manoeuvre. However, it was not possible with the Me 262, as with the Bf 109, to execute a tight curve in preparation for the landing. This had to be started quite early on in order to reduce speed and come in for a landing at a small angle and at a reduced speed. In doing so, the engine throttles had to be moved most carefully, and at best, one left them to run at the revolutions one had selected for the landing approach and only reduced power gradually shortly before touchdown. For well trained pilots, the Me 262 was no problem. Admittedly the technology, and certainly the engines, sometimes caused annoyance, but these stayed within limits. Due to the war situation, the conversion of young pilots to the Me 262 took place under very great time pressure which followed in a very much superficial manner and was pursued at too fast a pace, when one thinks of the completely new method of propulsion and the high speeds involved. Several accidents thus occurred in the operational units which could have been avoided.'

Based on the training programme and on the flight logbook of Unteroffizier Eduard Schallmoser of III./EJG 2, conversion training on the Me 262 proceeded as follows: 14 hours of theoretical instruction on the airframe, powerplants, weapons and radio equipment; four hours of practical training on the

On 2 November 1943, the Luftwaffe C-in-C Reichsmarschall Hermann Göring visited the Messerschmitt-Werke in Prüfening and Obertraubling. To his left is Generalíng. Lucht on leaving the Aministration building in Prüfening. In the meeting that took place there, it was decided that effective immediately, the Me 262 was to be put into series production, and as early as January 1944 the first Me 262 fuselages were completed. (Photo Schmid)

147

NEST OF EAGLES

In September 1944, the first of 335 Me 262s was in final assembly at Obertraubling. Under the greatest of secrecy, their manufacture was begun in October 1944 in the Waldwerk 'Stauffen'. The photograph shows Me 262 A-1 W.Nr. 500071 which was ferried by Einflieger Gerhard Ertelt on 20 January 1945 from Obertraubling to Erding. The aircraft was later operated by 9./JG 7 and was flown to Switzerland (see page 152). (Photo DM Munich)

Regenburg's Chief Test Pilot, Wendelin Trenkle is shown climbing into an export Bf 109 E for a test flight in the Autumn of 1939. A good proportion of Bf 109 Es in the 2300 Werknummern batch went to Switzerland.

Me 262; two hours of engine starting practice in an exercise fuselage, and eight hours of flying the Me 262 for a duration of 5.04 hours. Conversion to the Me 262 was thus completed before being assigned to an operational unit. With the low amount of flying hours, it was not easy for even an experienced pilot to be ready for normal flying operations with the Me 262, let alone aerial combat with superbly trained Allied fighter pilots.

Final assembly of the world's first operational jet fighter began in September 1944 at the Obertraubling Fliegerhorst. According to information from Flugkapitän Trenkle and Frau Seitz, who at that time, worked in the flight operations control office, the first Me 262 take-off with Trenkle in the cockpit was on 19 September 1944. Right up to the first take-off of an Me 262 from the fully bombed-out Fliegerhorst, innumerable technical problems as well as differences of opinion in the RLM existed that needed to be eliminated. Hitler had declared the Me 262 as a 'Chefsache' ('top-level matter') and called for what was designed as a fighter to be used operationally as a fighter-bomber in defence against the Allied invasion expected on the Channel coast.

The Me 262, codenamed 'Schwalbe' ('Swallow') and, from 1945, 'Silber' ('Silver'), represented the beginning of a new, revolutionary epoch in aviation, whose effects we feel to the present day; it was the start of the 'jet age'. German development in the realm of turbojets with axial-flow compressors has since then revolutionized both military and civil aviation. In this sphere, German powerplant specialists conducted pioneering work, with the same holding true for Willy Messerschmitt who created the Me 262 which, with its gently swept wings created a completely new era of aerodynamics. The Me 262 attained flying speeds which only a few years previously, would have been regarded as utopian. With its heavy armament of four 30 mm MK 108 cannon as well as R4M air-to-air rocket projectiles that were introduced shortly before the end of the war, it was the most potent fighter of its day. It was Hitler's last hope of countering the destructive enemy air offensive and of turning the tide of war. Altogether, between September 1944 and April 1945, 335 Me 262s underwent final assembly at Obertraubling and many of these were actually flown.

That production of the Me 262 only really got underway in the autumn of 1944 is confirmed by several facts. Particularly decisive were the problems with the turbojets which represented a completely new field of endeavour, where all knowledge about this new type of propulsion had first to be acquired. Since the necessary high quality steel alloys could not be made available in the required quantities, it was necessary for their series manufacture to inlcude compromises, which in turn influenced technical reliability in flying operations or else reduced operating hours. Hence, the engine throttle levers had to be moved very slowly. If they were moved too fast, too much fuel was injected into the combustion chamber and led to overheating of the turbine, causing the turbine blades to catch fire.

On this point, Flugkapitän Trenkle commented: 'The first jet engines were of an extremely sensitive design and forgave no mistakes in their handling. If one pushed forward the throttle levers too fast, the engine literally swallowed too much injected fuel and cut out. If, on the other hand, one throttled back too rapidly in order to reduce the revs, the turbojets also cut out. At altitudes over 8,000 m (26,250 ft), it was best not to touch the throttle levers at all, otherwise the turbojets cut out and a relight in flight was not always successfully accomplished.'

In order to avoid overheating or extinction of the turbojets upon too sudden a movement of the throttles, a throttle lever attenuation with an acceleration governor was installed. Despite continual design improvements, the turbojets produced by the German aero-engine firms to the end of the war had their idiosyncrasies, and even after the war, British and American pilots were killed testing captured German jet fighters whose engines failed. Nevertheless, it must be said that the German aviation industry, especially in the manufacture of high-performance jet engines and aircraft which operated in the high-speed regime, possessed an unimaginable technological leap over the other belligerents. Messerschmitt in Regensburg played a decisive role at the beginning of this new era of aviation, and the US aircraft industry profited in no small measure from German developments and projects. Thus, certain post-war US jet fighters such as the North American F-86 Sabre quite clearly display their ancestry to proposals made by German aircraft designers. At the end of the war, across the Atlantic, a massive technological change began, which spared American industry an expensive ten-year period of research and development work in the sphere of aviation and rocket propulsion.

To return to powerplant testing with the Me 262: between 10 June-26 September 1944 there were 43 turbojet failures. Some of these failures were due to servicing errors. Other problems existed with the Riedel starter unit, a two-stroke motor which started the

Civilian technicians and engineers prepare a Me 262 for a test run at an unidentified production plant. The photograph shows a 'wet start': occasionally a small amount of fuel leaked into the base of the Me 262s engine cowling causing a sheet of flame to pour from the turbojet when ignited. Such an event, although spectacular, rarely resulted in any damage to the aircraft.

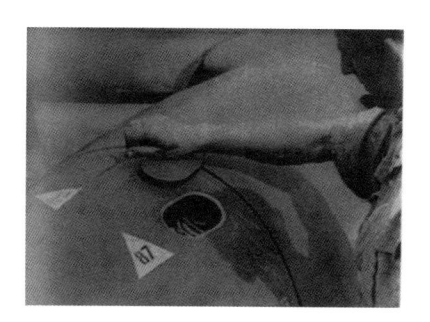

The nose cone within the cowling housed the Riedel starter unit, a two-stroke motor which started the turbojet.. It was started by the ground crew pulling on a cable, whose handle can be seen resting against the aperture in the cone. Initial problems with this unit resulted from it not decoupling when the turbojet started, resulting in it over revving and destruction of the starter unit. The yellow 87 octane triangle denotes the fuel filler point for the starter motor.

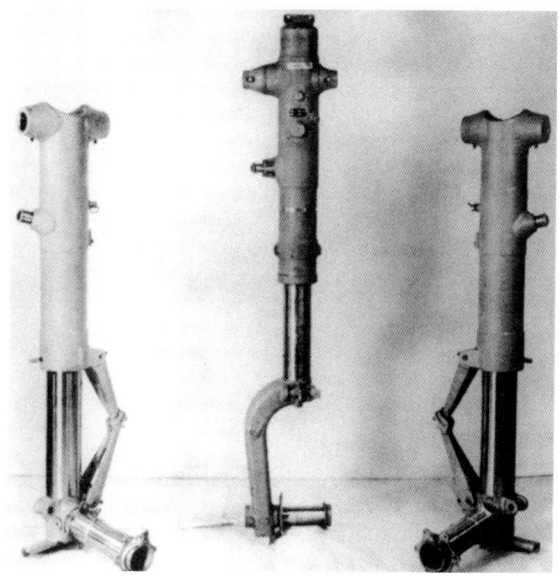

The standard undercarriage legs as manufactured by Opel for the Me 262, showing the nosegear in the centre, flanked either side by the port and starboard maingear. Several modification proposals were investigated relative to the 'scissor link' shock absorbers in the mainwheel legs as development of the Me 262 progressed. Undercarriage failures were commonplace with some 34% of accidents being attributed to this cause, while engine problems were responsible for 33%.

Left and far left: These photographs show a standard series production nosewheel as fitted to a Me 262. Note the absence of a scissor link which had been removed after the nosewheel leg had been modified to accommodate an internal friction damper which had previously hindered the efficient working of the flutter/shimmy dampers.

turbojet and which was attached to it by a coupling. After the turbojet had started-up, the Riedel starter was supposed to decouple automatically, but at the beginning, this coupling did not always function reliably, so that at higher turbine revs the two-stroke motor was over revved, resulting in its destruction. Despite all manner of technical problems with the turbojets, speeds in the region of sound were attained with them, and here one came up against previously partially unknown problems, such as rudder flutter or too-sudden loss of elevator control at speeds above 800 km/h (497 mph) for which there was no explanation. In this respect, Flugkäpitan Trenkle related: 'In diving or in steep curving flight, the speed of the Me 262 increased very quickly. The control column then locked solid like concrete, and even when pulled with both hands, it could not be moved by even one millimetre. With increasing speed, the airflow hummed around the aircraft such that one became most anxious, and it was only through careful operation of the elevator trim that one could level out. If everything went off well, one shot upwards into the sky at around 900 km/h (559 mph) or more!'

With the undercarriage of the Me 262 too, there were also not inconsiderable problems from the beginning. The initial prototypes were still fitted with a tailwheel. At take-off, the airstream did not grip the elevator and it was only by touching the brakes that at a high take-off speed the tailplane lifted up and allowed the elevators to exercise a control function in the airstream. For operational flights with a fully-fuelled and armed aircraft, this was an unacceptable condition. In great haste, a nosewheel undercarriage was designed, whose 660 x 190 mm (26 x 7.5 in) nosewheel came from the Bf 109 G-6. The mainwheels, measuring 770 x 270 mm (30.3 x 10.6 in) on pre-production aircraft, were replaced by 840 x 300 mm (33 x 11.8 in) wheels on production machines. Operational use revealed that the Me 262 undercarriage, due to the aircraft's high landing speed and the particular forward slant of the sprung legs, was not up to the loads imposed on it. To enable introduction of the larger 840 x 300 mm mainwheel tyres on series-built aircraft without modifying the

Eight Me 262s are seen here recently arrived at Lechfeld from Leipheim and carrying the white tactical numerals of Erprobungskommando 262, the first Me 262 military trials unit, on their noses and yellow recognition bands applied to the fuselage forward of the Balkenkreuz. The three aircraft in the foreground are 'White 2', W.Nr. 170071, 'White 3', W.Nr. 170067 and 'White 5', W.Nr. 170045.

fuselage, the sprung legs were set at an angle, which did not permit a problem-free functioning of the leg as the range of travel of the spring was too limited. On landing, this led to shock rents in the tyres, to deformations in the sprung legs, and even partially to bending of the undercarriage mainwheel legs in their shafts inside the wings. By means of comprehensive trials and drop-hammer tests at the Erprobungsstelle Rechlin, the source of the problems was found and eliminated. Alterations to the undercarriage (oil filling, shock absorbance, manoeuvring arrangement, etc.) became possible without considerable modifications to make the undercarriage fit for mass production. Decisively engaged on this work was a young Rechlin engineer – the later designer of the post-war Messerschmitt commercial cabin-roller – Fritz Fend. After the war, Prof. Messerschmitt confirmed that it was thankfully largely due to the work of Ing. Fritz Fend that the Me 262 undercarriage reached the stage of production maturity. The nosewheel also had its weaknesses and was somewhat under-dimensioned. On landing, the nosewheel had to touchdown extremely softly and under no circumstances was the aircraft to be ground-towed by its nosewheel. In some instances, in hard landings, the entire fuselage nose broke away. This was clearly due to manufacturing faults in the realm of point-welding which was traceable to the use of concentration-camp inmates, PoWs and foreign workers in the aircraft industry – a problem that had already occurred in connection with Bf 109 production. Further problems lay in the tyres, which only withstood five to six take-offs and landings. Through alterations to the undercarriage and changing the tyres to a higher layer thickness by using artificial silk and thin cord, the tyres now withstood 120 take-offs and landings. A strengthening of the profile raised its braking capability and service life and a considerably weaker undercarriage springing also reduced the impact loads on the wing main spar.

Beginning in mid-1944, when the Me 262 A-1 and A-2 (for technical data and Werknummern see Appendix 17) arrived in small numbers at the Luftwaffe flight-test centres, it was anything but a matured design, as it featured numerous innovations which were pioneering and which pointed the future path for modern aircraft. Technical difficulties were one facet of the Me 262, but there were also other episodes in the development of this groundbreaking aircraft such as problems with turbojet manufacture, as the necessary high-alloy heat-resilient steels for the turbine wheel were absent due to the lack of raw material (nickel). Also, there was the withdrawal of all designers from the Me 262 project and their transfer to the Me 410 project on 17 March 1943; the far-reaching damage or destruction of the jigs for the Me 262 fuselage through the bombing raid on the Regensburg plant on 17 August 1943, and termination of flight trials in Leipheim at the end of 1943 because the airfield was occupied by Italian night-fighters! Furthermore, there was the transfer of its fuselage construction jigs from Regensburg to Passau was as a result of the bombing raids of 22 and 25 February 1944 on the Fliegerhorst Obertraubling.

Although from mid-1944 the Me 262 only appeared in limited numbers over the skies of the Reich, it created as much of a furore in the Luftwaffe as with the Allied air forces. The first to experience its presence were the Mosquito reconnaissance aircraft which penetrated the skies of southern Germany. Where once the wooden construction of the Mosquito had previously provided almost a life insurance for its crews, the first losses now began to be encountered. Erprobungskommando (Ekdo) 262 led by Hauptmann Werner Thierfelder operated from June 1944 from the Fliegerhorst Lechfeld in Bavaria with a handful of Me 262s. Operational trials also encompassed interception sorties against constantly intruding RAF and USAAF reconnaissance aircraft. In this way, Oberfeldwebel Helmut Recker of Ekdo 262 was able to shoot down a Mosquito of 60 (South African) Squadron, RAAF, near Ponsdorf on 26 August 1944. The Mosquito crew, consisting of Lieutenant Christian Johannes Mouton of Bulawayo and Lieutenant Daniel Krynauw of Capetown, were killed in the attack. Both pilots were buried in the military cemetery near the Tegernsee in Bavaria. Shocked by the reports of the increased appearance of the Me 262, American bomber formations immediately began to attack its associated aircraft plants and airfields. These attacks, however, had only a limited effect, as Me 262 manufacture had been decentralized to a just tolerable degree. Divided into the smallest of production centres, its manufacture, in which the parent firm in Augsburg and Regensburg was involved, was increased month by month, where work on the aircraft was divided up between the two plants. Whilst Augsburg built the wings and empennages, Regensburg was responsible for the fuselages. Each production line for the Me 262 was, as a rule, available in duplicate, so that in the event of fall-out of one production centre due to a bombing raid, final assembly could still continue. A gigantic transport system took care of connections between the individual manufacturing centres and thus enabled a relatively problem-free production. This only began to break down towards the end of the war due to the effects on the German transportation network caused by increased bombing and low-level raids. Even the final assembly lines were often undisturbed, since these were located in well camouflaged Waldwerken (forest factories) near Leipheim and Schwäbisch Hall, which produced the Me 262 for Messerschmitt AG, whilst final assembly for the Messerschmitt GmbH took place in Regensburg and Neuberg/Donau. Final assembly of smaller numbers were accomplished in the Bergwerk Kahla near Jena, and in Budweis, Czechoslovakia, for the reconnaissance version; factory flight-testing was undertaken on the airfield at Eger. With the exception of the Waldwerk in Neuburg, which was situated in the immediate vicinity of the airfield, the final assembly lines were not attacked from the air as they could not be discovered by enemy reconnaissance aircraft. Responsible for entire Me 262 production was the Regensburg plant Direktor Linder, who had been given comprehensive powers for this purpose.

That the Me 262 in its introduction to Luftwaffe units was not a mature design, is borne out in the report by engineer Hilber of Messerschmitt AG Augsburg, following visits he paid to the Me 262 Einsatzkommandos of Major Wolfgang Schenck of KG 51 on 21 and 22 September 1944, and Major Walter Nowotny on 22 and 23 September 1944: 'At the time of my visit, [Me 262 operational readiness was 80% at Kommando Schenck and 90% at Kommando Nowotny. An exchange of experiences was held at the former with Fliegering. and TO [Technical Officer] Mascheck as Major Schenck was absent, and at the latter, with Major Nowotny, TO Hauptmann Streicher and communications officer Leutnant Preusker.

'Although the high percentage of operational aircraft was well acknowledged, they nevertheless had three important problems, whose elimination was considered to be extraordinarily important. Wear and tear levels at the fuselage nose is today still very high, and according to their information, up to three nosecaps per aircraft were necessary. From my observations, I have the following explanation as to the cause of this:

'In weapons-firing flights, the loose barrels fall out as their anchorings have not been strengthened in all the nosecaps and as a result, the locking pins do not project sufficiently into the barrels.

'Destruction of the nosecaps due to nosewheel flutter. With the current ground equipment, no satisfactory setting of the flutter brakes to 12 mkg is possible. I have therefore forbidden its use until it is improved, and a somewhat more inconvenient but in all cases more secure setting is indicated. As to what extent the 12 mkg setting due to wear and tear over the course of time becomes reduced, has first to be learned from experience. It is however, certain that with 12 mkg, no nosewheel flutter occurred at Lechfeld.

'The aircraft that are ready for operations still do not have the final strengthened external skinning on the fuselage noses as is required by Mitteilung (Notification) 262 A B1/44. According to earlier data, this is to be carried out without exception from the 501st fuselage nose. Two instances indicate that the introduction of the nosewheel Y-forces in the fuselage nose is still too weak for operational requirements. As to how far the external skin on the nose, between frames 500 and 900 have already been strengthened, has yet to be established. A raising of frame 830 up to the next longeron is, however, to be recommended, in that it would not involve a major alteration. In one particular known case, the nosewheel does not lock in time, so that the aircraft tips over onto its nose.

'The mechanics have enormous problems after an engine exchange to attach the engine cowlings. The one day needed for doing this is by no means a rarity when taking into account the current state of the parts delivered. Even so, stepwise differences exist between the individual cowling parts by up to 10 mm as well as extensively visible folds in the sheeting as a result of bracing. These differences cost not only speed, but also disturb the distribution of aerodynamic forces, which can have dangerous effects on the strength of the cowling. The harmonization of wings, engines and airframe is urgently required.

'Fuel leakage spills oil onto the W/T equipment, whose function is impaired so that the aircraft cannot be properly vectored. This is the principal objection which very much affects operational readiness, and tests are urgently necessary to overcome this. Until then, it is proposed that the W/T equipment be protected by a canvas covering.

'With regard to already known objections of a lesser nature are the following: upward twist of the wing trailing-edge above the engine; the ventilation flap cannot be moved at high speed, and anchoring by means of rivetheads is insufficient. Access to the operating lever has to be improved. Furthermore, this flap is not available on all aircraft, so that a strong smell of fuel is experienced.'

Hilber's report further detailed various problems with the nosewheel leg, a replacement for which lasted up to seven hours, and which was also the same for the fuselage nosecap; loosening of the mainwheel brake fastenings as a result of towing over long distances; too-slow retraction and extension of all three wheels; re-adjustment of the undercarriage retraction mechanism following hard landings; the need for removal of the 200-litre fuel tank to make room for electrical switches; the need to raise the mainwheel extension above the permissible 300 km/h (186 mph) as the aircraft lost speed too slowly in the landing phase which could lead to an overshoot. He finally added that the high percentage of operational aircraft should not encourage delay in removal of all the problems encountered, as this would lead to disadvantages when larger Luftwaffe Me 262 formations became available for operations. In such cases, maintenance crews would not be as numerous as they were at the time of the report. Between September and December 1944, Messerschmitt Regensburg had delivered a total of 49 aircraft, the majority of which consisted of the Me 262 A-2 with which KG 51 was equipped.

NEST OF EAGLES

Regensburg-built Me 262 A-1a, W.Nr. 501232, 'Yellow 5' was operated by KG(J) 6 or KG(J) 54, units formed in 1945 of former bomber and multi-engined pilots, retrained to fly the Me 262 in fighter operations – with dubious results. The aircraft is seen here shortly after the cessation of hostilities at München-Riem, when it was selected by USAAF personnel for shipment to the USA where it underwent further evaluation. It was eventually moved to the USAF Museum at Wright Patterson AFB in Ohio as an exhibit.

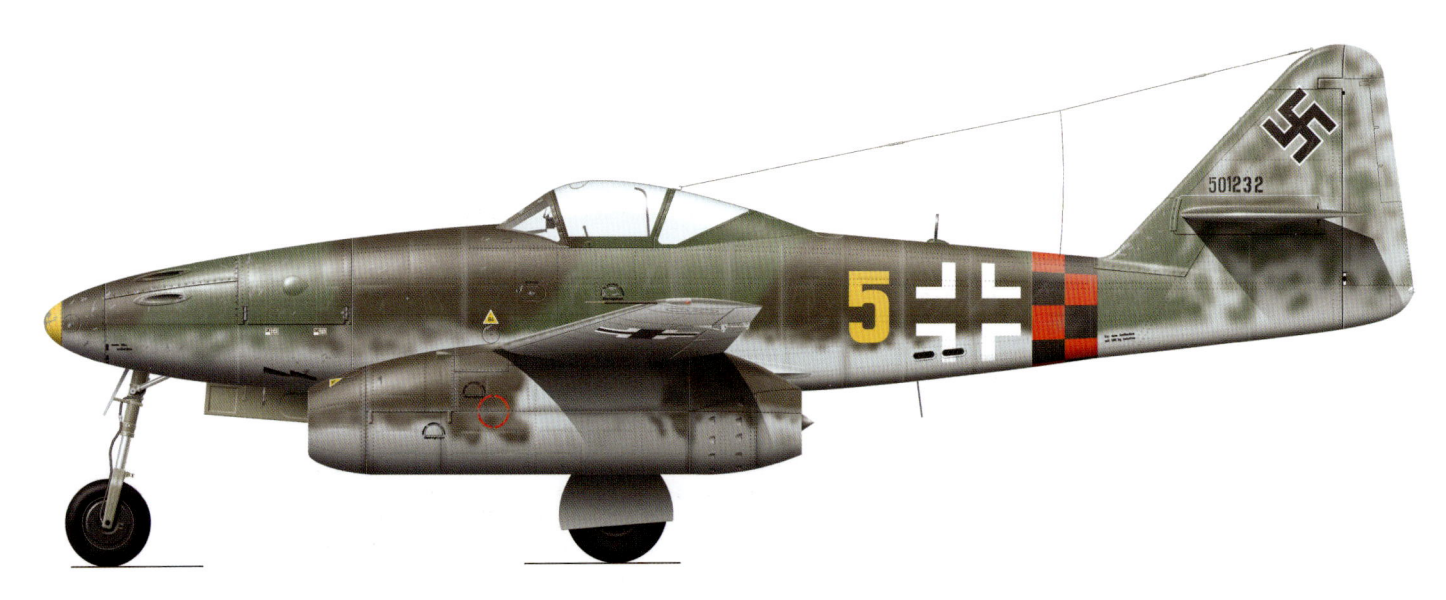

Me 262 A-1a, W.Nr. 501232, 'Yellow 5', KG(J) 6 or KG(J) 54, München-Riem, May 1945

152

A Me 262 A-1a of JG 7, believed to be that of the Geschwader Kommodore, Major Theodor Weissenberger and seen at either Brandenburg-Briest or Kaltenkirchen in late January 1945.

At 1545 hrs on 12 October 1944, a US reconnaissance aircraft flew over Obertraubling. Evaluation of its aerial photographs showed that not only were 30 Bf 109s parked on the airfield at Obertraubling, but also that four of the new and dreaded Me 262s were discovered for the very first time, parked at the southeastern extremity of the field. The USAAF was thus aware relatively quickly of the Messerschmitt 'secret' and over several reconnaissance flights, maintained frequent observation of the Fliegerhorst. Already in November 1944, 12./KG 54 relocated to Obertraubling to take over the Me 262 A-2. At the beginning of 1945, the Staffel was redesignated 12./KG(J) 54, the 'KG(J)' signifying 'Kampfgeschwader im Jagdeinsatz' ('Bomber Wing on Fighter Operations').

That a number of technical problems both at Messerschmitt as well as in the Luftwaffe still existed with the Me 262 as late as February 1945, is shown in a report by Messerschmitt test pilot, Flugkapitän Fritz Wendel who made an inspection trip to JG 7 (the first and still embryonic Me 262 fighter Geschwader), KG 51, and Kommando Welter – the latter an experimental unit that tested and operated the Me 262 as a Nachtjäger (night-fighter). In his report to Messerschmitt AG Augsburg, Wendel wrote: 'Kommando Nowotny, which in October/November [1944] after a brief period of missions had lost 27 of its 30 aircraft, freshened up in Brandenburg-Briest. In the meantime, pilots received better training at Lechfeld. Each pilot at Lechfeld had 12 flying training hours. This Kommando now forms the III. Gruppe in the newly established JG 7. The Kommodore, initially Oberst Johannes Steinhoff, is currently Hauptmann Theodor Weißenberger (200 victories). This Geschwader, and especially the III. Gruppe, is to be the first Jagdgeschwader to utilize the Me 262 for Reich defence. Since 12 February, the III. Gruppe has 50 operational aircraft.

'The I. Gruppe, under the leadership of Kommandeur Major Erich Rudorffer (212 victories), has essentially been completely retrained. Still unaccomplished are formation training and practice in close formation flying (use of the FuG 16 ZY and FuG 25a). Up until 9 February, this Gruppe had only 12 aircraft. With normal availability of a maintenance unit in Brandenburg-Briest, this Gruppe would likewise be operationally ready by the end of this month. The last, in other words, the II. Gruppe, would then be subsequently immediately re-equipped. The operational deadline is dependent upon the availability of the aircraft and pilot training at Lechfeld. Since Ergänzungsgruppe (EJG) 2 at Lechfeld at the present time only has four out of 19 aircraft in flyable condition due to the lack of engines, the supply of pilots is unable to keep pace with availability of the aircraft.

'Hauptmann Weißenberger has prepared the first large-scale mission well, which as a result of pilot training, promises to be a complete success. However, the technical state of readiness following the first missions will sink rapidly, because the replenishment situation with regard to airframe and engine replacement parts is very bad. Responsible for equipment supply is the Jüterbog location, where stores are very poor. A speedy improvement is necessary. Eventually, in the operations area of JG 7, a well-equipped engine parts distribution depot has to be available.

'With almost all aircraft of the III. Gruppe, we have installed adjustable control columns. In installing these, it was shown that the installation documents were incorrect in a number of places, i.e.:

In the autumn of 1944, Fritz Wendel, the Messerschmitt test pilot, visited the headquarters of KG 51 at Rheine to assess bombing operations using the Me 262. Wendel is seen here (right) in discussion with Major Heinz Unrau, Kommandeur of I./KG 51.

Another Me 262 whose construction fell under Messerschmitt Regensburg's control, was Me 262 A-2a W.Nr. 500200, 'Black X' of 2./KG 51. It surrendered at Fassberg on 8 May 1945, and the two photographs show it after the national markings had been overpainted though retaining the 'Black X'. This aircraft is now on display at the Australian War Memorial in Canberra.

1) The stop positions at the foot of the column must be altered by 1 degree 30 minutes in accordance with the C-position column alteration. A notice to this effect is missing.
2) The elevator stop positions in the "depress" direction should be 20°. In fact, the extension is 26°.
3) There are far more bumpers delivered than should be exchanged according to the drawings, and in particular for the rudder control.

'The pilots, especially Hauptmann Weißenberger, are extremely delighted with the adjustable control column and it is the belief that through the manoeuvrability attained with it, the shoot-down rate against enemy fighters will increase. It is desirable, however, that the adjustment button be enlarged and that on this button, the words "take-off/landing" and "flight" be denoted.

'With several aircraft (produced at Leipheim) the trailing-edge control stops are incorrect. There were differences of up to 6° in the ailerons and elevators.

'At the wish of Hauptmann Weißenberger, the General der Jagdflieger, on 5 February, issued instructions that in single-engine landings, a belly-landing should be made. I have already pointed out in one of my recent reports that this instruction has to come about if accidents in single-engine landings are to be avoided. Although the incidence of single-engine landings has fallen considerably, this instruction has now been given in order to avoid further loss of personnel due to the dearth of Me 262 pilots. As long as no skids are mounted beneath the engine nacelles and engine suspension is not strengthened, there will always be considerable damage to the airframe and engines.

'In the aircraft of III./JG 7, the heating system was adjusted. In general, complaints were made of the cockpit heating up too much. Even with closed sliding panels, the temperature at this time of year is unacceptably high. In this connection, it must be once more pointed out that the current ventilation flap has to be altered. The new flaps have to be fitted to all aircraft at the latest by the onset of warm weather. The heating panels crack very often, and especially a few minutes after switching off, these cracks appear. The temperature differences which occur on cooling down are apparently too much for this panel. I have arranged that with some aircraft, the inner panels be sealed and sprayed with warm-air circulation from the heating system.

'With snow and ice-covered runways, several take-offs and landings have resulted in nosewheels remaining skew. When is the cropped nosewheel fork going to appear? Why is its introduction into series production still being delayed? The reason given, that this fork will first appear in conjunction with the hydraulic buffet brake is wrong, for with this fork we shall probably no longer need a hydraulic buffet brake.

'For some days now, Kommando Welter, which reports to NJG 11, has been located in Burg near Magdeburg, where Oberleutnant Kurt Welter is conducting nightfighting operations with the Me 262 using the "Wilde Sau" (Wild Sow) tactic. As opposed to the normal version, his aircraft only have ultraviolet lighting, map illumination and a emergency turn indicator. Welter, who up to now has been the only one to have carried out such operational flights, has already achieved five victories with this aircraft, and his five pilots are still on conversion training. The Kommando possesses 6 aircraft, all of which are expected soon to fly such missions. A further three pilots of this Kommando have all suffered fatal crashes on daytime training flights. One of them even mentioned prior to his crash that he lost elevator trim that was followed by a vertical dive. In another vertical dive and crash near Burg, in which a ferry detachment pilot was killed, the elevator was likewise completely nose-heavy. In altering the adjustment switch, the cruising position slot has been covered over, so as to avoid the adjustment lever from hanging fast in this slot. In addition to that, JG 7 has introduced an interruption button on the adjustment lever for trim activation. The accidents, however, were presumably caused by the pilots, e.g. with their arm or with their left knee, having accidentally pressed the adjustment lever forward. I have pointed out to all pilots that by self-adjustment of the elevator, to pay attention to this.'

In order to avoid overheating or a shut-down of the turbojet due to too rapid movement of the throttle, a throttle lever damping with an acceleration governor had been installed.

Despite all the problems with the turbojets, speed advances were made which bordered on the 'sound barrier' where new and hitherto unknown phenomena began to be experienced, such as control surface flutter, or insufficient control effectiveness at speeds above 800 km/h (500 mph), for which there was no explanation.

CHAPTER 13

'Götterdämmerung'—1945

IN the early hours of New Year's Day, 1945, in an attempt to strike a decisive blow against the Allied tactical air forces, the Luftwaffe launched a surprise low-level attack against 21 enemy airfields in North West Europe. Codenamed Operation 'Bodenplatte', it had been conceived under great secrecy by Gen.Maj. Dietrich Peltz, a former bomber ace who had been appointed to direct II. Jagdkorps, the main fighter command operating on the Western Front. Peltz was assisted by an experienced staff comprising fighter veterans Oberst Walter Grabmann, Oberst Hanns Trubenbach and Oberstleutnant Gotthardt Handrick. The attack deployed 41 Gruppen drawn from 10 Jagdgeschwader and one Schlachtgeschwader as well as Me 262 and Ar 234 jet bombers from KG 51 and KG 76 – in all a force of more than 900 aircraft. It was a monumental effort for the Luftwaffe to mount such an operation at this stage of the war; to the planners' credit it achieved significant surprise and – for a brief period – probably served to lift the spirits of many a war-weary or doubting Jagdflieger. It is believed that 388 Allied aircraft were destroyed or damaged as a result of Bodenplatte. The effects on the German side, however, were at best questionable and at worst, very grave.

A total of 271 Bf 109s and Fw 190s were lost in the raid, with a further 65 damaged. Just under half of these fell to Allied anti-aircraft fire over sensitive front line areas, while just under a quarter were shot down by Allied fighters. Those aircraft shot down, were, to a great extent, flown at low level by young, poorly-trained and thus inexperienced pilots who provided easy prey to Allied fighter pilots already airborne on early morning sorties. Even today, some 40 pilots who took part in 'Bodenplatte' are still regarded as missing and whose fate has forever become a mystery. They were shot down largely by their own Flak for in order to preserve secrecy, the German Flak units were not informed in advance of the large Luftwaffe offensive that was carried out at low-level.

In many cases however, the German formations failed even to find their allocated targets, as with Obstlt. Johann Kogler's JG 6 over Volkel, whilst elsewhere they became lost or collided, as happened to Major Gerhard Michalski's JG 4 over Le Culot. In this case, of the 75 aircraft, only around 12, or 15 per cent of the strike force, actually attacked whereas the Geschwader suffered a 47 per cent loss rate during the operation. This is comparable to JG 53 which lost 30 Bf 109s out of 80 attacking, or 48 per cent. One hundred and forty three pilots were killed or went missing, with a further 21 wounded and 70 more captured. These debilitating figures included no fewer than three experienced Geschwaderkommodore, five Gruppenkommandeur and 14 Staffelkapitäne. Obstlt. Johannes Kogler, the Kommodore of JG 6 confessed to American interrogators after being shot down on 1 January 1945, 'Whatever we did was too soon or too late. One almost felt ashamed to go out in Luftwaffe uniform at home.'

Whereas the Allies were able to replace their losses relatively quickly due to their materiel superiority, the Luftwaffe found itself in no position to overcome the loss of well-trained pilots. Its back was finally broken and its last reserves senselessly expended. In the West, the Allies inexorably approached the borders of the Reich and the Rhine river as the last natural obstacle. On 13 January, the Red Army advanced from the Baranov bridgehead and along the Vishla front to start a great offensive that was only able to be brought to a standstill at the Oder river. The population panicked, and in their flight from the Soviets, indescribable scenes were played out. Responsible for the civilian victims were the Gauleiter, who often against better judgement ordered evacuation with insufficient means of transport. What then followed can best be described as a case of 'save yourself - whoever can'. From the middle of March, the

155

Allied armies set out on their last 'storm'. A few weeks later, in a symbolic gesture, the Americans and the Russians shook hands at Torgau on the Elbe river, and Hitler's Third Reich effectively ceased to exist.

In the end phase of the war, the airspace over the Reich was utterly dominated by the USAAF and RAF. In its daily incursions into Reich territory, the USAAF alone deployed three to four thousand aircraft and more. The last German operational day and night-fighter units lay camouflaged in wooded areas and took off – as far as the fuel situation allowed – to combat low-flying aircraft or otherwise to shoot at advancing Allied tank columns. The Luftwaffe had long since given up attacking the fleets of four-engined bombers, as only the Me 262 units still had any real chance against them and the escort fighters. The entire transportation system and related infrastructure in the Reich broke down; the political leadership either committed suicide or gave themselves up. What remained was a ruined landscape, a populace living in indescribable misery, totally disoriented and without hope.

Me 262 Final Assembly at the 'Gauting' and 'Stauffen' Waldwerk

After valuable experience had been gained with the Waldwerk 'Gauting' near Hagelstadt, the search was begun in June 1944 for a suitable forested area for the erection of a final assembly line for the Me 262 in the neighbourhood of Regensburg, and reconnaissance flights in this area were again conducted with a Fieseler Storch. It became clear that the Fliegerhorst Obertraubling had to be retained as the main focus of support and that acceptance flights had to be made from there. An ideal location was found east of the Fliegerhorst, to the north-east of Wolfskofen in the forests owned by the Thurn & Taxis family near Mooshof. A large forested area between Reichsstrasse 8 in the south and the Reichsautobahn in the north provided ideal traffic communications – the prerequisite for the erection of final assembly for the Me 262. An already existing forest road network was correspondingly expanded, the area extensively cordoned off and camouflaged against discovery from the air. The latter was so successful that although the Fliegerhorst was attacked several times in 1945, such final assembly was never discovered. The entire area was allowed to be entered only with a special pass and was strongly guarded. Construction work began here in the summer of 1944. In the middle of the forest, concrete tunnels for the erection of conveyor-belt assembly and floors for construction jigs were built, as well as light construction manufacturing halls built of wood covered with Heraklith and corrugated metal sheeting. Here, the delivered wings, empennages, fuselages and turbojets were kitted out for the final assembly line, and cranes for unloading the delivered parts were erected in almost all the halls. The largest building, with a length of around 120 m (394 ft), served for final assembly and was covered with innumerable camouflage nets, the building being connected to all the other halls by a railtrack system. Further there were well-camouflaged barracks and tents in which offices, kitchens, canteens, lodgings and various material storage installations were located, and electric power and telephone connections were laid down from Reichsstrasse 8 into the forest. Production of the most modern aircraft of its time was begun in October 1944 under the most primitive conditions, where hundreds of forced-labourers and Russian PoW officers were employed on production. For the layout plans of the Waldwerke 'Gauting' and 'Stauffen', see Appendices 17 and 18.

A report on the Waldwerk 'Stauffen' by Electromeister Josef Liebl of Regensburg recorded: 'Based on my function at Messerschmitt GmbH Regensburg, I was in the Waldwerk at Mooshof on several occasions. The entrance to the Försterhaus (forest rangers' house) just as it does today, led over the course of the small stream. Already at the turn-off from the Reichsstrasse was the first control point. Beside the Försterhaus was a good usable path that led deep into the forest, where a number of branch paths led to hidden barracks, assembly halls and tents. The entire installation, most heavily guarded, could only be entered with a special pass, and was superbly camouflaged against discovery by low-flying aircraft by trees and camouflage nets. A never-ending stream of traffic and trucks could be observed. It was already a paradoxical situation, where Russian officers worked together with foreign workers from various countries as well as some German personnel on the Me 262 – Hitler's last hope of securing the initiative in once more winning the war in the air.'

Using transport trucks, parts were brought from Reichsstrasse 8 to the Waldwerk in Mooshof, including fuselage noses, main and rear fuselages, cockpit sections, fuel tanks, wings, empennages, engines, and main- and tailwheel undercarriages. Firstly, the rear fuselage was joined to the empennage on the jig. The main fuselage rested on its mounting on the four wing attachment points. The centre and rear fuselages were then joined together by 32 bolts. The fuselage nose was then fitted with two or four MK 108 cannon and attached to the fuselage. The cockpit trough enclosure, which had previously been completed with all its installations such as the pilot's seat, instruments, electricals, control column and foot pedals, was then installed in the fuselage to which it was anchored by rivets in the upper and four fittings in the lower fuselage. After all electrical, hydraulic and oxygen systems, conduits and control cabling had been installed, the fuselage was raised from its mounting onto the fully-assembled wings to which it was attached by 4 bolts, the rear fuselage being supported during this process by a work platform. This was then followed by attachment of the fuselage nose, under-carriage and the two fuel tanks. The latter, also pre-equipped ready for installation in the fuselage, were mounted from beneath it, the tanks being suspended by two cables and hauled up by a lifting device. Once the tanks had been fixed, the cables were removed and the openings sealed.

Final assembly of an Me 262 at one of the main production plants in Southern Germany, 1944-45. There were five of these; at Leipheim, Schwäbisch Hall, Obertraubling, Neuberg an der Donau and Kuno, the latter a code name for a Waldwerk (forest factory). Prior to being delivered to their allocated operational units, each Me 262 underwent stringent manufacturing proving tests. Following successful completion of these tests, many aircraft were then handed over to the Flieger Überführungs Geschwader who would then deliver them to their assigned units.

The engines were placed on a trolley-mounted hoist, wheeled beneath the wings and hoisted into position in the engine nacelles. In the Me 262 A-2 fighter-bomber version, a third auxiliary fuel tank was installed in the rear fuselage. Finally, the cables, leads and rods were connected up and and checked for proper assembly. Following several tests, the hatch coverings and panels were then attached. All of the electrical and hydraulic systems including the undercarriage and the control rods underwent thorough functional testing. After the aircraft had been lowered onto its undercarriage, it was rolled into the paint shop. Final assembly took place on a raised travelling conveyor belt that had a length of about 100 m (328 ft) and which passed through five pre-assembly stations: fuselages, cockpits, wings, engines, and fuel tanks.

The entire final assembly was arranged for a minimum of work processes, since all Baugruppen (component construction groups) had been pre-assembled as far as possible, so that only a few bolts and rivets were needed to join the parts together. The manufacturing tolerance here was merely two-tenths of a millimetre. When production reached its zenith in February 1945, four to five aircraft left the final assembly daily. What then followed was transportation to the Fliegerhorst Obertraubling. On the stretch of Reichsautobahn, railtracks had been laid down for a Feldbahn (military or narrow-gauge railway). The Me 262s were lifted onto special railcars and pulled along to the airfield by a small Diesel locomotive. On arrival there, the aircraft were freighted to a large field shed situated between Birkenfeld and Lerchenfeld east of the Fliegerhorst. This shed had been specially modified for the purpose and had a large door at each end.

Rudolf Melzl recalled: 'At that time, 1945, I was 16 years old and worked as an apprentice at the Fliegerhorst Obertraubling. With other apprentices, I worked in a field shed east of the airfield on Me 262 final assembly. To our admiration, several Czechoslovak aircraft examiners dressed in white work-coats, under the supervision of German craftsmen and technicians, once more conducted thorough checks on the aircraft. We installed the radio and compass items; the bomb clasps for the Me 262 fighter-bomber version were also installed here that were tested functionally with cement bombs. We managed to get through five aircraft per day. After fastening the last inspection hatches, which were partly pop-riveted in place, the aircraft were towed by a caterpillar tractor over a small field path to the Fliegerhorst. The tractor was manned by Russian PoWs and it sometimes happened that the combination slid into the small drainage ditches beside the path. The Russians, out of fright, made themselves scarce in the vicinity and we had quite a job to get the Me 262 out of the ditch again. Most of the time the aircraft became somewhat damaged and had to be brought back to the shed. Since the caterpillar tractor had a rather high fuel consumption, someone came up with the fabulous idea of using a car for this purpose. Said and done, a car was requisitioned and used for towing the Me 262. After towing the second Me 262, the coupling became useless as it was not designed to handle the towing weight of an Me 262. On the Fliegerhorst, the aircraft were parked under camouflage nets in the areas where the greatest damage had been done, so that it was hoped the Americans would not suspect there were any aircraft located there. As far as I can remember, it was at the beginning of February 1945 when the 100th Me 262 was decorated with a plaque and floral garlands and rolled out of the final acceptance point.'

At Messerschmitt, there were other worries. Although the fastest jet aircraft was being built, there was no airfield there suitable for Me 262 factory flight-testing, as the airfield had only one grass strip about 1,200 m (3,940 ft) long, which from the bombing raids of February and July 1944 had been left pitted with a number of bomb craters that had been provisionally filled in so that the whole airfield was thus correspondingly uneven. In periods of lengthy rainfall, puddles developed and the grass runway became soft. The acceptance test pilots at that time – Trenkle, Stemmler, Riedmeir, Scheffl and Lohmann, told the author about some take-offs where they just about managed with great difficulty to lift off at the airfield boundary. In such airfield conditions, every take-off was a hazardous life and death event, and resulted in losses. Feldwebel Scheffl recalled: 'It was at the beginning of January 1945. It had rained and snowed for days and was weather such that even the birds went on foot. We pilots all sat in the control centre and waited for an improvement in the weather. On this particular day, a sharp west wind blew one rain and snow shower after another across the airfield. The cloudbase lay at 400-500 m (1,300-1,650 ft). The door suddenly opened and the Gauleiter appeared with his entourage. He bellowed at us loudly: "The Front needs aircraft, so get up off your arses and fly!" When the Gauleiter had finished, Feldwebel Gerhard Ertelt suddenly sprang up, went over to the 'golden pheasant'[1], turned up the lapels of his uniform, beneath which was his Party badge and said: "We will test-fly the aircraft when we consider it appropriate to do so and when the weather conditions permit, but not today! To attempt to take-off in this weather would in the circumstances lead to the total loss of the pilot and the aircraft." The Gauleiter was almost on the point of exploding, but the sight of the gold Party badge certainly had its effect on him. With a highly red face he stormed off and was not seen again. The rest of us pilots watched this encounter with astonishment, but it was a good indication how, towards the end of the war, all manner of officialdom wanted to interfere in our flying domain, even when they understood nothing at all about it.

'On 30 January 1945, the same Feldwebel Ertelt took off on a test flight with an Me 262. It rolled down the runway howling and hissing, throwing up an enormous fountain of water behind it. In that sunken ground, the Me 262 appeared to accelerate even more slowly than it did anyway. It had not quite reached take off speed at the

Taken in December 1944, this photograph (from left to right) pilots Josef Haid, Heinrich Beauvais, Gerhard Ertelt and Franz Scheffl.

Feldwebel Gerhard Ertelt pictured wearing his Eisernes Kreuz I beside his Golden Nazi Party emblem which came in useful one day in January 1945.

---

[1]. Slang for a Party official due to the colour of the Nazi Party uniform and its golden decorations.

edge of the runway, when Gerhard attempted to lift off. The Me 262 leapt briefly into the air but immediately sank back down, and at the small slope of the railway track and the connecting road to Obertraubling, to the west of the airfield, the aircraft exploded in a ball of fire. There was no hope of saving the pilot, and we were forced to watch how he was helplessly burnt alive. A later examination revealed that dirt presumably thrown up by the nosewheel entered the air intake of one of the turbojets and led to its failure. On the following days also, bad weather prevailed or else brought hardly any improvement to the airfield, so that we were again not able to conduct flight trials. The aircraft, so urgently needed by the front line units, thus piled up at the airfield.'

When the weather improved in mid-February, acceptance flying was once more able to be resumed. But the USAAF knew from which side a danger still threatened, and the Fifteenth Air Force made preparations for a new blow against the Me 262. From the beginning of February, Obertraubling airfield was under almost uninterrupted aerial surveillance, and based on evaluation, the Allies were able to register most precisely how the numbers of Me 262s at the Fliegerhorst Obertraubling increased. On 16 February, 263 B-24s dropped 515 tons of bombs on it, including thousands of small fragmentation bombs. Due to the high losses in aircraft on that day, 20 Me 262s were written off and 20 others were heavily damaged. A most unconventional method was then decided upon by Regensburg as to how a concrete runway could be secured for the jet fighter. The road that ran by the east side of the assembly halls was lengthened by some 100 m (330 ft) in a southerly direction into the airfield, as a result of which a concreted runway some eight m (26 ft) wide and 1,200 m (3,940 ft) in length was created. On an aerial photograph taken in April 1945 of the Fliegerhorst Obertraubling, this road used for take-off is clearly visible.

Flugkapitan Trenkle undertook the first test flight on this provisional runway: 'I rolled my aircraft to the extreme end of the concreted stretch and pointed it precisely in the direction of take-off. Through the small front windscreen the strip looked damned small and I hoped that no vehicle would just happen to drive onto the runway and cut across my path. There were two barricade positions on the road, but one could not be careful enough. After I had received the OK for take-off, I pushed the throttles for the engines slowly forward and stood fully on the wheelbrakes. When the turbines had already begun to develop thrust in an orderly manner, I released the brakes. The Me 262 of course, accelerated very slowly, but did not cause me any problems in holding the nosewheel in the take-off direction. I thus thundered along, getting faster all the time, past the destroyed assembly halls, and after about 1,000 m (3,280 ft) I had so much speed that the Me 262 almost lifted off by itself. In a wide curve I flew past the Walhalla in the direction of Regensburg and headed back to the airfield. For safety reasons I landed on the grass runway, because the road was too narrow to do so. Now, we at last had a hard runway for take-off which ran in a direction from roughly south-east to north-west that not exactly corresponded to the main wind direction. But for an experienced pilot, the take-off distance with it was no problem for the Me 262.'

But it was not only limited space that hindered flight-test operations at Obertraubling, as the continual low-level attacks were also a problem in themselves. To quote yet again a report by Flugkapitän Trenkle: 'The constant low-flying attacks were a further hindrance to our works test flights, and as soon as the weather permitted this activity to continue at the beginning of 1945, the 'myo' was in operation – the code for warning of enemy aircraft in our airspace. For us works pilots, 'myo' normally meant a take-off ban, but in the spring of 1945 (possibly 25 March 1945 – author), I took-off despite 'myo' in Obertraubling and attacked several P-38s over Regensburg, which continually flew low-level attacks on the town. The P-38 Lightnings were so concentrated on their approach flight in the railway station area that they noticed my attack relatively late. But I had all the advantages on my side: high speed, greater firepower, as well as a better tactical position than they did. I was able to open fire on one P-38 to good effect, because it smoked quite appreciably on flying away, but I could not observe the crash of the aircraft due to the air battle that now ensued. My attacks were like a stab into a wasps' nest, and by the flying movements of the American pilots, I was clearly able to see how surprised they were from being attacked by an Me 262. After making a few further attacks I broke off the air combat, and following my landing, the rumour arose that I would be penalized for taking off without permission, but that was not true. In fact Hitler, after being informed of this air battle, had immediately ordered via his adjutant, Nicholas von Bülow, that at Messerschmitt in Regensburg, we were to form an Industriestaffel to combat low-flying aircraft. But we were neither in terms of personnel nor materially in a position to do so.'[2]

Rudolf Melzl of Regensburg remembered: 'In the air attack on 13 March 1945, my parents' home in Neuprüll was totally destroyed. A few days after this date, an air battle took place over Regensburg. My parents and I tried to save whatever was still usable from the debris. On this particular day, low-flying aircraft were almost constantly over the town and shot at everything that moved. The US fighters continually put themselves in breathtakingly steep dives and had the railway station area in particular in their gunsights. From my parents' house at that time, one could still see as far as the Fliegerhorst in Obertraubling where today the University stands, when on the airfield the sound of howling jet engines could suddenly be heard. Since I myself worked at Messerschmitt, I knew the sound of those turbines only too well. Out of a cloud of dust an Me 262 lifted off in the direction of Walhalla and then flew in a wide turn to the town. The Lightnings still continued to blithely make their low-level attacks when the Me 262 travelling at high speed pounced. It was really a marvellous sight, as one could clearly see how shocked the American pilots were at the appearance of a single Me 262. A little later, the muffled sound of shots from its cannon could be heard. The Me 262 pilot heavily damaged one Lightning which, belching smoke, flew away southward, followed by the other P-38s while at high speed, the Me 262 continued to fire at the US fighters before descending. It was impressed with what ease and superiority the Me 262 was able to handle this air battle against six enemy fighters. Since the air battle had moved over to the south, the aircraft went out of my range of visibility.'

[2.] At 0831 hrs on 25 March 1945, 45 P-38s of the 1st FG took-off from Salsola for low-level attacks on the general area of Regensburg. The fighters reached their target area at 1050 hrs and according to US records, the 1st FG lost one P-38 on this day.

Since the USAAF constantly flew over the Regensburg area with its reconnaissance aircraft no large numbers of Me 262s, were to be parked on the Fliegerhorst Obertraubling. Feldwebel Lohmann's recalled: 'We even flew the Me 262 in the worst of weather conditions from Obertraubling to Neuburg, Erding or München-Riem. The way back was mostly made via an old requisitioned taxi which regularly suffered from tyre defects. As the other airfields, especially Neuburg, had been heavily bombarded, one soon did not know where to go to with the aircraft. Although we flew certainly the fastest aircraft in the world, we were, however, helpless on the ground against bombing attacks. The numerical superiority of the USAAF was unimaginable. In April 1945, the rigidly-led organisation of the Luftwaffe broke down in increasing measure. At München-Riem, General Adolf Galland had in the meantime established his fighter unit, Jagdverband 44, to which we ferried several Me 262s. For this purpose, Messerschmitt had established an acceptance flight together with Lufthansa employees. At Regensburg, Me 262 production continued far into April and was ended only shortly before the entry of US troops. I ferried probably the last Me 262 on 23 April 1945 directly in front of the eyes of the Americans who were already on the march towards Regensburg, from Obertraubling to München-Riem. On this day, I flew at low level over the town in order to take leave of my wife. We had agreed I would do this and I knew that she would be standing somewhere down below and would wave to me, and that because of the war situation my immediate return to Regensburg would be very unlikely. As a precaution, I had also given my wife my valuable pilot's wristwatch which we have rescued from all the chaos of war. On flying over the old part of the town, I also saw a great mass of people standing on what today is the Dachauplatz. It was only later that I learned of the demonstration by the Regensburg populace who protested against defending the town and demanded that it be handed over by the Nazi bigwigs to the US troops. I delivered the Me 262 according to orders at München-Riem. My return to Regensburg was no longer possible, so that I had to await the end of the war near Holzkirchen.'

The Me 262 production run took place as follows: The wings consisted of a relatively simple construction, assembled from larger, shaped wing ribs and with only three stiffeners which served to hold together the main and auxiliary spars. The wing halves were manufactured individually and mated together on the final assembly line, which made their transportation by road and rail easier. Each wing half consisted of five main sets of construction components: the spar, the forward inner and outer wing profiles and the rear inner and outer wing profiles, which were manufactured in stationary construction jigs. They were first joined together in a jig and subsequently riveted together in rotatable jigs. Assembly of the five main component groups was then accomplished in special construction cradles. The fittings for the engines and main undercarriage attachments were then added to the wings. The attachment points for the wing nose slats, ailerons and landing flaps were already in place. The two main fuselage sections were manufactured separately. The fuselage half-shells that emerged from the presses were then placed on the jigs and rived to the fuselage frame. The construction parts were so subdivided during manufacture that riveting was accomplished mechanically. According to statements by former Messerschmitt employees, 85% of all riveting on the Me 262 was done mechanically.

The Messerschmitt engineers were successfully able to keep to a minimum the number of individual parts. The connecting points for the separate fuselage portions were already worked into the half-shells. For manufacturing reasons, the entire fuselage consisted of four main construction sets which were bolted together during final assembly. In this way, it became possible to conduct final assembly of the Me 262 under the most primitive conditions, in caves and forests.

Aircraft Production in 1945

Bf 109

January	=	555 (1 G-6, 3 G-10, 1 G-14, 211 G-14 AS, 338 K-4)
February	=	315 (82 G-14 AS, 233 K-4)
March	=	204
April	=	50[1]
Total:	=	1,124

Me 262			**Me 262 fuselages**
January	=	50 (43 A-2)	277
February	=	134	86
March	=	67	362
April	=	30[2]	★
Total:	=	**281**	**1,025 plus**

[1]. Handwritten notice of the RLM Quartermaster-General in the National Archives, Washington
[2]. Source: USSBS
★ No information available. It can certainly be assumed that Me 262 fuselages were still being manufactured in April 1945.

An oblique aerial view of the Fliegerhorst Obertraubling as seen in May 1945. In the foreground is the road that served as a take-off runway for the Me 262, which still exists today in Neutraubling. At centre is the totally destroyed Halle 5. To the left and right of it were Hallen 4 and 6, of which only portions of the walls remain standing. At top centre the relatively intact Werfthalle is visible and to the left of it, what remains of Halle 2. (Photo USAF)

Me 262 production in the various dispersal centres in March 1945, is shown in Appendix 17. The workforce in April 1945 comprised 11,474 people, of which 5,124 were German and 6,350 foreigners, plus 1,350 appprentices, giving a total of 12,824 altogether.

16 February 1945

Production by Messerschmitt GmbH, even at a continually reducing pace, continued well into April 1945. As already mentioned, bombing and low-level attacks almost brought industrial production to a standstill, so that in that month it was only due to available stocks that production could be continued. The USAAF in particular, had its eye on Me 262 production. In ever-increasing numbers the jet fighters, called 'Turbos' by the Luftwaffe, appeared in the skies over Germany and caused the US bomber crews anxiety and fright, especially after the Me 262 had been equipped with the 55 mm R4M air-to-air rocket projectile that caused some bomber units to suffer considerable losses. A further problem for the bomber crews was the high closing speed of the Me 262. Their electrically-operated gun turrets could not keep pace with the fast approach speeds of the jet fighter, so that defensive fire was effectively reduced to an untrained barrage fire. The four 30 mm MK 108s in the Me 262 fuselage nose caused havoc on the light metal construction of a B-17 or B-24, and only three or four hits were sufficient to bring down a four-engined bomber. For the USAAF, the Me 262's appearance came as a shock. It was believed that the Germans had almost been beaten, when these aircraft now began to appear in the skies in ever-increasing numbers. Obertraubling was under continual aerial surveillance and records were kept of the Me 262s that were parked ready for acceptance flights. After the passing of the bad weather period, no acceptance flights were possible because the grass airstrip at Obertraubling was waterlogged. American reconnaissance flights had identified a continually growing number of Me 262s, and when a stock of 48 jets had been counted, attack preparations by the Fifteenth Air Force were put in train. On 16 February 45, a formation of 263 B-24s flew towards Regensburg from their bases in Italy. Shortly before the raid, 56 operationally-ready Me 262s had been registered. From 1305 to 1325 hrs, in the true sense of the word, 630 high-explosive 500 lb bombs, 19,722 20 lb fragmentation bombs and 3,615 cluster bombs weighing a total of 515 tons, rained down on the Fliegerhorst. Damage to buildings there was appreciable: 25 aircraft were destroyed, 30 badly damaged of which 20 Me 262s were a write-off, while 20 others were heavily damaged in one way or another and even two Bf 109 K-4s were reduced to scrap. Further USAAF reconnaissance flights followed and on 14 and 16 March 1945 they detected seven operationally ready Me 262s at Obertraubling.

Oberfeldwebel Stemmler's recalled the 16 February 1945 bombing raid: 'Because of bad weather, acceptance flight trials almost came to a standstill. On the one hand, due to the wet, the runway had been significantly softened and on the other, the cloudbase lay so low that a take-off in an Me 262 would have been irresponsible. As I recall, some 50 to 60 Me 262s were parked far from each other at the Fliegerhorst. Some of the aircraft were covered by camouflage netting and parked in the neighbourhood of the Fliegerhorst that had been destroyed the most, in the hope that no bombs would fall here. Hardly had the weather improved, when the American bombers made their approach. A strong bomber formation attacked Obertraubling. Following the first alarm, we had already left the area and braced ourselves for what was to come. From a safe distance we were able to observe how whole showers of bombs descended. A huge cloud of smoke and dust rose over the Fliegerhorst. It was a brief, but concentrated attack. After the all-clear, we drove back to the Fliegerhorst. From afar, our Me 262s appeared to be undamaged. But when we looked at them from close-up, we saw the mess. Small bomb splinters in several aircraft had severely damaged the wings and airframes; fuel was flowing out, turbines were defective, and tyres flattened. It was a disconsolate sight, but work nevertheless continued, even if we could not grasp the senselessness of it all. Yet there was no purpose to anything anymore and any effort to keep going merely resulted in casualties. After the raid, Me 262 parking became even more decentralized, so that it often took 30 minutes or more until they were towed to the airfield. As far as the weather permitted, the aircraft were immediately flown to other airfields, e.g. to Neuburg, Erding, and München-Riem. But even at these locations the Me 262s were not safe from air attacks.'

11 April 1945

On 11 April 1945, a further raid on the Fliegerhorst took place. This time, it was mounted by the 2nd Bomber Division of the Eighth Air Force with 79 B-24s equipped with 160 tons of bombs which throroghly ploughed up the already shattered Fliegerhorst. In the meantime, no building remained standing anymore that had not been destroyed or damaged in some way by bombs. After the air raid, hundreds of concentration camp inmates had to fill in the bomb craters on the runway. The Me 262 final assembly line that was hidden in the forest east of Obertraubling was not hit by any of the bombing raids and was probably not recognised as such. For a table of all bombing raids on Regensburg and Obertraubling, see Appendix 15.

Production at the Flossenburg and Mauthausen concentration camps

A particularly grim chapter in the history of aircraft production in 1943 and 1944 was the use of concentration camp inmates, initiated by the RLM in the search for ever newer sources of manpower. For the Messerschmitt GmbH in 1943, this entailed the erection of production facilities in the Flossenburg camp and later, at Mauthausen (St. Georgen) in 1944. In August 1943, 800 inmates from Flossenburg are said to have worked for the enterprise. In the Flossenburg stone quarries under the command of the SS-owned DEST (German Earth and Stone Works), Jews, PoWs and anti-Nazis were annihilated by being forced to work under the harshest conditions, given poor food, subjected to brutal terror by the guards and Kapos in sub-human accommodation. The suffering and deaths in the concentration camps took on immeasurable and unimaginable proportions in terms of crimes against humanity and they should not be forgotten. Above all, it should not be forgotten that all of this happened in the name of the German Reich and its people and that the post-war generations of all nations carry the responsibility to ensure that it should never happen again.

Beginning in spring 1943, a part of wing production was transferred to the Flossenburg camp. For those inmates involved, it meant that they at least could now work in closed Hallen and were no longer subject to heavy work in all kinds of weather in the quarries. Prof.

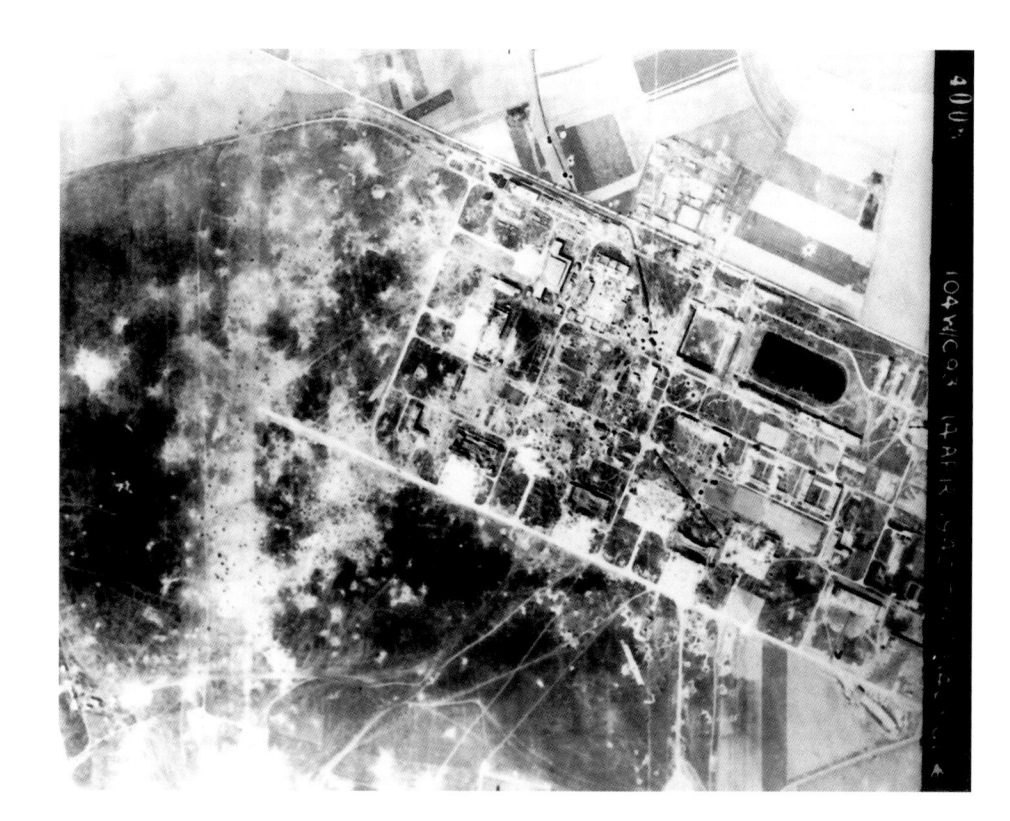

An overhead view of the Fliegerhorst Obertraubling taken on 14 April 1945. Visible is the lengthened road that was used as a take-off strip for the Me 262. Besides this road, some 1,200 m long and 10 m wide, still referred to today in Neutraubling as the 'Rollbahn', levelling work had begun in parallel for another take-off runway on the east side of the Fliegerhorst by PoWs and concentration-camp inmates. At upper left is the PoW camp adjacent to the connecting road between Obertraubling and Barbing.

The result of the bombing raid on 11 April 1945 on the Fliegerhorst Obertraubling. Numerous Me 262 fuselages, nose cones, wings and empennages lie in this bombed-out Halle. Standing behind Me 262 W.Nr. 500480 (or 488?) in the centre foreground is an American soldier taking notes. (Photo USAF)

Messerschmitt sought to obtain better nourishment for the inmates and argued with the SS that only a reasonably nourished person would be able to produce satisfactory work. Despite that, little was changed for the inmates as the SS controlled all of the installations. The work demands on the inmates were so high that under the existing circumstances they were simply unable to fulfil them. The external camps were notorious, to where the relocation of inmates meant nothing other than a death sentence. An almost forgotten external camp was the one in Saal on the Danube. Here, at the end of 1944, work was begun on digging a tunnel and a system of galleries in the Ringberg to secure a bomb-proof final assembly line for the Me 262. Construction of the

When the war ended, these Bf 109s, partially unpainted, were left abandoned on the Fliegerhorst Obertraubling. (Photo Schmoll)

Me 262 fuselage construction was begun in two smaller halls in the Flossenburg stone quarry. The first hall had four construction jigs for the fuselage halves, whilst in the second fuselage final assembly was undertaken. When US troops entered the area, only four fuselages were under construction whilst the empennages for four others were on hand. In Flossenburg, around 2,000 camp inmates worked on aircraft production under SS control, and numerous Messerschmitt technicians were there to supervise production, eliminate manufacturing deficiencies and to instruct the inmates. Production took place in two shifts with 1,400 and 600 workers.

necessary airfield for it was begun on the other side of the Danube near Hermsaal. Everywhere in the Reich, concentration camp inmates and forced labourers were hard at work digging tunnels and galleries so that armaments production would be safe from the ever-increasing volume of Allied bombing attacks. The manufacture of aircraft parts in Flossenburg saw, according to information in US documents, as of April 1945, the manufacture of wings and fuselages for the Bf 109, the dismantling and repair of damaged Bf 109s and the commencement of Me 262 fuselages. Production of Bf 109 wings in Flossenburg, according to US data, proceeded as follows: The pre-assembled parts for the wings were delivered to Flossenburg and were put together in a Werkhalle there. The wing spars together with the wing ribs were put together on appropriate mounts in an assembly hall. In 24 vertical construction jigs that were erected in two rows, the sheet-metal skinning for the upper and lower wing sides were riveted. These two assembly lines occupied almost the entire length of the Halle. The wings were then moved to the final assembly line, where 18 travelling and turnable installations were available. It was here that the radiators and landing flaps, ailerons and wing leading edge slats as well as the requisite electrical equipment was added. In two shifts, 12 pairs of wings were manufactured per day. The Halle measured 40 x 100 m (131 x 328 ft). The Bf 109 fuselage assembly line was located in Plankenhamer, some 4 km (2.5 mls) south of Flossenburg. The assembly hall had the same dimensions as that of the wing assembly hall in Flossenburg. One section concerned itself with installation preparations for the engine which was moved on rails to the fuselage final assembly line. There were two fuselage assembly lines on which twelve complete fuselages were assembled. The Bf 109 was completed to the extent that only the wings and tailplanes needed to be added. The wings and fuselages were transported to Vilseck and put together at the airfield there, where the radio, armament and camouflage paint were added.

The dismantling and repair of damaged Bf 109s took place in a so-called Industry Repair Shop, in an appropriately modified hall that had been moved from the Flossenburg stone quarry to the railway line to Flossenburg. Here, the damaged Bf 109s were stripped and reusable parts extracted. Less damaged aircraft were repaired using the reusable parts. The installation equated to a final assembly line, but suffered from a lack of spare parts and equipment. Shortly before the end of the war,

The Mauthausen concentration camp had two subsidiary camps, Gusen I and II, at St. Georgen. Manufacturing for Messerschmitt Regensburg began at both locations around mid-February 1944. In various stretches situated in a stone-breaking quarry near St. Georgen, Messerschmitt Regensburg began construction of a manufacturing line for Bf 109 fuselages and other aircraft parts. Production in the concentration camp was undertaken by the SS with logistical support provided by the SS-owned DEST, aircraft production technology and the necessary personnel being provided by Messerschmitt. The camp inmates produced the aircraft parts, which the SS in turn sold to Messerschmitt GmbH. For some time, the German aircraft industry had been placed in an extremely dangerous position in being dependent upon the SS, which in 1944, had become a State within a State. It also controlled further areas of armaments production, and its influence and position of power grew from day-to-day, reaching its apex when SS General Dr.-Ing. Hans Kammler took over control of the rocket and jet aircraft programme. In Gusen I and II in July 1944, there were about 6,000 inmates engaged on production of Bf 109 fuselages and Me 262 parts, and an average of around 77 railway freight cars filled with aircraft parts left the camp each month to supply the other decentralized production centres in eastern Bavaria, and with necessary parts for Bf 109 further assembly. At about the same time, around 9,000 inmates were occupied with building tunnels and galleries to form a completely underground town. On average, 140 railcar loads of cement were used for the production of concrete. In mid-1944, the death rate stood at some 200 inmates per month and were the highest among inmates working on gallery construction. Production of Me 262 fuselages began in St. Georgen in November 1944, the necessary parts having been largely supplied at the beginning from production of the Olympia Tunnel near Eschenlohe. Already in December, 18,500 inmates in St. Georgen worked on armaments production and a further 5,000 were still engaged in gallery consruction. Altogether, at the end of 1944 over 24,000 inmates from Gusen I and II were engaged on gallery construction. The death rate at that period lay at around 1,000 inmates per month and reached 2,084 in February and with 3,271 in March 1945, reached its macabre zenith. Even in June 1945, 1,433 former Gusen concentration camp inmates perished. From the start of armaments production in February 1944 up until June 1945, the total number of deaths from Gusen I and II inmates was 14,131, and immeasurable suffering is hidden in these

American troops take a rest on a bare-metal Me 262 fuselage section outside the underground production facility at St. Georgen, east of Linz in Austria. This underground complex was served by a purpose-built narrow-guage railway and was staffed by slave labour from the nearby concentration camp at Gusen. (Photos Forsyth)

naked figures. For those belonging to post-war generations, it is difficult to comprehend what tragedy was involved. Half-starved inmates performed the most difficult work for an inhuman regime, and shootings took place on a daily basis for no clear reason. The Camp Commandant, Ziereis, took pleasure in having several inmates shot daily before he had breakfast. More than 2,000 of them were shot 'attempting to escape' and 1,500 committed suicide because they could no longer bear the daily taunts and hunger anymore.

Deliveries of Me 262 fuselages from Mauthausen, which had already largely been equipped with technical installations, were made to all final assembly centres such as Leipheim, Schwäbisch-Hall, Regensburg, Neuburg and Kahla. On average, 65 rail freight cars per month left the concentration camp with Me 262 parts and several of the fuselage group components were sent for final assembly to Obernzell near Passau. The entire decentralized manufacture of the Me 262 is visible in documents captured by the US Army which, at the time of writing, are held in the National Archives in Washington, USA. Towards the end of the war, preparations were being made for Me 262 wing production in the underground centre in St. Georgen. It only needed a few more weeks before one of the largest underground aircraft manufacturing plants would have started production to its fullest extent, and most probably, final assembly and acceptance flight-testing would have taken place in the vicinity of St. Georgen or Linz. Thus, the ruling powers in the Third Reich would once more have had a possible centralized and protected production centre unaffected by long transport distances and from air attacks.

A former Messerschmitt employee recalled: 'As far as I remember, it was a few weeks after the bombing raid on 17 August 1944 when together with three other colleagues, I was ordered to erect, adjust, and prepare construction jigs for wing and fuselage production in the Flossenburg concentration camp. We were obliged to maintain the highest secrecy, and under threat of the strongest punishment, were not allowed to talk about this even to our families. On the special Pass, the travel ticket and the moving order, there was no destination shown. We were travelling on official business for the RLM. Already on the journey to Flossenburg we came up against the first problems because we were not allowed to reveal our destination to the ticket inspector on the train. At the next station, we were taken off the train and had to present all our travel documents, which only caused even more mistrust. We merely mentioned that all four of us were travelling on a secret mission, and after an endless number of telephone calls, we were allowed to continue our journey.

'At Flossenburg, we were accommodated in private quarters for the duration of our stay of some three weeks. The production halls set aside for Messerschmitt were located in the stone quarry area. My colleagues and I did not enter the camp itself. When we reported to the guard at the stone quarry, the double fence that was much higher than normal human height immediately caught our eye. The inner fence was electrified, and between the two rows, SS men with loaded rifles patrolled constantly. At specific distances encircling the camp were watchtowers equipped with machine guns. During the first hours of our stay we felt as if we were hard criminals, as cocked rifles were constantly aimed at us by the guards. It was here that I saw concentration camp inmates for the very first time in their grey striped suits, shaven heads and wearing enforced caps. As soon as any guard crossed their path, the camp inmates tore off their caps and saluted them. If the guard felt they had not saluted quickly enough, they were kicked, punched on the face or beaten with their rifles. This was the first, totally shocking impression that we had. The inmates were at that time erecting a new building and had to carry the stones and other construction materials at quick march to the building site. At particular distances apart stood the dreaded Kapos - likewise camp inmates, and as soon as one of the inmates did not maintain the tempo or just because one of the Kapos was in a bad mood, the inmate received a shower of blows on all parts of his body with sticks. For the victims, it was like running the gauntlet. We stood there speechless and could not believe such things were happening. It should be mentioned here that we had all grown up in the Hitler Youth and shall we say, had been rather Nazi-indoctrinated. But what we came to witness here was incomprehensible and we were facing a situation against which we were helpless and powerless to do anything about.

'We were even more shocked a few days later, when suddenly a siren sounded and someone shouted: "Alarm!" and right away the machine guns in the watchtowers opened fire into the camp. Everyone lay flat on the round, and we trembled to our bones. An inmate had approached too close to the fence and fire was opened into the camp from all sides. The inmate was shot dead at the fence. We complained to the Camp Commandant, stating that we were civilians and would refuse to undertake work if we were shot at. From then on, the instruction was issued that fire would only be opened along the fence. Because of overcrowding in the camp, beatings were provoked so that inmates were driven into the electrified fencing. In the stone quarries accidents constantly took place which one could also term as murder. The starting point for these here were the camp guards and the dreaded Kapos. This was told to me by inmates who later on worked together with myself and my other colleagues, and it happened in this way: The numerous construction jigs that were delivered, stood out in the open and on the exposed parts, rust had already set in. In order that these be cleaned and made free of rust, Russian PoWs were assigned to us. Two of them who worked with me were a captain (from a Russian motor patrol boat) and a lieutenant-colonel. Blows were constantly showered here too, on the prisoners by the guard personnel. As a result, we again complained to the Camp Commandant, as no kind of coordinated work became possible. It was like a little miracle, for the guards were thereafter instructed not to enter the Halle anymore during the work period. In our complaints, we had to present our arguments extremely cautiously and think over very carefully what we said. We called upon our very important task within the framework of the armaments industry - the highest priority status - and in so doing, always managed to get our way.

'Contacts with prisoners were not allowed to be made and were forbidden under threat of punishment. But because of the daily nature of the work, these interim human contacts could not be avoided, insofar as most of the Russians spoke a little German. Thus, in all secrecy, private conversations did take place. The Russian colonel requested me politely to get some salt for him. I was startled at first, because if I was searched by the SS, I would definitely have been punished. This in fact later happened to some Messerschmitt employees who were simply arrested and about whose whereabouts we were able to ascertain absolutely nothing. But when it became clear to me what food the prisoners were given - unwashed cabbage stumps sliced and put into large containers and cooked as a soup, to which they were given bread which did not deserve to be called that, I then obtained salt for the Russians. I took a small packet with me to my workplace and hid it inside a pipe that was the nearest to me in one of the construction jigs. The prisoners several times assured us that it was a matter of good fortune that they had been allowed to work here in the Hallen, without being exposed to the weather, the constant beatings and subjected to the hard physical work in the quarry. When I left the camp in Flossenburg after some three weeks, in view of the injustices that were practiced here, my Nazi world ideology had been given a tremendous wrench. The worst was, however, that I could and ought not talk about it to anyone as the danger existed of being betrayed and arrested, and could not trust a second person to believe or want to believe when told about all the things that went on here. After my return to Regensburg, it did not take long before we were assigned a new task. This time, we journeyed to St. Georgen where the quarries there belonged to the Mauthausen concentration camp.

'In Mauthausen, the same conditions reigned as in Flossenburg. In the Hallen at the quarry, we erected the construction installations for the aircraft parts. After us came other Messerschmitt technicians who taught the camp inmates. Production in these camp facilities naturally did not run free of problems, since here as well, the aircraft parts made had a tolerance of one- to two-tenths of a millimetre. The SS made short shrift of sabotage: the inmates were simply hanged on the spot. A noose was attached beneath the ceiling where installation conduits ran; the inmate was placed on a wooden crate which was then kicked away by an SS man. As a discouragement, the corpse was left to hang for some hours. In the quarry, work was in train on two galleries each of some 4 m (13 ft) height and width in which installations for fuselage manufacture of the Me 262 was later added. Shortly before the end of the war, preparations were made in Mauthausen for Me 262 wing production.'

Jan Szopa of Krakow, a former camp inmate at Flossenburg, recalled conditions there: 'The Flossenburg concentration camp was erected in 1938 as a Category II camp, to which criminals and anti-social individuals were sent. After the outbreak of war in September 1939, political prisoners from Dachau were also transferred to Flossenburg. The camp was originally built to house 1,600 inmates and was later expanded to house 3,000. During the war it was continually overcrowded and in the last months, hopelessly so. The main camp had almost 100 subsidiary camps that were widely separated from it in terms of distance. A considerable number of the 140,000 prisoners that were registered in 1938-45, were housed in these external camps. As a result of the inhuman conditions that existed in all the Flossenburg camps, some 80,000 died during this period. The death rate was particularly high during 1944-45, when epidemics such as typhoid snatched away the already weakened prisoners in large numbers. Those prisoners who were ill were transferred to the sickbay where they were often killed with a Phenol injection. The standard for provisions conformed to a directive issued by the Reichsführer-SS Heinrich Himmler on 1 April 1940 and consisted of a weekly ration of of meat and meat products 250 gm, fats 170 gm, bread 2,450 gm, sugar 80 gm, jam 100 gm, flour 125 gm, potatoes 3,500 gm, and vegetables 2,800 gms. In 1944, the rations were far less, so that we in the Lengenfeld camp, on paper, received per day: bread 250 gm, margarine 20 gm, jam 20 gm, meat products 50 gm and 500-700 ml of soup consisting only of kohlrabi, and with great good luck, with some potato skins as well. Very often it was much less, and we suffered from continual hunger. One enlightenment were the Red Cross parcels, but we got them much too rarely. The camp inmates were often beaten and maltreated. One torture for the inmates were the often held roll-calls. For these, we had to stand in rows for up to three hours in pouring rain or in icy cold in the open air on the roll-call ground. The accommodation barracks had no heating in winter and we froze. I can still remember well the Christmas evening of 1944 when a Christmas tree stood on the roll-call ground and right next to it on a gallows hung six inmates. In 1943, new production halls were built for Messerschmitt, where fuselages and wings for the Bf 109 were manufactured. The detachment that worked for the firm was designated '2004' and worked in two shifts of workers - 1,912 during the day and 1,117 during the night. Next to the assembly area, doping work was carried out. The inmates were overseen by supervisors and specialists. The Lengerfeld camp was erected in September 1944, where the camp inmates worked in halls and galleries, mainly on tooling machines such as lathes, milling and polishing machines, etc, in 12-hour shifts.'

Josef Zeyar of Krakow recounted: 'I worked from 7 September 1944 until 23 April 1945 in the Flossenburg concentration camp for Messerschmitt '2004' in the Kommando 'Schtych' in the old Halle. This Detachment was later renamed 'Altenhammer'. Beside the Halle was a dwelling in which the prisoners were accommodated. The daily provisions consisted of bread 400 gm, margarine and jam 30 gm, tea and kohlrabi soup. On the last day, we were freed from our great misery by the Americans.'

The 'Me-Ringberg' and 'Weingut II' Projects

Despite undisturbed production in the Waldwerken (forest factories), a feverish attempt was made in 1945 to relocate into bomb-proof tunnels, galleries and bunkers, for which purpose vast underground construction projects were commenced for Messerschmitt Regensburg such as at Saal on the Danube in which inmates of the Flossenburg concentration camp were tasked to work.

Under what conditions this occurred, is described by Wilhelm Evers of Nijmegen, Holland: 'At 18 years of age, as a trained carpenter I was rounded up to perform forced labour in Germany. At first, I went to Bochum for bunker construction and in 1944 wound up in Eschenlohe near Garmisch-Partenkirchen, where I was assigned to the Regensburg construction firm of Klug. After the tunnel entrances in Eschenlohe had been covered over with massive concrete, I reported for work on a construction site of the Klug firm at Saal on the Danube. Here I was a little closer to my beloved Holland. Having arrived in Saal, I was quartered in a barracks behind the Gasthof 'Alte Post'. The reason for the presence of foreign workers was the construction work undertaken by the OT [Organisation Todt] on the Ringberg in Saal at the Teugner Straße. It was here that an extended tunnel system for the Messerschmitt Werke was to be erected. We had to work at high pressure 12 hours a day, seven days a week, to complete the installation. The performance required had been set inhumanly high and was unachievable as there was hardly any rest. We at that time built the concrete encasements for the tunnels and had to erect the tracks for the narrow-gauge railway. After each blasting, the blown-up rocks had to be removed from the tunnel and a new stretch of rail with its sleepers had to be carried for its extension into the tunnel. Shortly after the start of construction work in November 1944, the first camp inmates appeared at the construction site. They were taken off the train in Saal and arrived in darkness on foot at the camp in the Teugner Straße. The inmates, controlled by SS guards accompanied by fierce watchdogs, were led to the construction site about 600 m (660 yards) away. It was a disconsolate sight, when one saw how the emaciated figures dragged themselves along to their workplace. They bored the holes in the rock for the explosives and carried away and loaded the rubble from the tunnel into railway trucks. When blasting was to take place, we all headed for safety outside the tunnel. At each detonation, a bright brown, thick cloud of dust shot out, and immediately after that, the inmates were driven with kickings and beatings into the still smoky tunnel to get to work. The SS showed no mercy, and new transports always kept coming from Flossenburg. It was planned extermination through sheer work. Inmates later on told me that a work detachment was constantly on the move in the forests to chop up construction wood for the tunnel and combustible wood for burning the corpses. The latter was carried out in a small quarry on the Ringberg. Due to the poor provisions and lack of hygiene, a dysentery epidemic broke out in the camp at the end of 1944 and resulted in several victims among the weakened inmates.

'At an angle across from the gallery entrance and directly beside the road to Teugn were two barracks in which the OT construction heads were housed. Behind it, somewhat higher, were the canteen and the kitchen barracks. Each day a detachment appeared from the camp, equipped with pails to collect the meal. And every day, it was cabbage soup with a piece of wet bread, which had been impregnated with potatoes and straw. One day, supplies of provisions were driven by a horse-drawn vehicle to the kitchen. On the way, a barrel of jam fell to the ground and began to ooze out. That part which emptied out was covered over with sand and dirt. When the meal collectors emerged from the camp, some of the inmates bent down and attempted to eat some of the spilled jam. The guards beat ferociously with their rifle butts at the bent and kneeling figures, and several remained motionless. Powerless, we had to watch was going on, and at 19 years of age, I just could not believe it. Why does God allow such a thing to happen, that human beings can be so cruel?

'Any kind of contact with the inmates was strictly forbidden and we were also not allowed to walk in the direction of the camp. But on looking out from the canteen, we could see very well, and my colleagues and I surmised all what was going on there. There were guards everywhere, some of them with dogs. A short while later, I came into contact with a Dutch camp inmate. There was not much I could do for him, but was able at a particular spot to leave a for him piece of bread which he quite furtively hid. His eyes expressed more than a thousand words of thanks. In doing that I myself became very fearful of becoming caught and winding up in the camp. Among the SS there were many Ukrainians who became conspicuous because of their especially brutal behaviour; they were supervised by German SS men.

'We foreign workers had it somewhat better as we were not subordinated to the SS, but to the construction leadership. Our provisions consisted of about 100 gm of bread per day, and sometimes there was some sausage. For lunch in the canteen, we got cabbage or vegetable soup and potatoes with brown sauce. For us young men and with our strenuous work, that was of course much too little, and we were always hungry. But there were also Germans who were ready to help, like the Süß family in Untersaal. From them I always got a tidbit to eat; at one time it would be potatoes, some fruit and, what was almost sensational for me, a piece of bacon - secretly of course. Up until the present time, I have not forgotten the way the family helped me and my friends in our great need. That the battle fronts came ever nearer, we noticed from the ever-increasing numbers of of low-flying aircraft. We could even observe how low-level flyers had shot-up a fuel train in flames near Bad Abbach.

On one occasion, we were just at the railway flyover in Untersaal when two red-nosed Lightnings approached very low, flying at the most 10 m (33 ft) over the Danube. The SS took cover in the roadside ditches, but the Americans did not open fire. Never had aircraft flown by so close to me, and I could see how the pilots looked over towards us and waved. Feeling completely homesick, I looked back at them. One morning, a few weeks before the end of the war, were were loaded onto trucks and were driven for two days to Regensburg to undertake clearing-up work in the railway station area. After a heavy bombing raid it looked catastrophic, and everywhere there were bomb craters. As the US troops got ever nearer, the camp was cleared out and construction work on all the galleries was stopped. One of the main galleries was was about 100 m (330 ft) and the other about 30-40 m (100-130 ft) long. We foreign workers were ordered to erect tank barriers at the railway crossing in Untersaal. For this purpose, concrete discs were rolled up, connected to each other by steel rails and covered over with concrete. I awaited the arrival of the US Army in the cellar of the Süß family. After we were liberated, we were driven to a barracks in Regensburg. The war ended on 8 May; on the 9th, it was my father's birthday and on the 10th, after an almost two-year spell, I happily returned home.'

The works pass issued by Messerschmitt Regensburg GmbH for Alfons Pichelmeier who was employed in Werk I at Prüfening and in Werk II at Obertraubling. (Photo Pichelmeier)

With the aid of eyewitness accounts, the author has been able to construct a conceivable overview of the Ringberg installation. Production of the Me 262 was doubtlessly planned here. The four side galleries were probably stores galleries which would have been supplied by rail or trucks delivering aircraft parts into the cavern(s) and which would have been prepared for final assembly. Based on the two large galleries towards the Teugner Straße, it can be surmised that in one of them fuselages, and in the other, wing assembly would have taken place. With the wingspan of the Me 262, the width of the galleries would only have permitted production of one line of wings and fuselages in a longitudinal direction. The mating of wings and fuselages would then have followed in a final assembly hall. This, together with the engines, would presumably have taken place at the Hernsaal airfield still in the process of construction, where the initial planning work for a runway had begun, likewise by camp inmates. Transportation of fuselages and wings on trailers over the Danube was - at least in the initial phase, was to have taken place with the available Herrnsaal-Untersaal river ferry. The start of production was planned for the end of 1945. In the cemetery at Saal are the mass graves of 20 dead and the ashes of 360 camp inmates. Ironically, after the war, the camp at the Teugner Straße was used by the US Army as a PoW camp solely for the SS. The entrances to the galleries were later blown-up at the order of the military government.

A further massive project was the underground bunkers for aircraft manufacture near Mühldorf on the Inn. Here, according to similar plans as at Lechfeld near Augsburg, a mammoth bunker was to have been erected, codenamed 'Weingut II', where over ten thousand camp inmates from Dachau as well as forced labourers slogged to complete a roughly 400 m (1,320 ft)-long and 85 m (215 ft)-wide bunker for Me 262 production, but although it could not be finished before the war ended, caused several deaths among the inmates.

Recollections of an Eyewitness

Alfons Pichelmeier of Langquaid, born in 1928, recounted his time at Messerschmitt GmbH Regensburg in Werk I at Prüfening and in Werk II at Obertraubling: 'Already as a schoolboy, I became interested in aviation. In the Langquaid Volksschule, in the 6th to 8th Classes, there was an aircraft modeller's fraternity, of which I was naturally a member. When the time drew near to leave school, we had to undergo professional training advice. For myself, I had long decided upon taking up metalworking, where I would be involved with aircraft. The careers advisor explained to me that the only possibility that existed for this was the Messerschmitt-Werk in Regensburg. I immediately wrote an application to Regensburg, and soon afterwards, received a reply with an invitation to appear for an acceptance test and medical examination. Both worked out positively for me. On 14 May 1943, I began my apprenticeship as a metal-aircraft builder at Messerschmitt with simultaneous acceptance into the Works-owned apprentices lodgings. In the first apprenticeship year, I was paid RM 25, of which RM 20 was retained for accommodation and meals. For me, there began a wholly new phase in my life. The old school comrades were suddenly not there anymore, and new friendships had to be made. The first few days were occupied with taking care of formalities, assignment in the apprentice lodgings, and it was here that uniform work clothing was also handed out to us. Then followed our assignment to classes in the trade school and to the various specialists and instructors. A Works inspection was also arranged for us newcomers. That was, naturally, highly interesting for us since one could not simply enter all areas of the plant. For particular Hallen, a special pass was necessary. When we came to the lacquer shop, for the first time I saw an Me 163, a sleek aircraft with a tiny propeller in the fuselage nose. This aircraft looked completely different from all that were hitherto known to me, for it did not even have a tailplane. Because of its size, the propeller could hardly have represented the powerplant, and we were puzzled as to what kind of engine powered it. The circular opening at the tail end led to some speculation, but no explanations about the aircraft were given to us. In this conducted tour, the Me 163 was completely ignored, and for us remained completely enigmatic. After the tour, considerable discussion ensued about this unknown aircraft. It was only much later that we learned something about its type designation and that the Me 163 was the world's first operationally-capable rocket fighter.

'In the apprentice workshop there now began the daily routine of an apprentice. Each one of us was given a basic plan of the course with all practice pieces and their illustrations. As the first item, we were given a U-shaped piece of iron and then told to file it down, followed by another 5 mm of filing down, until almost all of us had blistered hands. Later, when working on light-metal sheeting, the saying proved itself: 'First expand it till you bust, then compress it again, so that in the end you can no longer make use of it!' For those of us who were housed in the apprentice lodgings, our day at the end of the workshift was not yet over. After the evening meal there were many sporting activities; for some, music instruction, communal writing of school tasks or, when something did not work out as intended, a march to the airfield. There was hardly any activity there in the evenings, so that on the airfield there was military drill and refinement, so that much dust was raised.

'After a good three months, when basic instruction was just about over, the inferno of the 17 August 1943 bombing raid on the Messerschmitt plant took place. We just so happened to be in the apprentices' canteen for lunch when the air raid warning sounded. As had already been practised on some previous occasions, we went into the air raid shelter beneath the training building. I stood there with Horst Weiß, one of my best friends who was already in his second year of training, in the northern part of the shelter. It was purely by accident that I discovered there our apprecenticeship lodgings leader, Wastl Weigert, who ordered me to go to the washroom that was situated at the southern end of the shelter, to join the other first-year apprentices. I therefore made my way to the southern end of the shelter and placed myself with the others against the shelter wall. The roaring of heavy aircraft engines could now be heard. One of my comrades stood at the shelter window and through the light shaft, looked upwards. Suddenly, he cried out: "Hey, those are four-engined aircraft!" Just when I wanted to go to the window to take a look outside, the first bombs detonated and the window-pane blew in. An enormous pressure of air swept through the room. It now became clear to all of us that we were the target of a bombing raid. After a few minutes, the next wave arrived, and one of our trainers - the old Kaltenecker, soothed us in his strong Bavarian dialect with the words: "Boys, have no fear - not every bomb hits!" We also survived the second attack wave. But it was not long before a third wave threatened. All of us cowered on the floor and put our hands over our heads.

This time, our training building also got hit. We in the washroom were fortunately uninjured. A thick cloud of dust spread through the cellar. Suddenly, one of our instructors appeared out of the dust and smoke and called out to us: "Everybody out of the cellar and head towards the Danube, otherwise we'll all be dead!" For me, that was like the relief from a heavy burden and I ran up the cellar staircase, my one thought – to get out of the building. When I ran around the corner of the undamaged part of the building, I got a terrific shock. The apprentice barracks and half of the training building was a heap of rubble. None of the survivors remained standing for even a moment. The hurry to get out of the inferno was too great. I should also mention at this point that one first-year apprentice, Franz Laßleben, came over to the apprentice workshop during the raid to fetch a steel saw in order to free someone who was jammed in wreckage. For this heroic act, he was later awarded the War Service Cross. We ran towards the Danube, across the Hochweg and diagonally across the fields. Once we believed we were at a safe enough distance, we stood still, and in the meantime we could hear no more aircraft. We waited, and after some 15 minutes, the sirens sounded the all-clear. Over the Works were huge pillars of smoke and dust. It was only upon our return to the Works grounds that we first became aware of the extent of the destruction. The northern part of the training building in which I had been before the first bombs fell, was completely destroyed. There, there were mainly the second-year apprentices, of whom only a few survived. My friend Horst Weiß, whom I had spoken to only a short while before, was dead. Likewise, some of the instructors; among them the one from my trainee group (Landgraf) who did not survive. It now became clear to me that I owed my life to Wastl Weigert. Since the apprentice barracks had been almost destroyed, we were sent home. The trainee workshop was only slightly damaged, so that our work continued after one week. For the almost 400 killed, among them over 80 apprentices, a large funeral service was held at the Upper Catholic Churchyard. We were now accommodated in very primitive conditions in the old brewery building in Winzer and had to take the ferry every day over the Danube to get to our workplace. But the event had one advantage: there was no time for punishment exercises or other similar amusements.

'After the bombing raid, some 15 metres of the large apprentice training building was cordoned-off by an interim wall. What was that supposed to mean? In one of the workbreaks, I was able to take a look into the cordoned-off space where there were four or five fuselages of an aircraft that again had no propeller and which looked quite different from the Me 163 - much more elegant, but also, it seemed, more threatening. Our instructors, who often carried out work on these fuselages, were very secretive. But, bit by bit, the secret was revealed. At that time in Regensburg, we were witnesses to the design and manufacture of the world's first operational jet fighter, the Me 262. Work was conducted at high pressure on completion of the Turbinenjäger, as the Me 262 was called at that time, so as to be able to successfully combat the air attacks on the Reich. For us apprentices, our training took place on the lathes, milling and joining machines. I still have none too good memories of my time on the milling machine, for it was then that I was given my first and only slap across the ears during my training period. The instructor Harry Schmid gave me a workpiece on which he had already long worked upon and which belonged to a former of the Me 262. I was tasked to mill down half a millimetre at a particular point on it. When he thereafter measured it, the tolerance limit on the workpiece, and presumably on his nerves as well, had been exceeded.

'In the meantime it had turned to winter and we were still housed in emergency quarters in Winzer. The crossing on the Danube ferry in conditions of ice and high water were very dangerous. At the beginning of February 1944, we relocated to the Obertraubling Fliegerhorst. Here, we were housed in so-called stepped-construction apartments and were delighted about the pleasant four-man rooms in these barracks. The sanitary rooms were superbly equipped, and lunch was taken in a large mess hall. The generously laid out Fliegerhorst with all its installations was available to all of us Messerschmitt employees.

'There were no destroyed buildings or temporarily-repaired Hallen here like in Prüfening, but instead, enormous Hallen and endlessly long buildings characterized the Fliegerhorst. The apprentice workshop was set up in a large aircraft Halle and training took its customary course. But this idyllic situation only lasted three weeks, for on 22 February 1944, the first bombing raid occurred at the Fliegerhorst. In the lunch break, the alarm sounded once more and the sirens howled. We were instructed to go into the basement air-raid shelters. However, the majority of us had our noses full of the air-raid cellars and beat it over the fence in the direction of Barbing. There were about ten of us trainees and we had just reached the edge of the village when the first wave of bombers approached. On the outskirts of Barbing, in the direction of Donaustauf, there was a small concrete bunker in which we sought cover. After the all-clear, we went back to the Fliegerhorst. The first horrible sight, from still beyond the Fliegerhorst fence where the Russian barracks was located, was a torn-off leg wrapped in a puttee. As we approached our area, crossing over much debris, we were able to recognise that our accommodation had been destroyed. It was a miracle that from those who remained behind, no-one was injured or killed. We apprentices were thereupon sent home. On the way to the Obertraubling railway station, I saw the remains of a shot-down bomber.

'Three days later, on 25 February 1944, there was a further heavy bombing raid on the Fliegerhorst. From a safe distance, I was able to observe the bombers as they headed for Regensburg, and my thoughts were with those who had to once more fear for their lives. On its approach to Regensburg, one B-17 was shot down by a Bf 109, and crashed and exploded near to the desolate and miserable area between Hellring and Dünzling. (The bomber was shot down by Major Walther Dahl, the Kommandeur of III./JG 3 – author). As a result of this second bombing raid, we apprentices were given leave until the beginning of April. During this time, together with several other apprentices I enrolled for glider pilot training encompassing an A-Certificate examination at the Reisberg near Regenstauf. It was already a quite exciting time until we were able to take off on our first short flight, which lasted only a few seconds. Take-off was with the aid of a rubber bungee. After landing, the Schneider SG 38 glider had to be laboriously towed by hand up the slope, back to the take-off point. It was really quite strenuous, but we all very proudly returned with our A-Certificates at the beginning of April. Our lodgings had once more been acceptably repaired, and in fact, a fine period had now begun for us. We were assigned to the production phase. I was in one of two groups, each 30 strong, who had to take apart the Bf 109s that had been damaged in the bombing raids. At our hearts' content, we were able to work away and keep on working. All reusable components were extracted and the rest scrapped. In this way, I learned a lot about the construction of the Bf 109 and its technical aspects. This work lasted throughout the whole of April, since the number of heavily damaged Bf 109s parked on the airfield had been so great. At the beginning of May came the news that the entire apprenticeship department would be transferred to Marienthal near Deggendorf. Hardly had the move arrangements been completed, when the new apprenticeship year began. We 'old ones' now had, in part, to make readily usable artifacts such as drawing-board stands and stencils for the workshops, partly also work on aircraft production and partly catch up on our training which we had not yet completed, such as forging, welding and soldering.

'During the 1944 summer vacation, I reported with some other apprentices for my glider pilot's B- and C-Certificate training at Moos, near Plattling, and at Landshut. Although the glider pilot training at that time was a severe sweat, there were cheerful times. In the B-course, we practised flying in turns. Here, in an SG 38, we were towed to a height of about 30 m (100 ft) with a winch, had to make a right and left turn, and then land. One of the trainee pilots in the SG 38 made a 180°-degree turn and flew directly into an enormous oak tree at the edge of the woods. It crumpled, and parts of the empennage fluttered down, the rest of it remaining hanging in the branches. The pilot was afraid to make any kind of move and sat firmly at a lofty height in the tree. We eventually fetched the fire brigade ladder from Moos to bring our colleague down from the smashed-up glider. After about two hours, he once more had firm ground beneath his feet and stood in front of the flying instructor for the customary report: "Pilot Trainee Hahn reports being back from take-off!" Loud laughter now broke out, and not even the stern flying instructor, Schweighard, was able to hold himself back. The crash pilot then had the honourable task of spending the rest of the course at the winch. Upon our return to Marienthal, we already all felt ourselves to be 'half-pilots'. But the daily routine soon caught us up, as the work portion of production became continually raised. At the end of January 1945, we completed yet another – as it was called at that time, emergency specialist examination. At the beginning of February, my course-year was called up for Reichsarbeitsdienst (labour service). At the beginning of April, I went to the Unteroffizierschule (NCO School) in Tetschen in northern Bohemia. Four weeks later, the war was over and with it, my dream of flying. Via some adventurous paths I was able to battle my way back home, for it was with cunning and cheek that I just barely managed in Brüx to avoid falling into Russian captivity. On my long march home, I passed by the totally destroyed Fliegerhorst Obertraubling. The once proud airbase had been heavily damaged and from the outside, gave the impression of being a ruin. At Obertraubling railway station lay some Me 262 fuselages and on the platform in the direction of Landshut were several open freight cars on which one jet engine beside the other were stacked. On looking at these – what were then highly modern artifacts, I thought ironically to myself: There in Regensburg, we built the fastest and most modern aircraft in the world, and still we lost the war.'

Appendix 1

Letter to Theo Croneiß from Prussian Ministerpräsident Göring
(Original letter opposite)

Berlin, 20 October 1933

Strictly Confidential!

Dear Croneiss,

In this strictly confidential letter, I should like to inform you that I regard your new task, to organise anew the aircraft industry in Bavaria, as a matter of extraordinary importance. I expect from your drive that you will push forward immediately with complete enthusiasm, the creation of an aircraft firm which hopefully, will soon bring out a first-class transport aircraft !!! Equally important, however, is the development of a very fast courier aircraft that need only be a single-seater. In case up to now you have not yet had anything to do with the development of such aircraft, we can however, suggest that the plant could initially be entrusted with licence manufacture, so that it is already in a position to secure employment of a large workforce and as a result of the proof attained thereby, promote the development of new types.

I request accordingly, that you examine all these things and to personally advise me soonest of your views. It would certainly be in our interest if a large plant could be erected in Augsburg. In other respects, I request you once more to regard the step that I have taken towards you as necessary for me. I honestly wish that no ill feeling whatsoever will exist between us. - I further request that after reading this letter, for reasons that are clear to you, to destroy it.

With Heil Hitler and best wishes

(signed) Göring

Appendix 2

Overall aircraft production by Messerschmitt GmbH Regensburg, 1938-1945

Details of overall aircraft production stem from the Messerschmitt GmbH Regensburg Production Control Report documents (Regensburg Stadtarchiv), the Annual Company Reports examined by the Trustee (Bundesarchiv), and from the USSBS. In the documents, differing figures appear, so that the overall total is to be regarded as a minimum total for each individual type of aircraft.

	Bf 108	Bf 109	Me 163	Me 210	Me 262 fuselages	Me 262	Me 323
1938	175						
1939	147	144(+1)					
1940	77	349					
1941	59	353		32			
1942	58	486	8	62			16(+7)
1943		2,166	62				86
1944		6,316			49	1,027	1
1945		1,074*			281	1,025	
Total:	516	10,888(+1)	70	94	330	2,052	101(+7)

For the year 1938, a total of 181 Bf 108s were reported, of which 6 were not yet taken on charge. For 1939, the Annual Report lists 198 aircraft and airframes for the Bf 108. A small part of these were sold to private individuals. In 1939, a Bf 109 E-3a (+1) was destroyed in acceptance testing. On hand from RLM delivery documents, relatively precise data is available for production, except that for April 1945 no official documents have been found to exist.

*Production status according to Messerschmitt Regensburg manufacturing control report documents up to 31 March 1945. From a handwritten remark of the RLM Quartermaster-General, up to 11 April 1945 some 50-60 Bf 109s were accepted from industry. By reason of the geographical location of Regensburg and the general war situation, it can be assumed that at least a part, if not all of these aircraft, came from Messerschmitt GmbH Regensburg. Source: National Archives, Washington. According to the USSBS, there were a total of 335 Me 262 [fuselages], whereas only 330 are listed by the manufacturing control report. For the Me 323, the USSBS registered 101 aircraft. In 1942, however, 23 Me 323s (of which +7 were prototypes) were built, and not 16 as reported in the USSBS.

Appendix 3

Total personnel employed at Messerschmitt GmbH Regensburg, 1936-1945

In numerous documents on personnel strength, various figures continually appear. The personnel strength figures listed here originate from a document in the US National Archives, Washington.

Month/Year	Apprentices	Germans	Foreign Workers/ Forced Labourers	Workforce Total
12/1936				1,336
12/1937	241	1,090		1,331
12/1938	452	2,537		2,809
12/1939	765	3,815		4,580
12/1940	933	4,275		5,208
12/1941	974	5,150	305	6,429
12/1942	1,159	5,546	4,710	11,415
12/1943	1,283	5,460	4,720	11,463
06/1944	1,352	5,449	4,886	11,687
04/1945	1,350	5,124	6,350	12,824

Appendix 4

Bf 108 B-1 data

Powerplant:	1 x Argus As 10 C
Engine power:	240 hp for 5 mins at 2,000 rpm (short-duration power)
	220 hp at 1,940 rpm (increased continuous power)
	200 hp at 1,880 rpm (continuous power)
Wingspan:	10.60 m (34 ft 9.3 in)
Length:	8.30 m (27 ft 2.8 in)
Height:	2.80 m (9 ft 2.2 in)
Wing area:	16.40 m² (176.52 ft²)
Undercarriage track:	1.50 m (4 ft 11.1 in)
Empty weight:	880 kg (1,940 lb)
Payload:	500 kg (1,102 lb)
Loaded weight:	1,380 kg (3,042 lb)
Maximum speed:	305 km/h (190 mph)
Cruising speed:	265 km/h (165 mph)
Landing speed:	85 km/h (53 mph)
Rate of climb:	3.15 mins to 1 km (3,280 ft)
Range:	1,000 km (621 mls)
Service ceiling:	5,000 m (16,400 ft)
Endurance:	3 hrs 40 mins

Messerschmitt Regensburg-built Bf 108s:
1938 = 75
1939 = 147
1940 = 77
1941 = 59
1942 = 58
Total = 516

Messerschmitt Regensburg-built Bf 108 Werknummern, identifications and their whereabouts, as far as is confirmable (list not complete) were as follows:

W.Nr.	Call sign	Remarks (Dates in Day/Month/Year order)
1640	TV+OA	
1655	NA+JU	
1658		On 26.12.43, 10 % damaged on landing (Erg.Gr.Süd)
1667		On 26.06.43, 70 % damaged through engine damage (Stab JG 27)
1685		On 15.03.43, 35 % damaged on landing (JG 107)
1690		On 10.08.41, 40 % damaged in emergency landing through lack of fuel (I./KG 77)
1691		On 22.11.42, 10 % damaged on landing (NJSch.1)
1692		On 04.05.42, destroyed through bombing (Stab KG 30)
1696		On 17.07.41, 15 % damaged through engine damage (Gen.Kdo. II.Flakkorps)
1897		On 24.04.41, 80 % damaged in crash (IV./KG 3)
1908		On 20.08.42, 90 % damaged in crash (Erg.Zerst.Gr.)
1910	W+AL	
1916	D-IWAN	
1923		On 22.11.42, 15 % damaged on landing (Flugbereitschaft GLM)
1925		On 19.08.41, 100 % damaged through engine damage (III./KG 1)
1926	A-203	Delivered to Switzerland (Acceptance on 25.01.39)
1982		On 28.09.43, 75 % damaged through engine damage (JG 105)
1986		On 13.09.43, 30 % damaged through engine damage (II./KG 2)
1988	A-201	Delivered to Switzerland (Acceptance on 23.11.38)
1989	A-202	Delivered to Switzerland (Acceptance on 23.11.38)
1992		On 17.08.43, 25 % damaged on landing (Stab LLG 1)
1995		On 26.04.43, 60 % damaged through bombing (Flugzeugleitstelle Lfl-Kdo 2)
1999	D-ICRO	This Mtt GmbH executive aircraft, was stationed in Regensburg from 04.10.41 as NI+QA, and from 23.10.41 in Rangsdorf.
-	A-204	Delivered to Switzerland (Acceptance on 25.01.39)
2003	A-205	Delivered to Switzerland (Acceptance on 25.01.39)
2007		On 10.01.41, 25 % damaged on landing (Stab StG 3)
2008		On 19.07.43, 100 % destroyed through bombing (1. Fallschirmjägerdivision)
2009		On 07.11.43, 15 % damaged on take-off (II./SG 2)
2010		On 10.01.41, 25 % damaged on landing (I./StG 1)
2011		On 14.09.43, 20 % damaged through bombing (NAGr 4)
2013		On 26.03.41, 35 % damaged on landing (Transportstab I. A.K.)
2014	F8+CA	On 11.09.43, desertion (Stab KG 40)
2019	D-IROS	Was owned by civilian pilot Elly Beinhorn
2021		On 29.08.43, 100 % destroyed after air battle (SG 101)
2024		On 16.08.43, 80 % destroyed through bombing (OKM Kurierstaffel)
2025		On 31.05.43, 15 % damaged through engine damage (FAGr 1)
2033		On 15.11.40, 20 % damaged on landing (Stab KG 76)
2035	GJ+AZ	
2045	DQ+NV	On 22.06.41, 100 % destroyed in crash (Stab JG 3)
2048	A-206	Delivered to Switzerland (Acceptance on 06.07.39)
2049	KZ+BZ	
2050		On 09.06.41, 20 % damaged through engine damage (Jagdfliegerschule 1)
-	A-207	Delivered to Switzerland (Acceptance on 06.07.39)
-	A-208	Delivered to Switzerland (Acceptance on 07.07.39)
2057	TU+AZ	
2060		On 10.11.41, 80 % damaged through engine damage (Fliegerbereitschaft Luftflotte 4)
2061		On 18.07.42, 20 % damaged through engine damage (II./JG 27)
2067		On 05.10.41, 10 % damaged after air battle (Flugbereitschaft V. A.K.)
2070		On 14.08.41, 95 % destroyed in crash (I./KG 3)
2071		On 04.10.43, destroyed through bombing (I./TG 4)
2074		On 15.11.41, 15 % damaged in ground movement (Zerstörerschule 1)
2081	GF+HI	
2083	A-209	Delivered to Switzerland (Acceptance on 06.07.39)
2084	A-210	Delivered to Switzerland (Acceptance on 06.07.39)
2085	A-211	Delivered to Switzerland (Acceptance on 01.08.39)
2086	A-212	Delivered to Switzerland (Acceptance on 01.08.39)
2087	A-213	Delivered to Switzerland (Acceptance on 01.08.39)
2088	A-214	Delivered to Switzerland (Acceptance on 01.08.39)
2089	A-215	Delivered to Switzerland (Acceptance on 04.08.39)
2090	D-IHTR	
2092		On 03.11.42, blown up by own troops (Stab JG 7)
2101		On 25.07.41, transported to Les Mureaux
2102		On 31.05.41, 35 % damaged through engine damage (II./KG 76)
2104		On 09.11.43, 25 % damaged at I.KG 51

W.Nr.	Call-sign	Remarks (Dates in Day/Month/Year order)
2107		On 14.07.43, destroyed through bombing (JG 105)
2109		On 13.06.41, 25 % damaged after lack of fuel (Stab XI. A.K.)
2123	DE+IB	
2133	DH+DE	On 05.10.40, 60 % damaged on take-off (JFS 3)
2134		On 24.10.41, 25 % damaged on landing (Stab Jafü 2)
2139		On 13.05.41, 80 % damaged in ground accident (JFS 2)
2151	IH+JB	On 28.03.42, 70 % damaged through engine damage (I./KG 26)
2154		On 18.07.43, 80 % damaged on landing (Flugbereitschaft II. Fliegerkorps)
2156		On 31.10.43, 25 % damaged on landing (Flugbereitschaft I. Fliegerkorps)
2200	KK+DH	
2209		On 15.07.43, 70 % damaged on landing (JFS 4)
2210		On 02.10.42, destroyed through bombing (Stab JG 26)
2214		23.06.41, 30 % damaged through engine fault (JFS 4)
2222		07.03.40*
2225	TL+AV	03.04.40* On 20.05.43, destroyed through bombing (III./KG 26)
2230	TM+AA	03.04.40*
2231	NF+MA	
2232	NF+MB	
2233	NF+MC	11.04.40*
2234	NF+MD	11.04.40*
2235	NF+ME	17.04.40*
2236	NF+MF	15.04.40*
2237	NF+MG	17.04.40*
2238	NF+MH	
2239	NF +MI	17.04.40*
2240	NF+MJ	25.04.40* Blown up on 17.12.41 (Fliegerführer Afrika)
2241	NF+MK	26.04.40*
2242	NF+ML	27.04.40*
2243	NF+MM	28.04.40*
2244	NF+MN	29.04.40* On 11.02.42, 40 % damaged on landing (Flugbereitschaft II. Fliegerkorps)
2245	NF+MO	29.04.40*
2246	NF+MP	
2247	NF+MQ	
2248	NF+MR	07.06.40* On 22.04.41, 25 % damaged on take-off (JFS 4)
2249	NF+MS	10.06.40*
2250	NF+MT	
2251	NF+MU	15.06.40*
2252	NF+MV	21.06.40*
2253	NF+MW	25.06.40*
2254	NF+MX	25.06.40*
2255	NF+MY	28.06.40*
2256	NF+MZ	29.06.40* On 13.04.43, 15 % damaged in ground movement (Kurierstaffel ObdL)
2257	NF+LT	29.06.40*
2258	NF+LU	29.06.40*
2259	NF+LV	30.06.40*
2260	NF+LW	08.07.40*
2261	CI+CE	10.07.40*
2262	CI+CF	10.07.40*
2263	CI+CG	22.07.40* On 09.12.41, 10 % damaged on landing (I./KG 77)
2264	CI+CH	22.07.40*
2265	CI+CI	30.07.40*
2266	CI+CJ	30.07.40*
2267	CI+CK	17.08.40*
2268	CI+CL	09.08.40* On 24.04.40, 40 % damaged in ground accident (III./KG 53)
2269	CI+CM	16.08.40*
2270	CI+CN	22.08.40*
2271	CI+CO	03.09.40*
2272	CI+CP	04.09.40*
2273	CI+CQ	06.09.40*
2274	CI+CR	12.09.40*
2275	D-IKRK	05.04.41*
2276	TI+EB	On 11.04.42, 35 % damaged on landing (I./NJG 3)

W.Nr.	Call-sign	Remarks (Dates in Day/Month/Year order)
2277	TI+EC	14.03.41*
2278	TI+ED	30.11.40*
2279	TI+EE	30.11.40*
2280	TI+EF	14.01.41*
2281	TI+EG	18.12.41*
2282	TI+EH	22.01.41* On 16.12.41, 100 % destroyed in fighter-bomber attack (2./H 14)
2283	TI+EI	06.02.41*
2284	TI+EJ	28.01.41*
2285	TI+EK	
2286	TI+EL	23.02.41*
2287	TI+EM	08.02.41*
2288	TI+EN	On 04.05.41, 25 % damaged on landing (I./JG 7)
2289	TI+EO	06.02.41*
2290	TI+EP	06.02.41*
2291	TI+EQ	18.02.41*
2292	TI+ER	16.02.41*
2293	TI+ES	22.02.41*
2294	TI+ET	22.02.41*
2295	TI+EU	07.03.41*
2296	TI+EV	
2297	TI+EW	30.05.41*
2298	TI+EX	
2299	TI+EY	
2300	TI+EZ	
2774		On 17.10.43, 30 % damaged on landing (NAGr 102)
2847		13.07.41, 60 % damaged through bombing (Stab KG 1)
3001	VK+WA	26.06.41*
3002	VK+WB	09.07.41*
3003	VK+WC	11.07.41*
3004	VK+WD	23.07.41*
3005	VK+WE	01.08.41*
3006	VK+WF	23.07.41*
3007	VK+WG	On 16.10.41, destroyed in crash (II./KG 3)
3008	VK+WH	
3009	VK+WI	
3010	VK+WJ	
3011	VK+WK	
3012	VK+WL	
3013	VK+WM	22.09.41*
3014	VK+WN	17.09.41*
3015	VK+WO	29.10.41*
3016	VK+WP	27.10.41*
3017	VK+WQ	29.10.41*
3018	VK+WR	10.11.41*
3019	VK+WS	10.11.41*
3020	VK+WT	12.10.41* On 04.04.42, destroyed in crash (Stab JG 3)
3021	VK+WU	12.11.41* On 03.06.42, destroyed in air battle (Stab KG 6)
3022	VK+WV	11.11.41*
3023	VK+WW	18.11.41* On 02.04.42, destroyed in crash (III./JG 27)
3024	VK+WX	18.11.41*
3025	VK+WY	20.11.41*
3026	VK+WZ	24.11.41*
3027	VF+EA	26.11.41*
3028	VF+EB	29.11.41* On 19.06.43, 80 % destroyed through engine damage (Lfl. Kdo.2)
3029	VF+EC	27.11.41*
3030	VF+ED	07.12.41*
3031	VF+EE	11.12.41* On 18.03.42, 10 % damaged on landing (I./StG 77)
3032	VF+EF	09.12.41* On 25.12.43, 50 % damaged through bombing (3./F 121)
3033	VF+EG	09.12.41*
3034	VF+EH	13.12.41*
3035	VF+EI	17.12.41*
3036	VF+EJ	19.12.41*
3037	VF+EK	19.12.41*
3038	VF+EL	23.12.41* On 25.03.43, shot down by own flak (Fl.Ber. Moscow)
3039	VF+EM	07.01.42*

W.Nr.	Call-sign	Remarks (Dates in Day/Month/Year order)
3040	VF+EN	26.02.42*
3041	VF+EO	
3042	VF+EP	13.01.42*
3043	VF+EQ	14.01.42* On 30.01.43, destroyed in crash (Fliegerführer Crimea)
3044	VF+ER	03.02.42*
3045	VF+ES	23.01.42*
3046	VF+ET	06.02.42*
3047	VF+EU	03.02.42*
3048	VF+EV	09.02.42* On 15.12.42, 90 % destroyed through bombing (Stab JG 52)
3049	VF+EW	09.02.42*
3050	VF+EX	12.02.42*
3051	VE+LA	12.02.42* On 23.08.42, 10 % damaged on landing (Fl.Ber. Don)
3052	VE+LB	27.02.42*
3053	VE+LC	27.02.42* On 12.10.43, 25 % damaged through engine damage (Stab StG 151)
3054	VE+LD	27.02.42*
3055	VE+LE	02.03.42* On 18.11.42, destroyed in crash (II./StG 1)
3056	VE+LF	
3057	VE+LG	02.03.42* On 21.07.42, 90 % destroyed on take-off (III./KG 26)
3058	VE+LH	02.03.42*
3059	VE+LI	02.03.42*
3060	VE+LJ	
3061	VE+LK	
3062	VE+LL	
3063	VE+LM	
3064	VE+LN	
3065	VE+LO	
3066	VE+LP	
3067	VE+LQ	14.04.42*
3068	VE+LR	14.04.42*
3069	VE+LS	16.04.42* On 23.10.42, 40 % damaged through bombing (Stab StG 77)
3070	VE+LT	22.04.42*
3071	VE+LU	22.04.42*
3072	VE+LV	05.05.42*
3073	VE+LW	05.05.42*
3074	VE+LX	05.05.42*
3075	VE+LY	06.05.42*
3076	VE+LZ	07.05.42*
3077	VG+FN	07.05.42*
3078	VG+FO	
3079	VG+FP	
3080	VG+FQ	
3081	GL+YA	On 24.01.43, destroyed in crash (Stab KG 55)
3082-3085		
3086		On 23.08.42, destroyed through bombing (Verbindungsstaffel 64)
3087	VG+FX	22.06.42*
3088	RE+EG	On 11.12.42 10 % damaged on runway (Fliegerbereitschaft VIII. Fliegerkorps)
3089	RE+EH	
3090	RE+EI	25.01.43, destroyed through engine damage (NAGr 10)
3091	RE+EJ	
3092	RE+EK	10.08.42, 45 % damaged through bombing (III./JG 51)
3093	RE+EL	
3094	RE+EM	03.06.42*

To Werknummer 3040, were Bf 108 B-1s; from 3041, Bf 109 D-1s. According to an alteration instruction, a 'cold-start' installation was built into Bf 108 Wernummern 3041 to 3094 by Messerschmitt GmbH Regensburg.
The call-signs that were not mentioned in Josef Haid's flight logbook, have been approriately expanded.

Appendix 5

Bf 109 G-6 Salient data

Powerplant:	Daimler-Benz DB 605 A
Take-off power:	1,475 hp
Wingspan:	9.92 m (32 ft 6.6 in)
Length:	8.94 m (29 ft 4 in)
Height:	2.50 m (8 ft 2.4 in)
Wing area:	16.02 m² (172.43 ft²)
Empty weight:	2,680 kg (5,908 lb)
Payload:	520 kg (1,146 lb)
Loaded weight:	3,200 kg (7,055 lb)
Maximum speed:	630 km/h at 7 km (391 mph at 22,965 ft)
Time to climb:	10.5 mins to 8.4 km (27,560 ft)
Range:	650 km (404 mls)
Service ceiling:	12,000 m (39,370 ft)
Armament:	2 x MG 131 + 1 x MG 151

List of Bf 109 Werknummer produced by Messerschmitt GmbH Regensburg

Due to gaps in surviving documents, not all of the Werknummer blocks have been captured. From a file remark by Messserschmitt AG Augsburg on 03.12.1939, it transpires from W.Nr.1955, that Mtt GmbH Regensburg delivered the Bf 109 E. The basis for the available Werknummer table are the flight logs of the Einflieger (Works acceptance test pilots) and Luftwaffe loss reports. From 1939 to 1945, the following Bf 109 models were manufactured at Regensburg:
Bf 109 E-3, E-3a, E-4, E-4B, E-4BN, E-7
Bf 109 F-0, F-1, F-2
Bf 109 G-1, G-2, G-2/trop, G-3, G-4, G-4/trop G-6, G-6/trop, G-6/AS, G-10, G-14, G-14/AS
Bf 109 K-2, K-4

The E-3a consisted of aircraft for export to Switzerland and Yugoslavia.
The G-1 examples, W.Nr. 14001 to 14005 (VJ+WA to VJ+WE), are not listed in Messerschmitt Regensburg documents as G-0s, but as G-1s.
The overall total of Bf 109s manufactured by Regensburg is approximately 10,888. For April 1945, no complete production figures are available, save for the RLM Quartermaster-General handwritten remark that in the period 01-11 April, 250 Bf 109s were taken over by the Luftwaffe. Production figures were:
1939 = 144, 1940 = 349, 1941 = 353, 1942 = 486, 1943 = 2166, 1944 = 6316, 1945 = 1074; Total = 10,888.

Bf 109 E Werknummern and Stammkennzeichen (factory call-signs)

W.Nr.	Call-sign	Month/Year built Type & and Remarks
2180	BY+BA Later converted into F-0.	1939/1940
2159 – 2198 (Switzerland)		
2300	BY+	1939
2351 – 2364 (Switzerland)		1939
2373 – 2381 (Switzerland)		1939
2385 – 2386 (Switzerland)		1939
2392		1939
2403 – 2409 (Switzerland)		1939
2420 – 2422 (Switzerland)		1939
2424 – 2449	SK+AA – SK+ZZ	6 & 7/1940
2711 – 2736	SK+CA– SK+CZ	7/1940
2741 – 2766	KF+SA – KF+SZ	7/1940
2782	GA+HP	8/1940
3015	TM+AF	
3709 – 3734	CI+DA – CI+DZ	8/1940
3735 – 3760	CI+EA – CI+EZ	8 & 9/1940
3761 – 3786	CI+FA – CI+FZ	
3799 – 3824	GA+LA – GA+LZ DH+KA DH+KJ	

Bf 109 F Werknummern and Stammkennzeichen (factory call-signs)

Werknummer	Call-sign		Completion ca. Month/Year
5601	CE+BM		
5602	CE+BN	V21	
5603	CE+BP	V23	
5604	VK+AB	V24	
5604	VK+AC	F-0	(total for 1939-1941 at Regensburg were 16 F-0 completed)
5622	PI+IK	F-0	
		F-1	10, 11/1940
5626 – 5631	SG+GU – SG+GZ		
5632 – 5657	SG+EA – SG+EZ		
5658 – 5683	RC+EA – RC+EZ	F-1	12/1940
5685	RN+GZ		1/1941
5686 – 5711	NA+YA – NA+YZ	F-1	1, 2/1941
5712 – 5735	ND+IA – ND+IX	F-1	(ND+IQ missing)
5736 – 5756	KH+DA – KH+DU	F-1	3/1941
5757	SG+PZ		3/1941
5758 – 5761	KH+DW – KH+DZ	F-2	3/1941
5762 – 5786	KK+SA – KK+SY	F-2	4/1941
8107	DE+FJ		4/1941
8907 – 8921	PK+HL – PK+HZ	F-2	4/1941
8922 – 8930	PK+SA – PK+SI	F-2	5/1941
8937 – 8939	PB+SP – PB+SR	F-2	5/1941
8955 – 8976	GB+KE – GB+KZ	F-2	5/1941
8977 – 9000	GG+KA – GG+KZ	F-2	5/1941
9153 – 9170	GB+QH – GB+QY	F-2	6/1941
9172 – 9196	NJ+XB – NJ+XZ	F-2	6/1941
9197 – 9222	PK+ZA – PK+ZZ	F-2	7, 8, 9/1941
9223 – 9248	TH+TA – TH+TZ	F-2	7, 8, 9/1941

Bf 109 G and K Werknummern and Stammkennzeichen (factory call-signs)

Werknummer	Call-sign		Completion ca. Month/Year
14001 – 14005	VJ+WA – VJ+WE	G-1	11/1941
14006 – 14009	BD+GA – BD+GI	G-1	12/1941
14010 – 14014	BD+GE – BD+GI	G-1/R-2	1, 2/1942
14015 – 14027	BD+GJ – BD+GV	G-1	2/1942
14028	BD+GW	G-2	2/1942
14029 – 14030	BD+GX – BD+GY	G-1	2/1942
14031 – 14035	NI+BA – NI+BE	G-1	2/1942
14036	NI+BF	G-2	2/1942
14037 – 14056	NI+BG – NI+BZ	G-1	3/1942
14057 – 14068	SG+LA – SG+LL	G-1	3, 4/1942
14069 – 14074	NH+PA – NH+PF	G-1	4/1942
14075 – 14094	NH+PG – NH+PZ	G-1/R-2	4/1942
14095 – 14120	NI+SA – NI+SZ	G-1/R-2	5/1942
14121 – 14135	DF+CA – DF+CO	G-1/R-2	5/1942
14136 – 14149	DG+UA – DG+UN	G-1/R-2	6/1942
14150 – 14161	DG+UO – DG+UZ	G-2	6/1942
14162 – 14187	DN+YA – DN+YZ	G-2	6/1942
14188 – 14213	BI+GA – BI+GZ	G-2	7/1942
14214 – 14235	BL+IA – BL+IU	G-2	7/1942
14236 – 14245	CC+PG – CC+PP	G-2	8/1942
14246 – 14255	CC+PO – CC+PZ	G-2/Trop	8/1942 in August/September 42
14256 – 14268	CH+KN	G-2/Trop	8/1942 conversion to 'Tropical'
16001 – 16026	DF+FA – DF+FZ	G-4	9/1942
16027 – 16038	DH+XA – DH+XL	G-4	9/1942
16039 – 16052	DH+XM – DH+XZ	G-4/Trop	9/1942
16053 – 16078	KG+OH – KG+OZ	G-4/Trop	10/1942
16079 – 16092	SO+KA – SO+KN	G-4/Trop	10/1942
16093 – 16104	SO+KO – SO+KZ	G-4	10/1942
16105 – 16130	CD+WA – CD+WZ	G-4	10, 11/1942
16131 – 16156	PE+KA – PE+KZ	G-4	11/1942
16157 – 16182	BE+WA – BE+WZ	G-4	11, 12/1942
16183 – 16199	RB+IA – RB+IQ	G-4/Trop	12/1942
16201 – 16226	CL+EA – CL+EZ	G-4/Trop	12/1942
16227 – 16232	CO+ZA – CO+ZF	G-4/Trop	1/1943
16233	VF+SD		1/1943
16234 – 16235	CO+ZG – CO+ZH	G-4/Trop	1/1943
16236	GN+IZ		1/1943
16237 – 16250	CO+ZT – CO+ZW	G-4/Trop	1/1943
16251 – 16253	CO+ZX – CO+ZZ	G-3	1/1943
16254 – 16279	SG+JA – SG+JZ	G-3	1, 2/1943
16280 – 16300	SP+EA – SP+EU	G-3	2/1943
16301 – 16310	KO+DA – KO+DJ	G-4/Trop	
16311 – 16312	BK+BA – BK+BB	G-4/Trop	
16313 – 16320	BK+BC – BK+BJ	G-6	
16321 – 16333	GN+MN – GN+MZ	G-6	↓
16360 – 16385	NI+YA – NI+YZ	G-6	2, 3/1943
16386 – 16411	NJ+MA – NJ+MZ	G-6	
16412 – 16437	DQ+IA – DQ+IZ	G-6	
16438 – 16463	DS+SA – DS+SZ	G-6	
16464 – 16489	SL+EA – SL+EZ	G-6	
16490 – 16500			↓
16501 – 16526	KT+CA – KT+CZ	G-6	3/1943
16527 – 16552	KT+DA – KT+DZ	G-6	4/1943
16553 – 16578	KT+EA – KT+EZ	G-6	
16579 – 16604	KV+GA – KV+GZ	G-6	
16605 – 16630	KV+OA – KV+OZ	G-6	
16631 – 16634	KN+PW – KN+PZ	G-6	
16635 – 16644	CJ+IA – CJ+IJ	G-6	
16645 – 16652	GK+OA – GK+OH	G-6	
18001 – 18020	GK+OG – GK+OZ	G-6	
18021 – 18046	GP+IA – GP+IZ	G-6	↓
18047 – 18072	SO+SA – SO+SZ	G-6	4/1943
18073 – 18098	SO+WA – SO+WZ	G-6	5/1943
18099 – 18110	SB+YO – SB+YZ	G-6	
18111 – 18136	KN+TA – KN+TZ	G-6	
18137 – 18162	KT+WA – KT+WZ	G-6	
18163 – 18188	TH+XA – TH+XZ	G-6	
18189 – 18214	TO+IA – TO+IZ	G-6	
18215 – 18230	IM+MA – IM+MP	G-6	
18231 – 18256	SQ+JA – SQ+JZ	G-6	↓
18257 – 18282	PL+DA – PL+DZ	G-6	5/1943
18283 – 18308	PP+TA – PP+TZ	G-6	6/1943
18309 – 18334	BF+QA – BF+QZ	G-6	
18335 – 18360	BJ+IA – BJ+IZ	G-6	
18361 – 18386	TL+DA – TL+DZ	G-6	
18387 – 18412	TO+QA – TO+QZ	G-6	
18413 – 18438	CJ+MA – CJ+MZ	G-6	
18439 – 18464	CH+IA – CH+IZ	G-6	
18465 – 18490	CD+TA – CD+TZ	G-6	↓
18491 – 18516	SI+OA – SI+OZ	G-6	6/1943
18517 – 18520	SN+LA?	G-6	7/1943
18521 – 18542	SN+LE – SN+LZ	G-6	
18543 – 18568	PH+XA – PH+XZ	G-6	
18569 – 18594	PM+FA – PM+FZ	G-6	
18595 – 18620	RJ+TA – RJ+TZ	G-6	
18621 – 18646	RG+CA – RG+CZ	G-6	
18647 – 18671	TN+JA – TN+JZ	G-6	
18672 – 18692	TQ+CA – TQ+CZ	G-6	
18698 – 18701			↓
18702 – 18727	CJ+JA – CJ+J	G-6 documented to CJ+JF

Werknummer	Call-sign		Completion ca. Month/Year
18728 – 18731			
18732 – 18749	CN+VI – CN+VZ	G-6	
18750 – 18775	PO+SA – PO+SZ	G-6	▼
18776 – 18801	PL+SA – PL+FZ	G-6	7/1943
18802 – 18827	SL+SA – SL+SZ	G-6	8/1943
18828 – 18853	SO+XA – SO+XZ	G-6	
18854 – 18879	KN+CA – KN+CZ	G-6	▼
18880 – 18903	KI+OA – KI+OX	G-6	8/1943
130110 – 130355		G-10	built in Regensburg 11/44 – 1/45
160001 – 160004	KD+PF – KD+PI	G-6	8/1943
160005 – 160030	KO+PA – KO+PZ	G-6	
160031 – 160033			
160034 – 160053	IM+ZG – IM+ZZ	G-6	
160054 – 160079	CR+DA – CR+DZ	G-6	▼
160080 – 160105	NA+TA – NA+TZ	G-6	8/1943
160106 – 160288	DC+WC		9/1943
160289 – 160314	NL+VA – NL+VZ	G-6	9, 10/1943
160315 – 160321			10/1943
160322 – 160347	PJ+SA – PJ+SZ	G-6	
160348 – 160366	PN+R		▼
160367 – 160392	SI+PA – SI+PZ	G-6	10, 11/1943
160393 – 160418	SN+NA – SN+NZ	G-6	11/1943
160419 – 160444	DK+OA – DK+OZ	G-6	
160445 – 160583			
160584 – 160609	BK+OA – BK+OZ	G-6	
160610 – 160635	BO+IA – BO+IZ	G-6	
160635 – 160640	BM+SS – BM+SW	G-6	
160641 – 160666	GK+FA – GK+FZ	G-6	
160667 – 160692	GP+OA – GP+OZ	G-6	▼
160693 – 160718	KP+YA – KP+YZ	G-6	11/1943
160719 – 160744	KS+ZA – KS+ZZ	G-6	▼
160740	KS+ZV	G-6/AS	11/1943
160745 – 160770	KT+LA – KT+LZ	G-6	12/1943
160771 – 160797	PI+IA – PI+IZ?	G-6	
160798 – 160800			
160801 – 160822	PP+WE – PP+WZ	G-6	
160823 – 160848	PR+GA – PR+GZ	G-6	▼
160849 – 160874	ND+VA – ND+VZ	G-6	12/1943 – 1/1944
160875 – 160968		G-6	1/1944
161001 – 161026	PP+BA – PP+BZ	G-6	
161027 – 161052	PO+JA – PO+JZ	G-6	
161053 – 161078	RL+JA – RL+JZ	G-6	
161079 – 161104	RP+FA – RP+FZ	G-6	
161105 – 161130	SS+MA – SS+MZ	G-6	
161131 – 161156	SU+NA – SU+NZ	G-6	▼
161157 – 161182	KQ+LA – KQ+LZ	G-6	1/1944
161183 – 161207	KP+FA – KP+FZ	G-6	2/1944
161208 – 161299			
161300 – 161325	NP+PA – NP+PZ	G-6	▼
161326 – 161351	NP+QA – NP+QZ	G-6	
161352 – 161377	NP+RA – NP+RZ	G-6	2/1944
161574			2/1944
161575 – 161706			3/1944
161707 – 161948			▼
162000 – 162025	RW+BA – RW+BZ	G-6	4/1944
162026 – 162051	RW+CA – RW+CZ	G-6	4/1944
162052 – 162077	RW+DA – RW+DZ	G-6	5/1944
162078 – 162101			
162102	RW+EY	G-6	
162104 – 162129	RW+FA – RW+FQ	G-6	
162130 – 162155			
162156 – 162181	RW+HA – RW+HZ	G-6	
162182 – 162309			▼

Werknummer	Call-sign		Completion ca. Month/Year
162310	BR+YP	G-6	
162311 – 162347			
162347	BR+HA	G-6	
162348 – 162371			
162372	BR+RZ	G-6	
162400 – 162424	TV+KA – TV+KZ	G-6	
162425 – 162450			
162451 – 162476	BF+VA – BF+VZ	G-6	
162477 – 162483			
162484	BE+RH	G-6	
162485 – 162527			
162528	BE+SM	G-6	
162529 – 162530			
162531 – 162556	RU+EA – RU+EZ	G-6	
162557 – 162600			▼
162601	RU+CS	G-6	5/1944
162602 – 162738			6/1944
162739 – 162764	RU+OA – RU+OZ	G-6	
162765 – 162999			
163000 – 163033	TS+TA – TS+TZ	G-6	
163060 – 163064			
163065 – 163085	TS+UA – TS+UU	G-6	
163086 – 163111	TS+VA – TS+VZ	G-6	
163112	ST+RB (Switzerland)	G-6	
163113 – 163136	ST+RC – ST+RZ	G-6	
163137 – 163162	ST+SA – ST+SZ	G-6	
163163 – 163188	ST+TA – ST+TZ	G-6	
163189 – 163214	ST+UA – ST+UZ	G-6	
163215 – 163239	ST+VA – ST+V?	G-6	
163240	RQ+BD	G-6	
163241 – 163242			
163243	RQ+BR (Switzerland)	G-6	
163244			▼
163245 – 163262	RQ+BI – RQ+BZ	G-6	6/1944
163263 – 163282	RQ+CA – RQ+CZ	G-6	7/1944
163283 – 163311			
163312	RQ+DY	G-6	
163313 – 163429			
163430 – 163435		G-6/AS	
163575 – 163600	RQ+SA – RQ+SZ	G-6	
163601 – 163764		G-6	
163765 – 163787		G-6/AS	
163788 – 163799		G-6	
163800 – 163825	NF+FA – NF+FZ	G-6/AS	
163826 – 163837		G-6/AS	
163838 – 163869	VT+FI – VT+FR	G-6	
163870 – 163902		G-6	
163876		G-14/R-2	▼
163903 – 163984	VW+DA – VW+DZ	G-6	7/1944
163976	SR+ZU		8/1944
163985 – 163994		G-6/AS	
164283		G-14	
164380		G-6	
164901 – 164910		G-6	
164911 – 164936	NY+AA – NY+AZ	G-6	
164937 – 164961		G-6	
164962 – 164999		G-6/AS	
165001 – 165117		G-6	
165019	NP+IE	G-6	
165058	NP+ER	G-6	
165118 – 165138		G-6/AS	
165138 – 165196		G-6	
165160	NJ+PP	G-6	
165197 – 165222	NH+LA – NH+LZ	G-6	▼

Werknummer	Call-sign		Completion ca. Month/Year
165223 – 165272		G-6	
165273 – 165298	BV+UA – BV+UZ	G-6	
165299 – 165475		G-6	
165476 – 165503		G-6/AS	
165504 – 165688		G-6	
165689		G-14	
165690		G-6	
165691		G-14	
165692 – 165727		G-14	
165736 – 165999		G-6/G-14	
165741		G-14/AS	
165742		G-14	
165756		G-14/AS	
165813		G-14	
165974		G-14	
165999		G-6/AS	
166001 – 166104		G-6	
166023	KW+YW	G-6	
166105 – 166130	CR+RA – CR+RZ	G-6	
166131 – 166156	CW+ZA – CW+ZZ	G-6	
166151		G-14	
166157 – 166260		G-6	
166261		G-14	
166262 – 166281		G-6	
166287 – 166293		G-14/AS	
166294		G-6	
166297 – 166308		G-14/AS	
166313 – 166350		G-14/AS	
166343		G-6/AS	
166351 – 166470		G-6	
166473		G-6/AS	
166475 – 166495		G-6	
166644		G-6	
167211 – 167310		G-6	
167337		G-14	12/1944
330105 – 330491		K-4	completion of K-4 in Regensburg and Vilseck 9/44 – 3/45, in Cham 11/44 –3/45
330917		K-4	
331323 – 331510		K-4	
332247 – 332998		K-4	
333876 – 333995		K-4	
334060 – 334263		K-4	
335170 – 335210		K-4	
600056		K-2	
780319 – 780394		G-14/AS 7/1944	
780665		G-14/AS	
780666 – 780669		G-6/AS	
780672 – 780697		G-14/AS	
780703 – 780783		G-14/AS	
780785 – 780793		G-6/AS	
780816 – 780892		G-14/AS	
780904 – 780943		G-14/AS	
780944		G-6/AS	
781117 – 781207		G-14/G-14/AS	
782288 – 782342		G-14/AS	
782340 – 782344		G-6/AS/G-14/AS	
782353 – 782391		G-14/AS	
782402 – 782430		G-14/AS	
782731 – 782760		G-14/AS	
783815 – 783954		G-14/AS	
784096 – 784118		G-14/AS	
784745 – 784986		G-14/AS	
785039 – 785189		G-14/AS	

Werknummer	Call-sign		Completion ca. Month/Year
785376		G-14/AS	
786311 – 786533		G-14/AS	
787067		G-14	completed in Cham
787453 – 787524		G-14/AS	completed in Cham 3/1945

Appendix 6

Me 210 A-1 data

Powerplants:	2 x Daimler-Benz DB 601 F
Take-off power:	1,350 hp
Wingspan:	16.40 m (53 ft 9.7 in)
Length:	11.20 m (36 ft 8.9 in)
Height:	3.70 m (12 ft 1.7 in)
Wing area:	36.20 m² (389.64 ft²)
Empty weight:	7,070 kg (15,587 lb)
Payload:	2,390 kg (5,269 lb)
Loaded weight:	9,460 lb (20,856 lb)
Maximum speed:	573 km/h at 5.9 km (356 mph at 19,355 ft)
Time to climb:	4.2 mins to 6 km (19,685 ft)
Range:	1,850 km (1,150 mls)
Service ceiling:	8,900 m (29,200 ft)
Armament:	2 x MG 151/20, each with 350 rounds (fixed, fwd-firing)
	2 x MG 17, each with 1,000 rounds (fixed, fwd-firing)
	2 x MG 131, each with 500 rounds (rear-firing B-Stands)
Bombload:	8 x 50 kg (110 lb) or 2 x 250 kg (551 lb) or 2 x 500 kg (1,102 lb) or 2 x 1000 kg (2,205 lb)

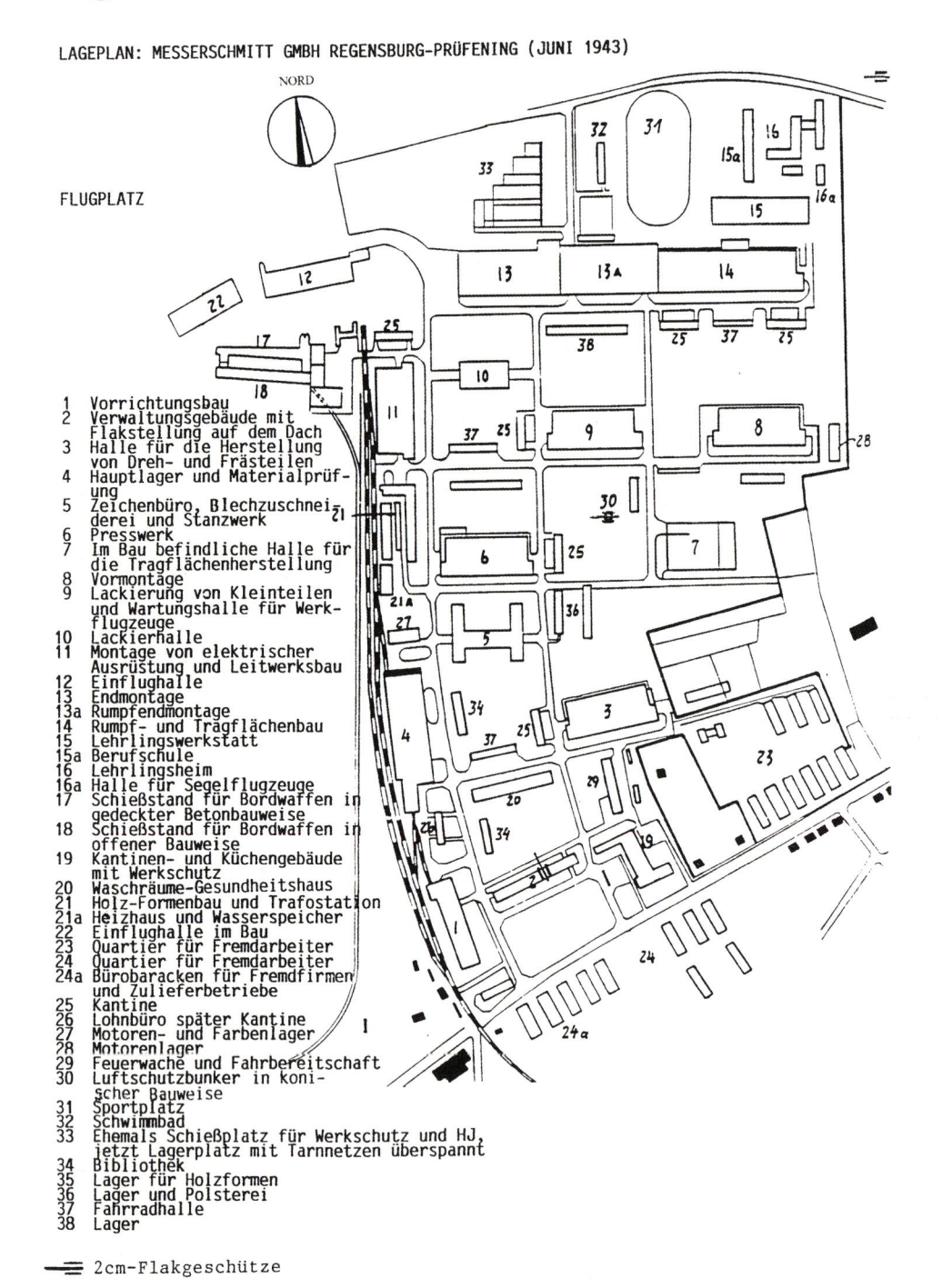

LAGEPLAN: MESSERSCHMITT GMBH REGENSBURG-PRÜFENING (JUNI 1943)

FLUGPLATZ

1 Vorrichtungsbau
2 Verwaltungsgebäude mit Flakstellung auf dem Dach
3 Halle für die Herstellung von Dreh- und Frästeilen
4 Hauptlager und Materialprüfung
5 Zeichenbüro, Blechzuschneiderei und Stanzwerk
6 Presswerk
7 Im Bau befindliche Halle für die Tragflächenherstellung
8 Vormontage
9 Lackierung von Kleinteilen und Wartungshalle für Werkflugzeuge
10 Lackierhalle
11 Montage von elektrischer Ausrüstung und Leitwerksbau
12 Einflughalle
13 Endmontage
13a Rumpfendmontage
14 Rumpf- und Tragflächenbau
15 Lehrlingswerkstatt
15a Berufschule
16 Lehrlingsheim
16a Halle für Segelflugzeuge
17 Schießstand für Bordwaffen in gedeckter Betonbauweise
18 Schießstand für Bordwaffen in offener Bauweise
19 Kantinen- und Küchengebäude mit Werkschutz
20 Waschräume-Gesundheitshaus
21 Holz-Formenbau und Trafostation
21a Heizhaus und Wasserspeicher
22 Einflughalle im Bau
23 Quartier für Fremdarbeiter
24 Quartier für Fremdarbeiter
24a Bürobaracken für Fremdfirmen und Zulieferbetriebe
25 Kantine
26 Lohnbüro später Kantine
27 Motoren- und Farbenlager
28 Motorenlager
29 Feuerwache und Fahrbereitschaft
30 Luftschutzbunker in konischer Bauweise
31 Sportplatz
32 Schwimmbad
33 Ehemals Schießplatz für Werkschutz und HJ, jetzt Lagerplatz mit Tarnnetzen überspannt
34 Bibliothek
35 Lager für Holzformen
36 Lager und Polsterei
37 Fahrradhalle
38 Lager

≡ 2cm-Flakgeschütze

Appendix 7

Layout of the Messerschmitt-Werke, Regensburg-Prüfening (June 1943)

1	Halle for construction jigs and formers
2	Administration building with roof-mounted Flak positions
3	Halle for manufacture of lathe- and milled components
4	Main storage and material examination
5	Drawing office, sheet metal cutting and stamping
6	Sheet metal moulding
7	Halle for wing manufacture (under construction)
8	Halle for pre-assembly
9	Halle for doping of small parts and aircraft maintenance
10	Paintshop
11	Electrical equipment installation and empennange manufacture
12	Flight-test hangar
13	Final assembly
13a	Fuselage final assembly
14	Fuselage and wing manufacture
15	Apprentices workshop
15a	Trade school
16	Apprentices lodgings
16a	Halle for gliders
17	Armament shooting stand (concrete covered)
18	Armament shooting stand (open construction)
19	Works canteen, kitchen and Werkschutz (Works protection)
20	Washrooms and employee health
21	Wood-shaping and transformer station
21a	Heating and water storage building
22	Flight-test hangar (under construction)
23	Lodgings for foreign workers
24	Lodgings for foreign workers
24a	Office barracks for foreign workers
25	Canteen
26	Pay office, later canteen
27	Engine and paint storage
28	Engine storage
29	Fire brigade and vehicle park
30	Air raid shelters/bunkers of conical construction
31	Sports field
32	Swimming baths
33	Former shooting ground for Werkschutz and HJ, currently storage area covered with camouflage netting
34	Library
35	Storage for formed wooden parts
36	Storage and upholstery Halle
37	Bicycle Halle
38	Storage Halle

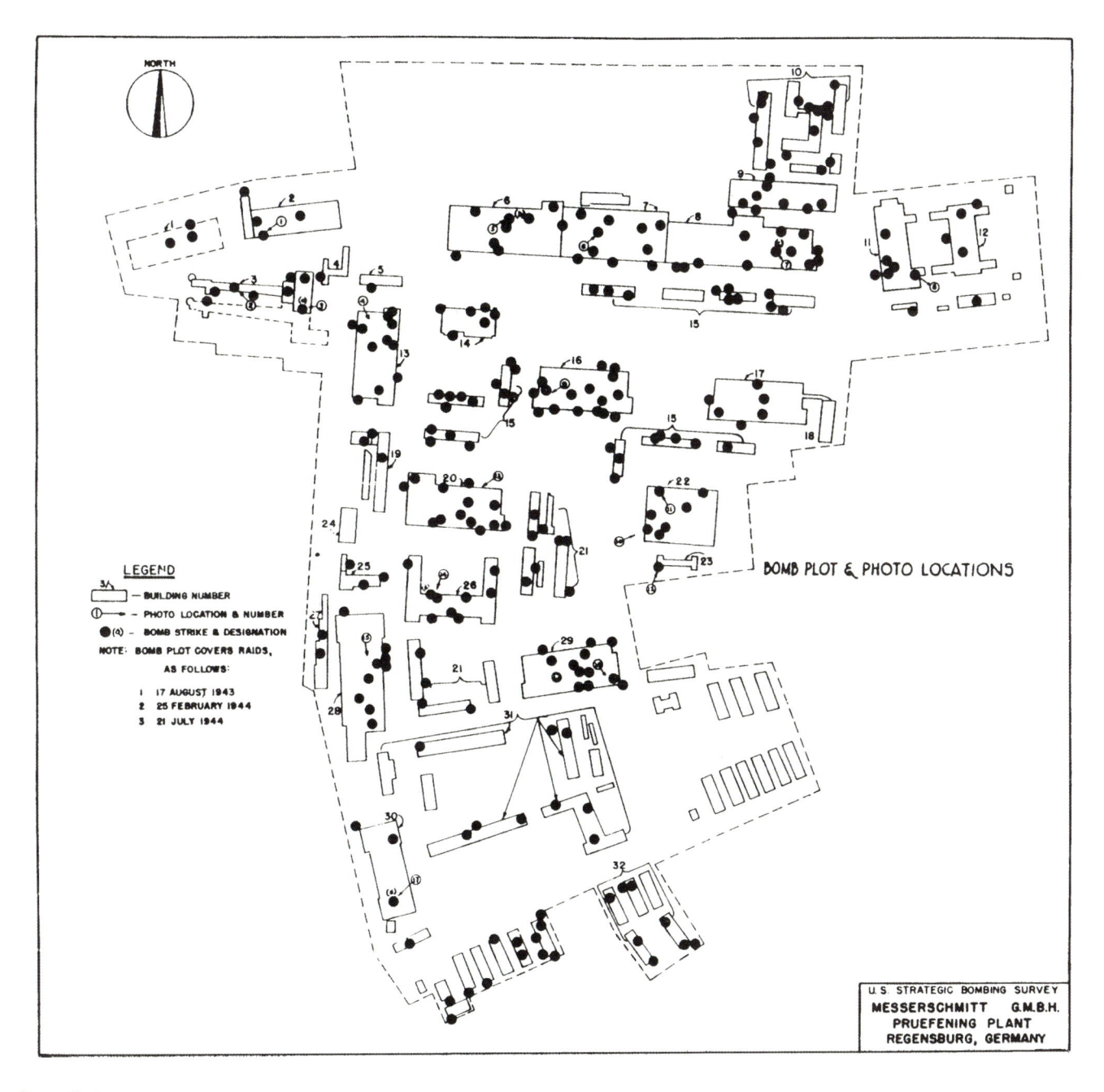

Appendix 8

Bomb hits on Prüfening in bombing raids of 17.08.43, 25.02.44 and 21.07.44

See Appendix 7 for numbered building functions. Buildings that were not hit are not included in the following list which shows damage inflicted only on 17.08.43.:

1) Construction jigs: direct hit on the south side; Maschinenpark 50 % damaged. Jigs for Me 262 fuselages heavily damaged.
2) Administration buiding: building centre hit; Flak stand ripped apart and direct hit at eastern end. Conference room destroyed.
3) Mechanically-made components: 2 or 3 direct hits; Maschinen partly destroyed
4) Material storage: building completely burnt out
5) Sheet-metal cutting: building completely destroyed
6) Sheet-metal forming: building 100 % destroyed; the adjoining canteen received a direct hit
8) Pre-assembly building: largely destroyed
10) Paintshop: completely destroyed by direct hit; canteen nearby received a direct hit
11) Empennage manufacture: largely destroyed
12) Flight-test building: offices destroyed; slight damage suffered by parked aircraft
13) Final assembly building: no direct hits (window-panes damaged)
14) Metal construction building: sub-assemblies destroyed; fuselage and wing assembly untouched, office rooms untouched, building roof partly destroyed by 5 to 10 bomb impacts
15) Apprentice and training workshop: direct hit in centre of building, 40 % destroyed. Maschinenpark undamaged.
15a) Works school: 50 % damaged
16) Apprentices barracks : 70-80 % destroyed; apprentices canteen 30 % destroyed
17 & 18) Works school buildings: completely destroyed by several bomb hits
19) Housekeeping buildings: hits on northwest corner, Works protection office totally destroyed
20) Washrooms: hit in west corner, no extensive damage
22) Flight-test hangar: completely destroyed
28) Engines building: 100 % destroyed
29) Fire-brigade: direct hit on west side, extinguisher vehicles all buried by debris, extinguisher vehicles in the open made unusable due to bomb shrapnel
38) Metal parts storage: completely destroyed. The Leichtmetallbau firm, east of the apprentices centre (not included in the layout plan), 100 % destroyed. The Reichsbahn (German railways) installations suffered only light damage.

NEST OF EAGLES

Messerschmitt GmbH Regensburg

Dezentralisierte Fertigung der Bf 109 G und K im Dezember 1944. Die wichtigsten Fertigungsstandorte ohne Materiallager:

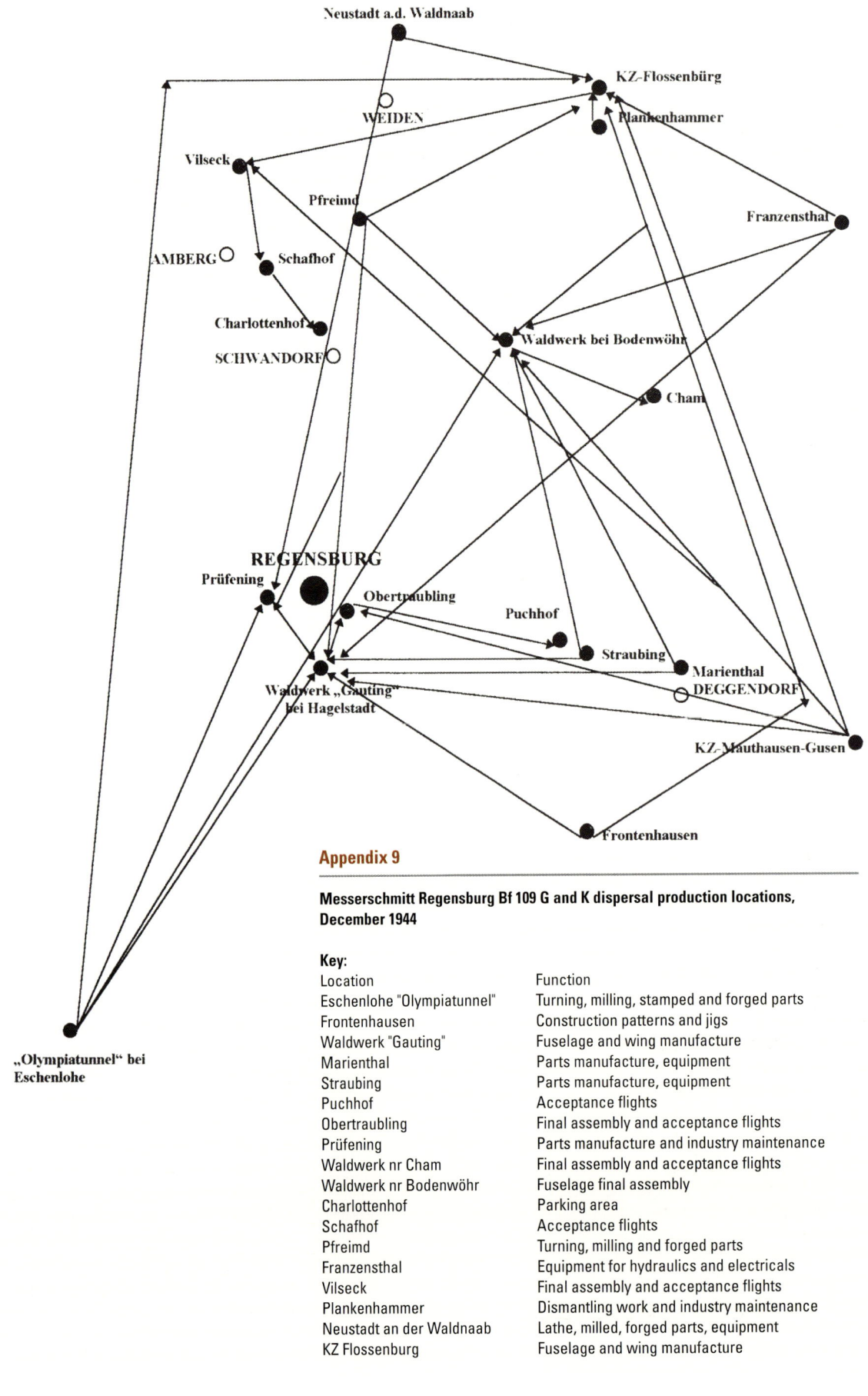

Appendix 9

Messerschmitt Regensburg Bf 109 G and K dispersal production locations, December 1944

Key:

Location	Function
Eschenlohe "Olympiatunnel"	Turning, milling, stamped and forged parts
Frontenhausen	Construction patterns and jigs
Waldwerk "Gauting"	Fuselage and wing manufacture
Marienthal	Parts manufacture, equipment
Straubing	Parts manufacture, equipment
Puchhof	Acceptance flights
Obertraubling	Final assembly and acceptance flights
Prüfening	Parts manufacture and industry maintenance
Waldwerk nr Cham	Final assembly and acceptance flights
Waldwerk nr Bodenwöhr	Fuselage final assembly
Charlottenhof	Parking area
Schafhof	Acceptance flights
Pfreimd	Turning, milling and forged parts
Franzensthal	Equipment for hydraulics and electricals
Vilseck	Final assembly and acceptance flights
Plankenhammer	Dismantling work and industry maintenance
Neustadt an der Waldnaab	Lathe, milled, forged parts, equipment
KZ Flossenburg	Fuselage and wing manufacture

Appendix 10

Manufacturing sections in the Eschenlohe 'Olympiatunnel'

Key: To above diagram
Vorderansicht = Frontal view   Draufsicht = Overhead view
Overall length approximately 500 m (1,640 ft)

1 Sand spray shop
2 Acetylene generation
3 Welding and assembly
4 Lathe and milled parts manufacture
5 Sheet-metal cutting shop
6 Ventilation and air-conditioning installations
7 Offices and canteen rooms
8 Heating installation
9 Offices and materials preparation
10 Approach road
11 Forging plant
12 Forging tools
13 Forming shop
14 Forging plant

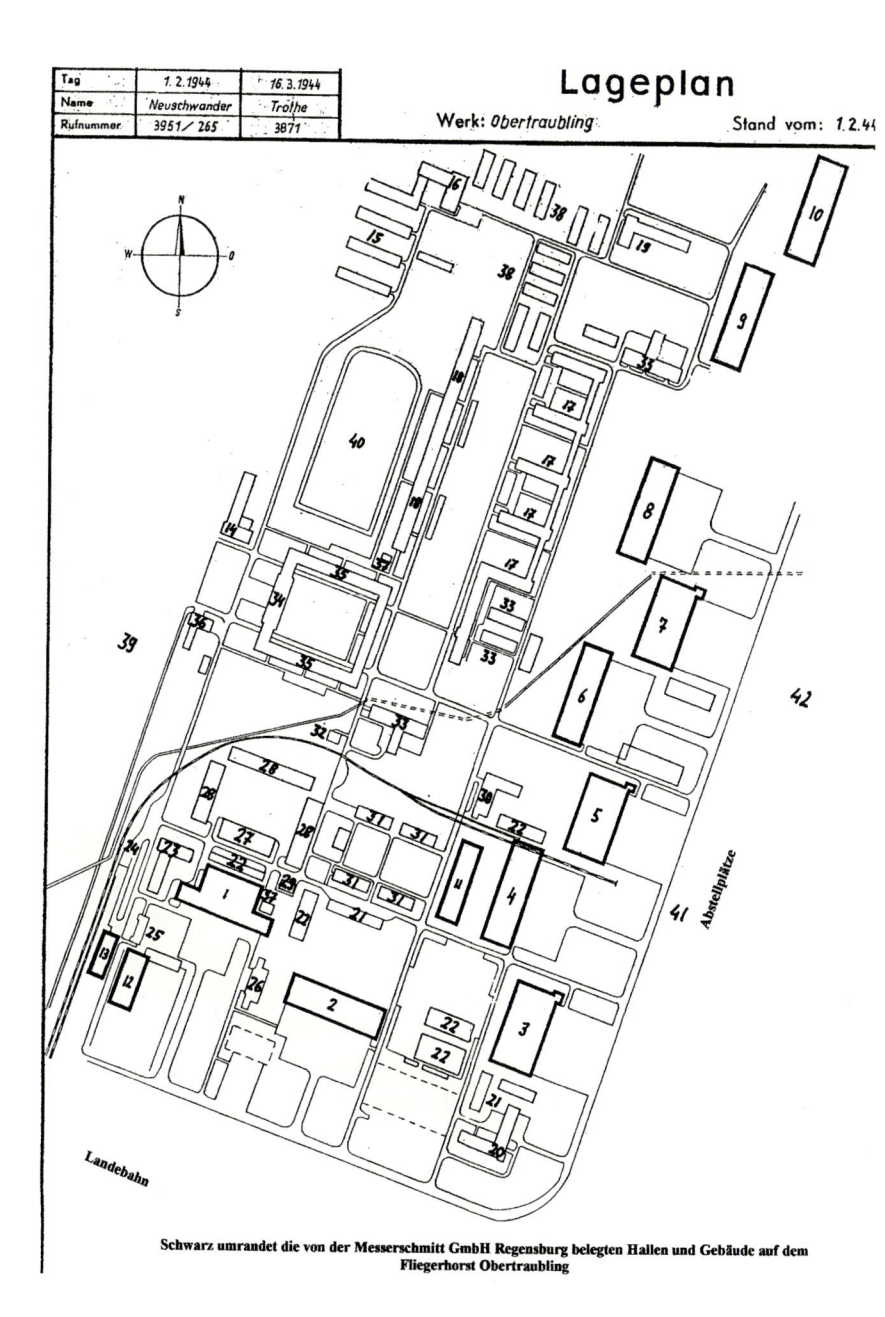

Appendix 11

Layout of Fliegerhorst Obertraubling as of 1 February 1941

Location of buildings and Hallen occupied by Mtt GmbH Regensburg at the Fliegerhorst Obertraubling.
Abstellplätze = Parking area, Landebahn = Landing runway

List of buildings at Fliegerhorst Obertraubling

1) Aircraft workshop
2) to 10) Aircraft Hallen
11) Works Halle
12) Storage and offices
13) Heating Plant II and railway station building
14) Construction directorate; later on, offices
15) Officers quarters
16) Mess hall
17) Barracks for flight personnel, alias 'Staffelbau' (stepped construction)
18) Barracks for ground personnel; because of its length, alias 'Schlangenbau' (snake construction)
19) Police station / Field hospital
20) Air traffic control with control tower, homing beams, weather station and fire-brigades
21) Garages
22) Storage areas
23) Heating Plant I
24) Locomotive sheds
25) W/T centre
26) Weapons centre and parachute storage
27) Vehicle workshop
28) Garages for the vehicle park
29) Paint storage
30) Garages and offices
31) Lodgings barracks
32) Telephone bunker
33) Canteen
34) Kommandantur (Garrison HQ / Commander's office)
35) Fliegerhorst Administration
36) Main Guardhouse
37) Transformer station
38) Barracks for forced labourers and PoWs (Russians)
39) Large storage area with planned capacity for 4,000 persons: PoWs, forced-labourers, and shortly before war's end, for KZ (concentration-camp) inmates
40) Dredging lake
41) Fuelling point in front of Hallen 4 and 5
42) Shooting stand for centring of airborne weapons

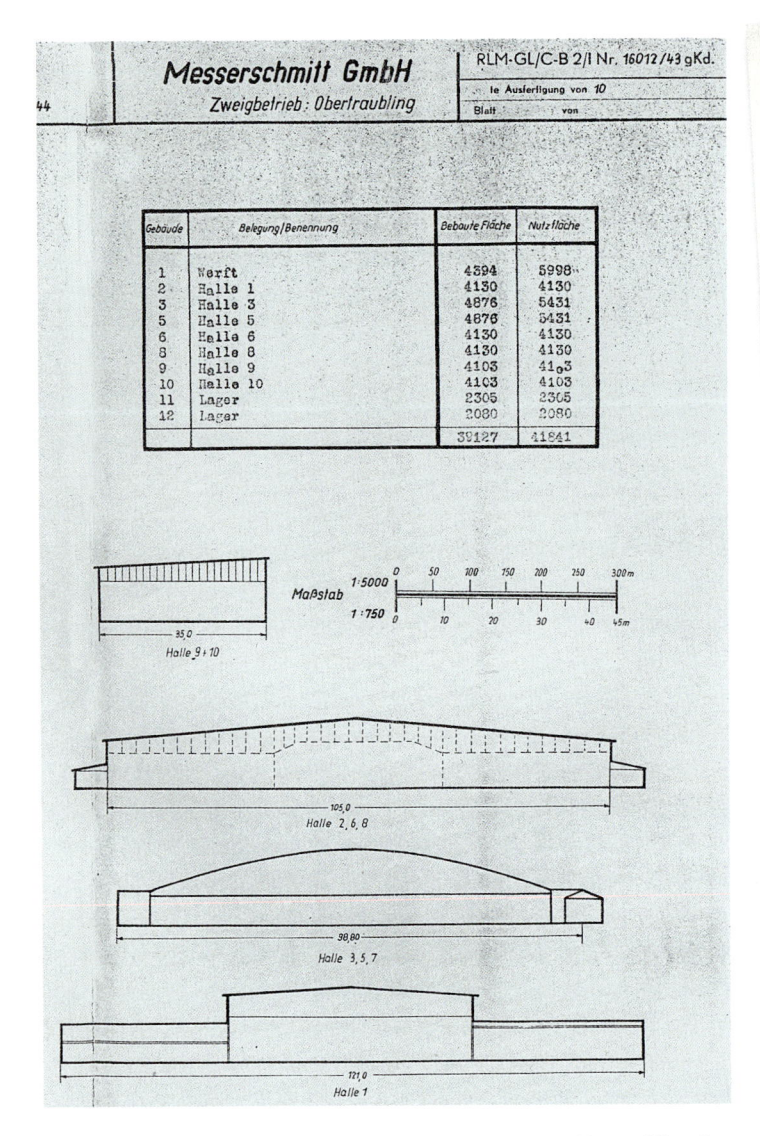

Cross-sections and widths in metres of the Messerschmitt Obertraubling plant, Hallen 1 to 10.

In centre box:
Gebäude = Buildings
Belegung/Benennung = Function/Halle number
Bebaute Fläche = building area,
Nutzfläche = Usable area (in square metres)

Appendix 12

Me 321 data

Powerplants: None
Wingspan:	55.00 m (180 ft 5.4 in)
Length:	28.15 m (92 ft 4.3 in)
Height:	10.20 m (33 ft 5.6 in)
Wing area:	300 m² (3,229.1 ft²)
Empty weight:	11,290 kg (24,890 lb)
Equipped weight:	12,000 kg (26,455 lb)
Useful load:	23,000 kg (50,706 lb)
Flying weight:	35,000 kg (77,161 lb)
Towing speed:	230 km/h (143 mph)
Landing speed:	115 km/h (71 mph)
Armament:	4 x MG 15

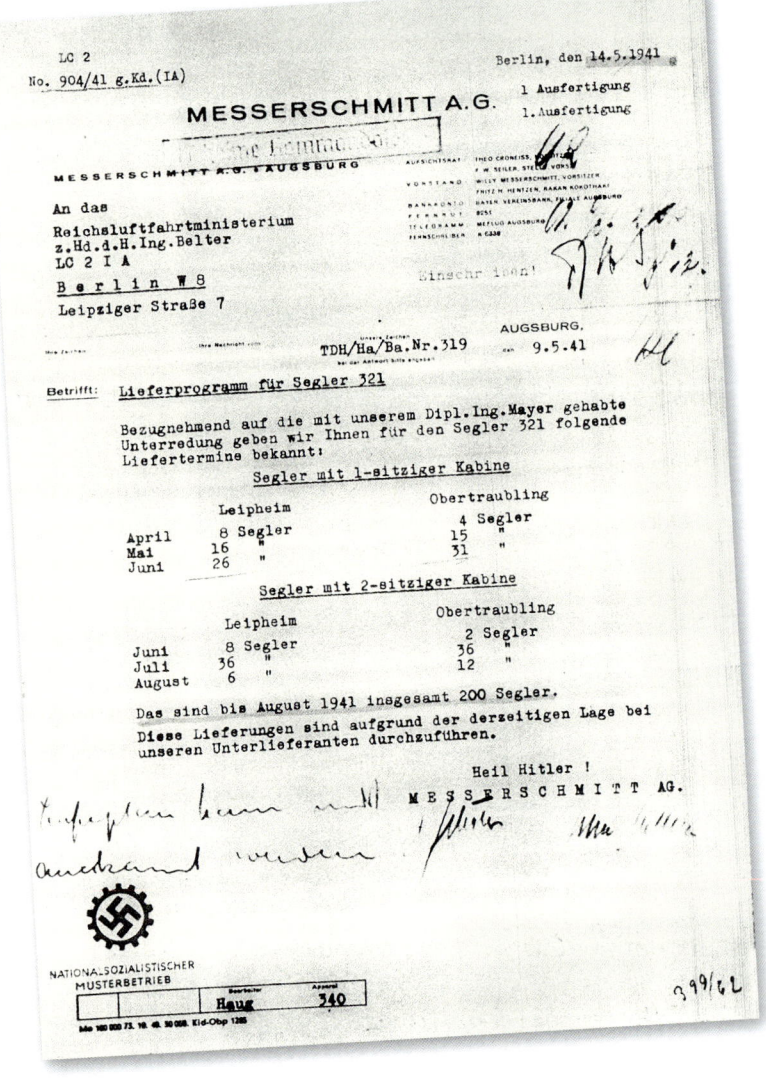

Messerschmitt AG letter of 14 May 1941 to the RLM Berlin re Me 321 Delivery Programme

To: The RLM
Attention: Ing. Balter, LC 2 IA
Leipziger Strasse 7,
Berlin, W8

Reference: TDH/Ha/Ba. Nr. 319, Augsburg, 09.05.41
Re: Delivery Programme for the Me 321 Glider

With reference to the meeting held with our Dipl.-Ing. Mayer, we herewith advise you of the following delivery periods for the Me 321:

Glider with 1-seat cockpit

	Leipheim	Obertraubling
April	8 Gliders	4 Gliders
May	16 Gliders	15 Gliders
June	26 Gliders	31 Gliders

Glider with 2-seat cockpit

	Leipheim	Obertraubling
June	8 Gliders	2 Gliders
July	36 Gliders	36 Gliders
August	6 Gliders	12 Gliders

Up until August, this makes a total of 200 gliders. Based on the current situation, these deliveries are to be carried out by our subcontractors.

Heil Hitler !
Messerschmitt AG
(signatures)

Me 321 deliveries from Obertraubling, with dates and call-sign
The following 68 Me 321 aircraft, confirmed in a list prepared by the Obertraubling Fliegerhorst Kommandantur, were delivered on dates (day/month/year) below to the following locations:

Date	Call-sign	Location and Remarks
02.07.41	W2+SB	To Merseburg
03.07.41	W2+SA	To Merseburg
05.07.41	W2+SH	To Merseburg
06.07.41	W2+SK	To Merseburg
07.07.41	W2+SZ	To Merseburg
22.07.41	W2+SF	To Merseburg
24.07.41	W2+SE	To Merseburg
04.08.41	W2+SC	To Merseburg
29.08.41	W2+SM	To Schroda-East
29.09.41	W1+SD	To Merseburg (Me 321 built at Leipheim)
29.09.41	W2+SR	To Merseburg
30.09.41	W6+SB	To Merseburg
07.10.41	W2+SN	To Öttingen
07.10.41	W2+ST	To Öttingen
09.10.41	W2+SD	To Öttingen
10.10.41	W4+SQ	To Öttingen
10.10.41	W4+ST	To Öttingen
13.10.41	W4+SS	To Öttingen
16.10.41	W4+SR	To Öttingen
16.10.41	W2+SS	To Öttingen
17.10.41	W2+SO	To Öttingen
20.10.41	W4+SP	To Öttingen
20.10.41	W4+SX	To Öttingen
22.10.41	W4+SU	To Öttingen
22.10.41	W2+SQ	To Öttingen
24.10.41	W6+SL	To Öttingen
24.10.41	W6+SK	To Öttingen
29.11.41	W3+SS	To Posen
30.11.41	W6+SA	To Schroda-East
30.11.41	W2+SP	To Öttingen
01.12.41	W4+SV	To Öttingen
01.12.41	W4+SF	To Deiningen
01.12.41	W6+SD	To Schroda-East
01.12.41	W2+SW	To Deiningen
02.12.41	W2+SV	To Deiningen
02.12.41	W2+SU	To Deiningen; emergency landing nr Monheim
02.12.41	W2+SJ	To Deiningen; emergency landing nr Erding
08.12.41	W4+SA	To Deiningen
08.12.41	W4+SC	To Deiningen
09.12.41	W4+SJ	To Deiningen
09.12.41	W4+SN	To Deiningen
09.12.41	W6+SO	To Deiningen
09.12.41	W4+SK	To Deiningen
10.12.41	W4+SM	To Deiningen
10.12.41	W4+SB	To Deiningen; crashed nr Kelheim
13.08.42	W8+ST	To Leipheim
14.08.42	W8+SZ	To Reims
14.08.42	W8+SR	To Reims
15.08.42	W8+SF	Emergency landing nr Sinzing
16.08.42	W8+SB	To Reims
16.08.42	W8+SH	To Reims
17.08.42	W8+SQ	To Reims (fetched back due to tailplane damage)
17.08.42	W6+SR	To Reims
18.08.42	W6+SQ	To Reims
25.08.42	W8+SM	To Leipheim
27.08.42	W8+SN	To Leipheim
24.10.42	W8+SS	To Lechfeld
24.10.42	W6+SU	To Lechfeld
25.10.42	W6+SZ	To Lechfeld
25.10.42	W6+SX	To Lechfeld
25.11.42	W6+SV	To Dijon
25.11.42	W8+SL	To Dijon; emergency landing nr Sigmaringen
26.11.42	W8+SD	To Dijon
07.12.42	W8+SP	To Langendiebach

Date	Call-sign	Location and Remarks
07.12.42	W8+SQ	To Langendiebach
11.12.42	W8+SM	To Dijon
25.11.42	W6+SV	To Dijon
25.11.42	W8+SL	To Dijon

Me 321s coded W2, W4, W6 and W8 were built at Obertraubling, whilst W1, W3, W5 and W7 were built in Leipheim. (Sources: Daily War Diary and various Flight Logbooks.)

(4) Me 321 Special Flight by Unteroffizier Geisbe, 12 May 1943

The document below, authorized Uffz. Geisbe and the named crew members to deliver Me 321 (W8+SV) on 12.01.43 from Obertraubling via Jasionka and Zhitomir-South to Stalino, flying at between 300 m and 3,000 m (9,840 ft) altitude.

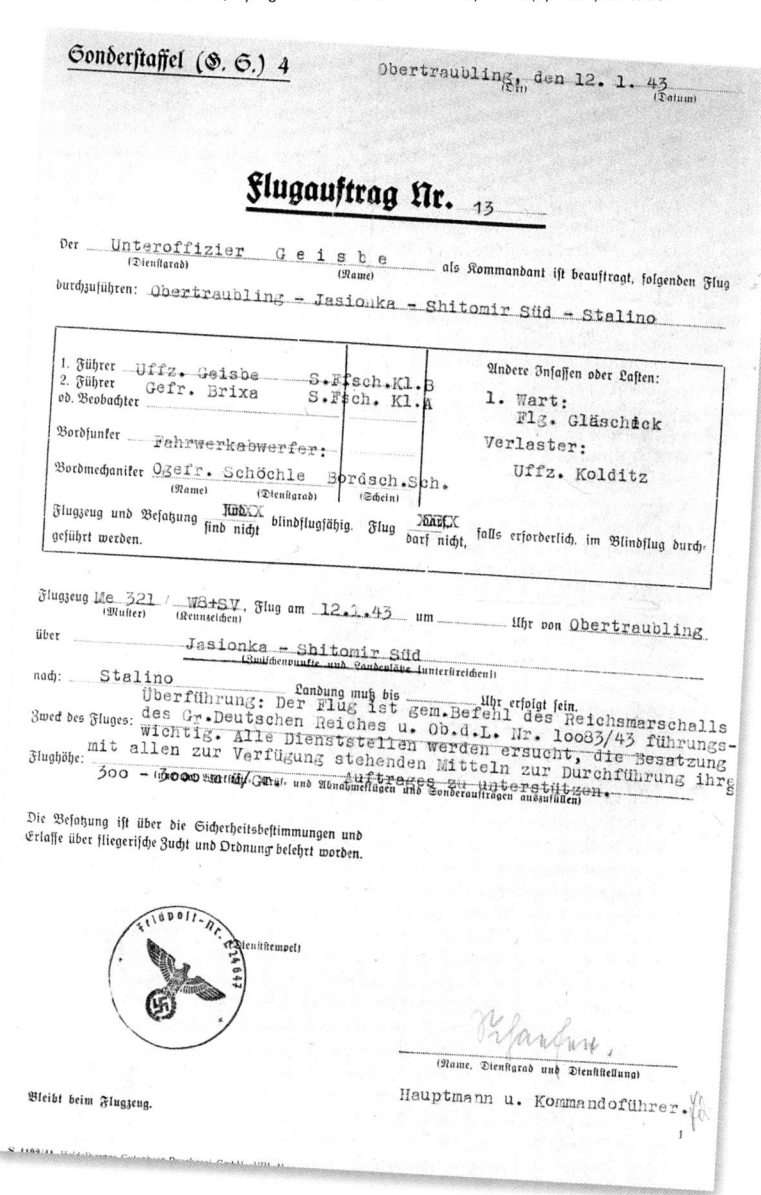

Appendix 13

Me 163 B data:

Powerplant:	1 x Walter HWK 509A
Static thrust:	1,600 kg (3,527 lb)
Wingspan:	9.30 m (30 ft 6.1 in)
Length:	5.92 m (19 ft 5.1 in)
Height:	2.80 m (9 ft 2.2 in)
Wing area:	17.30 m² (186.21.97 ft²)
Fuel weight:	2,026 kg (4,467 lb)
Take-off weight:	4,100 kg (9,039 lb)
Landing weight:	2,100 kg (4,630 lb)
Maximum speed:	950 km/h (590 mph)
Time to climb:	3.35 mins to 12 km (39,370 ft)
Range: 80 km	(50 mls)
Service ceiling:	14,500 m (47,570 ft)
Armament:	2 x MG 151/20 or 2 x MK 108

Me 163 Bs built in Obertraubling

V-model	Call-sign	Werknummer	Remarks
V2	VD+EL	16300011	
V8	VD+ER	16300017	
V10	VD+ES	16310019	
V11	VD+ET	16310020	
V12	VD+EU	16310021	
V14	VD+EW	16300023	
V18	VA+SP	16300027	
V31	GH+IJ	16310040	
V33	GH+IL	16300042	
V45	PK+QP	16300054	
V48	PK+QS	16310057	On 11.10.44, destroyed in air combat.
V49	PK+QT	16310058	On 28.09.44, destroyed in crash landing
V53	GH+IV	16310062	
V55	GH+IX	16310064	
V61	GN+MD	16310070	On 07.10.44, destroyed on take-off to target area
V62	GN+ME	16310071	On 07.10.44, destroyed by Mustang fighters

Appendix 14

Me 323 D Salient data:

Powerplants:	6 x Gnôme-Rhone 14 N 48/49 radials
Take-off power:	6 x 1,180 hp (maximum)
Airscrews:	(Me 323 D-1) Bloch 175 with 3-blade Ratier variable-pitch
	(Me 323 D-2) LeO 45 with 2-blade wooden Heine fixed-pitch
	(Me 323 D-6) LeO 45 with 3-blade Ratier variable-pitch
RATO units:	Up to 8 x HWK RI-202b rockets possible
Dimensions:	As Me 321
Equipped weight:	27,600 kg (60,847 lb)
Payload:	5,500 kg (12,125 lb)
Maximum load:	11,000 kg (24,251 lb)
Flying weight:	43,000 kg (94,798 lb)
Cruising speed:	250 km/h at 2 km (155 mph at 6,560 ft) with Ratier variable-pitch airscrews
	200 km/h at 2 km (124 mph at 6,560 ft) with Heine fixed-pitch airscrews
Climbing speed:	(climbing power): 2.0 m/sec (394 ft/min) with Ratier variable-pitch airscrews
	(climbing power): 3.0 m/sec (591 ft/min) with Heine fixed-pitch airscrews
	(continuous power): 1.0 m/sec (197 ft/min) with Heine fixed-pitch airscrews
Climbing time to 2 km (6,560 ft):	16 mins with variable-pitch airscrews
	14 mins with fixed-pitch airscrews
Ceiling (climbing power):	4,500 m (14,765 ft) with Ratier airscrews
	3,600 m (11,810 ft) with Heine airscrews
Maximum range:	750 km at sea-level (466 mls) with Ratier airscrews
	850 km at 2 km (528 mls at 6,560 ft) with Heine airscrews
	950 km at 4 km (590 mls at 13,125 ft) with Heine airscrews
Take-off run at take-off power: 800 m (2,625 ft) with Heine airscrews	
Maximum permissible speed with flaps full-down: 180 km/h (112 mph)	
Normal gliding speed: ca. 160 km/h (99 mph)	
Landing run:	ca. 600 m (1,970 ft)
Fuel (normal):	6 x 890 litres = 5,340 litres
Oil (normal):	6 x 80 litres = 480 litres
Armament:	2 x MG 131 in fuselage nose + 2 x MG 15 in wings + 1 x MG 131 in fuselage sides + 1 x MG 131 in B-Stand

Me 323 Ds delivered from Obertraubling to Leipheim to KG zbV 323

Confirmed in Daily War Diary, Fliegerhorst Obertraubling

09.09.42	DT+IA
12.09.42	DT+DL
01.10.42	DT+QB
02.10.42	DT+IC
05.10.42	DT+ID
05.10.42	DT+IE
28.10.42	DT+IB
30.10.42	DT+IF
06.11.42	DT+IH
06.11.42	DT+II
17.11.42	DT+IJ
20.11.42	AT+ID
03.12.42	DT+IM
09.12.42	DT+IN
12.12.42	DT+IK
16.12.42	DT+IR
16.12.42	DT+IL

Obertraubling-built Me 323s and Werknummmern

W. Nr.	Call-sign	Remarks and fate (where known)
?	AT+ID	V-model
801?	DT+IL	V-3. On 12.09.42, ferried from Obertraubling to Leipheim to KG zbV 323.
?	DT+QB	V-model. Ferried to Leipheim on 01.10.42

Werknummern 1201-1226 : Me 323 D-1 and D-6

1201	DT+IA	On 09.09.42, ferried from Obertraubling to Leipheim to I./KG zbV 323. On 05.01.43, 45 % damaged in collision at Trapani, Italy.
1202	DT+IB	On 28.10.42, ferried from Obertraubling to Leipheim.
1203	DT+IC	On 28.10.42, ferried from Obertraubling to Leipheim. On 22.11.42, 60 % destroyed in unsuccessful landing in Piacenza, Italy.
1204	DT+ID	From 01.10.42, used in Leipheim for instruction and conversion training flights. On 24.11.42, ferried from Obertraubling to Leipheim. On 02.12.42, crashed into the Adriatic south-west of Termoli as result of engine fault; 3 crew killed.
1205	DT+IE	On 05.10.42, this D-1 was ferried from Obertraubling to Leipheim. On 10.03.43, was destroyed in bombing raid on Tunis.
1206	DT+IF	On 30.1042, named 'Hein', ferried from Obertraubling to Leipheim.
1207	DT+IG	Stabsstaffel aircraft named 'Peterle', after Oberleutnant Ernst Peter. On 17.10.43, 35 % damaged in crash landing near Radinov.
1208	DT+IH	On 06.11.42, ferried from Obertraubling to Leipheim. On 01.03.43, crashed near Trapani; 12 killed and 3 injured.
1209	DT+IL	On 06.11.42, ferried from Obertraubling to Leipheim. In service with I./TG 5 in Hungary, on 14.06.44 was destroyed in low-level attack by a P-38 Lightning.
1210	DT+IJ	On 17.11.42, ferried from Obertraubling to Leipheim. In service with II./TG 5, was 60 % damaged on 17.08.44 due to engine trouble on flight between Insterburg and Riga.

W. Nr.	Call-sign	Remarks and fate (where known)
1211	DT+IK	On 12.12.42, ferried from Obertraubling to Leipheim. In service with I./KG zbV 323. On 15.01.43, shot down by fighters in front of Tunisian coast; 12 occupants killed.
1212	DT+IL	Used as conversion trainer in Leipheim from 23 - 28.09.42. On 16.12.42, flown from Obertraubling to Leipheim. On 13.04.43, 60 % damaged in take-off mishap in Tunis.
1213	DT+IM	On 03.12.42, ferried from Obertraubling to Leipheim. In service with I./KG zbV 323. On 05.01.43, 50 % damaged in collision with a landing Me 323 in Trapani. On 08.08.43, once more reported as having suffered 65 % damage in Pisa.
1214	DT+IN	On 09.12.43, ferried from Obertraubling to Leipheim. In service with I./KG zbV 323. On flight from Tunis to Naples on 10.02.43, could not reach coast for emergency landing; 4 killed and 3 injured. Aircraft had to be booked as total loss.
1215	DT+IO	On 05.04.43, 45 % damaged in bombing raid in Tunis.
1216	DT+IP	On 30.09.43, shot down by fighters on flight from Corsica to Elba; 9 killed.
1217	DT+IQ	No details available.
1218	DT+IR	On 16.12.42, ferried from Obertraubling to Leipheim. On 05.01.43, 45 % damaged in collision with another Me 323 in Trapani.
1219	DT+IS	Later coded C8+MB in service with I./TG 5.
1220	DT+IT	Named 'Himmelslaus' in Leipheim in 1942. On 15.12.43, 15 % damaged in landing in Lemberg.
1221	DT+IU	On 13.04.43, destroyed in bombing raid on Castelvetrano.
1222	DT+IV	Service code C8+NF. On 22.03.43, after engine failure in Castelvetrano on take-off and sunsequent crash landing, burnt out; 3 killed.
1223	DT+IW	On 25.04.43, caught fire on fuelling at Castelvetrano; 2 injured and aircraft burnt out.
1224	DT+IX	Later coded C8+EP. On 22.04.43, shot down near Cap Bon; 9 killed.
1225	DT+IY	Later coded C8+CP. On 22.04.43, shot down near Cap Bon; 9 killed.
1226	DT+IZ	Later coded C8+DP. On 22.04.43, shot down near Cap Bon; 9 killed.

Werknummern 1253-1278 : Me 323 E

W. Nr.	Call-sign	Remarks and fate (where known)
1253	VM+IA	In service with I./KG zbV 323. On 22.04.43 shot down near Cap Bon; 6 killed, 3 injured.
1254	VM+IB	Later coded C8+CC with II./KG zbV 323. On 22.04.43, shot down near Cap Bon.
1255	VM+IC	Later coded C8+LF.
1256	VM+ID	Later coded C8+CG with I./TG 5. Destroyed 17.03.43 in bombing raid on Pomigliano.
1257	VM+IE	Later coded C8+ME by I.Gruppe.
1258	VM+IF	Was 90 % destroyed in crash landing in Obertraubling. 1 killed, 2 injured; among the injured was Major Markus Zeidler.
1259	VM+IG	Aircraft of I. Gruppe. On 22.05.43, shot down by allied fighters over the Mediterranean; 5 killed and 4 injured.
1260	VM+IH	Later coded C8+FN with II./TG 5 and named 'Mücke'. On 07.05 43, was blown up in Tunis by German troops during retreat.
1261	VM+II	Aircraft of I. Gruppe. Destroyed on 30.05.43 in bombing raid on Pomigliano.
1262	VM+IJ	Later coded C8+LB with I. Gruppe. On 05.08.43, 45 % damaged during ground taxi at Venofiorita airfield where it was later found by the Allies partially burnt out.
1263	VM+IK	No details available
1264	VM+IL	Later coded C8+QE with I. Gruppe. Was 35 % damaged on 16.04.43 in bombing raid on Pomigliano.
1265	VM+IM	No details available
1266	VM+IN	Aircraft of II. Gruppe. On 01.08.43, destroyed in bombing raid on Capodicino.
1267	VM+IO	Later coded C8+DG with I. Gruppe. On 26.07.43, shot down by fighters west of Cape Rera; 3 crew killed and 6 injured.
1268	VM+IP	Later coded C8+TE with I. Gruppe. On 05.09.43, 65 % damaged in raid on Grosseto.

W. Nr.	Call-sign	Remarks and fate (where known)
1269	VM+IQ	Later coded C8+CB, an Me 323 E-2 of I./TG 5. On 23.02.44, hit an obstacle after an engine failure and was 50 % damaged.
1270	VM+IR	Later coded C8+EG with I./TG 5. Shot down by fighters on 26.07.43 near Garibaldi; 5 crew killed and 4 injured.
1271	VM+IS	Lated coded C8+AF with I./TG 5. On 21.07.43, was 70 % damaged in raid on Grosseto.
1272	VM+IT	From 31.12.43 to 04.03.44, this Me 323 WT was used for trials at E-Stelle Tarnewitz.
1273	VM+IU	Aircraft of II./TG 5. On 17.08.43, 25 % damaged in bombing raid on Istres airfield.
1274	VM+IV	Aircraft of II./TG 5.On 30.07.43, shot down by fighters near Barcaglio on Corsica and was 80 % destroyed; 4 crew injured.
1275	VM+IW	Aircraft of II./TG 5.On 17.07.43, was 60 % destroyed in air raid on Pomigliano and after capture of the airfield by the Allies, was found there burnt out.
1276	VM+IX	No details available
1277	VM+IY	Acceptance flight of Me 323 E-1 made on 16.07.43 by Anton Riediger at Obertraubling.
1278	VM+IZ	Aircraft of II./TG 5. This example was equipped as a flying Werkstatt and was destroyed 21.07.43 in an air raid on Grosseto.

Werknummern 1279-1298 : Me 323 E-2

W. Nr.	Call-sign	Remarks and fate (where known)
1279	SL+HA	Found by the Allies burnt out at Castelvetrano airfield.
1280	SL+HB	One flight documented from Avignon to Pisa with Oberfeldwebel Lutz.
1281	SL+HC	No details available
1282	SL+HD	Formed postcard motif. Picture taken in summer 1943 at Obertraubling. From 09.03.44, a flight logbook entry of this aircraft by Oberfeldwebel Friedrich and Prüfmeister Ebner.
1283	SL+HE	No details available
1284	SL+HF	Aircraft of II./TG 5. From 10 - 15.07.43, a transport flight is documented by pilot Feldwebel Blanke from Dijon - Istres - Grosseto - Pomigliano -Istres - Grosseto.
1285	SL+HG	Aircraft of II./TG 5. On 30.09.43, was shot down on flight from Corsica to Elba; 3 killed.
1286	SL+HH	Aircraft of II./TG 5. On 23.09.43, was 55 % destroyed in air raid on Pisa.
1287	SL+HI	Aircraft of II./TG 5. On 23.09.43, was destroyed in air raid on Pisa.
1288	SL+HJ	Aircraft of II./TG 5. On 23.09.43, was damaged in air raid on Pisa.
1289	SL+HK	No details available
1290	SL+HL	No details available
1291	SL+HM	Found by the Allies destroyed at Trapani
1292	SL+HN	No details available
1293	SL+HO	Aircraft of I./TG 5. Coded C8+BE, was 85 % destroyed on 15.03.44 in a crash in Belgrade.
1294	SL+HP	Documented on 01.10.43 with pilot Obereldwebel Epke as a transport from Lemberg to Königsberg for wounded.
1295	SL+HQ	Aircraft of I./TG 5. Later coded C8+DF, on 28.08.44 made emergency landing near Kunki, about 14 km west of Tomaszow. On 31.03.44, cannibalized and presumably scrapped.
1296	SL+HR	No details available
1297	SL+HS	No details available
1298	SL+HT	Was equipped as Me 323 WT special variant.

Letter of 5 December 1942 to RLM GL/C Oberst i.G. Vorwald regarding Me 323 D-1, D-2 and D-6

[1.] D-1 Series

The 32 aircraft with Bloch engines and Ratier airscrews cannot be completed in Obertraubling in a continuous series, since after the 26th aircraft (the first four January machines) no operationally usable Bloch engines are initially available. This is traceable to the fact that a stocking-up by the Sonderausschuss T 3 (Special Committee) of individual parts for engine assembly has apparently not taken place, although the agreement between the Sonderausschuss F 2 and T 3 on 3.7.42 specifically stated therein that the stocking- up of Bloch and LeO engines for the Me 323 falls within the sphere of responsibility of Sonderausschuss T3. From the Arbeitsausschuss (Working Committee) F 2/d in my enterprise, the Sonderausschuss T 3, after the absence of the engines was established, was requested on 30.11.42 to comment on the matter. Independent of the outcome of these negotiations, I have authorised the Arbeitsausschuss F 2/d to take all necessary steps in order to retroactively arrange for the stocking-up of substitute parts for individual engine parts, in the event that no other arrangement can be attained with the Sonderausschuss T 3. The take-over by Bronzavia in Paris of SNCASO in Bordeaux of on-going work to re-equip the Bloch engines leads one to expect that from the end of January 1943, that further quick-replacement engines will follow. For the ca. 35 aircraft that have to be delivered by the end of the year, these must be forwarded to the responsible Luftzeugamt for stocking-up purposes. In order not to endanger the operational employment of the aircraft, the last 6 of the D-1 series in Obertraubling, with termination of the programme, are therefore planned only for July of next year.

2.) D-6 Series
These aircraft with LeO engines and Ratier variable-pitch airscrews will likewise not be completed in a continuous series of 29 aircraft in Obertraubling. The reasons which lead to this consideration are exactly the same as that for the substitute parts situation which apply to the D-1 series. In order not to endanger their operational employment due to the lack of variable-pitch airscrews and individual parts such as variable-speed engines, etc., after completion in Obertraubling of the first D-6 aircraft, production will be continued of the D-2 that is fitted with wooden airscrews. Since at the present time there are an insufficient number of LeO engines available for which the required soft supports for the Heine wooden airscrews are necessary, Obertraubling will therefore initially commence preparatory work for the D-6 series, for which the LeO engines on hand with normal (i.e. harder) supports will be used with the Ratier airscrews. Up to the beginning of next year, however, the delivery of LeO engines with soft support is assured in sufficient quantity, so that the D-2 series can be planned from February onwards.

3.) D-2 Series
As these aircraft are equipped with Heine wooden airscrews, only LeO engines are permissible, which necessitates the soft support.

Unfortunately, GL/C-E 3/V (Dr. Geiseler) has still not provided any conclusive comment on the considerations which our Project Office voiced on 26.6.42 concerning the installation of the Heine wooden airscrews. Should, if the airscrews be manufactured from wood that is not dry, and that which after centrifuging further function unpredictably, any kind of disruption for the planned completion of the aircraft result, I shall immediately advise you of this accordingly.

In conclusion, I must therefore stress that the fulfilment of the submitted proposal is dependent upon several prerequisites described above, for whose fulfilment I shall devote all my efforts.

I shall therefore be very grateful if you would, however, support me in this task in that you would further continue to provide the preferential furnishing of the agreed manpower. In addition, it will be necessary to instruct the GL Liaison Office in Paris and the heads of the Sonderausschuss T 3 and T 6 that the distribution of the engines and airscrews have to follow in series for stocking-up, in the way in which this was explained in detail in my letter of 1.12.42 addressed to the GL/C-E 2, in accordance with the attached copy.

Heil Hitler !
(signature)

Attachments:

1 Programme proposal of 1.12.42
1 Letter copy of 1.12.42

Copy of this letter to GL/C-B [and]GL/C-B 2

Above: Letter of 5 December 1942 to RLM GL/C Oberst i.G.Vorwald regarding the Me 323 D-1, D-2 and the D-6.

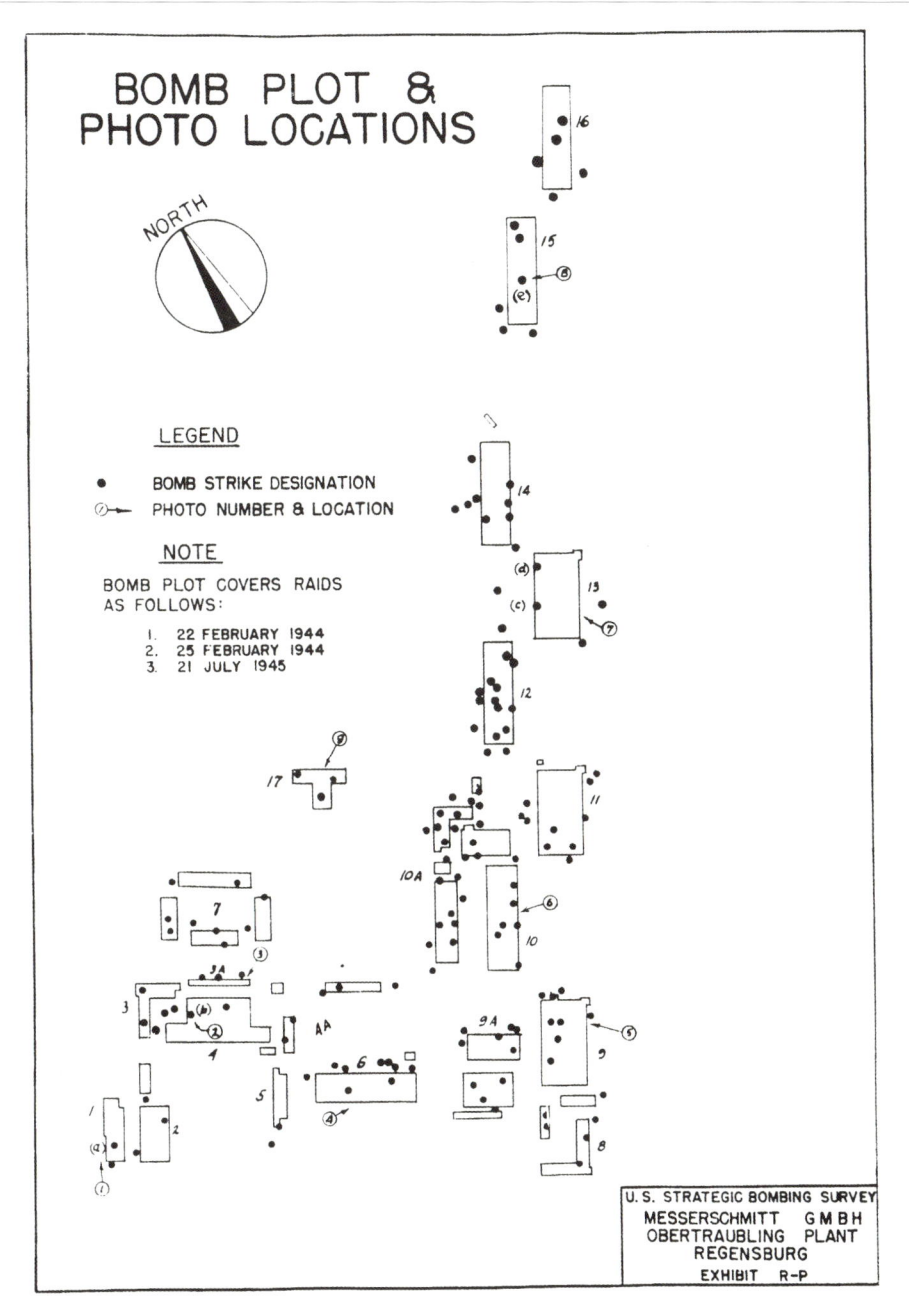

Appendix 15

Damage to Obertraubling in bombing raids of 22 Feb / 25 Feb / 21 July 1944

Bombing raids on Obertraubling, from 22 February 1944 to 11 April 1945

Date	No. of bombers	Type	Air Force	No. of bombs	Type	Weight (in tonnes)	Total (weight)	Target
22 February 1944	94	B-24	15th AF	741 306	227 kg* 45 kg**	168 t 14 t	182 t	Bf 109 production
25 February 1944	158	B-17	8th AF 3rd Air Division	1295 1028	227 kg* 45 kg**	294 t 46 t	340 t	Bf 109 production
21 July 1944	90	B-17	8th AF 3rd Air Division	500 fragmentation bombs 400 liquid incendiary bombs 5000 spiked incendiary bombs			210 t	Bf 109 production
16 Feb. 1945	263	B-24	15th AF	At least 630 At least 402 At least 20,000 fragmentation bombs	227 kg* 45 kg**		515 t	Me 262 production
11 April 1945	79	B-24	8th AF 2nd Air Division	315 535	111.5 kg* 227 kg*		159 t	Me 262 production
Total	684						1406 t	

Bomb weights: 45 kg = 100 lb, 112.5 kg = 250 lb, 227 kg = 500 lb.
*At least 4,000 heavy demolition bombs were dropped.
**2,136 liquid incendiaries dropped, plus 5,000 spked incendiaries and over 20,000 fragmentation bombs.

NEST OF EAGLES

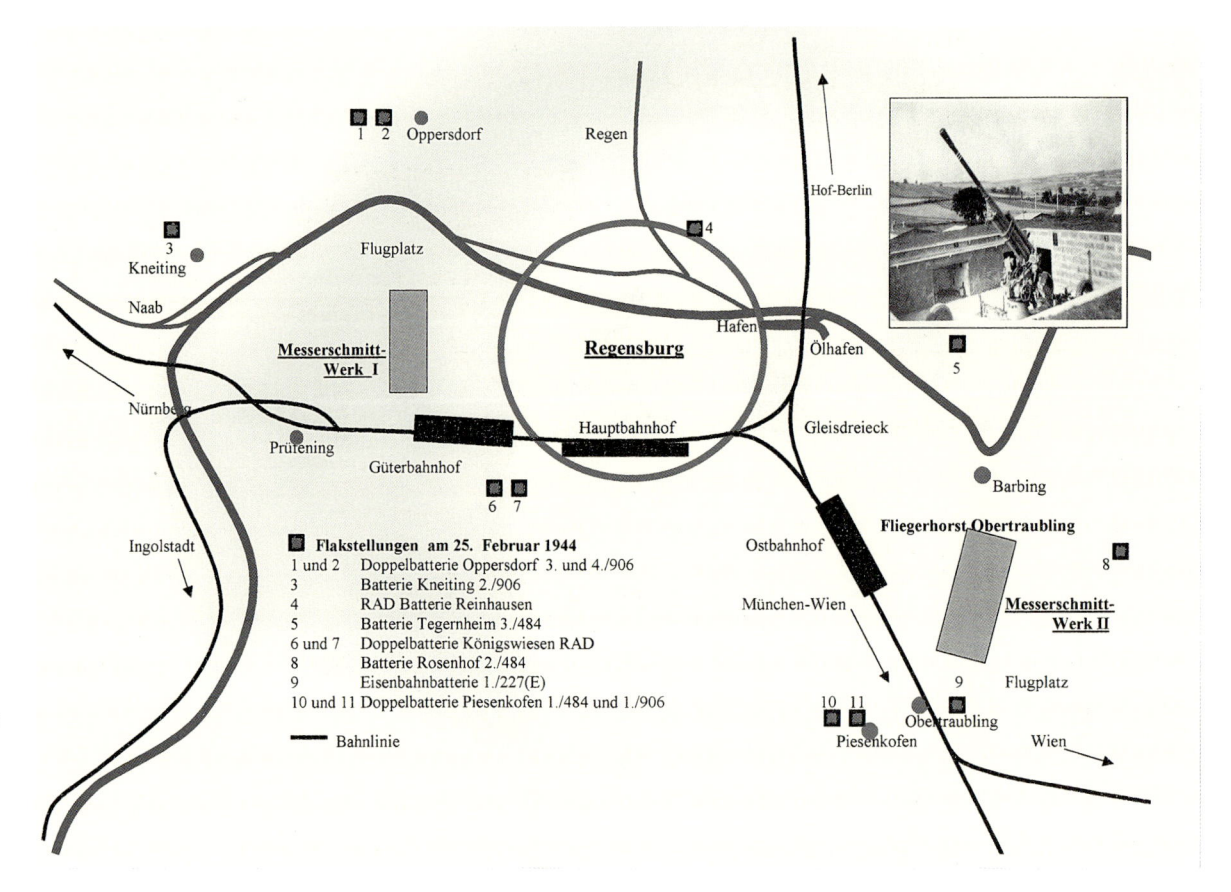

Plan showing the positioning of Flak Batteries, as of 25 February 1944 in the Regensburg and Obertraubling areas. See Appendix 16 below for translation of key.

Flakstellungen am 25. Februar 1944
1 und 2   Doppelbatterie Oppersdorf 3. und 4./906
3   Batterie Kneiting 2./906
4   RAD Batterie Reinhausen
5   Batterie Tegernheim 3./484
6 und 7   Doppelbatterie Königswiesen RAD
8   Batterie Rosenhof 2./484
9   Eisenbahnbatterie 1./227(E)
10 und 11 Doppelbatterie Piesenkofen 1./484 und 1./906

— Bahnlinie

Appendix 16

Flak Batteries on 25 February 1944 in the Regensburg and Obertraubling areas

Key to Flak Batteries as listed above on map:
1 & 2:   Oppersdorf - 3./906 & 4./906 Twin-Battery
3:              Kneiting - 2./906 Battery
4:              Rheinhausen - RAD Battery
5:              Tegernheim - 3./484 Battery
6 & 7:   Königswiesen - RAD Twin-Battery
8:              Rosenhof - 2./484 Battery
9:              Obertraubling - 1./227 (E) Railway Battery
10 & 11:   Piesenkofen - 1./484 & 1./906 Twin-Battery
===   Railway lines
Flugplatz = Airfield

Appendix 17

(1) Me 262 A-1 /A-2 data

Powerplants:	Junkers-Jumo 004 B-1 turbojets
Static thrust:	2 x 890 kg (1,962 lb)
Wingspan:	12.65 m (41 ft 6 .0 in)
Length:	10.60 m (34 ft 9.3 in)
Height:	3.60 m (11 ft 9.7 in)
Wing area:	21.70 m² (233.57 ft²)
Empty weight:	4,100 kg (9,039 lb)
Payload:	2,000 kg (4,409 lb)
Loaded weight:	6,100 kg (13,449 lb)
Maximum speed:	950 km/h up to 8 km (590 mph to 26,245 ft)
	900 km/h above 8 km (559 mph above 26,245 ft)
Max. diving speed:	1,000 km/h (621 mph)
Speed, flaps full down:	300 km/h (186 mph)
Initial climb rate:	20 m/sec (3,937 ft/min)
Time to climb:	11 mins to 8 km (26,245 ft)
Range:	1,000 km (621 mls)
Service ceiling:	12,000 m (39,370 ft)
W/T equipment:	FuG 16 ZY and FuG 25a
Armament:	(Me 262 A-1) 4 x MK 108
	(Me 262 A-2) 2 x MK 108
Bombload:	(Me 262 A-2) 2 x 250 kg (551 lb) underfuselage bombs
Fuel capacity:	(Me 262 A-1) 1,800 litres J2 in 2 x 900 ltr fuselage tanks + as below
	(Me 262 A-2) as above + 1 x 600 ltr and 1 x 170 ltr fuselage tanks
Fuel type:	When J2 not available, B4 could be used; Riedel starter used A3.

(2) Regensburg-built Me 262 Werknummern

Versions built in Regensburg were the Me 262 A-1 Jäger (fighter) and Me 262 A-2 Jagdbomber (fighter-bomber). Me 262 A-4 Aufklärer (reconnaissance) were converted in Budweis (Czechoslovakia) from the Me 262 A-2 from the 500.000-block. The following 183 documented Werknummern in the 500.000- and 501.000-blocks stem from pilots' logbooks and loss reports and are not claimed to be complete as full documentation was not available.

Production in 1944		
500.001	500.269	501.192
500.003 - 500.005	500.281	501.196
500.007 - 500.010	500.302	501.199 - 501.200
500.012 - 500.013	500.304	501.221
500.015 - 500.018	500.312	501.225 - 501.226
500.020 - 500.021	500.344	501.232
500.024	500.402	
500.026	500.426 - 500.428	
500.035 - 500.036	500.436	
500.038 - 500.039	500.438	
500.041 - 500.042	500.443 - 500.444	
500.049 - 500.050	500.449	
	500.451	
Production in 1945	500.455	
500.053 - 500.054	500.462 - 500.465	
500.056 - 500.059	500.467	
500.061	500.470	
500.063 - 500.065	500.472 - 500.473	
500.067	500.475	
500.069 - 500.072	500.488	
500.078	500.490 - 500.493	

500.089	500.498	500.555 - 500.556
500.093	500.500	500.561
500.095 - 500.097	500.503	500.724 - 500.725
500.100	500.505	500.729
500.103	500.510	500.863
500.124	500.512 - 500.519	
500.154	500.521 - 500.525	
500.200 - 500.258	500.029 - 500.031	
	500.034	
	500.539	
	500.542	

According to USSBS documents, total Me 262 production by Messerschmitt GmbH Regensburg from September 1944 was 345 aircraft. The following Regensburg-built Me 262s survived the war and are in the following museums:

Me 262 A-1 W.Nr. 500.071 - Deutsches Museum, Munich
Me 262 A-1 W.Nr. 500.210 - Australian War Memorial, Canberra
Me 262 A-1 W.Nr. 500.491 - National Air & Space Museum, Washington, D.C.

Messerschmitt GmbH Regensburg: Dezentrale Fertigung der Me 262 im März 1945

(3) Me 262 Dispersal Production in March 1945

Map key:
Düsentriebwerke = Jumo 004 jet engines
Triebwerksverkleidungen = engine nacelles
Rümpfe = fuselages; Rumpfspitze = fuselage nose-cones, Rumpfmontage = fuselage assembly
Gerätebank = instrument panel
Leitwerke = empennages; Leitwerkstelle = empennage station
Bewaffnung = armament
Treibstoffbehälter = fuel tanks
Bauteile = construction parts
Umbau im Aufklärerversion = conversion to reconnaissance variant
Wannenausrüstung = cockpit trough equipment installation
Einflug = acceptance flights
Endmontage = final assembly
Elt. Ausrüstung = electrical equipment
Elektrische Anlagen und Leitungen = electrical installations and conduits
Tragflächen und Leitwerke = wings and empennages
Blechteile = sheet-metal parts
Waldwerke = forest factories
Fertigung durch Luftangriff zerstört = production destroyed by air raid
Einflugbetrieb mit Unterstützung der = acceptance flying, with support of the Lufthansa facilities
Herstellung von Dreh-, Fräs- und Preßteilen = manufacture of turned, milled and formed parts

NEST OF EAGLES

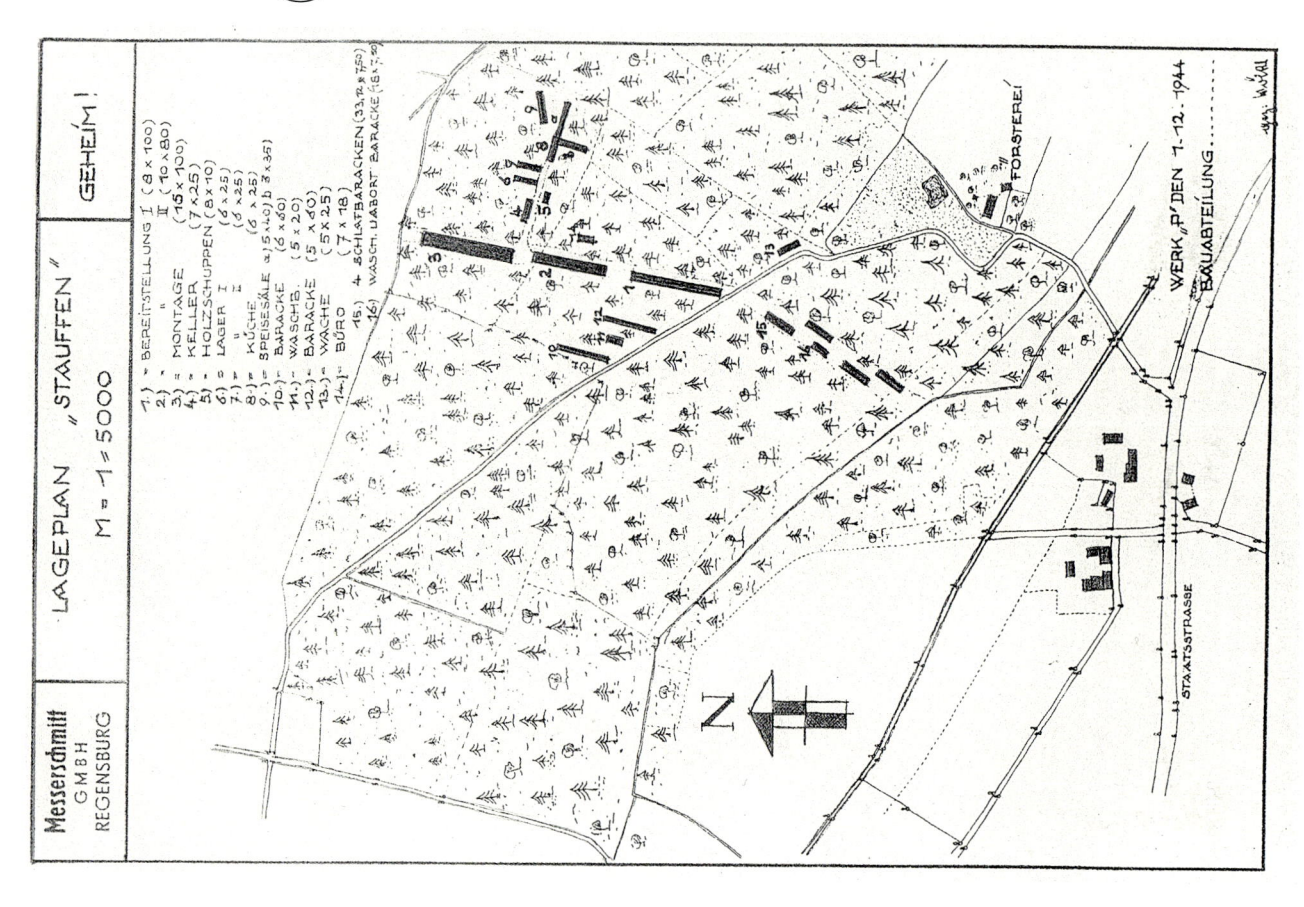

Appendix 18

The Obertraubling Waldwerke 'Stauffen' and 'Gauting' (left)

Map key:

1 & 2 Preparation areas
3 Assembly
4 Cellar
5 Wooden sheds
6 & 7 Storage
8 Kitchen
9 Canteen
10 Barracks
11 Washroom
12 Barracks
13 Guard Post
14 Offices
15 Sleeping accommodation
16 Wash and toilet barracks

Forsterei = Forestry buildings
Staatsstrasse = State road
Bauabteilung = Construction department

Appendices

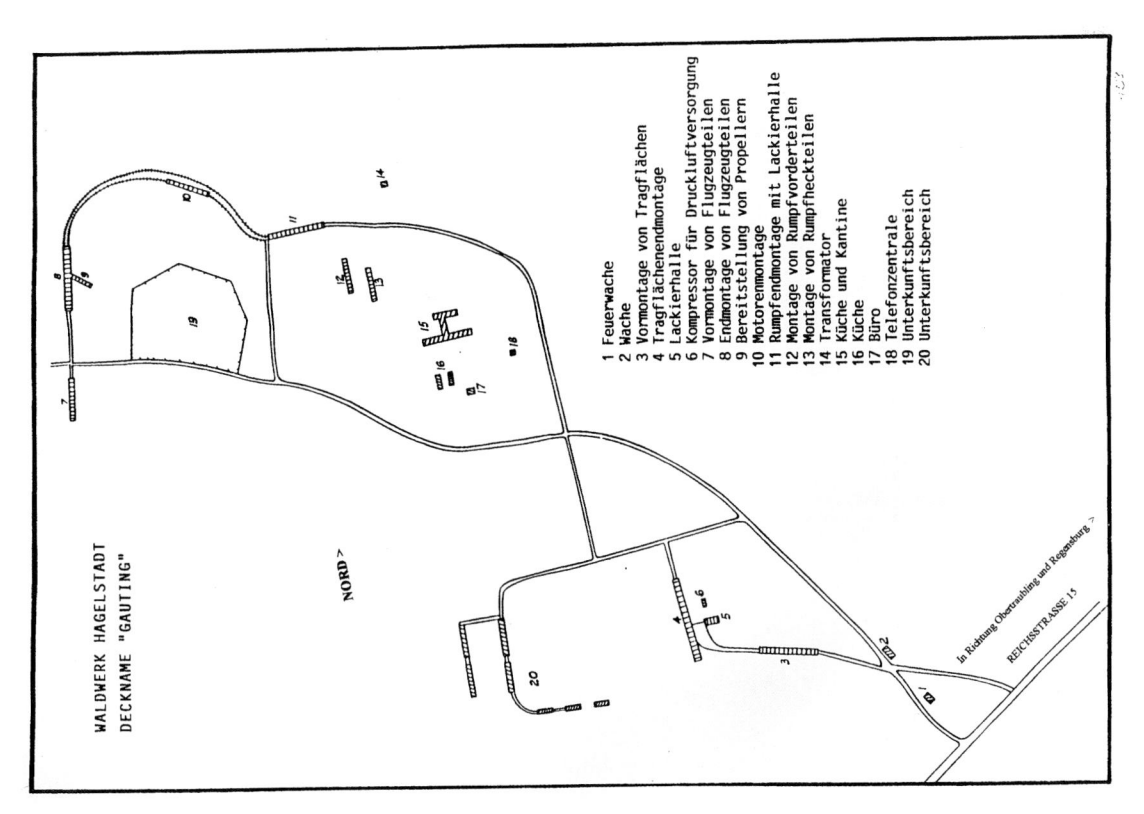

Photo 4 - Exterior view of fuselage assembly bldgs. 12 and 13.

Photo 5 - Interior view of fuselage assembly bldg.

Photo 6 - Interior view of fuselage assembly shop.

Photo 7 - Interior view of fuselage assembly shop.

Photo 8 - Interior view of engine mounting assembly shop.

Photo 9 - Transportation of engine to front assembly shop.

(See next page for details)

WALDWERK HAGELSTADT
DECKNAME "GAUTING"

NORD >

In Richtung Oberautahling und Regensburg >
REICHSSTRASSE 15

1 Feuerwache
2 Wache
3 Vormontage von Tragflächen
4 Tragflächenendmontage
5 Lackierhalle
6 Kompressor für Druckluftversorgung
7 Vormontage von Flugzeugteilen
8 Endmontage von Flugzeugteilen
9 Bereitstellung von Propellern
10 Motorenmontage
11 Rumpfendmontage mit Lackierhalle
12 Montage von Rumpfvorderteilen
13 Montage von Rumpfheckteilen
14 Transformator
15 Küche und Kantine
16 Küche
17 Büro
18 Telefonzentrale
19 Unterkunftsbereich
20 Unterkunftsbereich

Map key:
1 Fire Brigade
2 Guard Post
3 Wing pre-assembly
4 Wing final assembly
5 Paint spray shop
6 Compressor for compressed-air supply
7 Aircraft parts pre-assembly
8 Aircraft parts final assembly
9 Airscrew readiness station
10 Engines installation
11 Fuselage final assembly & paint shop
12 Forward fuselage assembly
13 Rear fuselage assembly
14 Transformer station
15 Kitchen and canteen
16 Kitchens
17 Offices
18 Telephone centre
19 & 20 Accommdation areas

NEST OF EAGLES

This and previous page: Although of poor quality, this selection of photographs, which was taken in July-August 1944, represents the only known German images of the 'Waldwerk Gauting', near Hagelstadt, south-east of Regensburg. They were discovered by the Allies and incorporated into a post-war report for the USSBS. (Photo USSBS)

Sources and Bibliography

(1) Archives, Collections and Documents:
Air Documents Division, T-2 AMC, Wright Field Microfilm R 2713 F 1025
Archiv Potsdam (Reports of the German Revisions- und Treuhand-AG Berlin on the Mtt Regensburg)
Bayerisches Hauptstaatsarchiv Munich (Reports of the Government President to the Reich Governor)
Bundesarchiv (German Federal Archive) Koblenz (Photograph Archive)
Collection : Carl E. Charles (Bf 109 Werknummern)
Collection : Jan Horn (Me 262 Werknummer list and losses)
Collection : Theodor Mohr (Messerschmitt GmbH development status for Bf 108 and Bf 109)
Collection : Willy Radinger (Messerschmitt Technical Directorate documents)
Deutsche Dienststelle (WASt) Berlin (Reports of losses of flying personnel)
Deutsches Museum Munich (Photograph and Aeronautical Archives)
Kriegstagebuch (Daily War Diary) of Fliegerhorst Obertraubling from RL 21/90 in BA/MA Freiburg, Industrielieferplan (Industry Delivery Plan) status 31.03.1943
Militärarchiv Freiburg (The Secret Daily War Diaries of the Wehrmacht Leadership - RL 2 III 1159, RL 3/1-63, RL 8/212, RL 19/87, 100, 103, 105, 106, RL 21/90, RW 21-52/2 and 3)
National Archives Washington (RGs 243/25/84A & B, 243/27/135, 18/7/1762-1764, 1863 and USSBS ADI [K] Reports RG 165, 573, 577 and 604/1944; 365/1945)
USAF Archive, Dayton, Ohio (Survey of Messerschmitt Factory & Functions, Report of Messerschmitt Engineering and Research Facilities (Report of Aeronautical Research Institute of Vienna)
Stadtarchiv Regensburg (Collection Eisenbeiß and records ZR III 719-722, 724-725 and 731)
Aircraft Handbooks: Bf 108 B, Bf 109 G-2, Bf 109 G/Trop, Bf 109 G-6/AS, Bf 109 G MW-50, Bf 109 K,
Me 163 B, Me 210 A-1, Me 262 A, Me 323, Jumo 004
Flight Logbooks of Luftwaffe and Acceptance pilots Haid, Lohmann, Riedmeir, Schallmoser, Fischer, Bergmann, Lotter, Illenberger, Bielefeld and Dahlitz.

(2) Books:
Blasel, Werner L.: *Me 108 Taifun / Me 109 Gustav*, Herford, 1987
Braun, Hans-Joachim: *Technikgeschichte*, Band 57, Nr. 2, Hamburg, 1960
Brückner, Joachim: *Kriegsende in Bayern 1945*, Freiburg im Breisgau, 1987
Dabrowski, Hans-Peter: *Giganten der Luft*, Friedberg/Hessen, 1993
Dabrowski, Hans-Peter: *Messerschmitt Me 321/323. The Luftwaffe's 'Giants' in WW II*, Schiffer, 2002
Dierich, Wolfgang: *Die Verbände der Luftwaffe*, Stuttgart, 1976
Freeman, Roger A.: *Mighty Eighth War Diary*, New York, 1981
Freeman, Roger A.: *Mighty Eighth*, London, 1989
Gersdorff, Kyrill / Grasmann, Kurt: *Flugmotoren und Strahltriebwerke*, Munich, 1981
Halter, Helmut: *Stadt unterm Hakenkreuz*, Regensburg, 1994
Hentschel, Georg: *Die geheimen Konferenzen des Generalluftzeugmeisters*, Koblenz, 1989
Irving, David: *Die Tragödie der deutschen Luftwaffe*, Frankfurt, 1975
Ishoven, Armand van: *Messerschmitt*, Vienna, 1978
Kaufmann, Johannes: *Flugberichte 1935-1945*, Schwäbisch Hall, 1989
Kosin, Rudiger: *Die Entwicklung der deutschen Jagdflugzeuge*, Koblenz, 1983
Monogram Close-Ups: *Bf 108; Bf 109 F-K*, Boylston, 1976
Peter, Ernst: *... schleppte und flog Giganten*, Stuttgart, 1976
Piekalkiewicz, Janusz: *Luftkrieg*, Munich, 1978
Powilleit, Heinz: *Flugerinnerungen 1938-1943* (Eigenverlag), 1998
Prien, Jochen: *Geschichte des Jagdgeschwaders 53, Band 3*, Hamburg, 1991
Saft, Ulrich: *Das bittere Ende der Luftwaffe*, Langenhagen, 1992
Schlaug, Georg: *Lastensegler* (undated)
Schramm, Percy E.: *Kriegstagebuch des OKW, Band 1-8*, Munich, 1982
Späte, Wolfgang: *Der streng geheime Vogel Me 163*, Munich, 1983

Index (People)

Altrogge, Dipl.-Ing. Werner 98, 99
Armbrust, Dipl.-Ing. 112

Bachmeier, Hauptmann 95
Ballewski, Helmut 80
Beinhorn, Elly 14, 18
Bergmann, Feldwebel 55
Bessler, Feldwebel 55
Birkholz, Heinz 133
Bräutigam, Leutnant Otto 95
Breunig, Oberfeldwebel 55
Brindlinger, Otto 14

Clarke, 1/Lt Robert C. 138
Croneiß, Theo 10, 11, 22, 25, 34, 40, 41, 44, 95

Dahl, Major Walther 168
Davis, 1/Lt Nelson H. 138
Dienstl, Heinrich 114
Dittmar, Heini 109
Dörfl, Gefreiter 96
Dürpisch, Kurt 122
Duttmann, Peter 74

Engel, Gefreiter Adolf 95
Ertelt, Feldwebel Gerhard 157
Evers, Wilhelm 165

von Falkenhorst, Oberleutnant Freiherr 129
Fischer, Arno 74, 75
Flinsch, Ing. Bernhard 95
Fuchs, Dipl.-Ing. 95
Furrer, Reinhard 18

Galland, Generalleutnant Adolf 37, 53
Gattinger, Martin 42, 81
Geisbe, Unteroffizier Karl 8 10
Gerlitz, Major 132
Gorbachov, Oleg 73
Göring, Reichsmarschall Hermann 10, 11, 12, 24, 25, 40, 41
Grabmann, Oberst Walter 155
Graf, Hermann 37
Gray, 1/Lt Delmar A. 138
Grasser, Major Hartmann 73
Groß, Ludwig 81, 129
Gymnich, Flugkapitän Alfried 8

Haid, Josef 'Sepp' 17, 22, 35, 49, 54, 55, 57, 58, 59
Hammon, Leutnant 96
Handrick, Oberstleutnant Gotthardt 155
Häussler, Unteroffizier 55
Heck, Hermann 80
Heiss, Erich 20
Hess, Rudolf 11, 24, 25
Hesselbach, Flugkapitän Peter 92, 94, 95
Hessler, Feldwebel 55
Himmelmeyer, Ing. Hans 19
Himmler, Reichsführer-SS Heinrich 165
Hitler, Adolf 10, 11, 21, 24, 37, 53, 65, 68, 148
Huber, Ulrich 101
Hübsch, Feldwebel Fritz 97, 104

Jödicke, Oberfeldwebel 115
Jung, Ernst 96

Kahdemann, Gerd 18
Kaltenbrunner, SS-Obergruppenführer Ernst 139
Kandler, Oberfeldwebel Ludwig 115, 117
Karelin, Leutnant Cyrill 73
Kaufmann, Johannes 38, 39
Kellnberger, Josef 22
Knippel, Leutnant 103
Kogler, Obstlt. Johann 155
Konrad, Michael 49
Kronseder, Hermann 19, 43
Krynauw, Lieutenant Daniel 150

Ladegast, Oberleutnant 54, 55, 63
Laßleben, Franz 167
Ley, Robert 22
Liebl, Otto 24, 42, 156
Linder, Karl 22, 34, 49, 55, 59, 118, 151
Lippisch, Dr Alexander 109, 112
del Littorio, Raduno 14
Lohmann, Unteroffizier 55, 57, 157, 159
Lucht, Generalingenieur Roluf 40, 44, 49, 134

Marseille, Hans-Joachim 37
Matysiak, Josef 26
Meier, Josef 24
Messerschmitt, Prof. Dr.-Ing. Wilhelm (Willy) 10, 11, 25, 26, 38, 40, 41, 43, 44, 47, 49, 88, 95, 109, 112, 113, 148
Metzel, Rudolf 65, 157, 158
Michalski, Major Gerhard 155
Milch, Generalfeldmarschall Erhard 10, 11, 38, 40, 44, 47, 139,
Mirter, Frau 2
Mittman, Arno 79
Mölders, Werner 36, 37
Morzik, Oberst Fritz 96
Mouton, Lieutenant Christian Johannes 150, 153
Mrotzek, Feldwebel 55, 61, 63
Müncheberg, Hauptmann Joachim 28, 29, 37

Nowotny, Major Walter 151, 153

Obermeier, August 57, 63
Obermeier, Flugkapitän Heinrich 115
Obermeier, Kurt 68, 75
Opitz, Oberleutnant Rudolf 109, 111
Oppitz, Kurt 97

Paulus, Generalfeldmarschall Friedrich 47, 53
Peltz, Generalmajor Dietrich 155
Pichelmeier, Alfons 166
von Podewils, Leutnant Heinrich Freiherr 132, 138
Popp, Director of Police 26
Posemann, Unteroffizier 55
Powilleit, Unteroffizier Heinz 96, 99, 115
Preusker, Leutnant 151

von Michel-Raulono, Frau Baroness 49
Recker, Oberfeldwebel Helmut 150

Reitsch, Flugkapitän Hanna 109, 111, 112
Riedmeir, Oberleutnant Adolf 37, 129, 157,
Riek, Feldwebel 100
Richter, Feldwebel 55
Röhm, Ernst 11
Römer, Oberleutnant 126
Rommel, General Erwin 33
Rudorffer, Major Erich 153

Sachse, Unteroffizier Helmut 102, 103
Sachsenhauser, Leutnant Josef 90, 97, 105, 114
Saur, Reichsdienstleiter Karl-Otto 139
Schäfer, Hauptmann 115
Schallmoser, Unteroffizier Eduard 147
Scharf, Unteroffizier 133
Scheffl, Feldwebel 157
Schenck, Major Wolfgang 151
Schieferstein, Karl 97
Schmid, Dipl-Ing. Karl 117, 118
Scholz, Unteroffizier Helmut 103
Schotterheim, Dr. 10, 25, 26,
Schreiber, Obergefreiter 55
Schwarz, Leutnant Fritz 95
Seidemann, Hans 14
Seiler, F.S. 49
Seitz, Frau 148
Semmler, Oberfeldwebel 49, 55, 59, 157 160,
Senoner, Oberleutnant 132, 138
Sevkin, Leutnant Ilya 73
Sinz, Josef 95
Sorgatz, Oberfeldwebel 55
Späte, Hauptmann Wolfgang 109, 112
Starbati, Walter 97, 98, 100
Steinhoff, Oberst Johannes 153
Stöhr, Willi 25
Streicher, Hauptmann 151
Stuhrmann, Feldwebel 55
Szopa, Jan 164

Thieme, Otto 22, 34
Thierfelder, Hauptmann Werner 12
Trenkle, Flugkapitän Wendelin 22, 54, 55, 57, 58, 148, 149
Trubenbach, Oberst Hanns 155
Tschassovnikov, Leutnant Alexei 73

Udet, Generalfeldmarschall Ernst 92
Utevikov, Leutnant Dimitry 129, 130

Vilsmeier, Hermann 103
Voigt, Woldemar 38
Voronzow, Hauptmann Peter 73
Vorwald, Oberst i.G. 114

Wagner, Josef 101
Walter, Erwin 124
Wedemeyer, Dr. 22, 118, 134, 49
Weiger, Kreisleiter 25
Weigert, Hauptmann 96
Weinlich, Major 96
Weiß, Horst 167
Weißenberger, Hauptmann Theodor 12
Weißmüller, Hauptmann Dr. Josef 28, 73
Welter, Oberleutnant Kurt 153, 154
Wendel, Flugkapitän Fritz 153
Willekins, Detlef 102
Wolf, Feldwebel 44

Yakovlev, Leutnant Alexandr 73
Yaresh, Leutnant Vassily 129, 130

Zeyar, Josef 165
Ziereis, Commandant 163
Zitter, Hermann 97